# Forbearance as Redistribution

Why do governments tolerate the violation of their own laws and regulations? Conventional wisdom is that governments cannot enforce their laws. *Forbearance as Redistribution* challenges the standard interpretation by showing that politicians choose not to enforce laws to distribute resources and win elections. Alisha C. Holland demonstrates that this forbearance toward activities such as squatting and street vending is a powerful strategy for attracting the electoral support of poor voters. In many developing countries, state social programs are small or poorly targeted and thus do not offer politicians an effective means to mobilize the poor. In contrast, forbearance constitutes an informal welfare policy around which Holland argues much of urban politics turns. While forbearance offers social support to those failed by their governments, it also perpetuates the same exclusionary welfare policies from which it grows.

Alisha C. Holland is Assistant Professor of Politics at Princeton University. She was previously a Junior Fellow of the Harvard Society of Fellows. Holland's research on redistribution, urban politics, and law enforcement in Latin America has appeared in the *American Journal of Political Science, American Political Science Review, Comparative Political Studies*, and *Latin American Research Review*.

## Cambridge Studies in Comparative Politics



**Other Books in the Series**

Christopher Adolph, *Bankers, Bureaucrats, and Central Bank Politics: The Myth of Neutrality*

Michael Albertus, *Autocracy and Redistribution: The Politics of Land Reform*

Ben W. Ansell, *From the Ballot to the Blackboard: The Redistributive Political Economy of Education*

Ben W. Ansell, David J. Samuels, *Inequality and Democratization: An Elite-Competition Approach*

Leonardo R. Arriola, *Multi-Ethnic Coalitions in Africa: Business Financing of Opposition Election Campaigns*

David Austen-Smith, Jeffry A. Frieden, Miriam A. Golden, Karl Ove Moene, and Adam Przeworski, eds., *Selected Works of Michael Wallerstein: The Political Economy of Inequality, Unions, and Social Democracy*

Andy Baker, *The Market and the Masses in Latin America: Policy Reform and Consumption in Liberalizing Economies*

(*Continued after the index*)

# Forbearance as Redistribution

## *The Politics of Informal Welfare in Latin America*

ALISHA C. HOLLAND
*Princeton University*

CAMBRIDGE
UNIVERSITY PRESS

University Printing House, Cambridge CB2 8BS, United Kingdom

One Liberty Plaza, 20th Floor, New York, NY 10006, USA

477 Williamstown Road, Port Melbourne, VIC 3207, Australia

314-321, 3rd Floor, Plot 3, Splendor Forum, Jasola District Centre, New Delhi - 110025, India

79 Anson Road, #06-04/06, Singapore 079906

Cambridge University Press is part of the University of Cambridge.

It furthers the University's mission by disseminating knowledge in the pursuit of education, learning and research at the highest international levels of excellence.

www.cambridge.org
Information on this title: www.cambridge.org/9781316626351
DOI: 10.1017/9781316795613



First published 2017

*A catalogue record for this publication is available from the British Library*

ISBN 978-1-107-17407-8 Hardback
ISBN 978-1-316-62635-1 Paperback

# Contents

# Figures

# Tables

# Acknowledgments

Classical Greek histories include discussions of whether leaders should punish mass deserters or "let the law sleep." Part of God's power in the Bible is represented through repeated decisions to pass over the sins of man. Illegal immigrants in the United States depend on executive choices to stay their deportation.

This book nevertheless started with a specific type of forbearance in mind: towards the poor in Latin America. Before starting graduate school, I witnessed a protest in Bogotá, Colombia, in which street vendors claimed a right to work. What struck me was that the participants did not want government jobs or unemployment programs. They wanted to work in city streets and cited the state's failures to generate work for them to justify their claims. In graduate school, I started to think about why models of European welfare states did not apply to the Latin American contexts that I knew. The protesters' basic point – that legal violations can substitute for state alternatives – kept coming back to me. I care about how laws that the poor violate are enforced because it matters for social welfare. It also tells us something important about how states address inequality and how the poor make claims on the state.

This book grew out of my doctoral dissertation at Harvard, and it blossomed with the guidance of my advisors. My chair, Jorge Domínguez, consistently provided sage advice. His insistence on thinking through the best way to allocate my words and energies spared me many additional years in graduate school and in revising the manuscript. Steve Levitsky helped me realize that I had hit on something with this project from the start. He managed to hone in on the gaps in the argument and deepened my thinking about issues of institutional strength, clientelism, and state capacity. Fran Hagopian's generosity with her time and her meticulous comments helped me understand how to write and think like a political scientist; I only can hope to repay this debt by doing the same for others with such insight and warmth down the line. Torben Iversen always posed sharp questions about dynamics foreign to him and helped me see where my own logic went awry.

Countless colleagues in Cambridge also took the time to read, discuss, and improve this project. In particular, I'd like to thank Matthew Amengual, Shelby Grossman, Peter Hall, Nahomi Ichino, Didi Kuo, James Loxton, Lindsay Mayka, Andrei Roman, Ben Ross Schneider, Prerna Singh, and Brandon Van Dyck for critical feedback and advice along the way. Members of my writing group, Jen Brea, Charlotte Cavaillé, Emily Clough, Yanilda González, Kyle Jaros, and Brian Palmer-Rubin, slogged through countless drafts of everything from the prospectus to the final chapters. Their personal friendships made graduate school a joy and their insistence on asking important questions (and then communicating their answers) pushed me to be a better scholar.

Feedback from far-flung scholars greatly enhanced the manuscript. I was fortunate to hold a book workshop at Harvard with Daniel Brinks, Candelaria Garay, Evan Lieberman, Vicky Murillo, and Hillel Soifer. They offered scores of important suggestions about the transition from the dissertation to a book, which greatly improved its structure and clarity. I am grateful to seminar discussants and participants at Boston University, Columbia, Oxford, Pontificia Universidad Católica del Perú, Toulouse School of Economics, Universidad de los Andes-Bogotá, University of California Berkeley, University of Colorado Boulder, University of Chicago, and Yale. Along the way, Andy Baker, Ruth Berins Collier, Natalia Bueno, Tim Dorlach, Kent Eaton, Dan Slater, and Adam Ziegfeld all read and provided terrific feedback on parts of the manuscript.

Financial support for this project came from many sources. At Harvard, I am grateful for grants received from the David Rockefeller Center for Latin American Studies, the Weatherhead Center for International Affairs, and the Institute for Quantitative Social Science. A graduate research fellowship (DEG 0644491) and dissertation improvement grant (1263778) from the National Science Foundation supported much of the data collection and analysis. The American Bar Foundation provided a supportive home to finish my dissertation, and numerous friends at the University of Chicago pushed the project forward. The Harvard Society of Fellows made completion of this book possible, both by providing an ideal place to write and by fostering intellectual community with remarkable scholars who stretched beyond their disciplines to read parts of the manuscript.

Joining Princeton's Politics Department has brought this project full circle. I first became interested in Latin American politics as an undergraduate at Princeton. I am especially grateful to Deborah Yashar, who provided my first walk up Sartori's ladder of abstraction and an introduction to academic research. She has been a generous mentor and colleague ever since. More generally, my colleagues here have showed me by example what deep and careful social science looks like.

The large and small debts incurred while conducting fieldwork are too numerous to name, but they are what made this book possible and what motivated the writing. I spent many evenings staring out my office window at the Universidad de los Andes at Bogotá's sharp contrasts. For the view and insights into Bogotá's contradictions, I'm indebted to Alejandro Gaviria, Juan Camilo Cardenas, and the Economics Faculty. The staff at Cifras y Conceptos helped make the survey component of the book come to life, and Angélica Camargo shared her attempts to document informal land markets and how to use the city's archives. Much of this project depended on close work with bureaucrats and politicians who helped show me how enforcement decisions are really made. Virgilio Rueda, Diana Paredes, and Elsie Guerrero, all let me shadow their daily work in ways that shaped my sensitivity to the issues at stake. For research assistance, I was lucky to have the help of Juan Carlos González, Dake Kang, Luis Mas, and Lucy Msall. Tuğba Bozçağa made my fieldwork in Istanbul possible, and also tremendous fun, by translating both the language and Turkish politics. Tan Oral's cartoons gave me direct access to Turkish political commentary, and I'm grateful to include one in the book.

Lew Bateman and Robert Dreesen have been a pleasure to work with as editors. Their support was complemented by the careful copyediting and production assistance of Cambridge, as well as Madeleine Adams. I am indebted as well to Erik Wibbels and Kathleen Thelen, the series editors, and to the anonymous reviewers for their enthusiasm about the project and suggestions to improve it.

As the following pages reveal, the normative complexities of forbearance are substantial and the book's cover image captures these tensions. It comes from a photo series called "Squatter Imaginaries" by the contemporary Spanish artist, Dionisio González. Dionisio photographs informal settlements around the world and then digitally superimposes contemporary architecture. The photographs challenge the viewer to think about what constitutes a squatter settlement and what evolution is possible. But the details of the images also reveal substantial poverty and neglect. This book likewise asks us to think of the value of squatter settlements, both to their residents and to politicians, while trying to avoid romanticizing their shortcomings. Art, perhaps more than political science, inspires people to see differently and I am grateful to Dionisio for allowing me to share his work here.

Finally, I owe the greatest gratitude to my family. My parents, Dona Kercher and Norman Holland, inspired me to become an academic long before they resigned themselves to my career choice. This book began with a conversation with my husband, Glen Weyl, on my parents' couch that is seared in my memory. Some ideas, like romantic partners, strike you as "the one." I am grateful to have found a project that hit on all my intellectual passions, for the law, social policy, and inequality. But I am even more grateful for a partner who has nurtured them. Although Glen has uprooted his life multiple times to support my career, the cover image most vividly captures the depth of his support. Glen surprised me for my thirtieth birthday with a trip to Sevilla, Spain. I thought the trip was to honor my love of flamenco dance, but Glen had a second trick up his sleeve. He had arranged a "tour" with a very special guide: my favorite contemporary artist, Dionisio. The act touched me to the core. Although these words cannot capture my gratitude for truly being understood by someone, this book is for you.

# Introduction

María Luz has a newspaper article plastered to her precarious house in a squatter settlement in Bogotá, Colombia. The article title reads, "Social Interest Housing: A False Promise?" It chides the Colombian government for excluding the poor from its housing program through onerous savings requirements. As María Luz reasons, the absence of state housing alternatives "protects" her house built in the city's slums without land title: "If the government will not provide a dignified house and living conditions for my family, then it has no right to take me off this land."[1]

María Luz is similar to tens of millions of Latin Americans who have accessed housing, jobs, and services not through state provision, but through the violation of property laws. These informal welfare benefits do not appear on any government balance sheet. Yet they often surpass government social expenditures in magnitude. Think about the case of housing: from 1950 to 2000, almost two-thirds of housing construction in Colombia occurred informally. The state built just 3 percent of the housing stock for the poor (DNP 2007: 8). This phenomenon is not confined to Latin America. In Turkey, the rent payments that squatters save by building their own houses on state or private land are worth more than triple the value of all government social assistance (Başlevent and Dayıoğlu 2005: 37). Legal tolerance thus can result in substantial transfers of land and resources. Yet rarely are enforcement decisions incorporated into analyses of politics or social policy.

The idea of choices to enforce the law may seem counterintuitive. Conventional wisdom holds that limited enforcement reflects an impotent

[1] Author interview with anonymous squatter, Bogotá, Colombia, September 5, 2012.

state that *cannot* act otherwise. On the one hand, a state can deter and penalize all offenses with sufficient police, judges, and bureaucrats. Few states, particularly in low- and middle-income countries, have this fiscal luxury (Becker 1968; Becker and Stigler 1974; Centeno and Portes 2006; Geddes 1994; O'Donnell 1993). On the other hand, enforcement can lag due to principal–agent problems in which politicians struggle to monitor their agents. Police and bureaucrats may accept bribes or shirk their responsibilities. North (1990: 59) emphasizes, "Enforcement in Third World economies is uncertain not only because of ambiguity of legal doctrine (a measurement cost), but because of uncertainty with respect to the behavior of the [government] agent." Weak administrative capacity thus limits enforcement (Dimitrov 2009; Gans-Morse 2012; Lipsky 1980; Markus 2015; McCubbins, Noll, and Weingast 1987).

In light of standard expectations, widespread violations of property laws are unsurprising in developing countries. Far more puzzling are instances when governments *do* enforce their laws. Ecuador and Rwanda evict squatters, while their equally poor neighbors Peru and Uganda long have not (Dosh 2010; Goodfellow 2012). State capacity tends to change over the course of decades (if not centuries). Yet enforcement fluctuates quickly. After decades of encroachments, in the late 1990s Colombia removed thousands of street vendors who had built entire stores in the middle of major avenues to sell everything from car parts to feather dusters. Enforcement then stopped again in the 2000s (Chapter 4). Equally nettlesome questions arise as to why "strong" states tolerate legal violations. The United States deports fewer undocumented immigrants than countries that face much smaller immigration flows (Ellermann 2009). Chile can compel the rich to pay taxes (Bergman 2009), but allows street vendors to operate in some city areas while enforcing vigorously in others (Chapter 5).

These scattered examples raise broad questions about enforcement politics: Why do governments tolerate the violation of their own laws and regulations? And when do they enforce them? Why is enforcement stable and uniform in some contexts, and volatile in time or space in others? These broad questions give rise to more micro-level questions about how ordinary citizens, bureaucrats, and politicians view enforcement. Does the public want more enforcement? Are these "bad" laws that do not reflect majority views? Do politicians try to pursue enforcement and hit bureaucratic resistance? Or do bureaucrats run into political obstacles when they enforce the law?

I investigate how well theories of distributive politics can make sense of variation in enforcement. My central argument, which is elaborated in the next chapter, is that politicians choose not to enforce the law, a behavior that I call *forbearance*, when it is in their electoral interest. Focusing on laws that the poor violate, I argue that politicians' incentives hinge on two factors: (1) whether government social programs offer an alternative to the legal violation in question, and (2) whether politicians depend on the votes of the poor to win office. Politicians turn to forbearance when welfare policies are inadequate and they need the poor's support to take or retain office. In these circumstances, forbearance functions as a form of informal welfare provision that politicians manipulate to improve the lives of those who violate the law and to signal their commitments to poor constituents more broadly. Enforcement becomes possible when politicians can offer the poor formal versions of the same goods, or they can cut poor voters out of their winning coalition.

The primary – but not exclusive – empirical focus is Latin America, a middle-income region where many governments have the money and manpower to enforce their laws. Latin America is the region with the most unequal income distribution in the world, which means that poverty rates are much higher than would be expected at similar development levels. Sharp inequality and residential segregation create different incentives to enforce depending on where politicians seek office. I select city cases that vary along the principal independent variables under both my theory and competing state capacity-based explanations. The cases span a city known for its capable institutions (Santiago, Chile) and cities with more middling capacities that either group all voters into a single catchall district (Bogotá, Colombia) or divide voters into many income-segregated districts (Lima, Peru).

The decision to compare enforcement across cities reflects substantive and methodological concerns. City governments have become increasingly important sites of policymaking and electoral contestation after a wave of decentralizing reforms in the 1980s and 1990s. Four out of five Latin Americans also live in cities. The governance of metropolitan areas thus affects the quality of democracy and life for the vast majority of Latin America's residents. Methodologically, there are ways in which the biggest cities across countries – Lima and Santiago, or Lagos and Accra – are more similar to one another than to the secondary cities or rural regions to which they are compared in more common within-nation subnational research designs. Lima, for example, has ten times more inhabitants than Peru's second-largest city, Arequipa. Flows of people, congestion, business organizations, and housing shortages all look quite distinct in the two cities. Lima's urban challenges are far more similar to those in Bogotá. Therefore, in this book I focus on Latin American capitals as a way to make valid inferences across similar units, and I use enforcement patterns both within and across cities to expand the number of testable observations.

My argument underscores the strategic – and deeply democratic – nature of enforcement of laws that the poor violate. "Weak" enforcement does not necessarily imply a weak state that cannot regulate the behavior of its citizens. To the contrary, forbearance can indicate healthy electoral democracy in which politicians are responsive to poor voters and choose not to enforce laws that conflict with local preferences. This theory naturally suggests counterintuitive policy conclusions: reforms to strengthen the welfare state may do more to build the rule of law than additional funding for police and bureaucrats. Successful democratization and reforms to increase the poor's political power, if unaccompanied by improvements in social policy, can erode enforcement.

I am hardly the first to notice that politicians manipulate enforcement for electoral ends. But the twin challenges of comparing enforcement effort given unknown offense levels, and separating situations when governments cannot enforce the law from those when they will not enforce it, mean that forbearance rarely has been documented empirically. I do not tackle these challenges all at once. Rather, I take a multi-method approach in which I use observations about how a variety of actors – citizens, bureaucrats, mayors, and presidents – behave. I document a series of anomalies in standard state capacity–based theories and show how an electoral theory of forbearance elegantly reconciles them. Varied types of evidence from qualitative interviews, administrative records, public opinion surveys, campaign platforms, and focused experiments mean that the combined findings are difficult to dismiss as just measurement error.

The concept and methods developed can apply to many types of forbearance, including those that benefit the rich, but the empirics focus on two legal violations that are most consequential for the lives of the poor: the taking of property for commercial purposes (street vending) and for residential purposes (squatting). Social and corporate welfare rarely are included in the same study; likewise, forbearance that aids the poor merits a separate analysis, which it has not previously received. It comes as little surprise that the rich can use their money and power to change enforcement outcomes, especially in an unequal region like Latin America. Instances when the poor turn the law in their favor are less expected. They also are more instructive about electoral politics because the poor have little to offer other than their votes.

In exploring how laws that affect the poor are enforced, I aim to shed light on the urban poor's political representation and organizing. Throughout the book, I refer to the poor, urban poor, and informal-sector poor interchangeably to designate those trying to get by in the city. Although a very heterogeneous group, their shared experiences of scarce earnings, uneven participation in formal labor markets, exclusion from contributory welfare programs, and residential segregation have helped the urban poor to forge a certain common identity and set of interests. The urban poor usually are portrayed as apathetic or locked into clientelistic relationships. Roberts (2002) goes the farthest in calling Latin America a case of "classless inequality" because poor majorities never coalesced into a political movement. Yet, any understanding of how the informal-sector poor relate to the political system must begin with the policies that most affect their lives. These historically have not been state welfare programs. Rather, I try to show that the informal-sector poor have shared a common agenda around enforcement of property laws, which has shaped local and sometimes even national politics.

The structure of laws that the poor and rich violate tends to differ: property owners are less interested in using their labor to appropriate capital and more invested in protecting their capital against seizures and taxation. As Anatole France (1905) famously observed, "The law, in its majestic equality, forbids the rich, as well as the poor, to sleep under the bridges, to beg in the streets, and to steal bread." In this spirit, laws against street vending and squatting chiefly affect the poor in need of property, who spend their time trying to obtain it, not the wealthy in need of property protection. Chapter 1 provides a general theoretical framework to classify different legal violations and then presents my argument for why politicians allow the poor to violate property laws.

Chapter 2 explores how ordinary citizens think about forbearance and social policy provision. The chapter examines an intuitive idea: if forbearance serves as a form of informal redistribution, then canonical models developed to understand redistributive preferences should apply (more cleanly) to forbearance. Many forms of social spending in Latin America historically have been truncated, meaning that whatever their degree of universality on paper, in practice they covered those with formal employment and middle incomes (De Ferranti, Perry, and Ferreira 2004; Díaz-Cayeros and Magaloni 2009; Haggard and Kaufman 2008; Lindert, Skoufias, and Shapiro 2010). There is little reason to expect the Latin American poor to support more state spending if they are not its beneficiaries. Instead, because the poor are the primary violators of laws against squatting and street vending, income divisions should be even sharper around forbearance toward these offenses. To test these claims, I combine original and regional survey data. I show that many tax-based social policies do not align the electorate along the income scale. In contrast, forbearance generates stronger class cleavages, provides more credible cues about the political spectrum, and motivates vote choice in a survey experiment.

Chapter 3 explores the mechanisms that link the structure of national social policies to local enforcement decisions. Chile, Colombia, and Peru have made different investments in housing policy. This variation shapes the electoral incentives for local politicians to evict squatters. Truncated and inadequate housing policies in Colombia and Peru have led the poor to demand and organize around forbearance. Voters perceive politicians who enforce as taking "anti-poor" positions. Politicians rightly believe that they lose votes if they enforce in the majority-poor districts where squatting tends to occur. Chile's housing policy, which entails substantial investments in affordable housing for the poor, in contrast, has focused popular demands on housing authorities and has associated forbearance with cheating the welfare bureaucracy. Mayors not only face fewer land invasions but also see a political mandate to control them.

Of course, countries that do not invest in social policy may lack the budgets and bureaucrats to enforce their laws. I separate these circumstances by showing that mayors create political bottlenecks in which they stop enforcement procedures after bureaucrats complete their jobs. I also adapt from economics the idea of elasticity, or how one variable (in this case, enforcement) changes in response to another (say, the costs of enforcement or the budget), as a way to observe intent. What the idea of intentional non-enforcement means empirically is that politicians are unwilling to increase enforcement irrespective of the costs. Enforcement, in other words, is inelastic to improvements in resources. Meanwhile, I expect enforcement to be highly sensitive to electoral conditions. Consistent with these predictions, some politicians in Lima and Bogotá have refused to increase enforcement as satellite imagery and economic growth have made it cheaper and easier to control squatting. But they have enforced when the political costs are low, as in the less common cases when the rich occupy land illegally.

Chapter 4 examines how mayors use enforcement against street vendors to appeal to voters in citywide elections in Lima and Bogotá. I use the same idea of elasticity to probe how enforcement responds to fiscal conditions over time since the introduction of direct elections for mayor.

I show that enforcement peaked in Lima and Bogotá following major economic downturns, when state capacity was close to its nadir. Bogotá reverted to forbearance in the 2000s, just as the economy and police force improved; it snapped back to enforcement as the economy soured in the mid-2010s. Lima continued to enforce. Enforcement thus varies independent of resources. I rationalize these patterns by considering the core constituencies of different mayoral administrations. Some mayors have incorporated forbearance into their political platforms to attract lower-class core constituencies. Other mayors alienate poor voters through enforcement. I suggest that voters use enforcement positions as cues of a mayor's broader affinities, generating income-based voting patterns even in elections with very weak standard left–right divides. In other words, forbearance can function like a quasi-programmatic issue in that politicians stake out public campaign positions on enforcement that align the electorate in predictable ways.

Chapter 5 tests a core prediction of my theory: that electoral rules produce different enforcement patterns. Specifically, I hypothesize that decentralized cities that elect multiple mayors in sub-city districts respond to the different desires of local voters across space, while centralized cities that elect a single mayor have enforcement patterns that are more uniform across space and vary with different core constituencies over time. I exploit the differences in electoral rules across the cities examined to test this hypothesis. Using data on both offenses and sanctions against street vending at the district level, I find that enforcement varies with voter demographics only when cities hold elections at the local level, as in Lima and Santiago. The number of street vendors is the main determinant of enforcement in centralized cities like Bogotá. At least one mechanism driving the results is voter demands, not just partisan ideology, as illustrated by the political careers of mayors who run for office in different types of districts. Even mayors from Chile's most conservative and self-disciplined party sometimes enforce rules against street vendors and sometimes forbear. Their choices depend on the poor's electoral weight where they run for office.

The patterns of enforcement uncovered in Chapters 3 through 5 suggest that forbearance frequently is offered to all poor individuals who stand to benefit. I consider this unconditional distribution of forbearance an *informal welfare policy*. Of course, politicians can use their discretion to provide forbearance in a clientelistic manner with explicit demands for electoral reciprocity, as jobs and contracts (patronage) or handouts of cash and goods (vote buying) tend to be in much of the developing world.

But for the most part, forbearance is not distributed in an electorally contingent manner. The reason is that using coercion, and especially public forms of coercion like evictions of squatters and street vendors, is highly visible and carries reputational costs. I find that politicians use forbearance to demonstrate that they care about the poor's welfare. They expect that the goodwill generated will yield its own electoral returns. Selective enforcement against political detractors undercuts these reputational benefits.

Whereas the bulk of this book focuses on politicians at the local and city levels, who cannot change the design of social policy in the short run, Chapter 6 turns to the national level. It considers why presidents and their parties, who have greater authority and resources to alter social policy, rely on forbearance rather than tax-based forms of redistribution. I suggest a theory based on several forms of policy feedback effects. Like public welfare policies, informal welfare policies foster widespread public expectations and alter institutional capacities in ways that become resistant to change. Although the evidence and variation are insufficient at the national level to pinpoint the effects of forbearance, I trace the history of social housing policy and (more briefly, given its inherent difficulties and multiple forms) employment policy, considering how major historical shifts, such as the dictatorship in Chile, were able to disrupt the informal welfare model. In countries that never underwent such political shocks, such as Colombia and Peru, informal welfare policies have proved resistant to change, even when broadly recognized as undesirable and inefficient ways to redistribute resources. I call this a *forbearance trap*.

Efforts to formalize informal property and business have only deepened the forbearance trap. In the late 1980s, the Peruvian economist Hernando De Soto advocated property titling and small business registration as a way to bring an end to informal economies and "unleash" capitalism. International financial institutions, such as the World Bank, have become strong advocates of such formalization measures. These policies make tremendous political sense: once legal violations are widespread, politicians see electoral rewards from measures to legalize and improve informal property. These policies can be provided more quickly and to more voters than standard investments in welfare programs. However, *post-hoc policies*, meaning those that provide state benefits after a legal violation has occurred, encourage illegality by making it more likely that a violation will end in a transfer of property or resources. I also show how post-hoc policies divert and demobilize the poor's demands for government welfare solutions. Perversely, although the assignment of property titles was pitched as a way to strengthen property law and include the poor in state institutions, I find that it perpetuates legal violations and exclusionary welfare regimes.

Exit from a forbearance trap is hard, but not impossible. Chapter 7 considers a case where forbearance toward the poor largely has ended, Turkey. As in the Latin American cases examined in depth, Turkish politicians historically relied on forbearance to win the poor's support and patch over welfare state deficiencies. But I demonstrate that the electoral incentives to enforce have changed in Istanbul. The growth of a lower-middle class has led to a sustained enforcement turn against squatters and vendors. Politicians also have tried to associate legal violations with ethnic and religious minorities, further reducing the electoral costs of enforcement. The implication is that the use of informal welfare could be on the wane if Latin America's equitable growth continues. The analysis of a more ethnically diverse city also opens up questions about how social cleavages and beliefs about the deservingness of the poor affect enforcement politics, both in Latin America and beyond.

Stepping back, this book makes three main contributions. First, it helps explain the form that welfare regimes take in much of the global South. A growing literature focuses on why Latin American welfare states are "laggards" in comparative perspective, and what explains their uneven progress toward more inclusive policies in the contemporary period (e.g., Carnes and Mares 2015; Garay 2017; Haggard and Kaufman 2008; Huber and Stephens 2012; De La O 2015; Díaz-Cayeros, Estévez, and Magaloni 2016; Mares and Carnes 2009; Segura-Ubiergo 2007; Pribble 2010, 2013). Looking beyond the confines of state social expenditures presents a different view on welfare state development. Far more transfers have occurred to Latin America's poor than are commonly recognized, through the active manipulation of laws in their favor. Including forbearance toward the poor in the picture also makes sense of why governments have made progress in reforming some social areas, such as cash transfers and health care, while other "big-ticket" policies with effective informal welfare substitutes, such as housing and employment policy, remain focused on formal-sector workers.

The benefits from forbearance matter because their redistributive effects can be so substantial. For example, in Lima, Peru, about 13 percent of the population currently live in houses acquired through land invasions and 10 percent work as street vendors. According to calculations in Chapters 3 and 4, forbearance toward these populations is tantamount to transfers of about $750 million each year. In contrast, cash transfer programs, which have been one of the main innovations to aid the poor, cover just 7 percent of households nationwide (and almost none in Lima) and cost the government about $250 million annually. Cash transfer programs spread in the 2000s, whereas as early as the 1960s, land invasions were recognized to be a "legitimate part of housing policy" and housed a half million people in Lima alone (Collier 1976: 29). Thus, informal transfers can dwarf targeted state assistance in their coverage and historical import. I also show that informal welfare involves more than the self-help, family-based, and clientelistic handouts usually emphasized (e.g., Gough and Wood 2008). Rather, it requires active decisions by state actors and sometimes quite substantial pressure by poor voters. Not simply a footnote or anomaly, informal welfare policies are at the heart of how governments in much of the developing world address the poor's most basic needs.

Allowing the poor to claim commonly held public resources, such as land, is redistributive in the same way that giving the poor commonly raised tax revenues is the backbone of modern welfare states. It is the politics of these processes that differ. Forbearance occurs through state inaction toward legal violations, which makes its costs less visible, its benefits less secure, and its politics less apparent. It also can empower exploitative intermediaries that capture some of the redistributive benefits. But precisely the fact that these informal transfers do not require a welfare bureaucracy or legislative debate also makes their implementation more credible, especially in contexts where politicians' promises of state welfare solutions often fail to come to fruition.

A deep normative tension runs through this book: forbearance offers much-needed support, particularly for groups outside the aegis of the formal welfare state, yet it also can perpetuate truncated welfare states, exclusionary citizenship regimes, and stratified economies. Whether forbearance is desirable depends on the willingness of governments to provide for the poor's social needs in other ways, and the time horizons over which we evaluate its effects. The ideal is that governments guarantee basic welfare goods like jobs, water, electricity, and housing to all citizens. When they do not complete this task, as in most of the global South, how laws should be enforced against the poor is a question with no easy answer.

Second, a focus on the distributive and redistributive consequences of law enforcement contributes to research on weak institutions. Different levels of law enforcement have implications for our theories about institutional design, effects, and change (Levitsky and Murillo 2009, 2013,

2014). But we still know little about the sources of different enforcement outcomes. If opinions about enforcement differ by class (or other attributes that cluster in space), attention to the way electoral boundaries are drawn can explain both when enforcement occurs and its variability across space and time. I show that forbearance is stable in contexts where politicians face electoral districts of mostly poor voters. In some districts, gaps open between the written law and behavior, what O'Donnell (1993) labels "brown areas." But in districts that mix different class groups, forbearance shifts with the constituency courted by politicians. Uneven enforcement across time, or what I call "brown periods," can be even more consequential for voting behavior.

Lastly, my findings challenge the assumption that the central axis of politics forms between the Left, which favors tax-based redistribution, and the Right, which resists it. Most scholars start with this view of the political spectrum, which is derived from advanced industrial democracies where the state has a long tradition of pro-poor redistributive action. They then struggle with what Kaufman (2009) calls the "inconvenient facts" that Latin America's poor do not demand more redistribution than the rich or vote for leftist politicians who advocate it. Clientelism, populism, or characteristics of informal labor contracts are the dominant explanations for why the poor fail to ally consistently with their natural representatives on the Left. But this view of politics is inappropriate for contexts where much downward redistribution happens by the state's leave, rather than through the state's hand. This book's contribution is to show that the poor do have shared material interests that motivate their organizing and electoral behavior. These interests often lie in forbearance. In other words, we may be looking for the wrong redistributive cleavage in developing democracies that have yet to develop modern and inclusive welfare states. Especially in urban elections, the political spectrum makes more sense when defined by enforcement positions.

# 1

# An Electoral Theory of Forbearance

> The old saying goes that the law is for the peasants ...
> but with democracy and social rights, it gets all reversed.
> You can't touch the poor with the law.
>
> – Lawyer, Bogotá, Colombia.[1]

In Latin America, a large gap exists between written law and lived norms. Labor standards with respect to working conditions, wages, and benefits are regularly ignored. Half of workers labor in the informal sector exempt from social protection. Five to ten percent of workers are street vendors, who violate property laws by using public space to set up stores in the middle of busy streets (Aliaga Linares 2010: 9; Bonner and Spooner 2012: 42). Similarly, detailed building codes and land use regulations are little more than aspirations. One in four Latin Americans lives in a legally precarious, underserviced neighborhood (UN-Habitat 2011: 32). Everything from abortion statutes (Htun 2003) to tax law (Bergman 2009) and environmental regulations (Amengual 2015; Ferraz 2007; Hochstetler and Keck 2007) is unevenly enforced.

O'Donnell's (1993) pioneering work identified these vast areas where the law is functionally and territorially absent. Yet it offered little explanation for the persistence of these gaps beyond state weakness, especially in the wake of Latin America's debt crises. Many other studies likewise interpret legal violations as evidence that Latin American states are

[1] Author interview with judicial coordinator, District of Usme, Bogotá, Colombia, August 26, 2011. The Colombian dictum goes, "*La ley es para los de ruana*," meaning that only the ignorant and the poor are required to follow the law as written.

unable to sanction the behavior of their citizens, and that citizens have grown accustomed to "paper norms" (Adelman and Centeno 2002; Bergman 2009; Centeno and Portes 2006; García Villegas 2009; Levitsky and Murillo 2009, 2013, 2014; Weyland 2002). But enforcement does not neatly coincide with state strength. Laws sometimes go unenforced in rich and capable countries and are rigorously enforced in poorer ones.

In this chapter, I take up the challenge of explaining why some governments tolerate violations of the law and others do not. Explaining this disparity requires a new conceptual and empirical apparatus to distinguish circumstances when governments *cannot* enforce the law from those when they *will* not enforce it. I therefore introduce the concept of forbearance, by which I mean *intentional and revocable government leniency toward violations of the law.* While forbearance can affect the poor and the rich, I focus exclusively on forbearance toward laws that the poor tend to violate.

As we will see, forbearance is most likely when politicians have no other way to meet the poor's distributive demands and depend on poor voters to win office. In these circumstances, forbearance functions as a critical distributive benefit that a politician can extend to win votes. Just as important, forbearance signals a politician's stance toward the poor. Voters expect politicians who forbear to serve the poor's interests, whereas enforcement communicates limited social sympathy and repels some poor voters. Enforcement therefore varies with the structure of the welfare state and electoral institutions that alter the poor's political weight.

In this chapter, I elaborate the logic of these arguments in more detail. Next I show how to distinguish forbearance from garden-variety state weakness and how my electoral theory makes distinct empirical predictions relative to alternative explanations. I then discuss my selection of city cases and legal violations, as well as the data sources used throughout the remainder of the book. I conclude the chapter by explaining the analogy of forbearance with redistribution. In much of the developing world, the poor receive little from government social policies, especially housing and employment policies, and the rich do not clearly pay them. Against this backdrop, I suggest that forbearance toward property laws has done more to allow the poor to secure basic goods and to produce class politics than traditional taxes and transfers. I do not imply that forbearance is "good" for the poor. Rather, it is good politics.

## 1.1 THE CONCEPT OF FORBEARANCE

I focus on forbearance as a phenomenon distinct from weak enforcement. Forbearance can take several forms, it can benefit the poor or the non-poor, and it can be allocated contingent on or independent of other political behaviors. I use these distinctions to separate different subtypes of forbearance and justify my own focus on forms that aid the poor.

### 1.1.1 Defining Forbearance

Three components – capacity, intention, and revocability – distinguish forbearance from related concepts (see Figure 1.1). First, institutional capacity distinguishes forbearance from forms of weak enforcement in which actors *cannot* enforce the law. It is nonsensical to talk about forbearance in parts of Sierra Leone or Haiti, where the state apparatus barely penetrates society. Very corrupt bureaucracies likewise preclude enforcement.[2] Surpassing a minimum level of institutional capacity does not require that a government be able to control all offenses, or that it allocate resources or institutions to enforcement at present. The theoretical bar is that politicians must be able to muster the infrastructure to punish offenses if they so desire. If they lack the resources, fail to

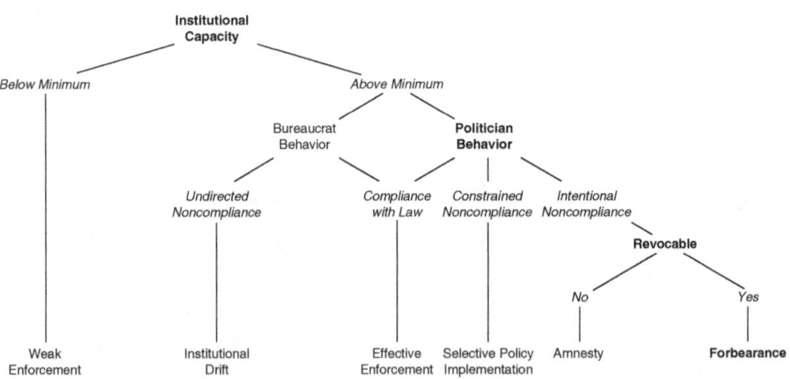


FIGURE 1.1 Situating the Concept

[2] For instance, Markus (2015: 202) rejects the possibility of forbearance in Ukraine due to the executive's inability to control the bureaucracy. President Viktor Yushchenko promised to ramp up property rights enforcement in Ukraine as part of the Orange Revolution, but a corrupt and intransigent bureaucracy thwarted his plans.

control predatory bureaucrats, or cannot revive neglected institutions, the outcome is weak enforcement, not forbearance.

Second, and most critically, forbearance requires a political choice not to enforce a law. A politician must act in some way to change the enforcement outcome, be it an attempt to demote bureaucrats who enforce, gut enforcement agencies, or stall sanctions for a type of offense or group. To make these choices, politicians must enjoy some discretion (formally or informally) over enforcement. If politicians face an insulated bureaucracy, then forbearance becomes impossible. This condition may seem to suggest that forbearance occurs only in "weak states," interpreted as those that lack insulated Weberian bureaucracies. However, the degree to which bureaucracy is insulated from electoral demands in a democracy varies. Many democracies place bureaucrats under the control of political appointees to increase electoral responsiveness, thus expanding discretion. More broadly, bureaucratic strength and autonomy do not always go hand in hand. Even large bureaucracies flush with resources may not be able to resist political pressure; some bureaucracies also sacrifice autonomy to expand their resources and capacity.[3] Forbearance depends on a bureaucracy with sufficient strength to execute politicians' desires, but imperfect autonomy so that politicians can intervene in enforcement.

I recognize the high evidentiary bar associated with showing political intent, but it is theoretically necessary to separate forbearance from other ways in which limited enforcement can be observed. Mahoney and Thelen (2010: 13), for instance, view enforcement as a locus for institutional change because state agents must enforce laws that they do not design. As Figure 1.1 illustrates, institutional drift results from bureaucratic noncompliance, as agents reinterpret or neglect formal rules. In contrast, forbearance suggests that politicians, not their agents, make the key decisions about whether to comply with the law.

Political intent also distinguishes forbearance from selective policy implementation, which refers to a decision to prioritize certain policies or laws and ignore others due to budget constraints. O'Brien and Li (1999), for example, develop the idea of selective policy implementation to describe the behavior of Chinese local cadres. Officials are assigned an array of policy targets, which they then choose among given limited time

[3] Amengual (2015: 25–6) questions the dichotomy between bureaucratic strength and autonomy. In many developing countries where states lack capacity to conduct enforcement on their own accord, societal cooperation can increase enforcement but reduce autonomy.

and money. Much work on Latin American informal economies focuses on a similar problem in which governments assume a heavy regulatory "load," and the combination of voluminous legal rules and finite budgets compromises enforcement (Centeno and Portes 2006; De Soto, Ghersi, and Ghibellini 1986). Selective policy implementation thus can be thought of as a variant of weak enforcement, except that politicians have the capacity to enforce if they divert resources and attention from one problem to another (or reduce the number of policies and regulations that they try to tackle in the first place). The implication is that a politician will enforce if resources or competing demands change.

In contrast, what forbearance – or intentional noncompliance by politicians – means is that *a politician is unwilling to change enforcement, even as resource constraints or competing policy demands ease.* Consider an example of enforcement against squatting in Bogotá, Colombia (Chapter 3). Although the city has invested in satellite imagery to track the expansion of squatter settlements and special teams of bureaucrats to monitor new construction, mayors refuse to sign legal orders to evict squatters and demolish their houses. More bureaucrats and money have not changed politicians' decisions to allow low-income squatters to remain.

A third core definitional element is that forbearance is revocable. The state reserves the right to enforce the law, and offenders believe that the rules can carry a sanction. This flexibility differentiates forbearance from cases of amnesty or legalization. There, the state formally surrenders its enforcement rights. A revocable decision can be formal, but more commonly, forbearance is expressed informally. Mayors in Santiago, Chile, for example, commonly give orders *not* to call in the police against street vendors as a way to win the support of poor voters (Chapter 5). Another example of revocable forbearance comes from riots in India. Some Indian politicians refused to call the police to prevent violence against Muslim protesters and transferred bureaucrats who tried to act (Wilkinson 2006: 61). Politicians could pick up the phone and reverse their choices at any moment.

It is easiest to recognize forbearance empirically when politicians maintain the resources and infrastructure to enforce at whim. But the ease with which forbearance can be revoked in practice varies. Vague and overlapping mandates can undercut enforcement, making it hard to distinguish political choices from bureaucratic constraints (Dimitrov 2009; Roever 2006). Politicians also can stop funding enforcement institutions or collecting information on legal violations altogether in a type of "benign neglect" or "standoffish state behavior" (Slater and Kim 2015). If prolonged neglect erodes institutional capacity so thoroughly that politicians have no control, then it is best described as weak enforcement. But institutional design and funding choices also can be endogenous to forbearance. In other words, politicians undercut enforcement institutions as a means of forbearance, as we will see in Chapter 3 with Peru's failure to create agencies or procedures to track squatters. As long as politicians credibly can increase enforcement, even if it requires reviving defunct procedures or using police capacity from other areas in new ways, these choices constitute forbearance.

### 1.1.2 A Typology of Forbearance

Enforcement (and its absence) has distributive consequences. More specifically, forbearance can be divided into subtypes, based on its distributive effects and mode of distribution. I define the distributive incidence as in the economic analysis of taxes and transfers. Progressive forbearance occurs when lower tranches of the income distribution receive greater absolute or relative benefits through the tolerance of law breaking than upper tranches. Regressive forbearance implies that upper tranches capture greater benefits.

There are two ways that a government influences the economic progressivity of enforcement through its decisions. First, choices about *which laws* to enforce have distributive consequences. In this case, progressivity depends on how the marginal utility of an offense changes with income. Forbearance that is directed toward laws that the poor tend to violate (or that primarily harm the rich) can distribute resources progressively. The criminalization of homelessness clarifies the point: although neutral on their face, vagrancy laws have a discriminatory impact on the poor, given that few wealthy individuals choose to sleep in the streets. Enforcement of laws that the wealthy tend to violate ("white-collar" crime), such as those against pure cocaine use, foreign tax shelters, or insider trading, has the opposite distributive consequences.

Other laws can benefit all income groups if ignored. In these cases, progressivity depends on *which groups* are targeted for enforcement. Consider the case of enforcement against squatting. If a government does nothing to prevent squatting, then the wealthy can take valuable pieces of land to build large houses and absorb the greatest absolute benefit from government leniency. However, the poor may receive the maximum relative benefit, given that they spend a greater share of their income on housing and they are potentially judgment proof in the case of prosecution. Weak enforcement thus has mixed distributive effects: it is likely regressive in absolute terms and progressive in relative terms. However, if the government prosecutes upper-class squatters and ignores lower-class ones, as I show in Chapter 3 in Bogotá, the result is solidly progressive. If only the very wealthy are allowed to violate land laws, as Sun (2015) finds in China, forbearance is regressive. The incidence depends not on the type of law, but rather on how governments use their discretion in enforcement.[4]

Just as with tax or social welfare programs, how to calculate distributive benefits can be tricky. Some laws are hard to categorize because the direct incidence (who violates the law and pays the direct costs) differs from the indirect incidence (who benefits once market prices have adjusted).[5] I focus on the direct incidence, although I agree that analyzing the indirect incidence of laws can lead to different conclusions, as has long been recognized in the case of social policies.

Thomas Malthus's (2008[1803]) famous analysis of poor relief in Britain underscores why studying the direct incidence makes sense. A direct incidence analysis of poor relief suggests that the poor receive the benefits and the nonpoor pay the costs through general taxes. Malthus proposed an indirect incidence analysis in which poor relief leads the poor to have more children, which raises the price of food. Higher food prices benefit agricultural interests but harm consumers. The increased food prices push those not receiving government benefits into poverty, perversely leading to greater poverty, disease, and starvation. Thus, poor relief – even when distributed to the poor and paid for through income taxes – actually harms the poor and serves the interests of the landowning class. This canonical example shows how quickly indirect incidence arguments can descend into absurdity. More important, they are inaccurate descriptions of politics. Most actors follow their immediate interests and struggle to see how economic forces will adjust in response to their individual choices. For this reason, most literature on the welfare state focuses on the direct incidence of who pays for and receives welfare programs. I do the same for forbearance, and as we will see in the next

[4] This feature is another way in which forbearance is distinct from selective policy implementation. Selective implementation focuses on the (non)enforcement of entire laws or policies, rather than their uneven implementation, as noted by Gobel (2011).

[5] In economics, the direct incidence also is referred to as the physical incidence, whereas the indirect incidence refers to the economic incidence.

chapter, the poor indeed see forms of forbearance that lead to direct benefits for them as serving their interests. The middle class mostly opposes forbearance and fails to appreciate the indirect benefits like a cheaper welfare state and an urban service class.

The second dimension distinguishes between modes of distribution. Forbearance can be provided in a contingent manner to individuals or groups as a reward for political behaviors, such as campaign contributions, bribes, votes, or turnout. Conversely, threats of enforcement can be used as negative inducements to compel political behaviors.[6] Most clientelistic exchanges raise credible commitment problems: a politician can renege on her promises of particularistic rewards once she wins an election, and voters can support their preferred candidate at the ballot box, ignoring the rewards they already received. But politicians can revoke forbearance at any point and therefore cement a more durable political dependency.[7] To be clear, if a voter supports a politician out of fear that enforcement will follow against him personally if he supports another candidate or fails to mobilize in a campaign, then it is a case of clientelistic forbearance. This definition excludes promises of forbearance (or threats of enforcement) that do not hinge on how an individual or a small group votes or acts politically.

In contrast, forbearance can be extended in a transparent and unbiased way. I distinguish this mode as noncontingent in that it extends to individuals or groups regardless of whether they supported or opposed a politician. So, if a voter supports a candidate because she promises not to enforce certain laws for all individuals in ways that a voter wants, then it is not clientelistic. A voter may feel compelled to support a candidate to guarantee the continuity of forbearance toward all similarly situated individuals, especially if a competitor promises enforcement, just as she may feel pressured to vote for candidates who will continue welfare programs that help her and other program beneficiaries.

These distinctions parallel those made between particularistic and programmatic policy. However, minimalist definitions of programmatic policy center on the ideas (1) that disbursements are made based on transparent criteria, regardless of whether a particular individual supported or opposed

[6] On the distinction between positive and negative inducements, see Mares and Young (2016: 268–71).

[7] Robinson and Verdier (2013) make a similar point about the advantages of using public-sector employment for patronage purposes, and Medina and Stokes (2007) theorize a set of politically monopolized goods that politicians can revoke.

the politician or party that designed the policy, and (2) that the criteria of distribution are formalized (Kitschelt 2000: 850; Stokes et al. 2013: 7). Noncontingent forms of forbearance fall short on the second component. Although politicians can be impartial and public in their position that laws should not be enforced, these decisions are by definition not codified in law. Forbearance is a frequent subject of political platforms and speeches; I therefore think of it as a quasi-programmatic policy.

Revocability cements relationships of political dependency in the context of contingent exchanges, while it has a more benign function in noncontingent exchanges. Politicians often rely on forbearance to change the effects of the law without the need to reform legislation and openly clash with powerful interest groups. Htun (2003), for instance, argues that removing abortion statutes would unleash the ire of the Catholic Church in many Latin American countries. Choosing not to sanction abortions de facto achieves similar objectives without the political costs. In addition, enforcement preferences can vary with electoral districts or economic conditions over time. As I show in Chapters 4 and 5, many politicians defend forbearance against street vending as a temporary accommodation to deal with economic crises and local unemployment. They want to be able to enforce against street vendors when macroeconomic conditions improve. Thus, forbearance can be extended in a noncontingent manner to tailor law to popular preferences and temporary exigencies.

These dimensions combine to generate four subtypes of forbearance, shown in Figure 1.2. The left side corresponds to intuitive regressive subtypes. When legal exemptions are provided to specific wealthy individuals, forbearance constitutes a standard form of corruption or cronyism. It is the flipside of targeted enforcement against political enemies. The quotation ascribed to Brazilian president Getúlio Vargas best captures the

| | *Economic Incidence* | |
|---|---|---|
| *Mode of Distribution* | Regressive | Progressive |
| Contingent | **Corrupt** | **Clientelistic** |
| Noncontingent | **Plutocratic** | **Welfarist** |

FIGURE 1.2 A Typology of Forbearance

sentiment: "For my friends, everything; for my enemies, the law." As long has been the norm in Latin America, forbearance can be manipulated as a favor to (or way to extract bribes from) the elite.

The lower-left corner corresponds to circumstances where forbearance extends to the rich as a class, or a type of plutocratic forbearance. The distinction from corruption is that the rich or powerful gain a general impunity that need not be negotiated by specific individuals. In highly unequal contexts, such as Latin America, legal immunity for the wealthy can extend to most areas of law. Scholars have called this the "misrule of law" (Holston 2008), the "unrule of law" (Méndez, O'Donnell, and Pinheiro 1999), and "legal apartheid" (De Soto, Ghersi, and Ghibellini 1986). Yet these concepts have been used to describe numerous legal injustices – lawless violence, flaws in the written law, and state absence – so I prefer the more precise idea of plutocratic forbearance to describe when wealthy citizens stand above enforcement.

The typology also yields two economically progressive types of forbearance. The upper right, which corresponds to a particularistic distribution of forbearance to favor the poor, is a clientelistic subtype. While poor voters, like the rich, can exchange bribes for forbearance, their main assets are votes, not money. Thus, they tend to offer their political support to secure special legal treatment, and run the risk of enforcement if it flags. A classic example comes from Chubb's (1982) study of patronage machines in southern Italy. The failure of police to denounce unauthorized shops in return for electoral favors was central to machine politics. Club goods also can be exchanged for a small group's turnout or votes in which case the relationship still may be clientelistic (Kitschelt and Wilkinson 2007: 2). For instance, squatters in countries as diverse as India, Brazil, and Zimbabwe have negotiated their collective votes to prevent threatened enforcement against their land occupations.[8]

Last, forbearance can be extended to the poor in a generalized manner as an informal welfare policy. Politicians may use income or other notions of deservingness in their enforcement choices, and they generally hope to be rewarded at the polls for their enforcement positions, but

[8] There is a large literature on clientelistic exchange in squatter settlements, although much of it involves the exchange of services and local public goods for electoral support (rather than protection against eviction). Some examples include Auerbach (2016); Cornelius (1975); Dosh (2010); Fischer (2008); Gay (1994); Herbst (1989); Leeds (1974); Jha, Rao, and Woolcock (2007); Karst (1971); Ray (1969); and Stokes (1991, 1995).

they do not demand specific political behaviors in exchange. An example of this dynamic comes from the restoration of democracy in Venezuela in 1958. In the fragile democracy, leniency toward squatters was a way for the left-leaning Acción Democrática government to "offer the possibility of helping the poor without any threat to the rich" (Bromley 1978: 38). The government allowed squatter settlements to expand tenfold in the years following the democratic transition. The generalized acceptance of squatting by the poor contrasts with previous periods in which squatter settlements only formed and survived with the explicit backing of a political party and a negotiated electoral exchange (Ray 1969: 88).

Studying forbearance can take us many directions, from copyright law to immigration, pharmaceutical, and environmental regulations. I focus on laws that the poor tend to violate, or those located on the right side of Figure 1.2. I recognize that forbearance toward the propertied and wealthy is pervasive and, frankly, the norm in most countries. But legal violations by the poor merit special attention because they involve distributive claims by numerically important voters and thus are most relevant for understanding politics in the developing world. Like government social programs, forbearance toward the poor can mobilize moral sentiments and structure electoral politics in ways that the illegalities of the rich cannot. Legal exemptions toward the wealthy tend to be negotiated in private, outside of the electoral process, and are more likely to involve formal changes in the law. I return to the contrast between types of legal violations in the book's conclusion, and focus here on how enforcement of laws that the poor violate shapes electoral politics.

## 1.2 THE ARGUMENT

The room for choice over enforcement is manifest in its erratic use. In some time periods and places, politicians punish street vendors, squatters, electricity theft, illegal mining, and deforestation. In others, they let thousands of offenses occur, often in public view and with little change in budgets or police forces. How can we explain such swings in enforcement? Why does enforcement occur in some areas of a city or country but not others? I argue that two primary factors, the structure of government social policies and the electoral leverage of poor voters, affect a politician's electoral incentives and thus determine the patterns of enforcement over time, space, and legal sector.

### 1.2.1 Social Policy Context

The Arab Spring began when a street vendor set himself on fire in front of a local government office to protest the confiscation of his street cart in 2010. This concrete moment of a poor person faced with a coercive and unjust state galvanized the Tunisian public to topple President Zine El Abidine Ben Ali, who had ruled the country with an iron fist for over two decades. Yet this same type of enforcement – the removal of equipment and merchandise from street vendors – occurs on a daily basis in cities around the world. While multiple factors shape public reactions to enforcement, I argue that the structure of the welfare state plays a central role in how enforcement is perceived, especially in electoral democracies. As a Colombian bureaucrat in charge of enforcement captures the core logic, "You just can't impose the law on a social question . . . but welfare policies can turn social questions back into simple matters of law enforcement."[9]

Figure 1.3 previews the three main paths through which social policy affects the electoral costs of enforcement. The first, and most mechanical, links welfare policies to the poor's material need to violate the law. Legal violations pop up when there are gaps left by welfare programs. Second, social policy changes what the poor demand from the state. When states fail to provide basic goods for citizens, enforcement becomes a terrain of political contestation, leading citizens to mobilize around forbearance. Welfare bureaucracies are viewed as irrelevant and distant from the poor's lives. Third, social policy provision changes how enforcement is interpreted in the political environment. Politicians fear being viewed as insensitive to local conditions if they enforce without alternative ways to meet the poor's demands. Combined, *complementary social policy*, or social policy that is inadequate or targeted at other class groups, raises the electoral costs of enforcement, making it more variable and dependent on the electoral context. *Substitutive social policy*, meaning measures that address the poor's welfare needs, reduces the electoral costs and makes enforcement possible in a broader set of circumstances.

Social policy is a structural variable in my model in the sense that local politicians tasked with enforcement cannot change it. In many countries, major welfare policies are designed at the national level as a way to pool risks and resources. Even when welfare responsibilities are decentralized, local governments, especially in poor areas, depend on resource transfers

[9] Author interview with housing inspector, District of Engativá, Bogotá, Colombia, July 13, 2010.

| **Social Policy** | | *Material Needs* | *Societal Demands* | *Political Signals* | | **Enforcement Costs** |
|---|---|---|---|---|---|---|
| **substitutive**<br>targeted and scaled in-kind policies | → | *crowded out*<br>needs met through formal welfare system, symbolic violations | *demand reinforcement*<br>citizens pressure for state provision | *legalism signal*<br>enforcement cues rule of law | → | **low electoral costs**<br>enforcement constrained by budget |
| **complementary**<br>truncated, skeletal, or cash-based policies | → | *crowded in*<br>needs unmet through formal welfare system, materialist violations | *demand displacement*<br>citizens pressure for forbearance | *distributive signal*<br>enforcement cues anti-poor policy | → | **high electoral costs**<br>enforcement constrained by political geography |

FIGURE 1.3 The Effects of Social Policy on Enforcement Incentives

from the national level and struggle to alter welfare provision in the short run. In contrast, enforcement (formally or informally) falls under the control of subnational politicians. I therefore take social policy as given, and ask how its provision conditions the local electoral costs of enforcement. In Chapter 6, I relax this assumption to think about the determination of social policy at the national level.

I concentrate on the broad division between substitutive and complementary social policies. In general terms, policies are substitutes if the presence (or efficiency) of one decreases the returns (or efficiency) from the other (Hall and Soskice 2001: 17). For the purposes of this book, a social policy substitute decreases the need for forbearance. The most effective substitutes are in-kind transfers that provide the same type of good that can be secured through law breaking. The poor do not need to take land when they have a house at their disposal or to bootleg electricity when free service is provided by the state. All substitutive policies must cover the poor, but not all bottom-targeted policies are substitutive. In particular, the most widely adopted social policies to assist the poor in the developing world since the 1990s have been means-tested cash transfers. Through an income effect, cash transfers may reduce demand for lower-quality informal welfare goods. With additional income, a poor household can rent an apartment, rather than invade land; they can pay for, rather than steal, electricity. But cash is not equivalent to a decent house, job, or basic services. Transfer payments often are insufficient to cover the costs of "big-ticket" goods like the purchase of a house. Cash transfers even can make forbearance more valuable. In theory, means-tested transfers incent the poor to work in the informal sector, where income flows are harder for social assistance agencies to detect.[10] Small cash payments rarely eliminate demand for forbearance, so I limit substitutive social policy to in-kind expenditures on the poor.

Symmetrically, social policies are complementary if they raise the value of forbearance. The welfare state must accomplish two things: to generate transfer payments and to have them actually reach the poor. Some governments fail in the former. They simply collect little in taxes and spend little to provide basic goods and services to their citizens. Other governments lag in the latter. They offer truncated social policies that involve substantial expenditures, but do not reach the poor. As I

[10] Empirical evidence for this claim is mixed: to date, most studies show that cash-based programs result in at most small shifts to the informal sector (Levy 2008; World Bank 2012).

describe in the next chapter, most welfare policies in Latin America began as emoluments for public sector and organized workers. Although governments have made progress to provide a basic social safety net to the poor, significant gaps remain, especially in tricky areas like housing and employment policy.

Returning to the mechanisms that connect social policy to the electoral costs of enforcement, substitutive social policies by definition affect the first channel and crowd out material demands for forbearance. Complementary social policies, in contrast, leave the poor's basic material demands unresolved, increasing the desirability of legal violations to claim the same goods. This *crowding out* or *crowding in* mechanism is the most obvious way in which social policy influences societal compliance and enforcement costs. Take an extreme example of a social democratic welfare state: Sweden. In Stockholm, a visitor is hard-pressed to find a single unlicensed street vendor, presumably due to the extensive state support for the unemployed. The legal violations that do occur in functioning welfare states are more likely to be isolated occurrences or have instrumental purposes. For instance, a renowned squatter community in Copenhagen was a "social experiment" meant to challenge the capitalist economic system (Karpantschof 2011). Some legal violations are part of a repertoire of criticism, intended to change or amend state policies (Peñalver and Katyal 2010; Tsai 2015). Squatters in Chile, for instance, have used land invasions to draw attention to the quality and location of housing programs provided by the Chilean welfare state (Guzmán et al. 2009). In contrast, when social policy is complementary, legal violations are widespread ways to fulfill basic material needs.

Second, social policies structure popular demands and organizing. It has become commonplace to argue that social policies unleash path-dependent dynamics in which beneficiaries organize to protect and improve their benefits (e.g., Campbell 2005; Mettler 2011; Pierson 1993, 1994, 2000; Skocpol 1995). In the context of substitutive social policy, the argument is a familiar one. When social policies include the poor, citizens look to the state to address their needs and existing beneficiaries mobilize to protect coverage. Social expenditures thus can unleash a virtuous cycle in which initial benefit inclusion leads citizens to expect and mobilize around the improvement and continuation of state intervention. I call this a process of *demand reinforcement.*

What do the poor demand in circumstances when social policy does little for them? I argue that complementary social policies can lead to a process of *demand displacement* when legal violations function as a substitute means of securing basic welfare. Because important welfare benefits can be secured through the violation of the law, these informal welfare benefits spur popular demands and collective action. Crucially, the poor mobilize for forbearance because they see it as a pragmatic way to improve their welfare. It is hard for the poor to lobby to increase taxes, redirect spending in their favor, or reform welfare bureaucracies. But they can lay claim to physical property. They can ask government officials to suspend enforcement. Inaction, quite simply, is easier to request and receive than action.

Demands for forbearance are particularistic in the sense that they are embedded in local contexts and instrumental in orientation. Squatters do not demand that property laws be abolished; informal shop owners do not propose to eliminate business regulations. Rather, the poor form groups that can demand forbearance toward their particular situation, such as street-vending associations, informal mining cooperatives, and squatter associations. Such organizing often is seen as counterproductive to the programmatic goals and horizontal integration across organizations embodied in more traditional labor movements (Collier and Handlin 2009; Oxhorn 1995; Roberts 1998, 2002). Nevertheless, specific entreaties for favorable legal treatment can cumulatively result in important change in the use and distribution of property.

Once the poor violate property laws, they pressure for measures that protect, improve, and ultimately legalize property, or what I call *post-hoc policies*. Collective action becomes oriented toward policies that allow the poor to stay and, in some cases, negotiate the legal transfer of resources. Policies such as property-titling initiatives and credit programs have become increasingly national in scope, as we will see in Chapter 6. Furthermore, poor people's associations increasingly use the language of social rights to frame their claims and mobilize the law to protect entire populations. In countries that recognize social rights in their constitutions, such as Colombia, Brazil, India, and South Africa, court justices have issued injunctions to stop enforcement as a way to protect social rights when the welfare state fails (Chapter 6; also Arslanalp 2015; Gauri and Brinks 2010; Holston 2008). Thus, complementary social policy moves the target of the poor's claims away from welfare bureaucracies and toward local forbearance, post-hoc policies, and, in some cases, constitutional rights claims.

This account of the poor's demands in inadequate welfare states both builds on and diverges from existing work. One branch of scholarship sees a path-dependent sequence in which inadequate welfare policies demobilize the poor's redistributive demands. Khemani (2007: 59) suggests a vicious cycle of "low [state] performance and low expectations for broad development outcomes." The poor instead look outside the state to self-help, family-based aid, clientelistic handouts, and nongovernmental and religious organizations (Barrientos 2004; Cammett 2015; Cammett and MacLean 2011; Gough and Wood 2008; Kitschelt et al. 2010; Mares 2005; Martinez Franzoni 2008; Soifer 2013; Wood and Gough 2006). The poor thus "blow with the wind," and provide no pressure to change a system that has failed them or locked them into clientelistic relationships.[11]

Another opposed view is that the poor's exclusion from social policy unleashes a reactive sequence. Workhorse models assume that the more skewed the income distribution is, which is partially a product of existing tax and transfer policies, the greater the electoral support for government policies to rectify it (Meltzer and Richard 1981; Romer 1975). Reactive models hit a major empirical snag, however. Redistribution tends to be most limited in the unequal societies, including Latin America, where it is most needed (Bénabou 1997; Kaufman 2009; Lindert 2004; Perotti 1996). The usual explanations for this fact point to the barriers created by extreme inequalities: states are unable to tax the rich, existing beneficiaries prevent changes to program targeting, powerful landowning classes thwart land reforms, and poor majorities struggle to sustain collective action (Acemoglu and Robinson 2006; Boix 2003; Haggard and Kaufman 2008; Huber and Stephens 2012; Karl 2003; Roberts 2002; Robinson 2010). In Latin America, characteristics of labor informality – heterogeneity of employment, geographic separation, precarious income, and lack of experience with modern benefit arrangements – also are blamed for the poor's limited influence on redistributive policy (Collier and Handlin 2009; Dosh 2010; Kurtz 2004; Oxhorn 1998; Roberts 1998, 2002; Weyland 1996a). In other words, the poor "lean against the wind," clamoring for more taxation and a greater share of spending, but fail to challenge powerful elites and implement their claims.

I largely agree with the first perspective that the poor are skeptical that state social policies will serve their interests. I demonstrate that the poor do not see themselves as the main beneficiaries of social spending, or trust politicians to spend in ways that serve their interests (Chapter 2). But the poor do not simply demobilize. Accounts that emphasize the informal

[11] I adapt the metaphor of "blowing with" or "leaning against" the wind from Moene and Wallerstein (2003: 485).

sector's lack of shared interests and organization often assume that the poor should pressure for tax-based social welfare policies. But pro-poor social policy has not been a major feature of politics in the developing world until late. In some areas, such as housing and job provision, the state still plays little role in providing for the poor's welfare. Likewise, in many historical periods, far more land redistribution has occurred through land invasions than through state land reforms. For instance, just over 100,000 families received land from the Brazilian government in the decade following the transition to democracy, whereas three million people participated in land invasions (Hidalgo et al. 2010: 506–07). My argument is that the sites of mobilization shift to arenas in which the poor expect that politicians and bureaucrats can do more. I echo Scott (1969: 1142) in thinking that "A large portion of individual demands, and even group demands, in developing nations reach the political system, not before laws are passed, but rather at the enforcement stage."

Continuing with the final mechanism, substitutive social policies change how voters perceive politicians who enforce. Sanctions are rarely popular, but as governments invest in social policy, politicians can emphasize state assistance to the poor and normative obligations to respect the law. Individuals who violate the law are portrayed as cheaters; politicians who tolerate their violations are seen as incompetent or even corrupt. Enforcement thus serves as a *legalism signal.* The absence of substitutive social policy, in contrast, changes the idiom of enforcement. At least to some voters, forbearance is interpreted as a way to provide welfare to the poor when the state fails, and signals that politicians understand the lives of the poor. Enforcement, conversely, conveys a politician who is insensitive to the poor's situation, serving as a *distributive signal* about a politician's class affinities. These distributive signals can be attenuated by other circumstances like when those who violate the law are ethnic outsiders, as we will see in Chapter 7, or when substantial violence accompanies legal violations, as I return to in Chapter 8. My claim is that enforcement is more likely to be understood as a cue of a politician's distributive commitments in contexts where welfare programs are complementary, all else being equal.

In summary, complementary social policies leave material needs unmet, channel organizing to forbearance, and link enforcement to antipoor positions. The electoral costs of enforcement are high and, as I turn to now, they hinge on the type of district where a politician runs for office.

### 1.2.2 The Political Power of the Poor

The political power of the poor strongly influences the enforcement calculations of vote-seeking politicians. Politicians risk losing votes among the poor, but can gain votes among the middle class when they enforce. Therefore, how important poor voters are to a candidate's electoral success is central to understanding where and with what variability enforcement occurs.

Several factors can influence the poor's political centrality. Demographic variables, such as the number of poor people and their spatial concentration, alter the poor's electoral importance. Processes of electoral inclusion also matter. In some cities, recent migrants confront daunting hurdles when attempting to register to vote, especially when they live in squatter settlements or steal services that otherwise provide documents to establish residency. The poor also may not show up to vote in non-compulsory systems. Poor *residents* need to translate into poor *voters*.

Even when group size and turnout are held constant, differences in electoral rules, especially related to political decentralization, can affect the poor's leverage. District-level elections, as in decentralized cities, generally provide an electoral edge to geographically concentrated groups, including the poor. In at-large elections, by contrast, the entire city forms an electoral arena, which makes it more difficult for the poor to influence policy on a consistent basis. In this section, I first explain the theoretical reasons that poor and nonpoor voters have different enforcement attitudes (Chapter 2 will provide empirical support for these claims). I then expand on how voter demographics and electoral rules condition the poor's political power and thereby change politician's enforcement decisions.

Why do the poor support forbearance? First, by definition, the poor are the primary material beneficiaries of progressive forms of forbearance. Whether because the poor violate the law at the moment or value the chance to do so in the future, poor voters have a stronger material interest in forbearance against certain legal violations than the nonpoor.

Second, while some people make judgments based on their self-interest, a wealth of research shows that people also think in terms of group attachments. Gibson (2008), for example, demonstrates how group concerns shape attitudes toward squatting in South Africa. While 83 percent of black South Africans view squatter evictions as unfair, only 40 percent of whites find evictions to be unfair. Solidarities may reflect preexisting group identities, such as race in South Africa, but they also can develop through shared experiences of enforcement. Conflicts between the police and the poor may be especially prone to activate empathetic solidarities among the poor because they tap into asymmetries in power and a shared frustration in treatment by authorities.[12]

Third, the poor expect politicians who forbear to privilege their distributive needs in other policy areas. Voters must decide on candidates based on observable characteristics, but they often lack informational cues like those provided by party labels in advanced democracies or ethnicity in some developing democracies. In this spirit, Ostiguy (2009) argues that the main candidate "types" in Latin American politics are distinguished by manners, dress, accent, and legal attitudes. "Low" types dispense with the "formalities" of law to achieve their objectives, while "high" types value the rule of law. In his argument, these are symbolic affinities. I instead suggest that forbearance can signal a politician's distributive commitments. Political signals are clearer for enforcement, given that it requires the use of coercive force. Forbearance is a subtler cue, but it can be conveyed through public statements, alliances with groups in violation of the law, and plans to legalize those who previously have violated the law. As we will see in the next chapter, voters are good at picking out the rhetoric of forbearance. They see politicians who forbear as more likely to represent the poor, while those who enforce are seen as unlikely to represent the poor in office.

Flipping the logic, nonpoor voters are less likely to gain materially or identify with the distributive claims at stake from forbearance.[13] The nonpoor can suffer direct harms from forbearance, such as the loss of public goods, lower-quality services, and threats to private property. But most opposition from the nonpoor arises from the linkage between legal violations and other social ills, like crime, unsanitary conditions, and social unrest. These are long-standing tropes. A Lima weekly captured middle-class opposition in the 1960s by calling a squatter settlement "a dirty brothel where human life prostitutes itself each day."[14] In the 1990s, business leaders in Bogotá proposed to move street vendors to agricultural colonies because "it is the only way to end the scourge of insecurity in the

[12] For instance, street vendors in India are more likely to cooperate with one another and work across ethnic divisions when primed to think about common experiences of police repression (Thachil 2015b).

[13] I use the term "nonpoor" to refer to the rich as well as the middle class, which is more likely to have formal-sector employment.

[14] "Infierno en Lima," *Caretas* No. 195, Lima, April 1960, p. 27.

city caused by the indigent and street vendors."[15] Visible legal violations by the poor can be construed as embarrassing and indicative of an impotent, backward state unable to carry out day-to-day tasks, much as Weitz-Shapiro (2014) shows in the case of middle-class opposition to clientelism. Enforcement shows a "modern" government.

Some nonpoor voters do support forbearance, just as some wealthy individuals support redistribution. These individuals sometimes understand the indirect benefits of using forbearance to solve social problems or lower consumer prices. But I find that much of the middle class supports the law in the abstract. What they object to is coercive enforcement. Colloquially, these nonpoor voters might be thought of as bleeding-heart liberals. An analogy comes from debates over illegal immigration in the United States. Although many liberals support restrictions on immigration and oppose illegal border crossings, they still see the deportation of illegal immigrants as excessively harsh (Ellermann 2009). Nevertheless, in broad terms, poor voters are more likely to reward politicians who rely on forbearance than nonpoor ones.

Due to these differences in opinion by class, forbearance's effectiveness as a vote-getting tool turns on the demographics of the district where a politician runs for office. I focus on how political decentralization shapes enforcement incentives by affecting the poor's electoral leverage. In the 1980s and 1990s, many developing countries implemented reforms to decentralize political power and reorganize metropolitan governance. In the context of urban politics, political centralization refers to a system that invests power in a single mayor, usually elected in an at-large district. In large capital cities, these mayors rival the president in popularity and name recognition. The entire city represents a single, heterogeneous electoral district. Political decentralization, in contrast, entails the creation of sub-city electoral districts and the division of power among local mayors. District mayors tend to be less notable political figures. In district-level elections, each local area elects a mayor. The poor tend to be spatially clustered in certain districts where housing is less expensive. Many districts are internally homogeneous, meaning that they are composed largely of poor or nonpoor residents.

I assume that all politicians want to be elected and then reelected: even if they face term limits, they want to launch their next venture as a success.

[15] Fenalco president Dionisio Araújo quoted in, "Qué hacer con los indigentes," *El Tiempo* March 21, 1995; see also "Comerciantes aplazan paro," *El Tiempo* April 29, 1995. Hilgers (2008) notes similar class divisions in Mexico City.

In pursuit of these ends, a politician sets enforcement policy for her electoral district and, as in classic models of decentralization such as Oates (1972), disregards any negative externalities imposed on other districts. In politically decentralized cities, then, politicians respond to the preferences of their geographically defined constituents. In politically centralized cities, politicians consider the costs of their enforcement choices across urban space and set enforcement policy for the city.

Urban decentralization results in electoral districts with different class compositions. In a largely nonpoor district, the most viable electoral strategy is to enforce in line with voter preferences, displacing offenses to poor districts. A political challenger gains little from deviating from this policy because there is no electoral constituency of poor voters to counterbalance nonpoor interests. The poor who violate the law are unlikely to live or vote in the nonpoor district. In districts that are overwhelmingly poor, politicians forbear and attract more offenders due to their lax enforcement policies. Local politicians allow legal violations in line with the preferences of their constituents. Some districts mix class groups, leading to greater instability in enforcement policy depending on which group's interests a mayor represents. Overall, I expect enforcement to decrease with the fraction of poor voters in a district. Most variation in enforcement in politically decentralized cities comes *across space* as politicians choose different enforcement policies to reflect the makeup of their constituency. Decentralized cities thereby are peppered with "brown areas" (O'Donnell 1993), or parts of the city where laws are ignored.

As I explain more fully below, if most variation comes in how politicians set enforcement policy to respond to their constituents, then I expect to see a negative correlation between offenses and sanctions across space. In poor districts, politicians do less enforcement, which encourages more individuals to violate the law. For example, when asked why there are so many street vendors in his district, one mayor in a decentralized city explains: "I think that people know that I won't have the [police] throw them out so they come here."[16] In nonpoor districts, politicians do more enforcement, which discourages offenses or at least displaces them to poor districts. Thus, I expect to observe a pattern across a city in which more sanctions are associated with *fewer* offenses. The top row of Figure 1.4 lays out this logic.

[16] Author interview with Pedro Isla Farías, mayor, District of San Ramón, Santiago, Chile, June 21, 2012.

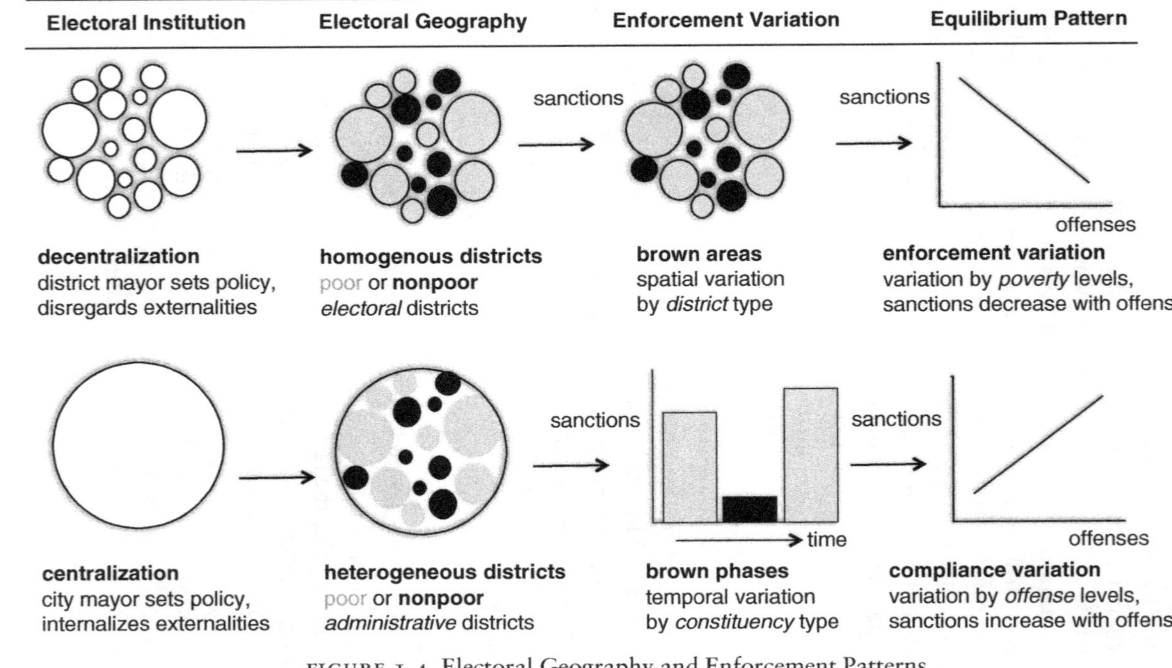


FIGURE 1.4 Electoral Geography and Enforcement Patterns

Political centralization results in different enforcement pressures and outcomes. Centralization concentrates all class groups in a single electoral district, which allows for multiple winning coalitions. Enforcement will vary with the social basis of a politician's core constituency, meaning the group that is most influential in providing her electoral, ideological, and financial support, and thus shaping her policy profile. Politicians who court poor core constituencies are more likely to promote forbearance because their key supporters benefit from it and the organized groups that support their campaign favor it. They also want to signal their affinity with the poor. Those with nonpoor constituencies tend to enforce in line with their voters and organized backers' preferences. Most variation in enforcement thus occurs *over time* as politicians who represent different core constituencies take office. Politically centralized cities have what I call "brown periods," or times in which laws are selectively jettisoned. These can punctuate periods in which politicians draw together nonpoor voters and enforce. Democratic alternation in power, in other words, produces swings in enforcement, just as it can in social or economic policy.

Although the level of enforcement varies with the politician in power, I expect more uniform enforcement across space once the politician sets the overall level in centralized cities. In theory, a politician charged with enforcement for the entire city could differentiate enforcement levels according to heterogeneous tastes in each neighborhood. However, the politician internalizes both the benefits of offenses and the costs imposed on others in the city. Her actions also send a political signal to all voters in a citywide district. Unlike in decentralized cities, I thereby expect the level of offenses, or compliance, to be the main driver of enforcement across space within a city. The police chief in a centralized city explains this logic: "[Some city mayors] take a tolerant view because they want to win votes by taking a social line . . . so we only go to places where there are problems, where there is more crime and conflict."[17] Most variation occurs over time, and the police direct more enforcement effort to places with more offenses, as shown in the bottom row of Figure 1.4.

I stress that enforcement varies with a politician's core constituency in politically centralized cities, rather than with political ideology. In advanced democracies, core constituencies and political ideology are taken as synonymous. Left parties are defined as those that represent the lower class. This association does not hold in much of the developing world. Labor-based left

[17] Author interview with chief of Public Space Unit, Bogotá, National Police of Colombia, September 8, 2011.

parties long drew their core support from more privileged segments of the middle class and formal-sector working class. The exclusion of the informal-sector poor allows elite parties using "segmented strategies" to build coalitions of poor and wealthy voters (Luna 2010, 2015; Thachil 2015a). It also can open the door to "neopopulist" politicians who unite rich and poor voters by railing against organized labor (Roberts 1995; Weyland 1996b). Left–right ideological distinctions do not capture which parties and politicians, if any, consider the informal-sector poor part of their core constituencies. I therefore identify a politician's core constituency by her pattern of electoral support and ties with organized groups, rather than by an ideological label.

An additional reason that I focus on core constituencies is that forbearance both aids and criminalizes the poor in ways that crosscut traditional ideological divides. The left–right cleavage tends to be viewed as a conflict around the politics of inequality and redistribution (e.g., Levitsky and Roberts 2011; Luna and Kaltwasser Rovira 2014). The Left refers to political actors whose central objective is to lessen social and economic inequalities. Strong disagreement exists over whether the tolerance of legal violations reduces social inequality. On the one hand, a materialist Left considers the economic claims of the poor to trump other concerns. Forbearance is justified because it allows the poor to fulfill their basic needs in the short run where the state fails. After all, enforcement involves the use of coercion against vulnerable populations who have made claims to legitimate goods like jobs, land, and basic services. On the other hand, a post-materialist Left seeks to advance a broader conception of social equality and citizenship rights. Forbearance creates a dual structure in which the poor access goods through illegal means that stigmatize them, harm collective rights, and leave them vulnerable to exploitation. Governments do not interact with the urban poor as rights-bearing citizens, but instead negotiate legal exceptions (Chatterjee 2004, 2011; Fischer 2008). The debate for the Left, then, is whether forbearance primarily promotes income equality or perpetuates legal inequality.

On the Right, ideological divisions arise between a libertarian and a liberal variant. The libertarian position underlines the corrosive impact of state regulations. Libertarians often support forbearance, seeing it as a way to reduce regulation and expand economic activity (De Soto 2000; De Soto, Ghersi, and Ghibellini 1986). In contrast, the liberal Right emphasizes the protection of property rights as a core state function, which requires a heavier state hand in providing the legal framework and enforcement to protect property owners.[18] The libertarian approach resonates among the poor, particularly when it involves the defense and legalization of informal activities. In contrast, the liberal position gains stronger support among the middle class. Hence, broad ideological labels miss these more nuanced views that can motivate politicians to promote forbearance and attract poor voters. Core constituencies serve as convenient shorthand to capture these different ideologies.

I assume that electoral victory is paramount to politicians, and other motives like ideology and competing career ambitions are secondary. But, as Aldrich (1995) skillfully points out, it also is naïve to conceive of politicians as devoid of ideology. Politicians also seek office to implement policies they believe to be in the public interest, which sometimes go against their constituents' immediate demands. Many subnational politicians also have ambitions to rise to national offices (and often the presidency) that require electoral strategies with an eye to national constituencies. All that my theory requires is that, when ideological beliefs or national office-seeking ambitions lead politicians to deviate from their constituents' preferences, enforcement results in the electoral consequences that I predict. Principally, politicians lose votes among the urban poor if they enforce in the absence of social policy substitutes, but this is counteracted by additional support from middle-class groups.

### 1.2.3 The Distributive Logic

The final piece of my argument concerns not just when and where forbearance occurs, but how it is distributed. As outlined above, forbearance can be provided as part of a contingent exchange in which politicians provide legal favors to supporters and enforce against detractors. The usual assumption is that politicians grant legal exemptions, rather than rights to certain goods, so that they can threaten to enforce the law and cement a relationship of political dependency. But this is an incomplete, and sometimes misguided, view of why voters and politicians support forbearance. Forbearance provides direct beneficiaries with valuable material resources and creates affective ties with non-beneficiaries.

[18] Ansell and Samuels (2015: 7–9) aptly summarize how the defense of private property, albeit primarily against the caprice of the state, is at the heart of Enlightenment liberalism. Historically, many liberal elites in Latin America, such as Chile's president Jorge Alessandri (1958–1964) and Peru's Manuel Prado (1956–1962), saw tolerance toward street vendors and squatters as an arbitrary use of government authority and a threat to private property.

Selective enforcement threats undermine the goodwill that politicians earn through inclusive commitments to alter the law in the poor's favor. Enforcement can end in protests. Rumors spread among poor voters that politicians do not care about them and end political careers. So, forbearance often is extended to all poor voters in a district.

When, then, do politicians distribute forbearance contingent on political behaviors? To answer this question, it is helpful to think about enforcement's reputational consequences. First, some types of enforcement are publicly observable and impose concentrated costs on those affected. As I explain below, the legal violations studied here – street vending and squatting – are visible and involve quite punitive sanctions. Other legal violations are less salient to the average voter and less disruptive to individual lives. I expect politicians to be more likely to negotiate sanctions in a clientelistic fashion when they can do so in private and the sanctions are small. Chapter 3 shows that quid pro quo exchanges are rare in the case of squatting because housing evictions are seen as a public and harsh punishment for political disloyalty. Clientelistic forbearance is somewhat more common for street vending because the fines are smaller (Chapter 4).

More broadly, the logic of removing and granting benefits differs. Many politicians are unwilling to impose concentrated harms on constituents and therefore refrain from making forbearance contingent on political behavior. But, they do engage in clientelistic negotiations around other goods. Moving away from the domain of losses, politicians prioritize certain loyal groups for local public goods and post-hoc policies. Of course, such targeting requires some capacity to monitor political behavior. In many parts of the developing world, political parties are weak, so it is dubious that the necessary party brokers exist to monitor voters' behavior. I show that association leaders often serve as critical intermediaries, or *organizational brokers*, in clientelistic exchanges (also see Holland and Palmer-Rubin 2015). Leaders bring their members to attend political meetings, plan events, and spread information about the candidate's positive attributes in exchange for private salary and group benefits. Concerns about reputational signals and societal mobilization prevent politicians from punishing associations that do not mobilize during campaigns or deliver the promised votes with coercive sanctions.

Second, district size changes the incentives to rely on clientelistic appeals. Politicians are more likely to make broad appeals in large districts because the costs of negotiating particularistic benefits rise (Hicken 2007: 56–7). Media outlets also tend to cover campaigns in larger districts, magnifying the reputational costs of enforcement. Conversely, monitoring recipients for quid pro quo arrangements and making targeted threats is easier in small districts. Following this logic, I demonstrate that forbearance is offered as a form of informal welfare provision in citywide elections and as a more clientelistic benefit in district elections, and especially in small districts where the votes of those who violate the law are pivotal.

Third, forbearance tends to be more programmatic in countries that recognize social rights in their constitutions. Politicians can claim to privilege a legal interpretation in which social rights trump other laws. Clientelistic enforcement against detractors then seems hypocritical. We will see this point most clearly in the contrast between Colombia, which recognizes social rights and where some politicians claim to protect the poor's constitutional rights through forbearance, and Peru, which does not constitutionally protect social rights and where clientelistic forbearance remains more common.

To review, my goal is to explain why some politicians enforce against legal violations by the poor and others tolerate them. I propose that national social policy bears on enforcement outcomes by influencing local electoral incentives. Substitutive social policies increase the chances that politicians will enforce the law because they directly crowd out the poor's distributive demands. Just as importantly, they reinforce the state as the authority responsible for social provision and reduce the reputational costs of enforcement. The electoral costs of enforcement are low. Conversely, the absence or truncation of social policy leaves local politicians with a distributive dilemma: they have no way to meet the poor's basic material demands. Popular pressure and organizing to offer informal welfare benefits encourage politicians to forbear, while the strong association between enforcement and anti-poor distributive positions elevates the electoral risks of enforcement. Social policy thus affects the overall stakes of enforcement decisions.

The second piece of the argument is attuned to how sensitive politicians are to poor voters and, thus, the patterns of enforcement across time and space. Decentralization has an impact on the poor's electoral clout at the local level. Political decentralization makes local mayors disregard the negative externalities of their enforcement choices on other districts. Politicians forbear in districts where the poor are geographically concentrated and thus represent pivotal votes. Meanwhile, urban political centralization means that mayors internalize all the negative externalities and reputational costs of their enforcement choices. Mayors are more likely to forbear when they represent poor core constituents for strategic or ideological reasons.

Electorally motivated forbearance can involve a contingent exchange of legal favors for votes. However, more often, politicians care about their reputations for serving the poor, and avoid selective enforcement that damages their standing in the local community. Especially in the case of visible sanctions, large electoral districts, and social rights constitutions, political actors who court poor voters prefer to stake out broad enforcement positions. They hope to build a reputation for goodwill, in addition to providing valued distributive benefits. Thus, my study joins others in questioning a narrow focus on clientelistic pacts as the way to mobilize the poor's votes (e.g., Golden and Min 2013; Min 2015; Thachil 2015a).

This electoral argument applies best to multilevel democracies with a minimum level of state capacity. Politicians must have some scope for choice in order to exercise forbearance. Although forbearance also occurs in authoritarian regimes (e.g., Bayat 1998; Collier 1976; Davis 1994; Dorman 2007; Sun 2015), it likely is motivated by different distributive pressures and national concerns, such as social stability, urban–rural migration, and regime legitimacy. As I expand on shortly, the theory also works best for legal violations that embed justifiable social claims, such as those to work, housing, water, electricity, and transportation.

## 1.3 EMPIRICAL STRATEGY

Although the idea that politicians manipulate enforcement to win votes is intuitively obvious to many who work in developing countries, how to document the phenomenon is not. How do we compare enforcement across governments that face different levels of legal violations? If perfect enforcement is unworkable, then what counts as reasonable or inadequate effort? And, perhaps most importantly, how can we separate circumstances when a government *chooses* not to enforce from those when it *cannot* enforce a law? These identification challenges bedevil empirical work on enforcement. In this section, I identify three general strategies that I use to separate forbearance empirically from garden-variety weak enforcement. I then discuss several other plausible political explanations for weak enforcement and their distinct empirical predictions.

### 1.3.1 Empirical Identification

Since enforcement is at the heart of this book, it is worth clarifying precisely what I mean by it. I focus on laws and regulations that are set by the government to proscribe mass behavior and that entail legal sanctions if violated. Enforcement encompasses any state activities that make sure that people do what the law says. Although there are many ways that states try to persuade the public to follow the law, including monitoring, verbal warnings, public campaigns, and working with social groups to control behavior, I downplay these persuasive efforts. Changing societal norms can be an effective way to boost compliance, but even persuasive efforts rest on the state's coercive power waiting in the wings. To use Levi's (1988) phrase, compliance is always *quasi*-voluntary. Sanctions, fines, and police operations are the meat of state efforts and the way that I operationalize enforcement. What I miss in the subtlety of comparing different enforcement "styles" and diverse tools to promote compliance, I hope I gain in the comparability of measures across contexts.

My approach harkens back to a law and economics tradition that draws more heavily from price theory than game theory.[19] The very idea of studying enforcement as a choice variable depends on breaking with certain game theoretic definitions. In North's (1990) widely adopted definition, for instance, institutions are shared expectations about the behavior of others. Enforcement exists as a mechanism to punish those who are cheating, and forms part of the institutional definition. In game theoretic models, any single individual's behavior affects the rules and thus the institution itself. I follow Mahoney and Thelen (2010: 10) in treating the institution as stable so that enforcement and compliance can be treated as variables. But rather than eschew rational choice modeling altogether, I show how a price theoretic tradition interested in observations of aggregate behavior and Marshallian equilibrium – that is, models in which no single individual can change the institutional equilibrium through their behavior – provides useful tools to distinguish forbearance. This approach works best for legal situations that involve a large number of similar violations, rather than interactions between a small number of parties, such as contract enforcement between a regulator and a single firm.

First, all studies of enforcement struggle with an issue of reverse causality between offenses and sanctions. This endogenous relationship has led some scholars to interchange the concepts of compliance and enforcement, as well as their measures. For instance, Levitsky and Murillo (2009: 117) define enforcement as "the degree to which parchment rules are complied with in practice," and advocate operationalizing enforcement

[19] The canonical examples of this tradition are Becker (1968), Stigler (1970), and Becker and Stigler (1974). For a definition of price theory, see Weyl (forthcoming).

through measures of offenses, sanctions, or inputs (like bureaucrats, cars, and budgets). But this approach to measurement provides limited leverage to understand whether citizens voluntarily comply with the law, reducing the need for sanctions, or whether politicians face resource constraints or electoral reasons to forgo enforcement. I instead adopt an equilibrium concept in which governments set enforcement levels and individuals make their compliance choices in response to the level of sanctions.[20] The goal is to characterize the related, but distinct, phenomenon of variation in sanctions due to government choices and due to the level of offenses, just as a supply and demand framework separates changes in production inputs from changes in consumer preferences in economic markets. A necessary, but not sufficient, condition for forbearance is that government actions, rather than offense levels, drive enforcement variation.

Sanctions and offenses are thought of as functions of each other, which jointly determine enforcement effort. On the one hand, the most basic assumption of crime control is that fewer individuals will violate the law as governments invest more in punishing offenses. We therefore can think of a demand curve (*Compliance*), which represents the level of offenses in a society as a function of government sanctions. This curve slopes downward because offenses decline with sanctions. On the other hand, the equilibrium is also determined by a government supply curve (*Enforcement*), which traces out the level of sanctions as a positive function of the level of offenses. Even governments that are not keen to enforce will apply more sanctions as the offense level increases because the negative externalities multiply, creating a rationale for additional sanctions, and more offenses are caught for a given resource investment.[21] The slopes of the enforcement curves vary across units because a government that engages in forbearance responds less to changes in offenses than one eager to enforce.

Figure 1.5 visualizes the two ways in which limited sanctions can be observed, through differences in the level of offenses or in government behavior. Think about two political units, *a* and *b*, which are alike in most ways. Citizens in *a* may have strong social norms against a given legal violation so the entire compliance curve is shifted inward relative to district *b*, as in the left panel of Figure 1.5. So, for any level of sanctions

20 Other works that adopt a similar equilibrium approach from law and economics include Gordon and Hafer (2014) and Ronconi (2010).

21 This reasoning stems from Becker's (1968) model of crime.

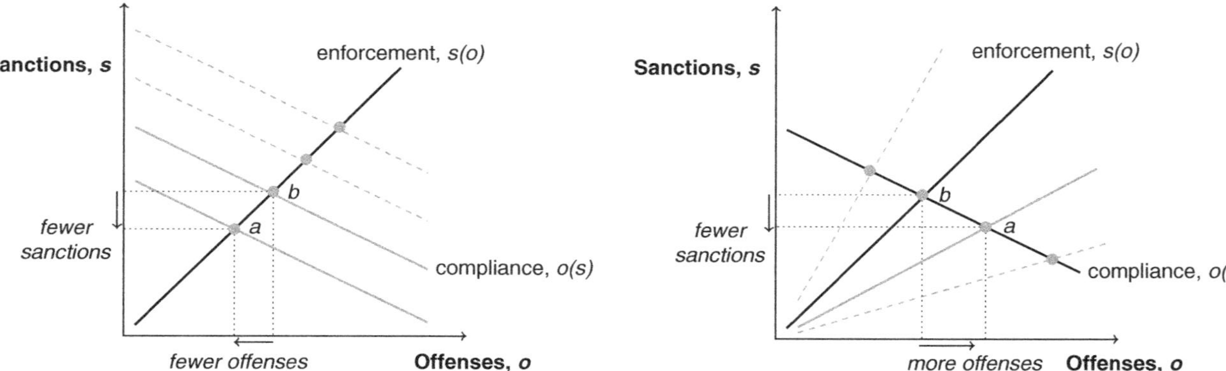


FIGURE 1.5 Compliance-Demand (left) and Enforcement-Supply (right) Shifts in the Enforcement Equilibrium

that government *a* does, it faces fewer offenses. Another possibility is that *a* has a similar culture of compliance as *b*, but government *a* cannot or will not enforce. The entire supply curve is shifted outward and flattened, as in the right panel of Figure 1.5. For any level of legal violations, district *a* does fewer sanctions than *b*. A comparison of sanctions alone gives us limited leverage to distinguish these two scenarios, and thus to infer what enforcement is like based on offenses alone (or vice versa).

The key insight is that information about the distribution of *both* offenses and sanctions can distinguish different causes of limited enforcement. Classic theory of identification of supply and demand curves, such as Working (1927), recognizes that supply-side shifts present different patterns of prices and quantities than those driven by consumer-side dynamics. In the same way, suppose the variation across units, such as political districts, is driven primarily by the demand (compliance) curve rather than the supply (enforcement) curve.[22] In this case, we see each unit has its own compliance curve, represented by the shifted dotted lines in the left panel of Figure 1.5. When we look across units (each in their own equilibrium marked by a point), the units trace out an upward-sloping relationship. This positive correlation corresponds to a "rational" enforcement model in the sense that governments engage in more sanctions when there are more offenses. As I show in Chapter 5, hard crime follows this pattern across districts.

If, on the other hand, the enforcement choices of governments fluctuate more than compliance (corresponding formally to more variation in the supply curves across units), a different pattern emerges. A line drawn to fit a range of political units will slope downward, as shown in the right panel. A "political" enforcement model predicts that governments exert less effort against offenses, which in turn encourages more legal violations. As I find in the case of street vending, mayors face different electoral pressures that lead some to oppose enforcement. Lax enforcement then encourages more residents to work as street vendors. Put another way, a positive correlation suggests the same enforcement policy, with sanctions allocated in proportion to offenses (compliance-side variation), while a negative correlation is indicative of different enforcement policy across districts (enforcement-side variation).

[22] A correlational strategy is based on the relative magnitude of the forces that shift the curves, given that both curves can shift at the same time. It therefore only reveals that one force is more important than the other.

The fact that enforcement variation stems from the government supply does not isolate whether politicians are unable or unwilling to enforce the law. One strategy is to control for observable differences in resources. Another is to select political units that share enforcement institutions. But, given possible unobserved institutional variation, the equilibrium strategy is most effective when there are exogenous shifters in the motivations for enforcement. In my model, plausibly exogenous differences in electoral rules, specifically the difference between decentralized and centralized cities, serve this role.

Second, I use a strategy to infer political intent by looking at the elasticity of enforcement. Elasticity refers to how responsive one variable, in this case enforcement, is to a change in another, like budgets, enforcement costs, or competing social concerns. Building off the equilibrium framework, I examine what factors lead to small or large shifts in the enforcement supply. Forbearance occurs when resources produce minimal changes in enforcement, while electoral factors result in large disturbances.

To see this reasoning, start with a budget constraint, representing government resources that can be spent on a set of goods and services. A politician allocates resources between enforcement and all other social goods, as shown by the budget constraint *B*. An exogenous change may reduce the cost of enforcement. For example, a technological advance like satellite imagery to track illegal logging decreases enforcement costs. Such a reduction moves the budget constraint to *B'*. If a politician wants to enforce the law, but previously was constrained by funds, the elasticity of response will be large. This responsiveness to changes in costs is represented visually by a steep indifference curve in which the politician is willing to trade substantial social goods for improvements in enforcement. In this case, the fall in the price of enforcement leads to a large increase in the amount of enforcement, as shown by the move from *a* to *a'*; in the left panel of Figure 1.6. This scenario corresponds to theories of selective policy implementation where the limiting factor is resources to act across a variety of policy areas.

A politician who does not want to enforce has an almost horizontal indifference curve. Additional enforcement requires a substantial sacrifice in other social goods, as shown in the right panel of Figure 1.6. The same change in resources from *B* to *B'* produces little increase in the level of enforcement (represented in the most extreme case in which *a* and *a'* are equivalent in the figure). Forbearance thus can be distinguished by a relatively inelastic response to changes in the cost or budget available

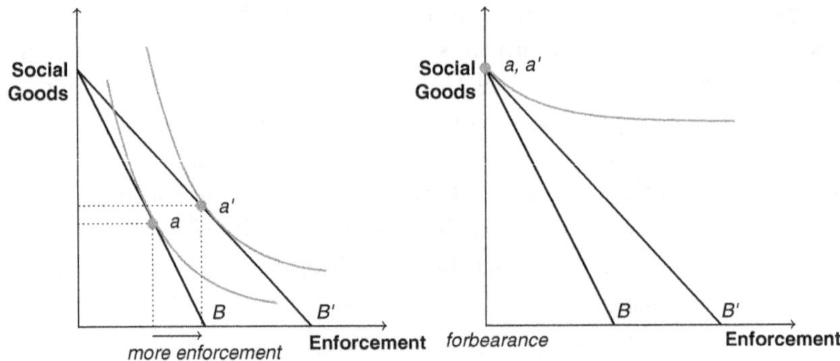


FIGURE 1.6 Elastic (left) and Inelastic (right) Responses to Enforcement Costs

for enforcement. It also makes clear that selective policy implementation and forbearance can be thought of along a continuum: the less willing politicians are to dedicate resources to enforcement, the more their behavior looks like forbearance.

While forbearance implies inelastic responses to resource changes, it involves a high elasticity to changes in the political costs of enforcement. The same electoral patterns predicted for other distributive goods apply to forbearance, such as electoral cycles and changes by administration. Observations of electoral patterns suggest institutional slack to change enforcement along with shifting political conditions, rather than binding capacity constraints.

A third empirical strategy to identify forbearance draws on measures of clearance rates, meaning how many cases that enter the legal system result in a sanction. Yet, rather than simply measure the endpoints (offenses and sanctions), as is common in clearance rate studies (e.g., Borg and Parker 2001; Cook 1979), I conduct a type of enforcement process tracing. Enforcement entails a sequence of behaviors that runs from the detection of an offense to administrative action to the imposition of a sanction. I trace how a given set of cases moves through each step of bureaucracy. Much like using a lagged variable, isolating reactions to a set of cases lets us set aside the issue of how past enforcement affects the offense level at present.

To separate forbearance from weak state capacity, we must have some notion of enforcement under institutional constraints as a counterfactual. Perfect enforcement is impossible. In any country, rich or poor, we expect some natural "loss" to occur at each step of an enforcement process. The challenge is that we do not know how hard each part of the process is, or more technically, the functional form of the loss function. A reasonable null hypothesis is one of constant attrition in which the same proportion of cases fails at each stage of the enforcement process (Holland 2016a). Compared to a null hypothesis of state weakness, forbearance implies that enforcement procedures stop at *political bottlenecks*. Politicians should make decisions to halt enforcement, even when bureaucrats and police perform their jobs. A sharp deviation from the trend occurs at the points at which politicians can influence the enforcement process. Bottlenecks also can occur because some procedural steps are harder than others. Additional causal-process observations, such as direct interventions where politicians act to bring about the bottleneck, larger drops for politically sensitive cases, or evidence about the relative difficulty of each step, strengthen a claim of forbearance.

In sum, none of these empirical approaches is a silver bullet. But they all offer falsifiable predictions that distinguish forbearance from often-confused ways that limited enforcement can be observed, such as societal compliance and weak state capacity. Before explaining how I combine these strategies throughout the book, I discuss some rival political explanations for why politicians manipulate enforcement and their distinct empirical implications.

### 1.3.2 Alternative Political Explanations

In policy circles and journalistic accounts, complaints about the need for "political will" to enforce the law almost always follow those about weak state capacity. But it borders on tautological to say that a government increases enforcement because those in charge make it a priority or decide to act. Instead, I try to make sense of why some politicians choose to enforce the law and others do not in terms of broader institutional factors, namely, the social policy context and the political power of poor voters. My model is an electoral one, in the sense that politicians incorporate the interests of average citizens, who are seen as empowered in different ways by the institutional environment. The main evidence for this model is that enforcement changes with majority preferences, and with the political institutions and social policies that affect them. Several alternative accounts likewise see enforcement changes as the result of political choices, but attribute them to different motivations like rent seeking, interest group activity, and culture. I emphasize the ways that my theory is "brittle," meaning that it is formulated in a way that it can be shown to be false and distinguishable, against these other political explanations.

First, a different theoretical tradition argues that politicians maximize their own rents, rather than their electoral prospects. In the enforcement context, the best example of this approach comes from Onoma (2010), who details how the extent of property protection in rural Africa varies with the ways in which leaders personally extract resources from land. In an urban context, several explanations for the tolerance of informal activities stress how politicians profit from its continuance either directly or indirectly through kickbacks from real estate brokers, lawyers, business groups, and property owners (e.g., Collier 1976; De Soto, Ghersi, and Ghibellini 1986; Fischer 2008; Tripp 1997). This class of explanation overlaps with some of those focused on state capacity, except that politicians, rather than bureaucrats, capture the rents.

The fly in the ointment of rent-seeking theories is that they cannot explain why politicians allow the powerless to violate the law. Rent-seeking theories expect that wealth and power make enforcement less likely because politicians will be attracted to take bribes from those with something to offer. A very tough test of my electoral theory – in the sense that it contravenes much conventional wisdom – is that sanctions against property laws are more likely when those who violate property laws are destitute. Under my theory, when those who violate the law are seen to gain wealth – squatters start to build bigger homes, street vendors gain capital, industrial firms steal electricity, and so on – the political costs of enforcement go down. When the poor engage in the same legal violations, and especially when they are perceived as destitute and victims of social injustice, the reputational costs from acting against them are higher. As one Ugandan development planner captures the intuition that some groups are "below" the law in the case of squatter settlements, "We are not lacking the capacity to demolish them, but these dilapidated housing structures belong to people you may find difficult to touch ... They belong to people *who are powerful in their own way*" (Goodfellow 2012: 137). Vote-seeking politicians thus should have stronger electoral incentives to enforce the law against better-off groups. Of course, I am not so naïve as to think that money never matters or changes hands around enforcement decisions. My more limited claim is that publicly enforcing against individuals who are perceived as vulnerable carries its own complications in an electoral democracy.

Rent-seeking theories also have distinct implications about how politicians who permit legal violations are perceived. If the poor must pay bribes to violate the law, then forbearance is unlikely to convey a politician who represents the poor's interests or implements other policies in their favor. Under my electoral theory, forbearance is a distributive benefit and thus signals a politician who represents the poor.

A second account focuses on how organized interest groups determine enforcement. Urban politics has a strong tradition of pluralist analysis, often traced back to Dahl (1961). Dahl's analysis of New Haven city politics focused on organized groups, but also active members of the general public, who managed to represent the wants and needs of average citizens. In this view, public policy shifts with the relative power of competing interest groups. Enforcement may depend on the outcome of power struggles between the representatives of the haves and the have-nots. A number of studies, for example, point to differences in the associational power of street-vending organizations and business actors to explain enforcement variation. (e.g., Aliaga Linares 2012; Bayat 1998; Cross 1998; Davis 2013; Donovan 2002, 2008; Moncada 2016; Tripp 1997).[23]

From a pure pluralist perspective, elected officials and the formal political institutions in which they operate tend to matter little. Pluralists predict the same patterns of enforcement in cities with different electoral institutions, as a common set of groups jostle for influence, strengthen local bureaucracies, and seek to pay off or mobilize for politicians. Electoral institutions, in my account, change the character and outcomes of group conflict. I find that enforcement varies with voter demographics only if cities hold elections at a local level. Otherwise, enforcement varies over time, but not space (Chapter 5).

I share with pluralists an interest in how those affected by law mobilize and pressure politicians for forbearance. But I accent that enforcement outcomes depend on the ability of interest associations to alter public opinion and influence mass electoral politics. What makes laws that the poor violate, and especially those that claim in-kind goods like jobs, services, transportation, and housing, unique is that they are plugged into broader debates about social welfare. Mass attitudes vary by class group and by local context, as groups try to influence public sympathies. Business groups in favor of enforcement try to emphasize the criminality and disorder associated with legal violations, while those in favor of forbearance link violations to structural causes like economic stagnation

[23] In an interesting twist, Hummel (2017) proposes that governments encourage informal-sector organizing as a way to promote compliance without the costs of coercive enforcement. Such organization also makes it easier to negotiate clientelistic bargains with leaders of informal-sector associations (for instance, see Hilgers 2008).

and poverty. In contrast to pluralists, I therefore see associational power as Janus-faced. While strong associations make it easier for the informal-sector poor to negotiate clientelistic deals with politicians, they can undercut efforts to turn public opinion in favor of those who violate the law. Chapter 4 shows that strong street-vending associations in central city areas proved vulnerable to enforcement because voters came to see them as mafias, slum landlords, and petty profiteers, rather than struggling poor families.

Third, it is often argued that a cultural disrespect for formal rules accounts for widespread law breaking in Latin America and hinders the state's ability to enforce the law. Cultural idioms ("Make the law, make the way around it"; "I obey, but do not comply") are taken as evidence of widespread cultural norms that reject paper constraints on behavior. Scholars who take a sociocultural approach stress that weak enforcement is rooted in Latin America's familial, Catholic, and clientelistic traditions (e.g., DaMatta 1991; García Villegas 2009; Mockus, Murrain, and Villa 2012; Mockus 2002). One implication is that legal attitudes look relatively similar across different areas of law and across individuals within the same milieu. Using survey data, I show that this is not the case. Legal norms are sometimes viewed as flexible and jettisoned by large segments of the population in Latin America, and particularly those who directly violate the law. However, support for forbearance is tightly bound to an individual's material interests and views about the state's welfare capabilities, not a generalized distaste for law. The poor, for instance, have more lenient attitudes than the nonpoor toward squatting and street vending, but these differences do not extend to legal violations by the rich, such as building code and tax violations. Another distinctive prediction is that enforcement runs into societal bottlenecks, rather than political ones, as low-income groups refuse to cooperate with state enforcement agents, such as refusing to report those who violate the law.

Socio-legal arguments more recently have focused on the emergence of a new social rights jurisprudence and the cultural changes that it engenders (e.g., Brinks and Forbath 2014; Gauri and Brinks 2010; Rodríguez-Garavito and Rodríguez-Franco 2015). Constitutions that embed social rights may formally tie the hands of governments to enforce laws against the poor, or at least create ambiguity in legal interpretation. Forbearance, in this case, will parallel the incorporation of social rights and vary little once accounting for different constitutional frameworks. I predict variation in enforcement across time, place, and sector, even in countries with constitutional protections for social rights. In my model, couching property law violations in terms of moral claims of rights to housing, work, and services in property law violations is nothing new or exclusive to countries with more expansive constitutions. I make a more limited claim that the legal recognition of social rights can tilt forbearance in a less clientelistic direction.

Table 1.1 summarizes the central empirical predictions under my theory and rival alternatives. The focus in the coming chapters will be to adjudicate between a model of forbearance and weak state capacity, or the leftmost columns. More than a simple strongman, the view that states cannot sanction and monitor legal violations continues to dominate much scholarship and therefore absorbs greater empirical attention. The power of the theory comes in its ability to explain a series of facts, rather than resting on any single observation.

## 1.4 RESEARCH DESIGN

The backbone of this book is a comparative analysis of enforcement politics in three Latin American capital cities (Santiago, Chile; Bogotá, Colombia; and Lima, Peru) and two types of legal violations (street vending and squatting). The empirical setting is Latin America because it is a middle-income region in which governments conceivably can enforce their laws. The scope condition, the ability to control enforcement, is most clearly met in capital cities.

City elections are relatively new to Latin America, so I begin with the introduction of direct elections for mayor in the 1980s and early 1990s. Prior to the third-wave democratic transitions, Latin American mayors tended to be appointees of civilian and military rulers. Elections for city mayors created a new set of actors with specifically urban interests and electorates. Yet the way that countries structured urban governance diverged depending on calculations about the desirability of strong city mayors.[24]

All cities are divided into sub-units, which I uniformly call districts. They differ, however, in whether they hold elections at the district level and, if so, whether mayors control their own police institutions. To guarantee variation on my explanatory variable, I selected cities with different electoral rules. At one extreme, Santiago is a politically decentralized city. The

[24] On the general differences of urban elections and their introduction, see Dietz and Myers (2002). Other scholars also have usefully documented the politics of political decentralization in Latin America, such as Eaton (2004); Falleti (2010); and O'Neill (2005).

TABLE 1.1 *Empirical Implications Summarized*

| | Electoral | State Capacity | Rent Seeking | Interest Groups | Culture |
|---|---|---|---|---|---|
| *Public opinion* | Poor voters prefer less enforcement if they benefit | Voters prefer enforcement | Voters prefer enforcement | Voters prefer enforcement | Poor prefer less enforcement in general |
| *Political signals* | No enforcement cues a pro-poor politician if no welfare alternatives | | No enforcement cues a corrupt politician | No enforcement cues a corrupt politician | No enforcement cues a pro-poor politician to poor voters |
| *Enforcement elasticity* | Responsive to political costs, not state or private resources | Responsive to state resources, not political costs | Responsive to private resources | Responsive to interest-group strength | Responsive to cultural change |
| *Clearance pattern* | Enforcement hits political bottlenecks | Constant case attrition | Enforcement hits political bottlenecks | Enforcement hits political bottlenecks | Enforcement hits societal bottlenecks |
| *Spatial variation* | By demographics only if politically decentralized cities | By resources if administratively decentralized cities | By demographics in all city types | By interest group strength in all city types | By demographics in all city types |

military regime initiated decentralization as an antidote to party politics and devolved responsibility for many local services to the district level. Chile reintroduced local government elections with its transition to democracy in 1992, but did not change the basic administrative structure. Each of thirty-four districts (*comunas*) elects a local mayor, but no mayor exists for the whole city. Many institutions remain centralized at the national level, including, most important for this book, the National Police (*Carabineros*).

At the other extreme, Bogotá is a politically centralized city. Colombia introduced direct election of mayors in 1988 for the first time in over a century, but maintained a centralized approach to urban administration. Citizens elect a city mayor, who appoints local administrators for each of twenty districts (*localidades*). As in Santiago, a national police force controls enforcement operations, but answers to the city mayor by law.

Lastly, Lima has a hybrid political structure. In 1981, Peru reinstated its system of local elections suspended by a revolutionary military regime. All forty-three districts (*distritos*) elect local mayors, but residents also elect a city mayor. While a prominent figure, the city mayor has far weaker formal powers than in Bogotá. Fujimori, in particular, strengthened district governments to undercut political rivals among Lima's city mayors in the 1990s. Among their many functions, district mayors manage their own police forces, creating very uneven local state capacity. Table 1.2 expands on these differences across cases.

Although each city also elects local and even city councilors (*ediles* or *concejales*), I focus on the role of mayors because they take most enforcement decisions. I will use the terms "mayor," "politician," and "local/district government" interchangeably to refer to the authority making enforcement decisions. I refer to the president or national government to refer to the higher level of government that takes decisions about welfare policy and the national legal framework.

These cities are situated in countries with different levels of state capacity. From a folk Bayesian perspective, if state capacity drives enforcement, as most analysts argue, then evidence of forbearance in a strong state (or enforcement in a weak one) provides greater confidence in the validity of my theory.[25] In addition to the extreme urban decentralization of Santiago – it is a rarity to have no city mayor at all in Latin

[25] On "folk Bayesian" logic and the idea of critical cases, see Gerring (2007); McKeown (1999); and Slater and Ziblatt (2013).

TABLE 1.2 *A Controlled Comparison across Latin American Capital Cities*

| | Bogotá, Colombia | Lima, Peru | Santiago, Chile |
|---|---|---|---|
| | ***Principal Independent Variables*** | | |
| Electoral structure | centralized | hybrid | decentralized |
| Number of electoral districts | 1 | 43 | 36 |
| Social policy context | complementary | complementary | substitutive |
| Housing expenditures as % GDP | 0.19 | 0.09 | 1.1 |
| Social expenditures per capita | $277 | $162 | $604 |
| Social expenditures as % GDP | 10.8 | 7.8 | 13.4 |
| | ***Competing Independent Variables*** | | |
| State capacity | medium | low | high |
| Government effectiveness | 62.6 | 20.9 | 83.9 |
| Corruption (% citizens who pay bribes) | 6.3 | 18.2 | 4.8 |
| Police structure | centralized | decentralized | centralized |
| Constitutional structure | social rights | no social rights | no social rights |
| | ***Controls*** | | |
| Population (millions) | 8.8 | 9.4 | 7.2 |
| Urban poverty rate (≈1990) | 37.6 | 33.6 | 32.1 |
| Political structure | unitary | unitary | unitary |

*Source:* Housing expenditure data come from national housing reports averaged from 2000 to 2010 (see Appendix C for details). Social expenditure, population, and poverty data from the Economic Commission for Latin America and the Caribbean (ECLAC). Government effectiveness is measured by World Bank. Citizens' reports of paying bribes come from AmericasBarometer 2010 and are calculated per bureaucratic transaction.

America – Chile has the highest state capacity and deep respect for law in Latin America. I then picked two cases with weaker state capacity, Colombia and Peru. Despite similar income levels and urban poverty rates, Colombia has a much more effective bureaucracy than Peru, especially at the city level. Observations of enforcement in Peru, in particular, cut against theories based on state strength.

In choosing Latin American cases to cover the range of state capacities, I necessarily sacrifice some comparability that I expand on in the next chapter. Chile, in particular, is one of the wealthiest countries in the region with a much smaller informal economy. I still see Chile's inclusion as worthwhile because it faced substantial urban poverty during its democratic transition and has stubbornly high levels of income inequality. I use the Chilean case in focused ways: to disentangle the role of social policy on enforcement incentives through process tracing in Chapter 3 and to show why forbearance emerges even in a strong state in Chapter 5.

Colombia and Peru, in contrast, are treated as comparable cases in which different electoral institutions predict different enforcement patterns. No case is a perfect match with Colombia due to its five-decade civil war. Almost 7 million people were internally displaced by the violence. However, Peru is the most similar because it also experienced a major internal conflict against the insurgent groups of Shining Path and Túpac Amaru. Beyond the magnitude of the fighting, a major difference between the cases is their embrace of social rights constitutionalism. Colombia has an activist court that has attempted to enforce the social rights included as part of a constitutional overhaul in 1991. Peru and Chile have unreformed constitutions from periods of authoritarian rule and conservative high courts.

I focus on two types of violations that are central to the lives of the urban poor: squatting and unlicensed street vending. For those who work in advanced industrial economies, squatting likely conjures up images of overcrowded inner-city apartments or communes in abandoned buildings. But in most of the developing world, squatting involves the unauthorized construction of homes. There is substantial disagreement on what qualifies as squatting, and what to call the neighborhoods produced by squatters. I define squatting as the physical occupation of a plot of land by an individual or group with either an absent or defective property rights claim. Squatting encompasses both land invasions in which individuals have no right to the land that they occupy, and illegal land occupations in which individuals have a partial claim to the land (such as a fraudulent title or a title to conservation or rural land where building is prohibited). As I expand on in Chapter 3, despite differences, these acts are supposed to end in evictions and have similar distributive impacts on the poor. Dozens of terms exist in Spanish for the neighborhoods produced by squatters; I refer to them simply as squatter settlements or informal settlements.

Street vending forms part of the broader concept of the informal economy, but differs from other forms of informal economic activity in that it involves a property law violation.[26] Street vending itself encompasses two different activities. First, there are vendors who roam city streets offering goods and services. Itinerant vendors concern governments less because they circulate and sell on a small scale. Second, I focus on the class of vendors that sells merchandise or services from a fixed point in public space. These vendors violate property laws by usurping public space for private commercial use. In their most invasive form, stationary vendors build "shops" on streets or sidewalks. Estimates show that less than 15 percent of vendors have fixed shops in Lima and Bogotá (Aliaga Linares 2012: 51). More common are stationary vendors who install carts, tables, or blankets for daily use. As I return to in the book's conclusion, my electoral theory applies relatively easily to enforcement against informal firms, where the penalties for violations (of tax, labor, zoning, or business codes) fall on lower-income business owners. It requires greater modifications to explain enforcement involving informal employment in large firms, where the incidence of fines is ambiguous.

Squatting and street vending are similar in that they involve the use of physical property and contain underlying social rights claims. In general, violations of property laws have the most potential for progressive economic impacts because land can be seized and put to immediate use without outside cooperation. Property holders then ask politicians to tolerate and legalize what already has occurred. Many other legal infractions that might serve the poor, such as violating drug patents or appropriating a health clinic to serve a poor district, depend on the government or a firm's initial complicity (Herbst 1989: 217). A comparative analysis of squatting and street vending limits the book to speaking most directly about certain types of legal violations that involve claims to basic social goods, such as housing and work. Accordingly, these are among the most important forms of informal welfare provision. But these infractions are not entirely unique. Water and electricity theft involves demands for basic services. Many legal violations involve a claim to work, such as informal transportation (unlicensed taxis, buses, and motorcycles), informal mining, domestic work, undocumented migration, and unlicensed small businesses. The conclusion discusses the fact that electorally motivated forbearance can be observed in a broad set of circumstances, but its extension tends to be more particularistic when no basic social claims are at stake.

[26] The most common definition of the informal economy is as a process of income generation that "is unregulated by the institutions of society, in a legal and social environment in which similar activities are regulated" (Portes and Castells 1989: 12).

These violations differ in their social policy substitutes and geography in ways that allow for a controlled comparison of each key explanatory variable. Squatting has a clear social policy substitute, housing policy, which varies by country. Chile is the regional leader in mass housing provision; Colombia and Peru assist the middle class with housing access and historically have done little for the poor (Chapter 3). Street vending has a less clear social policy substitute because job prospects are shaped by a host of macroeconomic and labor market policy choices. In all the countries studied, employment policy is complementary to street vending.

Squatting, with some exceptions, occurs on the urban periphery of cities, making it less visible to the nonpoor. There is less variation in the type of electoral district that confronts squatters. Street vending differs from squatting in that it often occurs in wealthy neighborhoods or central business districts where different income groups interact. Vendors are visible to broad segments of the public. By studying street vending, I thus can probe how enforcement policy varies across urban space, and how these spatial patterns differ with the electoral rules. Table 1.3 recaps how the selection of different types of legal offenses allows for a multidimensional test of the argument.

It is notoriously difficult to obtain data on enforcement activities. I therefore adopted multiple forms of data collection on the assumption that the best way to probe enforcement politics was through information from varied perspectives and sources. These data were collected during thirteen months of fieldwork split between Bogotá, Lima, and Santiago between 2011 and 2013, as well as a trip to Istanbul in 2014 to replicate my data collection. The appendix provides more detailed information on

TABLE 1.3 *Legal Violations with Different Social Policy Substitutes and Geographies*

| | Squatting | Street Vending |
|---|---|---|
| *Social policy* | *Variation by country*<br>Substitutive housing policy in Chile, complementary in Peru and Colombia | *No country variation*<br>Weak employment policy in all country cases |
| *Geography* | *No district variation*<br>Squatters take land mostly in poor districts | *Variation by district*<br>Vendors work in all types of districts |

the sampling procedures, survey instruments, unstructured interviews, and variables analyzed.[27]

I relied on five main sources of data. First, I conducted an original public opinion survey in Bogotá to probe the micro-foundations of my theory. I made use of an indirect measurement strategy with region-wide survey data to generalize my results. Second, to understand how interest associations interact with politicians, I supplemented the survey data with focus groups and in-depth interviews with leaders of street-vending and squatting associations. I located these association leaders through organized labor confederations and nongovernmental organizations. I also conducted dozens of interviews with squatters and street vendors in government offices, while waiting to meet politicians and bureaucrats. This strategy biased my sample toward more organized and active associations, so I rely on my survey to generalize about the attitudes of street vendors and squatters who do not participate in associations or petition government officials.

Third, I gathered original data on legal violations, enforcement actions, and political dynamics through a structured survey of bureaucrats. I personally interviewed 149 district bureaucrats in Bogotá, Lima, and Santiago. These were all "street-level bureaucrats" in Lipsky's (1980) sense that they interact with citizens directly and have discretion over decisions that matter for citizens' lives. To conduct the survey, I went to every district government office, sometimes multiple times, and spoke with the director or sub-director of the office in charge of street-vending and housing issues. I later replicated this process in Istanbul in a third of the city's districts selected in a stratified sample. Through these interviews, I collected data on offenses, enforcement actions, government resources, citizen complaints, decision-making, and bureaucrats' perceptions of enforcement politics. This original data collection was necessary because government agencies rarely keep records on local enforcement actions and district governments use different definitions of what constitutes enforcement, which in-depth interviews helped to standardize. The data are limited to a single moment in time, however, and may overstate enforcement operations if officials distort the information provided to portray a more effective administration. I therefore verified information on enforcement activities with local administrative records and also shadowed roughly a dozen bureaucrats in their everyday tasks to understand the

[27] Interview notes and protocols are archived through the Qualitative Data Repository (QDR).

constraints on enforcement firsthand. I supplemented this research at the district level with interviews with fifty-one city- and national-level bureaucrats from welfare agencies, property-titling agencies, prosecutorial offices, and horizontal oversight institutions.

Fourth, I conducted unstructured interviews with sixty-two local politicians (mayors, city councilors, and local councilors). During my survey of district offices, I always attempted to speak with politicians as well. Local politicians are hard to track down given that their political careers depend in large part on constituency service and local councilors often have second jobs. I only managed to interview politicians in about a quarter of the districts that I visited. My main concern in sampling was to complete interviews with politicians in districts with different socioeconomic profiles. I compensated for possible selection bias in the types of politicians who were in their office and willing to speak to an academic researcher by reviewing official campaign platforms. Peru, in particular, requires candidates to submit a platform to run for office, so I read and coded these documents across all poor and nonpoor districts.

Fifth, newspaper, archival, and secondary sources complement my original data gathering efforts. Given that districts rarely maintain records on their enforcement actions over time, I relied on secondary sources to understand the long-run dynamics. I followed enforcement politics around squatting and street vending in cases that held centralized city elections by systematically searching through a major national newspaper in each country *(El Comercio* in Peru and *El Tiempo* in Bogotá) from 1990 to 2010. I also collected reports and legal cases from the institutions responsible for street vending and squatting at the city and national levels. In Bogotá, I drew on a particularly rich database housed by the District Planning Secretary (*Secretaría Distrital de Planeación*, SDP), which includes all correspondence between the city and informal settlements requesting regularization since the 1950s.[28]

In explaining the data, it is important to be honest about what this book is and is not. It is not a study of contentious politics. Compared to a number of studies "from below," focused on the dynamics of street vendor and squatter associations, I chose to conduct a study largely "from above," centered on the ways that politicians and bureaucrats perceive and react to illegal behaviors. I spent most of my days shadowing bureaucrats on their jobs and waiting around municipal buildings to catch

[28] The Observatory of Informal Land and Housing Markets (*Observatorio del Mercado Informal de Suelo y Vivienda*) has coded and organized much of this archive.

mayors and councilors. In trying to span all district governments in a trio of cities, I also trade depth in the particulars of neighborhood and district dynamics for breadth in understanding how enforcement varies in systematic ways over space and in different national contexts. In so doing, I aim to provide a more nuanced picture of how the arms of the state – the police, courts, bureaucrats, and politicians – choose to enforce the law against the poor.

## 1.5 FORBEARANCE AS REDISTRIBUTION?

Even if we accept that forbearance involves the allocation of resources and electoral motivations, it may not be clear that this process involves any redistribution. I use the term "redistribution" very deliberately to underscore three of my bolder claims about the economic progressivity, class politics, and political logic entailed in forbearance toward violations of laws by the poor. This is a work of positive social science, so I do not make claims about the net effects of all types of forbearance or imply a normative judgment that this system is beneficial for the poor. As will become clearest in Chapter 6, I am deeply ambivalent about the effects of forbearance and believe that it has perpetuated inadequate social policies. But it also has alleviated the immediate needs of the poor and responded to their demands in important and largely unrecognized ways.

First, I take a classic view that all that redistribution requires – and indeed, how much redistribution occurs in modern welfare states – is that general resources belonging to the population as a whole are directed to those who have less. As Titmuss (1965) clarifies, redistributive policies "assign claims from one set of people who are said to produce or earn the national product to another set of people who may merit compassion and charity but not economic rewards for productive services." Robin Hood stole from the king's coffers, not from the purses of private citizens. European welfare states are funded through consumption taxes collected from all citizens. Such resource transfers obviously are less redistributive and less politically difficult than direct takings of income or land from the rich to give to the poor.[29] My point simply is that many redistributive social policies involve resources belonging to the public at large that go to those with less.

[29] For instance, Albertus (2015: 8) limits his study of land redistribution to expropriations of private land because they are more redistributive than the distribution of state lands, or what he calls "land colonization."

Furthermore, I find that tolerance of squatting and street vending involves more (although still not much) downward redistribution than many Latin American social policies. The resources at stake are publicly owned streets and land, and the harms fall on the public at large in the form of clogged streets, increased infrastructure costs, and insecure property rights. Meanwhile, the majority of squatters and street vendors come from the bottom segments of the income distribution. The very fact that forbearance requires individuals to violate the law can make it an effective way to target the poor or, more precisely, the poor who are willing to take legal risks. Consider the case of squatting: the poor are willing to live in squatter settlements without running water or light in the hopes of eventual property title. Most of the middle class will not stand for the inferior living conditions, and also has more to lose in the case of a conviction. For example, according to household surveys, more than four-fifths of squatters in Lima come from the bottom third of the wealth distribution (INEI 2011). As one former Lima city councilor and advocate for squatters put it, "If you have even slightly more money, you have other options and also know about the advantages of other living situations."[30] In contrast to the bottom-targeting achieved through forbearance, many housing programs in the developing world benefit middle-class groups able to save and document a steady income to repay mortgages. More than 90 percent of housing subsidies in Peru went to the middle class in 2011, for instance (Chapter 6). Forbearance thus can do a better job reaching the poor than state welfare programs, although it offers smaller benefits and still can exclude the absolute poorest.

Who benefits from forbearance is an empirical issue, and the redistributive effects can vary by place and time. On the one hand, it is possible that those who benefit are not poor because slum landlords, mafias, and other petty profiteers capture the benefits. According to this view, I should not refer to the poor at all, but rather middle-income groups, or "parasitic" actors to use Onoma's (2009) felicitous phrase. The trend that I find is that there is a long tail to the income distribution of street vendors and squatters: some individuals do quite well and profit off these activities, but they are a minority and capture only a fraction of the surplus. For instance, land traffickers, who often organize squatters and locate plots to seize, are paid anywhere from $50 to $2,000 in my sample. While

[30] Author interview with Samuel Yáñez Torres, city councilor, MML, and social worker at Centro de Investigación, Documentación y Asesoría Poblacional (CIDAP), Lima, Peru, June 7, 2011.

a sizable sum for poor households, most figures also show that properties rise in value, often reaching $10,000 once the poor convince the government to install services and recognize their plots. It is also worth noting that land traffickers, though not as poor as squatters, are hardly drawn from the upper strata of society. Many, in fact, are leaders of squatter settlements and street markets. It is not plausible that these traffickers appropriate all of the benefits, although they certainly can alter the losses and gains from forbearance. There are profits to be made off the poor's illegality.

On the other hand, a somewhat opposite view sees the idea of "benefits" from legal violations as nonsensical because the poor bear the costs.[31] But I try to let the poor speak and act for themselves. I present survey evidence to show how individuals value their possessions, based on how much street vendors and squatters think their property would be worth if rented or sold. In most cases, they report substantial values, which is consistent with observations that they also petition and vote to defend their property against enforcement. In some cases, as with job programs in Bogotá (Chapter 4) or housing programs in India (Barnhardt, Field, and Pande 2015), the poor also reject opportunities for formal goods like jobs and houses to retain their informal ones. Legal violations can be a first step to gain a foothold in urban life. As Holston (2008: 9) documents in his study of informal neighborhoods in São Paulo, Brazil, from an initial property law violation the urban poor "became landowners, made law an asset, created new public spheres of participation, achieved rights to the city, and became modern consumers." This is not an attempt to romanticize life in squatter settlements or street markets. But it also is wrong to see the possessions secured through forbearance as things without value to their owners.

It may seem strange to equate the failure to enforce a law with a transfer. But positive and negative forms of distribution can have equivalent economic consequences. It is easy to see how a program that allocates state land to poor families involves a transfer of resources. Allowing individuals to live on state land – and assigning them title to that property, as has become the norm in Latin America since the 1990s (Chapter 6) – has the same fiscal effects with different political ones. This point is analogous to that made about thinking of tax breaks as part of the welfare

[31] Perhaps no study more vividly captures this reasoning than Auyero and Swistun's (2009) ethnography of the Buenos Aires neighborhood of Flammable, where a combination of industrial pollution and government neglect imposes major health risks on residents.

state. To economists, the earned income tax credit is a transfer program. If taxpayers write a check to the government for their full liability and the government refunds them their money back if below a certain income level, these are government expenditures. The politics differ (Howard 1999). Transfers through forbearance likewise "count" because the government sets up a law, be it a tax schedule or a property law or a commercial regulation, which would result in public resources if followed.[32] Politically, of course, it should be much easier for governments to allocate such abstract resources than to impose direct costs on taxpayers.

This point leads me to the second reason that I refer to informal redistribution in this book: forbearance involves class politics. Past analysts have rejected the idea of the urban poor as a class due to the heterogeneous labor conditions and seemingly incoherent positions of workers toward the welfare state and the parties that defend it. Indeed, unlike the working class in its strictest Marxist definition, the urban poor do not share common working conditions. But this loose grouping does share common concerns based on their labor in the informal sector, their interactions with police and bureaucrats, and the reality of making do on scarce resources in a city. What it means to be part of the informal sector is that life depends on a certain amount of regulatory flexibility. Especially when enforcement threatens features central to the poor's livelihood, it makes sense that coherent material positions form around the ways that regulations are enforced, rather than state welfare provision and opposition to a capitalist class.

Counterpoised to the poor's claims to forbearance is the middle class's defense of an orderly, modern, and clean city. Slums, street vendors, service theft, and unlicensed transportation long have been blamed for society's ills and economic backwardness, even when they pose no direct threat to middle-class livelihoods. In many cases, forbearance has allowed the middle class to pay less in taxes and avoid funding a "real" welfare state. Informality is central to how cities function. Nevertheless, legal violations fuel debates about poverty because they make it visible and concrete to city residents. Street vendors and squatters, according to detractors, damage a city's image due to the poverty, dirt, and disorder on display. The poor (often rightly) see enforcement not just as an attack

[32] Centeno and Portes (2006) make a similar point that informality only exists when states attempt to regulate economic life; different "regulatory loads" create different possibilities for legal arbitrage and informal transfers.

on their livelihood, but as a larger class conflict in which the rich attempt to whitewash poverty. As Fischer (2014: 10) puts it, "Informal cities have frequently occupied center stage in Latin America's sociopolitical arena, but they have largely done so in the service of larger debates about the nature and tolerability of social inequality." Polemics about poverty, class, social rights, and redistribution drive debates about law enforcement.

My decision to limit this book to property laws that the poor violate reflects the unique class politics that undergirds these offenses. I could study how forbearance toward *all laws* changes the income distribution. As in many societies, the rich accrue tremendous benefits when able to use their power and money to escape regulations. This calculation is not tractable. More important, it is not consistent with how the public discriminates between different types of laws. Enforcement of laws that the poor violate, especially those, like squatting and street vending, that occur in public space, exposes concrete class divisions and has the ability to mobilize the lower class. The wealthy who evade taxes, pollute rivers, or steal electricity do not conceive of themselves as part of a class group defined by these acts.

Lastly, some scholars define redistribution based on the logic of allocation, rather than the economic incidence or the structure of sociological cleavages. As Lowi (1964: 690–1) puts it, distributive policies disperse benefits "in small units and in isolation from any principle." Redistributive policies differ in that "the categories of impact are much bigger, approaching social classes" and the principles are generalized. This definition of redistribution is the greatest stretch for my theory of forbearance. It also is the biggest difference in how forbearance operates in contemporary Latin America compared to other regions and historical periods. A central theme of this book is that many political actors and ordinary citizens defend forbearance as a matter of principle and as an informal welfare *policy*, rather than just a favor to their friends. Some city mayors and even presidents, ranging from populists like Alberto Fujimori in Peru to political insiders like Ernesto Samper and Luis Garzón in Colombia, view forbearance as advancing distributive justice. In the next chapter, I show that poor and nonpoor voters have different attitudes toward legal violations and enforcement on abstract surveys, not just because they want a personal favor from a politician. Citizens, bureaucrats, judges, and politicians alike think of forbearance as redistribution on the cheap.

# 2

# Who Votes for Forbearance

> Justice involves treating the equal equally and the unequal unequally in proportion to their inequality.
>
> – Aristotle

What do voters want from government? Especially in unequal democracies, many models assume the answer is redistribution. Poor voters want their representatives to take more resources from the rich to use to their benefit, and wealthy voters want to prevent this redistribution. Yet this theory of redistributive demands fails in Latin America – one of the most unequal regions of the world, where it should operate most seamlessly. Yawning income disparities do not translate into sharp differences in preferences over redistribution. Quite the opposite, poor and nonpoor voters have nearly identical preferences over many standard redistributive instruments (Blofield and Luna 2011; Holland 2016b). The middle class, not the poor, has been the strongest supporter of Latin America's left turn (Kaufman 2009).

This chapter reorients the conventional framework around redistributive demands in two ways. First, I suggest that the poor are ambivalent about tax and spend policies because they traditionally involved little downward redistribution. Many social insurance policies continue to be truncated to provide benefits to those *above* a certain level of income, rather than below it. Other policies benefit both poor and nonpoor groups, or offer such small-sized benefits that they constitute a weak source of social protection. Accordingly, the poor do not always expect to benefit from social expenditures. The wealthy also may have little to fear in how welfare states are designed (Ansell and Samuels 2015;

Soifer 2013). There are exceptions, of course: some policies, such as cash transfer programs, and some welfare states, such as those countries with longer democratic histories and wider coverage, have economically progressive impacts and generate the "expected" divisions between haves and have-nots.

Second, I argue that the poor have shared material interests in how laws are enforced and, specifically, whether property law violations by the poor are tolerated. Conversely, wealthy citizens dislike the disorder and property threats from legal violations. Thus, forbearance toward violations of property laws divides the electorate along class lines. As in the context of redistribution, people most likely form their attitudes by thinking about their material interests and group affinities. Even when individuals do not stand to benefit personally from legal violations, they can view enforcement as unnecessarily harsh and unfair to the poor.

Empirically, then, the thrust of this chapter is that models developed to understand attitudes toward redistribution apply to forbearance, and even more powerfully given that forbearance has been more targeted at the bottom tranches of the income distribution in Latin America. I examine three core hypotheses about how ordinary citizens view enforcement that underpin my theory: (1) poor individuals prefer less enforcement of certain property laws than nonpoor individuals, (2) popular support for enforcement is higher when individuals believe that social welfare substitutes exist for the poor's distributive claims, and (3) voters identify politicians who enforce as acting against the poor's broader distributive interests. I expect, in contrast, that voters are less divided in their opinions about state redistribution, and do not identify politicians who promise social expenditures as representing the poor's interests. I test these propositions with data gathered from a face-to-face survey of 900 voters in Bogotá, as well as data drawn from the Latin American Public Opinion Project (LAPOP)'s AmericasBarometer for more than 90,000 individuals across eighteen countries.

This chapter moves from the macro to the micro level and combines original observational and experimental data. I first provide some essential background on Latin American welfare states, emphasizing the historic exclusion of the informal-sector poor and reviewing some general political features in my three case studies. This context is necessary to develop my argument about public opinion, but it employs a broad brush and readers more familiar with the region's welfare regimes and politics may wish to proceed directly to the micro-level evidence. The second section describes how I operationalize attitudes and some descriptive statistics on the level of support for both forbearance and redistribution. The third section shows that material interest models developed to study redistributive preferences apply to forbearance attitudes. The fourth section then examines voters' evaluations of hypothetical mayoral candidates in a survey experiment. Together, these tests provide evidence that the public understands and justifies forbearance as an informal welfare policy.

## 2.1 TRUNCATED WELFARE STATES

Social programs are thought to play a major role in shaping the lives of the poor. But the role of the welfare state was not palpable for Latin America's informal-sector poor for much of the twentieth century. Pensions, health insurance, labor protections, and housing benefits concentrated their benefits on unionized workers and the middle class. To contextualize the role of informal welfare, I provide a very brief sketch of formal welfare state development in Latin America and then look at the political system and social policies in Chile, Colombia, and Peru. All three cases still have notable shortcomings in welfare coverage, thus opening space for informal welfare solutions.

### 2.1.1 Welfare State Development in Latin America

Much of the welfare state apparatus in Latin America dates back to the period of labor incorporation in the early to mid-twentieth century and the economic development model of import-substitution industrialization (ISI). A number of excellent studies link the push to industrialize through ISI to a unique logic of welfare expansion (Haggard and Kaufman 2008; Wibbels Forthcoming; Wibbels and Ahlquist 2011). To briefly recap the argument, capitalists needed labor peace to accelerate industrial growth, and a stable consumer base to warrant production for an internal market. Workers wanted protections against the low wages in traditional sectors. Governments therefore introduced protective labor codes to shield the industrial working class. Protection from external market competition allowed firms in the import-substituting sectors to incorporate generous social entitlements, which contributed to labor market dualism. Most spending went to social insurance programs – old-age pensions, health insurance, and disability benefits – for privileged segments of the workforce, such as state employees, the armed forces, and those working in favored industries.

Tying benefits to labor contracts left substantial tranches of the population in the informal and rural sectors without social protection.[1] The small size of the industrial working class meant that these choices led to less inclusive welfare states than similar European corporatist models (Huber and Stephens 2012: 22–4). For instance, Argentina and Brazil went the farthest with ISI due to their larger internal markets, yet manufacturing still employed less than a third of the urban labor force at its peak. Colombia, Chile, and Peru pursued more mixed development strategies. Not even accounting for the large rural sector, the share of the urban labor force in industry was just 21 percent in Chile and Colombia, and 18 percent in Peru at the height of ISI (Portes 1989: 26). Welfare states thus grew to be "deep but not wide" (Haggard and Kaufman 2008: 12).

Rural migration toward large capital cities accelerated during the ISI period, leading to the growth of squatter settlements and a rise in the proportion of unskilled workers. Capital city populations doubled in the span of two decades (ECLAC 2009). Unlike in Europe, where urbanization reflected the pull of industrialization, urban growth evidenced the poor conditions in the Latin American countryside and unfavorable terms of trade under ISI. Squatter settlements, although nothing new to the region, ballooned in size. Roughly half of all informal land development in Bogotá, encompassing almost 15 square miles of land, occurred between 1960 and 1980 (Camargo and Hurtado 2013: 84). Lima hit its apogee of informal construction in the same period. By 1980, 29 percent of Lima's population (1.3 million people) lived in informal settlements, up from 10 percent in 1955 (Riofrío 2003: 4). In response to intense political competition and leftist movements, 14 percent of Santiago's population seized land between 1967 and 1973 alone (Murphy 2015: 74).

Substantial debate brewed on whether the rapid urban growth and poor conditions in squatter settlements presaged political radicalization and redistributive demands. Urbanization held the specter of awakening the poor's consciousness and placed them in striking distance of seats of political power. But, most studies, such as Perlman's (1974) decisive rejection of the "myth of marginality," emphasize that migrants remained conservative and embedded in clientelistic networks. Squatters saw the ability to build their home as an important source of economic mobility

[1] Latin American countries of course varied in the extent of political incorporation of industrial workers (Collier and Collier 1991), as well as the extension of nondiscretionary social benefits to those outside of the industrial workforce (Garay 2017: chapter 3; Haggard and Kaufman 2008: chapter 2).

and relief from rent payments (for a review, see Nelson 1970). Most governments tolerated squatters and street vendors because they alleviated the need for "real" welfare programs. Moreover, tremendous political power came in the ability to distribute legal tolerance and accompanying urban services as favors rather than entitlements. Governments retained the upper hand to revoke their choices if elite interests so dictated or industrialization took off (e.g., Collier 1976; Fischer 2008; Ray 1969).

Rather than industrial growth bringing an end to property law violations, however, most Latin American countries suffered deep economic crises in the 1980s. Debt crises and market liberalization forced many governments to gut welfare programs. Temporary emergency assistance programs emerged to cushion the worse effects of market adjustments, but many governments slashed spending on the poor (Wibbels 2006). Exclusionary and increasingly privatized policies for the middle class and formal-sector working class were complemented by a largely informal system of family support, cash handouts, and self-employment for the poor (Barrientos 2004, 2009; Martinez Franzoni 2008). For instance in Peru, one of the countries hardest hit by an economic crisis and hyperinflation, informal employment shot up from 35 to 81 percent between 1985 and 1990 (Crabtree 1992; Glewwe and Gillette 1992).

With the return of democracy and economic stability, many Latin American countries extended social protections to informal-sector workers. However, as documented by several authors (e.g., Garay 2017; De La O 2015; Diaz-Cayeros, Estévez, and Magaloni 2016; Huber and Stephens 2012; Pribble 2013; Segura-Ubiergo 2007), progress was uneven across country and sector. The contours of political competition and legacies of previous social policy commitments shaped reform trajectories. In many countries, labor unions succeeded in protecting restrictive labor legislation and social insurance spending through deep state and market reforms (Carnes 2014; Haggard and Kaufman 2008; Murillo 2001; Wibbels Forthcoming).

Latin American governments still spend less on social policy and, critically, less on the poor than advanced democracies do. Despite high levels of inequality, social expenditures average 13 percent of GDP in Latin America compared to 20 percent in OECD countries.[2] On average, taxes and transfers reduce income inequality by 18 points in Europe and

[2] I compare Latin America to advanced industrial democracies, rather than other parts of the developing world, because most models of redistributive preferences have been derived in this context.

North America, but only by 3 points in Latin America.[3] Many Latin American governments leave inequality basically unchanged through their social expenditures, including Peru, Colombia, and (to a lesser extent) Chile, to which I now turn.

### 2.1.2 Varieties of Welfare State Development in Chile, Colombia, and Peru

Although their capital cities share important commonalities, Chile, Colombia, and Peru represent different political trajectories and variants of Latin American welfare state development. At one extreme, Peru went through one of the deepest economic crises in the region, decimating its already weak party system and welfare state. In the late 1980s, the Peruvian economy contracted by more than 10 percent. Squatter settlements swelled with an influx of rural migrants fleeing violence and poverty in the countryside. City life provided little respite. The Shining Path guerrilla movement terrorized urban popular neighborhoods, killing over one hundred community leaders in Lima's squatter settlements between 1989 and 2002 (Dosh 2010: 48; Roberts 1998: 250–62).

Peru's established political parties also fell into crisis. The collapse of the party system has been attributed to a range of factors, including profound structural changes, such as the elimination of the last barriers to suffrage, ongoing urban migration, the establishment of compulsory voting, and the growth of the informal economy. These shifts made it difficult for the traditional parties to provide adequate representation to growing urban sectors of society. Widespread anger around hyperinflation, economic inequality, and party corruption likely combined to lead underrepresented voters to turn to outsider candidates (for detailed discussions, see Cameron 1994; Levitsky and Cameron 2003; Morgan 2011; Seawright 2012).

The clearest manifestation of the party-system crisis came in the 1990 presidential election of Alberto Fujimori (1990–2001). Fujimori was a political amateur with no experience in government. Although Fujimori promised to avoid economic "shock" policies on the campaign trail, he pulled an about-face and implemented a draconian package of neoliberal reforms. He opted for an authoritarian strategy and closed the Congress, suspended the constitution, and purged the judiciary in a "self-coup" (*autogolpe*) in 1992. He then was reelected in 1995 by a multi-class

[3] These statistics are calculated from Solt (2016).

coalition backing his exceptional measures to fight terrorism and restore economic discipline. Peru was a competitive authoritarian regime in which the government ran elections, but Fujimori manipulated state resources to drive out the political opposition and engaged in increasingly corrupt tactics aided by his intelligence chief, Vladimiro Montesinos. Full democracy returned to Peru in 2001 after the release of videos that exposed Montesinos's corruption ring. The party system never recovered, and many institutions from the Fujimori period, from a new constitution to a flexible labor code, remain in place.

Since democratization, Peru has been governed from the center-right and presidents have done little to expand Peru's bare-bones welfare state. Limited industrialization in the mid-twentieth century meant that Peru's working class remained very small and contributory social insurance programs covered privileged segments of the population (Haggard and Kaufman 2008: 96; Segura-Ubiergo 2007: 233). Peru has a substantial (35–40 percent) indigenous population, which has higher rates of poverty and less access to basic social services than the national average (Pribble 2010: 209–10). Although a commodities boom greatly increased the budget available for social expenditures in the 2000s, democratically elected presidents, and even those claiming to govern from the Left, failed to follow the regional trend and expand social expenditures (Cameron 2011). Many social programs are targeted to the poor, but because Peru spends relatively little, the redistributive impact of social policy is among the worst in Latin America (Lustig, Pessino, and Scott 2014: 292).

In most respects, Chile and Peru represent opposite ends of Latin America's political and welfare state experience. Chile has a coherent party system with a strong Left and a growing social safety net. In the twentieth century, Chile went much farther with industrial development. It developed a coherent working class able to organize and push for redistributive demands and a much smaller informal sector. The Socialist and Communist Parties (and later the Christian Democrats) also were active participants in land invasions by the urban poor in the 1960s and 1970s, radicalizing and linking squatter claims to the party system in ways that did not occur in other Latin American countries. Large-scale mobilization among the poor and working class helped to elect the first socialist president, Salvador Allende, in 1970. Just three years later, the military launched a coup that brought Augusto Pinochet (1974–1990) to power.

The economy first faltered under the military regime, but recovered by the democratic transition. Pinochet slashed much of Chile's protective labor legislation and rewrote the Constitution. Efforts to break powerful unions largely were successful: the industrial labor force declined by 30 percent in the first decade of military rule (Schamis 1991: 208). The famous Chicago Boys spearheaded neoliberal economic reforms and some targeted anti-poverty policies. By the time the country transitioned to democracy in 1990, the economy had recovered and the military managed to secure favorable institutional rules.

The cleavages of the authoritarian period shaped Chile's party system and partisan alignments. Two conservative parties together formed the core of the opposition, known as the *Alianza*, from 1990 until it took the presidency in 2010. The center-left coalition, the *Concertación*, governed from 1990 to 2010, and again won the presidency in 2014. Chile's party system is praised for its high level of institutionalization, with a clear cleavage between supporters and opponents of military rule (Torcal and Mainwaring 2003). But partisanship is declining, along with the programmatic differentiation of the main parties (Hagopian Forthcoming; Luna 2015; Luna and Mardones 2010).

Although Chile elected center-left and left presidents in all but one election since democratization, progress toward welfare state expansion was slow. Authoritarian enclaves, such as lifetime senators and constitutional provisions governing budget procedures, as well as fear of regime destabilization, limited the scope for redistributive action in the early years of democracy. An exception to the generally slow expansion of social policy under Christian Democratic presidents, as we will see in Chapter 6, is housing policy. Fear of a return to the land invasions that destabilized the Allende government created a rare political consensus around the need for substitutive housing investments. Robust growth did improve the poor's lot, driving the poverty rate from 44 percent in 1990 to 29 percent in 1994 and just 13 percent in 2009. But extreme poverty and income inequality remained stubbornly persistent. Social policy expansions under Socialist-led governments in the 2000s finally began to dent inequality (Huber and Stephens 2012: 181, 198–8). Nevertheless, Chile's welfare state remains relatively small – costing just 13.4 percent of GDP – and decentralized social provision creates strong spatial inequalities in the coverage and quality of social services and unemployment protections.

Colombia, which is the main focus of the public opinion survey in this chapter, has a unique political and welfare state trajectory. Colombia largely escaped Latin America's debt crises, perhaps through prudent macroeconomic management at a time of economic populism or through the flows of illicit drug money that buoyed the economy (Urrutia 1991). It also remained a semi-democracy when much of the region fell to military rule. In 1958, the country's traditional Liberal and Conservative Parties formed a consociational pact, the National Front, to stabilize politics in the aftermath of a bloody civil war (*La Violencia*). The stable two-party system outlasted the formal arrangement. Clientelistic networks allowed the traditional parties to dominate politics, and important spheres of government were siphoned off for technocratic management (Dargent 2015: chapter 4).

Institutional reforms in the late 1980s and early 1990s marked an important break with the existing political regime and party system, akin to a democratic opening. Drug-related conflict made Colombia's cities some of the most violent in Latin America. Ongoing violence from the civil war and drug-trafficking organizations, as well as civic strikes across the country, pushed President Belisario Betancur (1982–1986) to establish direct elections for city mayors in 1986. Sustained pressure from subnational politicians and civil society culminated in a constitutional assembly in 1991 (Falleti 2010: chapter 4). The Constitution amalgamated neoliberal and social democratic threads. President César Gaviria (1990–1994), an economist from the Liberal Party, aimed to protect property rights, remove barriers to foreign investment, and allow for private ownership of former state enterprises, as part of Colombia's economic liberalization and state reforms. But a leftist guerrilla movement with middle-class urban origins, M-19, won the largest block of votes of any organized group at the Constitutional Assembly and joined with dissident factions of the Liberal Party. The left-leaning coalition wrote an extensive battery of social rights into the Constitution and devolved administrative responsibilities to municipalities. Drafters also rewrote electoral rules with the hopes of breaking the hold of traditional parties and regional power brokers.

Although traditional parties proved surprisingly resilient at first, Colombia's two-party system began to fragment. At the city level, as we will see in Chapter 4, independent politicians displaced urban political machines and won power based on their individual "brands" (Pasotti 2009: 74–88). Yet, in contrast to Peru, Colombian voters continued to elect presidents with links to the traditional parties. Every Colombian president has come from the political establishment and governed from the right or center-right. Even Álvaro Uribe (2002–2010) – who some consider a right-wing populist – was a career politician who rose through the Liberal Party ranks as a governor and never broke with the political establishment as president.

The Colombian welfare state blends elements of truncated social policies with aspirations for social inclusion. Historically, important social benefits were linked to formal-sector employment and administered through contributory funds (*Cajas de Compensación Familiar*, CCFs). Colombia extended the social safety net by establishing one of the largest and earliest noncontributory health programs in Latin America in the early 1990s and a targeted cash transfer program in the 2000s (Levy and Schady 2008). But income inequality remains among the highest in the region, and the coverage and quality of social benefits declines sharply with income.

Pressure for welfare state expansion in Colombia largely has not come through electoral politics or societal mobilization. Rather, the long-running civil war strengthened certain parts of the Colombian state, including the police and judiciary, and convinced some elites that strong state institutions and redistributive policies were essential to contain civil conflict. A special wealth tax to fund the security system is the best expression of elites' commitment to state building (Rodríguez-Franco 2016). The Constitutional Court has been the main advocate of additional social spending on the poor. Although some studies find a middle-class bias in the Court's interventions (Landau 2012), many claims taken up by the Court come from marginalized groups. The Court has forced national and subnational authorities to adopt a "developmental state" model in which they actively guarantee a minimum level of basic goods like water, health, housing, and education to vulnerable groups (Brinks and Forbath 2014). It also has prodded the government to do more to assist individuals internally displaced by the civil war (Rodríguez-Garavito and Rodríguez-Franco 2015).

Thus, despite significant differences in the economic and political context, all three countries have important deficits in their welfare states. The limited coverage of social programs has a crucial implication for the structure of public opinion: it cannot be assumed that the poor think social spending helps them. In contrast, squatting and street vending long have served as ways for the urban poor to cope with economic dislocations and integrate into urban life. The remaining sections of this chapter take up the question of how ordinary citizens think about forbearance and state redistribution, focusing on Colombia and then extending the findings to the rest of Latin America.

## 2.2 HOW TO MEASURE SUPPORT FOR FORBEARANCE

Examining popular support for forbearance requires thinking carefully about legal attitudes. I decompose legal attitudes into two distinct dimensions, attitudes toward *compliance*, meaning beliefs about the need to follow the law, and attitudes toward *enforcement*, meaning beliefs about how the state should act in response to legal violations. These beliefs do not necessarily move together. As we will see, some individuals want compliance but oppose enforcement, and some individuals support enforcement in the abstract and oppose it in concrete cases. I thus underscore the need for caution in drawing conclusions about the level of support for forbearance, and introduce the composite measure that I use to analyze how support for forbearance differs by income and social policy context in the next section.

Preexisting surveys rarely ask about enforcement attitudes or do so in imprecise ways. I therefore designed and administered my own survey to 900 voters in Bogotá (see Appendix A for details). The latitude to design my own survey instrument allowed me to ask a rich set of questions about both compliance and enforcement. I drew on my fieldwork and focus groups with squatters and street vendors to develop appropriate language to ask about legal violations. In particular, I did not want to impose normative judgments on an activity by labeling it as "illegal." I therefore asked about "informal," "unauthorized," or "unlicensed" activities so that respondents could arrive at their own judgments.

The main questions of interest involve attitudes toward squatting and street vending. Items about compliance ask whether a respondent "strongly disapproves" to "strongly approves" that people sell goods without a license in public spaces (*Street Vending*) or occupies land to build a house without appropriate title (*Squatting*). Enforcement items ask the degree to which respondents approve that the government implements the most common sanctions against these activities, the confiscation of merchandise from street vendors (*Decommission*) and the eviction of squatters (*Eviction*).

I use these two dimensions to produce a fourfold typology of legal attitudes summarized in Figure 2.1. I include the frequency of responses for street vending and squatting in Bogotá. The top row shows the fraction of respondents that approves or strongly approves of sanctions. The top-right cell can be thought of as the conventionally expected attitude toward legal violations, *state enforcement*. These individuals both disapprove of violations and support state sanctions. If we think of the case of murder, for instance, we expect that the population widely condemns the act and

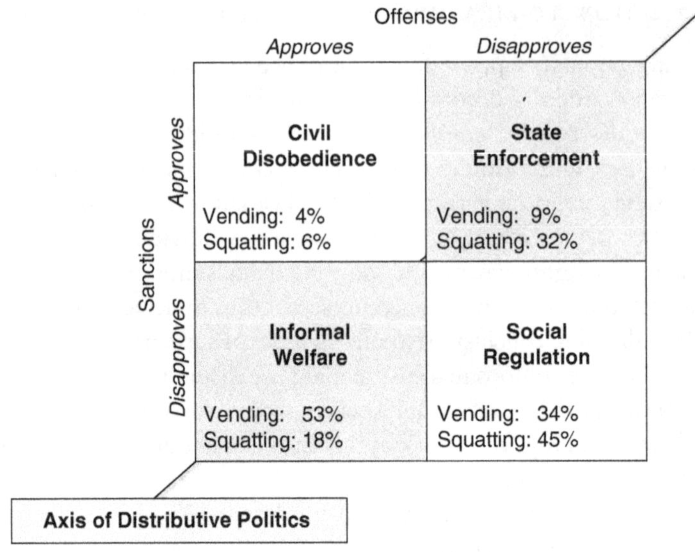


FIGURE 2.1 A Typology of Legal Attitudes

supports its punishment. If state enforcement beliefs predominate, then sanctions enjoy robust societal support. In the case of street vending and squatting, this viewpoint is in the minority and, as I demonstrate below, it concentrates among upper-class groups.

The upper-left cell is a rare combination where individuals approve of offenses and state sanctions. Theoretically, this combination reflects an attitude of *civil disobedience*. Individuals find the law unjust in certain circumstances, which merit its violation, but they believe that the state retains the authority qua state to enforce the law. For instance, black Americans who staged sit-ins in segregated public spaces during the civil rights movement were willing to go to jail to show their opposition to the law. In Latin America, individuals practicing civil disobedience might use a land taking to protest state housing policies at the risk of punishment; they are what Peñalver and Katyal (2010) call "property outlaws."[4] When surveyed, the category of individuals with these demands is miniscule (and possibly just respondent error). Intuitively, most individuals who justify

[4] Tsai (2015) similarly shows that some Chinese citizens justify legal violations as a way to provide feedback to the state on the appropriateness of laws. Although she does not analyze enforcement attitudes, it is plausible that some citizens who think it is justified to violate laws as a form of constructive feedback also think that the state has the right to punish those who disobey.

legal violations also think that the state should not sanction them, particularly on a survey where no symbolic political statement is being made.

The bottom row represents individuals who oppose or strongly oppose enforcement. The bottom-left produces the combination of beliefs of chief interest: individuals who both approve of offenses and eschew state sanctions. In the context of laws that benefit the poor if ignored, I consider this combination to indicate support for *informal welfare*. This attitude is quite different from a particularistic explanation of support for legal violations. DaMatta (1991) famously proposed that Latin Americans show limited support for law because they see their *personal* circumstances as meriting exceptions. Informal welfare attitudes, as measured on this survey, suggest principled stances in favor of legal violations. This view is widespread in reactions to street vending, making up about half of responses. It is less common in the case of squatting, perhaps because legal violations are more permanent or threatening to property rights. In cases where informal welfare beliefs are prevalent, the question becomes why the law exists at all. A slim majority in Bogotá, for instance, seemingly would support rewriting the law to allow street vending.

Lastly, the bottom-right cell captures opposition both to legal violations and to enforcement. A disjuncture forms between the ideal level of compliance and the use of state force necessary to achieve that outcome. Such an attitude, which I label support for *social regulation*, likely reflects the way in which enforcement is different from other policy areas. Sanctions impose concentrated costs on individuals and draw attention to the ways that the state actively can disrupt the lives of vulnerable groups. These views are clearest in the case of squatting because evictions constitute a harsh punishment. Three-quarters of respondents condemn squatting, but more than half of this group also opposes evictions. This finding coincides with Gibson's (2008: 707) work on South Africa, which shows general opposition to the redistribution of land through squatting but a frequent rejection of evictions as unfair. Hummel (2017) argues that governments encourage collective organizing as a way to have street vendors internally control the negative externalities without coercive sanctions. Notably, if social regulation views dominate, then having unenforced laws reflects the majority's will.

If concern about the effects of state actions on vulnerable individuals drives attitudes, then support for social regulation should increase when questions involve a concrete case. I asked questions about state enforcement activities framed as abstract decisions and as vignettes about a single case. Indeed, while 49 percent of respondents oppose evictions of squatters in general, a full 62 percent of respondents oppose the eviction of a family who occupies land illegally. Interestingly, middle-class respondents are most sensitive to these framing effects: support shoots up by almost 20 percentage points, while it barely changes among the poor.

I combine the survey items on compliance and enforcement into a single dimension to capture more stable attitudes and reduce noise from measurement error (Ansolabehere, Rodden, and Snyder 2008). The intuition is that, while opinions about compliance and sanctions are not the same, they have an underlying basis, just as opinions about taxation and spending are not equivalent, but strong support for both suggests more robust support for redistribution. Returning to Figure 2.1, what I want to measure is loosely the diagonal. The key groups – individuals who consistently back state enforcement and those who favor forbearance as informal welfare provision – are shaded in gray to indicate their centrality. Individuals who prefer social regulation can be understood as a swing group, which I suspect is more sensitive to the framing of enforcement actions. I use principal component analysis (PCA) to combine the questions into an underlying dimension of forbearance attitudes (*Forbearance*). I follow a similar method to measure redistributive attitudes (*Redistribution*), using a battery of questions about support for the general goal of inequality reduction and specific policies to tax the rich and spend on different social programs. A common dimension (the first component) loads positively on all questions and explains 37 and 45 percent of the variance in forbearance and redistributive beliefs, respectively. I now use these composite variables to analyze how attitudes vary with an individual's economic position and assessments of the welfare state.

## 2.3 DO POOR VOTERS FAVOR FORBEARANCE?

The most basic assumption of redistributive politics, usually associated with the Meltzer and Richard (1981) model, is that the poor prefer social welfare spending and the rich resist it. If forbearance serves as a form of informal redistribution, then it should divide preferences by income in a similar way. My chief independent variables of interest therefore are proxies for material interests. There should be a negative relationship between income (and related measures of wealth, education, and direct material stakes) and forbearance support. In addition, due to the truncated nature of welfare programs, I expect material interests to play a greater role in shaping attitudes toward forbearance than toward standard social policy tools. I begin with the correlational evidence from Bogotá, and then replicate the tests on data from across Latin America.

### 2.3.1 Material Interests in Bogotá

I test the material interest hypothesis with regression analyses of forbearance and redistributive attitudes in which income is included as an independent variable along with controls for potential confounders. Self-reported income measures have a number of known problems in developing countries where households do not receive regular paychecks (Handlin 2013). I try to surmount these issues by relying on the Colombian government's socioeconomic stratifications, a variable that I loosely call *Class*. Colombia divides the population into six strata based on household and neighborhood characteristics. Strata "1" is the lowest and "6" is the highest. Individuals are highly knowledgeable of their household's stratum, given that they are used to determine tax and service rates. Citizens and politicians alike speak in terms of "low" and "high" strata households. Strata measures thus come closer to capturing a broad notion of economic position than income measures. I expect the coefficient on class to be negative, given that upper-class groups prefer less forbearance. Because stratifications are made at the household level, I also include years of education (*Education*) to capture additional individual-level differences and lifetime earnings expectations.

Another implication of a material interest theory is that individuals who benefit directly from forbearance should be the most supportive. In particular, I expect that individuals who have worked as a street vendor (*Vendor Past*) or have occupied land illegally (*Squatter Past*) are more supportive of forbearance, given that they have a direct stake in the distributive benefits and perhaps greater sympathy for legal violations. Although a looser measure, individuals in the informal sector (*Informal*) also may be more likely to support forbearance due to their historic exclusion from formal welfare benefits and need for regulatory flexibility. I measure informality through a composite measure of whether an individual lacks a labor contract and does not have contributory health insurance or make pension contributions. This measure combines both contract- and benefit-based definitions of informality (Perry 2007: 28–40), offering the most robust sense of what it means to be an informal-sector worker.

In addition, support for law and order often is associated with conservative political ideology, which can correlate with income. To test if political ideology drives the results, I asked respondents to place their political views on a scale that runs from the political left to right (*Right*). I do not expect ideology to align with forbearance attitudes among political elites, as explained in Chapter 1. But among the public at large, support for law and order may correlate with support for the Right and enforcement.

In all models, I include several demographic controls. I expect that older respondents (*Age*) are less supportive of forbearance because they have a higher probability of owning property and may be more concerned about disorder. I also control for gender (*Female*). Women own less property and also are more reliant on flexible job opportunities like street vending. They therefore have more to gain from forbearance and may have higher levels of support. I rescale all categorical variables from 0 to 1 so that the coefficients can be interpreted as a change from the lowest to highest value of the independent variable.

Table 2.1 presents the results of an ordinary least squares regression model. Model 1 shows the basic model with class as the key explanatory variable. The coefficient on class, which is close to negative one, means that an individual in the highest class is about a standard deviation less supportive of forbearance than an individual in the lowest class. Model 2 adds the measure of political ideology. Individuals who identify with the Right are about a quarter of a standard deviation less supportive of forbearance than those on the Left.[5] Model 3 adds the direct benefits variables. Experiences as a street vendor or squatter or working in the informal sector all are associated with more support for forbearance. Crucially, class remains a significant predictor of forbearance attitudes, even accounting for political ideology and the direct violation of the law, suggesting that poor voters are more supportive of forbearance even when they identify with the Right and personally break the law.

Models 4 through 6 replicate the analysis using the index of redistributive attitudes as the dependent variable. As predicted in standard models, class is negatively associated with support for redistributive attitudes. However, consistent with my theory, it is a weaker predictor. A way to see the difference in explanatory power is through measures of model fit: despite using a battery of questions, demographic characteristics explain

[5] Because I lose 15 percent of the data due to nonresponse on ideology questions, and nonresponse is concentrated among low-income respondents, I multiply impute ideology using socioeconomic characteristics and past vote choice. Adjusting for missing data does not change the results.

TABLE 2.1 *Comparing Forbearance and Redistributive Attitudes in Bogotá*

| | Forbearance | | | Redistribution | | |
|---|---|---|---|---|---|---|
| | (1) | (2) | (3) | (4) | (5) | (6) |
| *Class* | -1.010* | -1.008* | -0.819* | -0.507* | -0.462* | -0.464* |
| | (0.133) | (0.138) | (0.133) | (0.142) | (0.152) | (0.146) |
| *Education* | -0.382* | -0.293* | -0.207* | -0.249 | -0.329* | -0.170 |
| | (0.139) | (0.146) | (0.141) | (0.150) | (0.161) | (0.156) |
| *Female* | 0.002 | -0.002 | -0.005 | 0.023 | 0.022 | 0.025 |
| | (0.062) | (0.066) | (0.061) | (0.066) | (0.072) | (0.067) |
| *Age* | -0.516* | -0.545* | -0.437* | -0.138 | -0.168 | -0.120 |
| | (0.104) | (0.110) | (0.103) | (0.111) | (0.121) | (0.113) |
| *Right* | | -0.235* | | | -0.041 | |
| | | (0.110) | | | (0.121) | |
| *Vendor Past* | | | 0.457* | | | 0.105 |
| | | | (0.076) | | | (0.084) |
| *Squatter Past* | | | 0.198* | | | -0.003 |
| | | | (0.101) | | | (0.111) |
| *Informal* | | | 0.245* | | | 0.142 |
| | | | (0.101) | | | (0.112) |
| N | 869 | 738 | 862 | 875 | 744 | 868 |
| Adjusted $R^2$ | 0.167 | 0.168 | 0.211 | 0.041 | 0.041 | 0.042 |

*Notes:* $^*p < 0.05$; robust standard errors in parentheses; two-tailed tests. The dependent variable is the standardized first component of a PCA analysis from a series of questions about forbearance (approval for squatting, street vending, evictions, and decommissions) and redistribution (approval for inequality reduction, taxation, cash transfers, housing, unemployment, and pension policies).

4 percent of variation in redistributive attitudes compared to 21 percent for forbearance attitudes. These results are consistent with past work on redistributive attitudes, which finds a less consistent and weaker relationship between income and support for redistribution in Latin America (Blofield and Luna 2011; Dion and Birchfield 2010; Holland 2016b). Interestingly, political ideology is not predictive of redistributive attitudes, despite dominant definitions of the political Left and Right based on orientations toward income inequality.

As a robustness check, I also look at the results separately for each question on legal and redistributive attitudes. Figure 2.2 plots the estimated coefficients and 95 percent confidence intervals on the horizontal axis from each of these regressions. I display the three main explanatory variables of interest: class, political ideology, and past violations of the law (socioeconomic control variables are included in the model but not

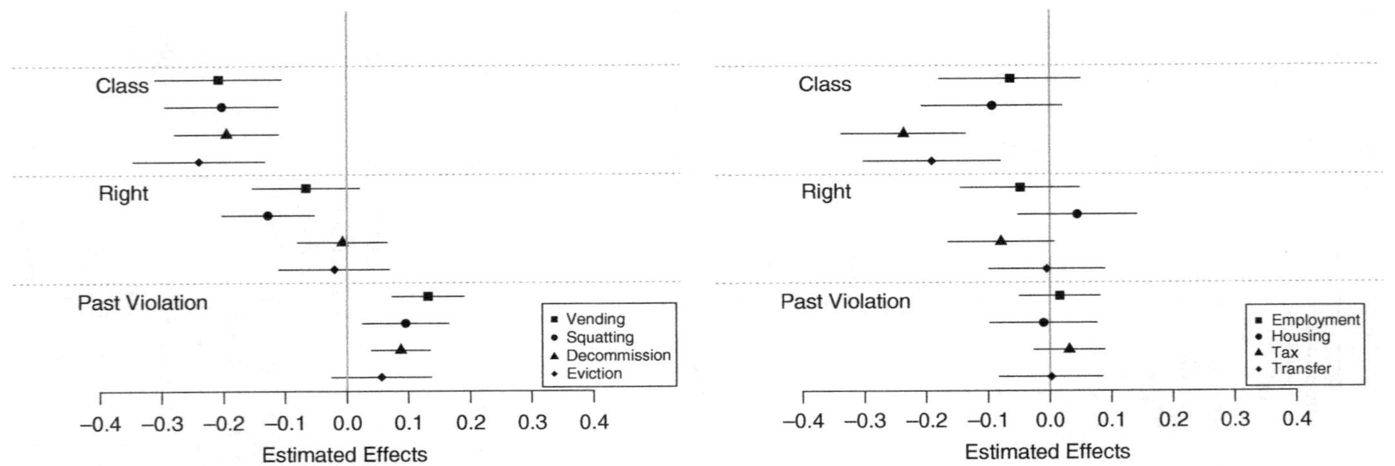


FIGURE 2.2 Predicted Effects of Class, Ideology, and Legal Violations

Notes: Horizontal bars represent 95 percent confidence intervals; controls for age, education, and gender not shown; the variable *Past Violation* takes on the value that matches the dependent variable specification (i.e., past history as a squatter for questions on squatting and evictions, etc.). Questions about sanctions are coded as opposition to the sanction so that a negative coefficient indicates that the wealthy are more likely to oppose forbearance/support enforcement.

shown). By looking at how many coefficients lose significance, shown visually by when the confidence intervals cross the vertical line at zero, the figure reveals the consistency of the results. The class coefficients on the forbearance questions are uniformly significant. Only some of the class coefficients are significant for redistribution, although they all have the correct negative sign. The results for political ideology are inconsistent. Ideology is associated with opposition to squatting (and street vending falls just shy of significance), but no differences in enforcement attitudes. Ideology also shapes tax, but not social spending, attitudes.

Breaking down the results by policy underscores the relationship between class, redistributive attitudes, and policy targeting. Only the more economically progressive social policies, such as taxing the rich or cash transfers to the poor, divide the electorate along class lines. These are policies that clearly benefit the poor. Housing and unemployment policy tend to favor formal-sector workers in Colombia, as I return to in subsequent chapters, and thus have weaker class divisions. The magnitude of class differences for progressive social policies is on par with those observed for forbearance.

The simplest way to give substantive meaning to these results is to analyze the fraction of respondents that holds a given legal attitude. State enforcement against squatting garners support among 47 percent of nonpoor respondents and 31 percent of poor ones.[6] Even more extreme, while 27 percent of nonpoor respondents support enforcement against street vendors, only 8 percent of poor respondents concur. Conversely, informal welfare beliefs concentrate among the poor. While 22 percent of poor respondents approve of informal welfare provision in the case of squatting, 6 percent of nonpoor respondents hold similar beliefs. Likewise, 63 percent of the poor hold informal welfare beliefs about street vending compared to 34 percent of nonpoor respondents.

In sum, I find strong evidence that class predicts forbearance attitudes. These effects are larger and more consistent than those observed for redistribution. I now consider whether these results generalize beyond Bogotá.

### 2.3.2 Material Interests across Latin America

Operationalizing support for forbearance cross-nationally is not straightforward, given that widely administered surveys rarely ask about attitudes

[6] I refer to Strata 1 and 2 as the poor, Strata 3 as the lower-middle class, and Strata 4 and above as nonpoor (or middle and upper class).

toward property laws. I use an indirect method to measure attitudes toward squatting using public opinion data from LAPOP's AmericasBarometer. The 2008, 2010, and 2012 waves ask respondents whether they approve "that people invade private property or land to protest." Response options range from "strongly disapprove" to "strongly approve" on a ten-point scale. This question thus probes compliance attitudes in a similar fashion to my survey in Bogotá. Levels of support for land invasions are low: I find that 16 percent of Colombians and 11 percent of the regional sample approve of private property seizures. But these results are not that far off the 21 percent who approve of squatting in Bogotá, and the difference may stem from the fact that AmericasBarometer asks about the taking of private land (whereas my survey left open whether the land was public or private).

The other catch is that the AmericasBarometer question asks about property invasions "to protest," and forms part of a block of questions about contentious behaviors. Responses thus likely mix beliefs about the general appropriateness of protest, the "response style" of an individual (meaning the tendency to give extreme or moderate answers), and reactions to land invasions. My aim is to isolate this latter aspect. To do so, I essentially only want to use the variation unique to the question on land invasions. I therefore create an index of general attitudes toward protest and then use this index in a first-stage regression on the question about property seizures as protest (see Appendix A for details). Controlling for the common component of views on protest, the remaining variation represents how individuals' responses differ when considering land invasions. I standardize the residuals to use as my dependent variable, so a change in any covariate can be interpreted in terms of a standard deviation change in support for land invasions.

Turning to redistributive attitudes, only one question has been used consistently: whether individuals believe that the government should take concrete measures to reduce inequality. This question elicits near-uniform positive responses because it poses no trade-offs in terms of taxation, growth, and so on. Nevertheless, it is the only question available to capture whether income predicts redistributive attitudes.

My main independent variable is income. Respondents self-report their household income range, *Income*. I take the log of the midpoint of each income bracket. Logged income is more normally distributed, and closer to theoretical expectations that a given percentage change in income should be associated with similar changes in attitudes. For robustness, I also consider household wealth (*Wealth*) based on durable assets that can be measured with less error. Support for squatting and redistribution should decline with income and wealth, and therefore the coefficient on both measures should be negative.

All models include a set of control variables similar to that used in Bogotá, *Age, Education, Female*, and *Right*. I also include an indicator variable for whether the respondent lives in a rural area (*Rural*) to account for the national samples. Both urban and rural land invasions involve distributive claims by the poor, so I do not expect differences in attitudes by geographic region. There are no questions on past history as a squatter or street vendor. Recent waves do include questions on whether an individual is self-employed, which I combine with information on education to create a category for self-employed unskilled workers (*Self-Employed*). Self-employment should be associated with more support for land invasions, but it is a much looser measure than used in Bogotá. As before, I rescale all categorical independent variables from 0 to 1.

Table 2.2 presents the regional results. I include country and time fixed effects (not shown) so the coefficient, say for income, represents how a move from the lowest to highest income level within a given country-year is predicted to shift attitudes toward squatting. Models 1 through 3 examine the determinants of attitudes toward squatting (my proxy for forbearance). Consistent with the findings from Bogotá, I find that poor respondents are more tolerant of squatting. This follows directly from my claim that property seizures constitute progressive transfers and thus gain greater support among the poor. Doubling one's income is associated with about a standard deviation decrease in the index of support for squatting. Being less educated, younger, and female also are associated with stronger support for squatting, perhaps because these groups are more likely to need to violate the law to acquire property or more sympathetic to squatters' claims. Wealth-based income measures produce substantively similar and significant results, as shown in Models 2 and 3. Identifying with the political Right is associated with less support for squatting, but does not change the coefficient on income. This result is consistent with my finding in Bogotá that political identification predicts attitudes toward squatting, while having a less significant association with other types of forbearance. The only surprising result is that self-employment is associated with less support for squatting.[7]

[7] It is possible that self-employment captures many small business owners, and that the dependent variable wording about seizure of "private property or land" invokes concerns about their businesses, rather than the taking of land for housing purposes.

TABLE 2.2 *Comparing Forbearance and Redistributive Attitudes across Latin America*

| | Forbearance | | | Redistribution | | |
|---|---|---|---|---|---|---|
| | (1) | (2) | (3) | (4) | (5) | (6) |
| *Income* | −0.010* | | | 0.003 | | |
| | (0.0) | | | (0.00) | | |
| *Wealth* | | −0.071* | −0.075* | | −0.132* | −0.128* |
| | | (0.02) | (0.02) | | (0.02) | (0.02) |
| *Education* | −0.256* | −0.223* | −0.241* | −0.021 | 0.053* | 0.090* |
| | (0.02) | (0.02) | (0.02) | (0.02) | (0.02) | (0.02) |
| *Female* | 0.038* | 0.037* | 0.036* | −0.016* | −0.016* | −0.028* |
| | (0.01) | (0.01) | (0.01) | (0.01) | (0.01) | (0.01) |
| *Age* | −0.083* | −0.066* | −0.066* | 0.026 | 0.049* | 0.062* |
| | (0.02) | (0.02) | (0.02) | (0.02) | (0.02) | (0.02) |
| *Rural* | −0.003 | −0.007 | −0.007 | 0.017 | 0.004 | −0.009 |
| | (0.01) | (0.01) | (0.01) | (0.01) | (0.01) | (0.01) |
| *Right* | | | −0.047* | | | −0.041* |
| | | | (0.02) | | | (0.02) |
| *Self-Employed* | | | −0.025* | | | 0.009 |
| | | | (0.01) | | | (0.01) |
| N | 64,180 | 73,672 | 60,322 | 68,743 | 79,300 | 64,154 |
| Adjusted $R^2$ | 0.036 | 0.034 | 0.036 | 0.049 | 0.052 | 0.054 |

*Notes:* $^*p < 0.05$; robust standard errors in parentheses; two-tailed tests; year and country fixed effects not shown. The dependent variable for forbearance is the standardized residuals from a first-stage regression of support for land invasions "as protest" on a series of questions about protest attitudes. For redistribution, the dependent variable measures standardized support for government actions to reduce inequality.

Models 4 through 6 compare the same specifications for redistributive preferences. Income does not predict support for redistribution in the pooled data, but wealth measures do produce the correctly signed coefficients. Surprisingly, education, another common proxy for socioeconomic status, is associated with either equal or more support for redistribution. It is possible that the inconsistent relationship between different socioeconomic measures and redistributive preferences at least in part reflects measurement error. However, income is more predictive of redistributive attitudes in countries where the welfare state is a relevant force in the poor's lives. Figure 2.3 makes this clear through a simple bivariate plot.[8] The vertical axis plots the predictive power of income on redistributive

[8] I test this idea through hierarchical regression analysis in separate work (Holland 2016b).

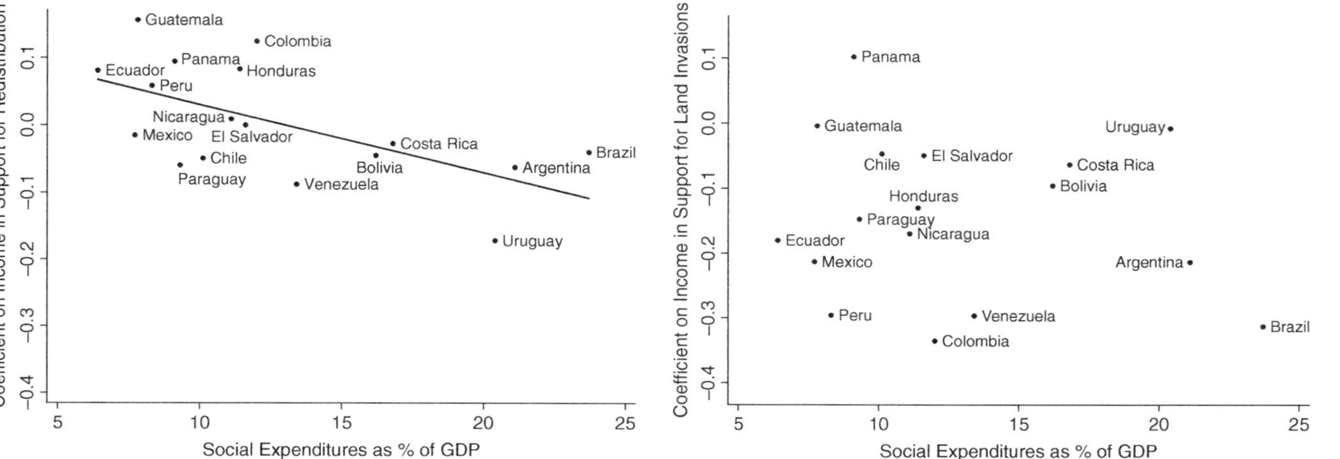


FIGURE 2.3 The Predictive Power of Income and Welfare State Size in Latin America

Notes: The coefficients are measured through a basic regression of income on support for land invasions and inequality reduction for the 2012 LAPOP wave in which the number of income categories expanded to allow for more precise measurements. Controlling for education, female, age, and rural residency produces the same results. Social expenditures come from ECLAC (2011).

preferences. In other words, a more negative coefficient means that a country comes closer to theoretical expectations that the rich support less redistribution than the poor. The horizontal axis plots the size of the welfare state in each country, as measured by social expenditures as a percent of GDP. I use social expenditures to proxy for the relevance of welfare programs to the poor's lives, but similar results obtain using the redistributive impact of spending. There is almost no relationship between income and redistributive preferences in countries with small or truncated welfare states, such as Colombia and Peru. But the poor do support more redistribution than the rich in countries with more meaningful social programs, such as Uruguay and Brazil.

The right panel of Figure 2.3 shows that income shapes attitudes toward land invasions across the region. In almost every country (save Panama), the relationship between income and support for land invasions is negative, as seen by the fact that the coefficients are less than zero. Countries best known for a history of land invasions, such as Brazil where the Landless Peasants' Movement has politicized land invasions, but also Colombia and Peru, have the strongest relationship between income and invasions. There is no clear relationship between the size of the welfare state and class divisions around land invasions, but I do not expect one given that a large welfare state does not guarantee substitutive housing policies to provide options for squatters.

Thus, class predicts forbearance preferences, both in Bogotá and across Latin America. While most theories focus on the class divisions that form around redistribution, I demonstrate that cleavages are at least as powerful around forbearance. In the remaining chapters, these class-based attitudinal differences will be at the heart of why elected officials make different enforcement choices depending on where they run for office.

### 2.3.3 Probing the Mechanisms

What explains the relationship between income and forbearance preferences? I suggest that forbearance gains support among the poor for material and sociotropic reasons: it provides direct material benefits to some poor individuals and elicits empathy among similarly situated individuals. I also expect forbearance to have greater acceptance when welfare states are failing. While not definitive tests, I consider the evidence in favor of these hypothesized linkages and several alternative explanations, such as legal culture, consumption benefits, and interest groups.

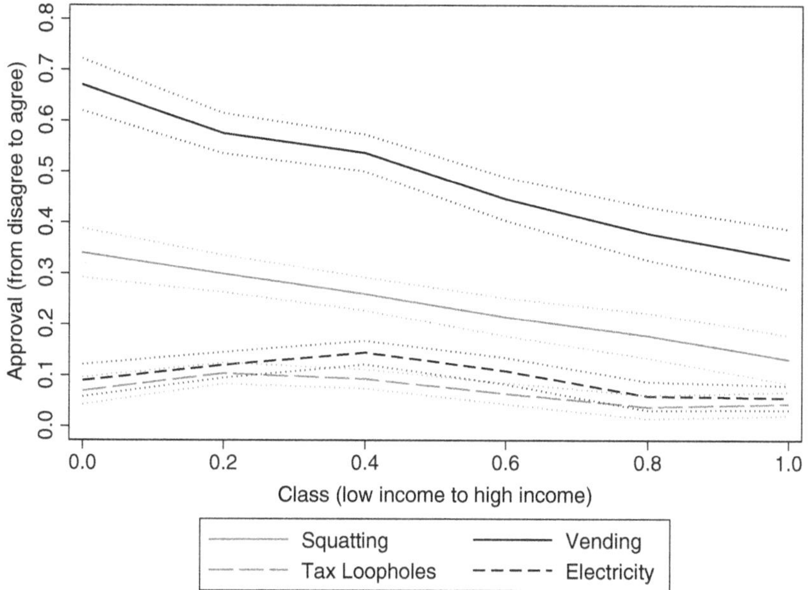


FIGURE 2.4 Support for Noncompliance by Class and Offense

First, a key test of my proposed mechanisms is the difference in attitudes across legal violations. If my theory holds, the poor's support for forbearance should not extend to instances when the wealthy violate the law. This prediction differentiates my theory from alternatives rooted in legal culture, which expect the poor to be less legalistic than the nonpoor in general. I asked questions about two common infractions with regressive effects, using business tax loopholes (*Tax Loopholes*) and tampering with industrial electricity meters (*Electricity*). Figure 2.4 compares approval for different types of offenses across class groups in Bogotá. The solid lines show approval for legal violations that benefit the poor, squatting and street vending, along with the 95 percent confidence intervals. The level of support for these violations is substantial, and it declines with income. In contrast, the dotted lines show support for the regressive violations (tax loopholes and electricity diversion). There is near-universal condemnation of these acts by poor and nonpoor respondents alike. Thus, consistent with my theory, only legal violations with progressive benefits polarize voters along class lines.

Second, this analysis by offense type suggests that viewing support for forbearance purely in terms of consumption interests is incomplete. In the context of market reforms, Baker (2010) proposes a consumer-oriented theory of preferences in which individuals primarily think about how policies affect prices. Applied to forbearance, street vendors often escape value-added taxes and offer lower-priced goods, which benefit all consumers (but especially price-sensitive poor consumers). Squatting has no clear effect on pocketbook issues – it might increase the housing stock, reducing housing prices, or it might reduce available land, raising housing prices. A consumer-oriented theory thus would predict more support for street vending than squatting, and stronger class cleavages around squatting given no offsetting consumer benefits to middle-class groups. Figure 2.4 reveals a modicum of support for this explanation: the level of support for street vending is higher than for squatting. But the class divisions are fairly similar, as seen in the parallel slopes. I did not ask whether individuals personally purchased goods from street vendors, which would have been an additional test of a consumer-interest theory (but also confounded by the fact that some individuals purchase from street vendors as a way to show their solidarity). I therefore cannot rule out that consumer interests motivate popular support for street vending, but they cannot account for why important segments of the electorate support squatting and why class divisions emerge toward both offenses.

Third, immediate material benefits from forbearance cannot fully explain attitudes. I expect that individuals who violate the law have the strongest support for forbearance, but even poor individuals who do not violate the law support forbearance based on their group affinity (or their concern that they too might need to violate the law one day). Thus, the negative relationship between income and forbearance attitudes should persist after accounting for whether an individual violates the law at hand. Returning to Table 2.1, we see that this is the case: the coefficient on class drops by about a quarter when including measures of direct dependence on legal violations, but income remains an important predictor of attitudes. This finding differentiates my theory from alternatives focused on interest groups. Interest-group theories imply that only direct stakeholders support forbearance, and they impose their preferences on the majority that supports enforcement.

A fourth way to probe whether distributive expectations undergird both formal and informal welfare attitudes is to see whether individuals believe that they benefit. To do this, I asked individuals if they believe that social expenditures benefit "people like them" (*Benefits*). This question is meant to judge perceptions that an individual receives benefits, whether

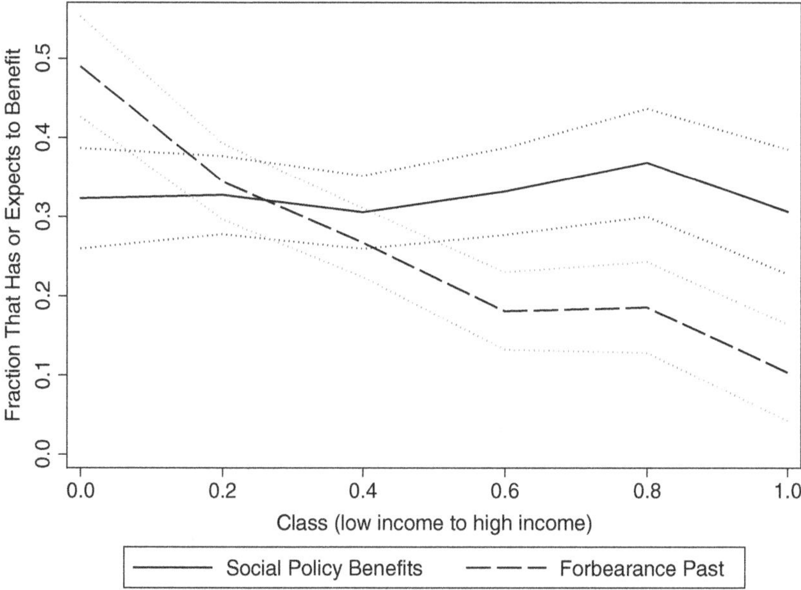


FIGURE 2.5 Expectations of Benefits from Social Policy and Forbearance

past or future, from the welfare state. The solid line in Figure 2.5 reveals that the fraction of respondents who believe that they benefit from social expenditures is amazingly constant across class groups. About a third of poor *and nonpoor* respondents believe that they benefit from state social policies. It is unsurprising that attitudes toward social policy differ little by class when the key mechanism that underpins material interest theories – differential benefits from the welfare state – does not vary at all based on class position.

Contrastingly, the dashed line in Figure 2.5 plots the fraction of the population that has benefitted from forbearance toward vending and squatting. For the poorest class group, the fraction that has benefited from forbearance is larger than those who expect to benefit from social expenditures. This difference is impressive given that the question scope (all social programs versus street vending and squatting) would lead us to think that social benefits should affect many more poor individuals. We can also see that the class difference across groups is very sharp for forbearance. Primarily lower-income respondents have worked as street vendors or lived in informal settlements, while all respondents expect to capture some social benefits in Colombia.

A final piece of my theory is that individuals are more likely to support forbearance in the absence of welfare state alternatives. If this is the case, then, support for forbearance will be lower among individuals who believe that the state provides welfare alternatives. To investigate this possibility, I asked respondents in Bogotá whether the government provided housing options to the poor or whether the poor needed to invade land to access housing (*Housing Availability*). Assessments of housing alternatives are dismal: 81 percent of respondents believe that the state offers no way for the poor to access housing. Beliefs that state alternatives do not exist indeed predict more support for squatting and less support for evictions (regression coefficients not shown). For instance, among respondents who believe that the state does not provide housing, 67 percent of poor respondents and 56 percent of nonpoor respondents oppose evictions. Among those who believe that squatters have other housing options, 37 and 40 percent of poor and nonpoor respondents, respectively, oppose evictions.

Similar patterns emerge in the regional data. I created an indicator variable for individuals who both believe that the government should take steps to reduce inequality and that it does not at present (*Social Deficit*). I find that perceived social deficits are associated with more support for squatting (the coefficient, not shown, is positive). Admittedly, it is hard to know whether individuals with varying beliefs about social policy alternatives differ in other unobservable ways that explain their enforcement views. An omitted variable, for instance, may be sympathy for the poor, which leads individuals to perceive welfare state failings and support forbearance.[9] Nevertheless, focus groups with leaders of squatting and street-vending associations support my interpretation: almost every participant brought up social policy failings to justify forbearance.

In short, the strong role of income in shaping forbearance preferences can be understood in light of the history and progressivity of Latin American welfare states. Many formal welfare benefits in Colombia and across the region have accrued to formal-sector workers. The greater polarization of attitudes around forbearance toward street vendors

[9] A better empirical test would look at whether attitudes varied with the availability of housing programs at a local level. In an attempted survey experiment, however, I was unable to change perceptions of welfare state alternatives by providing information about the size and targeting of housing programs. Respondents were uniformly skeptical that state housing programs generate real alternatives for the poor.

and squatters makes sense when their role in disproportionately helping the poor is considered. Welfare state failures and forbearance attitudes also seem to be intertwined: individuals who think the poor have few other welfare options tend to accept forbearance as a necessary substitute.

## 2.4 FORBEARANCE AS A DISTRIBUTIVE SIGNAL

Even if citizens understand the distributive functions of forbearance, it does not necessarily follow that they hold politicians responsible or change their voting behavior in response to enforcement choices. This section explores my final hypothesis: that politicians who propose forbearance are identified as sympathetic to the poor's broader interests, while those who run on enforcement platforms are viewed as anti-poor. Given the more progressive and credible nature of the benefits, I also expect that forbearance and enforcement platforms provide a clearer cue about distributive commitments than traditional social policy platforms in contexts where welfare programs lag.

To understand what enforcement conveys about a politician to the public, I designed a survey experiment. I focused on street vendors in the experiment because they create common problems across urban space so all respondents are equally familiar with their legal violations. Each survey respondent heard two short statements about a hypothetical candidate considering a run for city mayor with a platform about street vending or employment policy. The combination and order in which they heard the candidates varied. All of the statements were based on actual candidate proposals from past mayoral elections. Individuals heard one vignette about a candidate with a plan to create a government job program for unskilled workers (*Pro-Redistribution*) or to reduce business regulations to create jobs (*Pro-Business*). My goal was to simulate a classic left–right division on how to address unemployment. In addition, individuals evaluated a candidate with a plan for either forbearance (*Forbearance*) or enforcement (*Enforcement*) against unlicensed street vendors. The vignettes read as follows, where the italic type indicates wording that changed across vignettes:

Pro-Redistribution/Pro-Business: As a city councilor, the candidate criticized the lack of projects *for vulnerable sectors of the population/to generate private-sector investment*. If he were mayor, he would *invest in government job programs to help employ unskilled workers/cut government bureaucracy to help businesses grow and generate jobs.*

Forbearance/Enforcement: As a city councilor, the candidate criticized *the abuses/the permissive attitude* of previous mayors toward unlicensed street vendors. If he were mayor, he would *respect the rights of workers in the informal economy until the government provides other job alternatives/work for greater order in the streets and clear out unlicensed vendors.*

After hearing each candidate's proposal, respondents assessed the candidates separately to avoid consistency bias.[10] They evaluated the candidates on a four-point scale running from "highly unlikely" to "highly likely" on three items: (1) How likely is it that the candidate promotes the interests of the poor? (2) How likely is it that the candidate promotes the interests of people like you? and (3) How likely is it that you would vote for this candidate for mayor? The first pair of questions was intended to tap into representation and expectations of benefits, whereas the last analyzed vote intention. Finally, respondents placed the candidate on a five-point ideological scale ranging from the political Left to Right. I rescaled all responses from 0 to 1.

The groups hearing each candidate prompt were balanced with respect to class and other pretreatment covariates. A simple comparison of means can therefore be interpreted as the effect of hearing one platform versus the other.[11] There is no control condition because a candidate without any political stance is meaningless; instead, the effects are interpreted relative to each other so I can draw comparisons between and across candidate pairs.

Figure 2.6 shows the perceived likelihood that the candidate will promote the interests of the poor and the perceived ideological placement. I plot the raw means and 95 percent confidence intervals for each experimental condition. The vertical line at 0.5 indicates the point of indifference (i.e., the candidate is not seen as pro-poor or anti-poor, or from the Left or Right). The results confirm my hypothesis that enforcement/forbearance messages send clearer distributive cues than traditional social policy platforms. Provided with the enforcement message, 78 percent of respondents believed that the candidate is unlikely or very unlikely to favor the poor's interests. Just 33 percent of respondents thought the same about the forbearance candidate. The difference between these conditions is statistically significant (the raw scores on the one-point scale are 0.75 and 0.42, $p < 0.001$), suggesting that the information on a candidate's

10 A conjoint experiment might better test the theory that voters favor candidates who forbear over those who enforce or run on formal social policy platforms. This was a paper-based survey, however, which made it difficult to conduct a conjoint experiment.

11 See Appendix A for significance tests for differences of means using standard $t$-tests, $p$ values based on permutation tests, and regression analyses.

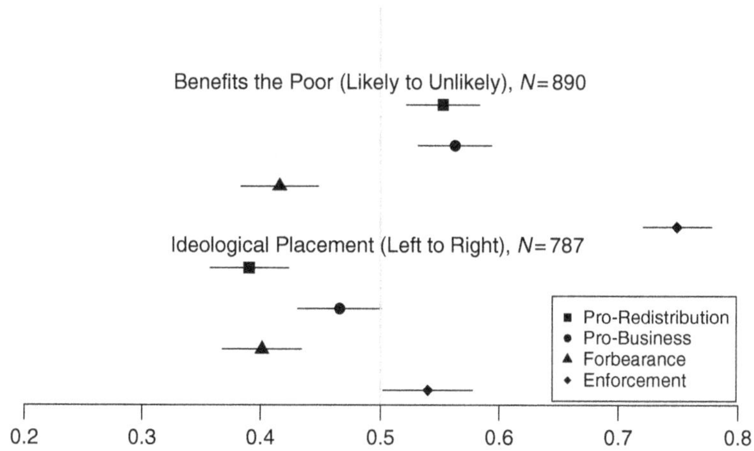


FIGURE 2.6 Perceptions of Distributive Benefits and Ideological Placement by Candidate
Note: Mean and 95 percent confidence interval by candidate statement. The vertical line shows the indifference point.

enforcement positions efficiently communicates a politician's affinities. In contrast, the traditional social policy candidates did little to signal pro-poor commitments: 57 percent of respondents viewed the pro-redistribution candidate as unlikely or very unlikely to favor the poor's interests compared to 59 percent for the pro-business platform (raw scores of 0.55 and 0.56, respectively). Learning that a candidate favors forbearance also signals a politician's affinity with poor voters more effectively than a pro-redistribution message does. While the pro-redistribution candidate was seen as slightly unlikely to favor the poor's interests, the forbearance candidate was seen as likely to favor their interests (visually, the forbearance candidate is to the left of the indifference line). Crucially, politicians not only avoid a reputation as an "anti-poor" candidate by eschewing enforcement, they also gain a reputation for representing the poor's interests through forbearance.

Although there were clear differences in views on which candidates would benefit the poor, only the enforcement platform differentiated the candidates ideologically. The pro-redistribution, pro-business, and pro-forbearance candidates all were perceived as slightly left of center, with no distinguishable differences between them. The enforcement candidate was identified as significantly farther to the right. The inability to place the candidates ideologically, other than the enforcement candidate, may be explained by the declining salience of left–right distinctions in Colombian politics. Nonresponse on the political ideology questions was substantial, particularly for low-income respondents (22 percent nonresponse, compared to 5 percent for the upper-income brackets). In contrast, the idea of whether a candidate "benefits the poor" evokes clear opinions and distributive expectations across the income spectrum.

Consistent with my theoretical expectations, poor and nonpoor voters respond differently when asked whether a candidate supports "people like you" and whether they would vote for each candidate. The phrase "people like you" was left deliberately vague so individuals could interpret their own class position or identity. To see how responses differ by class group, Figure 2.7 reports the mean response and standard deviation by class strata (shown with local polynomial smoothing and simulated 95 percent confidence intervals). The upper-left panel shows that poor respondents believe, by a wide margin, that the forbearance candidate is more likely to benefit them than the enforcement candidate is. Among the bottom strata, 60 percent of the poor believe that the forbearance candidate is likely to benefit them, compared to just 25 percent who hold that belief about the enforcement candidate. The lower-left panel shows similar results in terms of electoral behavior: 57 percent of voters in the bottom strata say they would vote for the forbearance candidate, compared to just 28 percent for the enforcement candidate. These are sizable proportions of the population, particularly for a competitive urban electoral context, where margins of victory can be small.

The comparison of the right and left side of Figure 2.7 confirms that forbearance and enforcement platforms more effectively cue a politician's distributive commitments than traditional social policy platforms. Although the poor do distinguish the pro-redistribution candidate as more likely to represent their interests and win their vote than the pro-business candidate, the difference is not statistically significant (right panels). This suggests that social policy promises are less credible than statements supporting forbearance.

A surprising aspect of the survey results is that there are no significant differences in the likelihood that upper-income respondents view the candidates as serving their interests or in their vote intention. One possible explanation for this non-finding is that the nonpoor may not view street vending as an issue and so disregard information about candidates' enforcement positions. However, nonpoor respondents are likely to care about the structure of business and redistributive policies, and therefore should have responded to the traditional social policy prompts. My suspicion is

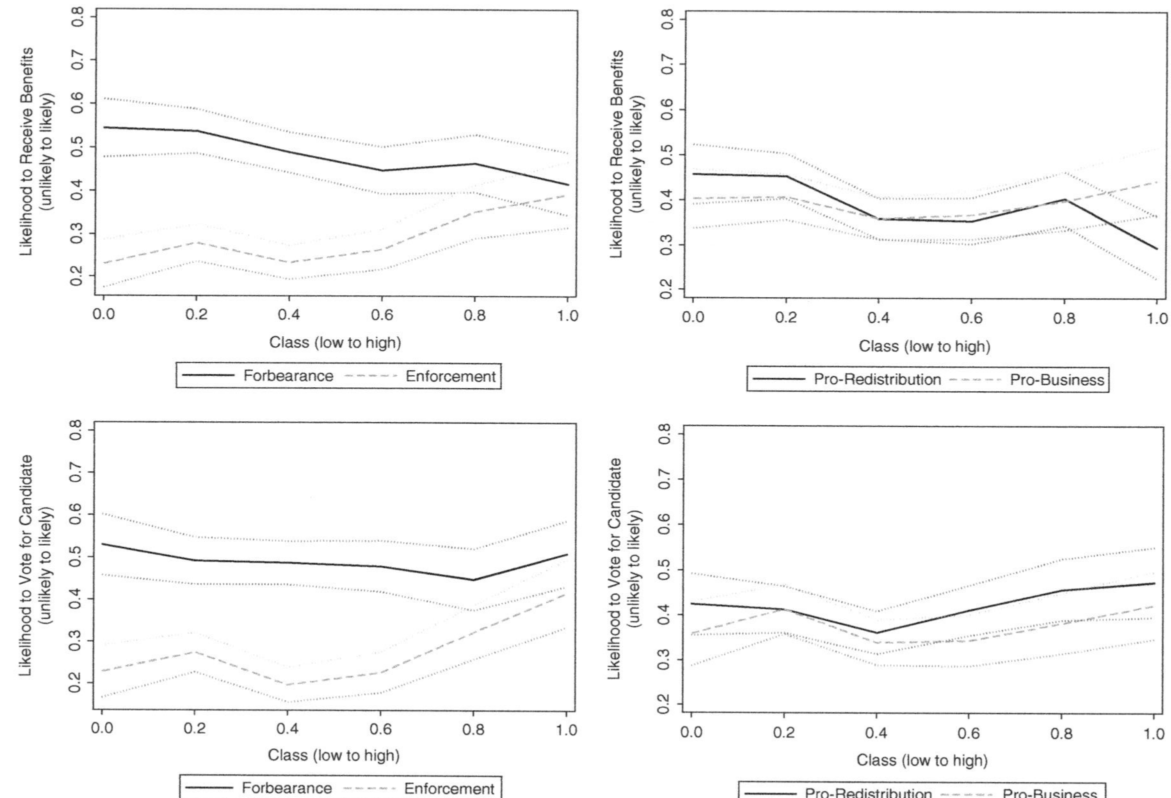


FIGURE 2.7 Perceptions That Candidate Will Benefit Respondent's Group (upper) and That Respondent Will Vote for Candidate (lower) by Class

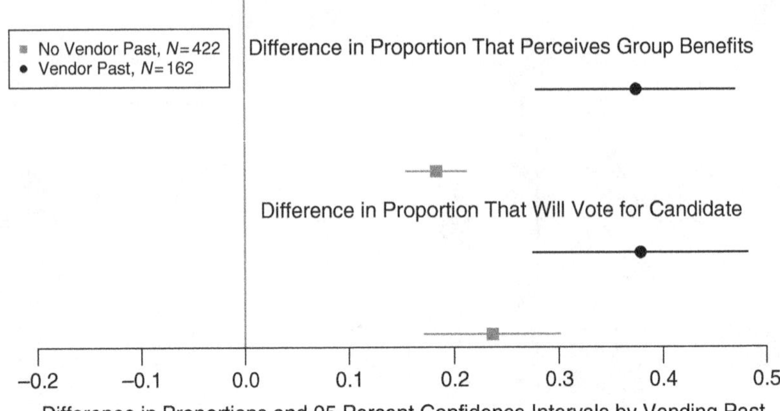


FIGURE 2.8 Average Treatment Effects for Lower-Class Respondents, Conditioned on Income from Street Vending

that the inability to budge perceptions indicates that nonpoor respondents know more about politics, which makes their preferences harder to alter in the context of a low-stakes survey experiment. Unfortunately, the survey did not include questions to test a respondent's knowledge or sophistication about politics, so I cannot disentangle whether more engaged respondents were less swayed by the information provided.

Finally, my model suggests that individuals with stronger material interests in forbearance should be the most responsive to informal welfare appeals, but that their responses should not entirely drive the effects. As we saw earlier, a past history of working as a street vendor or living in an informal settlement was associated with more support for forbearance. Likewise, I expect that individuals who once derived income from street vending (28 percent of lower and lower-middle class respondents) should be most sensitive to the forbearance information. Figure 2.8 compares perceptions that a candidate benefits "people like them" and vote intention for lower and lower-middle class groups who have worked as vendors and those who have not. I report difference of proportions in the respondents who say they find it likely or highly likely that the forbearance candidate will favor their interests and that they will vote for that candidate compared to the enforcement candidate. The differences between the conditions are statistically significant for both subgroups, suggesting that a forbearance platform has a positive effect on the poor's perception of a candidate. Direct experience as a street vendor conditions the average treatment effect in the predicted direction. The results are not consistent with an interest-group story in which only street vendors favor lax enforcement. But the small sample size means that these results are merely suggestive, and do not reach conventional levels of statistical significance.

In sum, the experimental results largely support the idea that enforcement signals the distributive positions of candidates, and that it does so more powerfully than traditional social policy platforms. The main drawback, as with all experimental work, lies in the generalizability of these claims. Although these vignettes present hypothetical candidates, they likely invoke associations with real politicians. Bogotá has elected mayors with sharply divergent positions on street vending that likely resonate with the vignettes, as we will see in Chapter 4. The mayor who pursued forbearance, Luis Garzón, is identified with the poor, workers, and the labor-based Left. Running the same experiment in Lima or Mexico City where mayors more identified with the Left (Susana Villarán and Marcelo Ebrard, respectively) evicted street vendors could offset the observed relationships between forbearance and pro-poor positions. Given that I do not have experimental data across countries, I draw on observational data in the rest of the book to suggest the broader association between pro-poor positions and forbearance.

Another concern is that the survey language artificially induced the gap between social policy and enforcement candidates. Enforcement positions may induce stronger class reactions in the experiment because the candidates use phrases like "order" and "abuses." However, these vignettes are drawn from candidate platforms from past elections and designed after extensive conversations observing how politicians discussed their enforcement views. I deliberately toned down the vignettes and excluded even stronger phrases like "police force" and "social cleanup," which some past candidates have used and would have biased my results toward finding an effect. Further dilution would have strayed from my argument's premise that enforcement conveys a politician's class commitments precisely because it can be linked to concepts like order. It also was not clear a priori that the phrases included in the social policy vignettes such as "vulnerable sectors," "unskilled workers," and "private-sector business" would not generate equally strong reactions.

Finally, it is hardly true that most of the time individuals have a single piece of information about a candidate and use that information to assess candidate attributes. This experiment cannot distinguish how enforcement combines with social policy information to alter candidate perceptions. Rather, I consider this experiment a necessary, but not sufficient, condition for my theory (i.e., a "hoop test"). If enforcement and forbearance positions were unable to communicate candidates' distributive commitments, particularly to poor voters who are at the core of my theory, it would have been disconfirming evidence of the signaling mechanism proposed. But studies of the natural world, as presented in the next chapters, are necessary to understand when and how enforcement information actually serves this role in political life.

## 2.5 CONCLUSION

This chapter provided a brief background on Latin American welfare states and then explored the individual-level determinants of attitudes toward forbearance and redistribution. Original and cross-national survey data, as well as a survey experiment, allowed me to show how enforcement pressures vary with individual and contextual variables. The core finding is that the poor support less enforcement than the non-poor, but only for offenses that involve progressive distributive benefits. Forbearance tends to be favored by the poor as a group and by those who perceive gaps in the welfare state. I showed that forbearance divides the public more sharply than standard redistributive issues, and suggested that this difference resulted from the poor's skepticism that social spending favors them.

In addition, I showed that forbearance platforms convey a politician's commitment to the poor and are more likely to win the support of poor voters in a survey experiment. Building from this micro-foundation, it follows that politicians' incentives to enforce will vary depending on the demographic composition of the electoral district where they seek office and the centrality of poor voters to their winning electoral coalitions. Subsequent chapters explore how politicians make choices depending on their calculations about the electoral and reputational repercussions of enforcement in the real world.

It may seem unsurprising that the rich are more enthusiastic about property law enforcement and politicians who support it. But this chapter also highlights that income does not fully account for enforcement attitudes. Beliefs about the functioning of the welfare state play a role in how citizens view squatting and street vending, and middle-income groups often want to find solutions to promote legal compliance without coercive actions against the poor. The next chapter on squatting dives further into how the availability of housing policy affects mass pressures and thus politicians' enforcement choices.

# 3

# What Enables Forbearance

## *Inadequate Social Policy and Squatting*

The only way to compete with a free house is with an almost free house.

– Bureaucrat, Finance Ministry, Chile

At the most basic level, the failure of government social policies gives rise to illegal behaviors by the poor. State welfare policies can offer functional substitutes and thus reduce the need to violate laws. But this chapter goes a step beyond the intuitive argument that social policy improves compliance to show that it also increases enforcement. I argue that social policy provision legitimizes enforcement operations, increasing societal collaboration with state officials, and reduces the electoral costs, encouraging politicians to engage in enforcement. Conversely, the absence of social policy raises the electoral stakes of enforcement. The poor mobilize in favor of forbearance and (as we saw in Chapter 2) view it as a signal of their political representation.

In this chapter, I investigate the link between social policy and enforcement politics through a close analysis of how national housing policies affect local politicians' enforcement against squatters. I examine housing provision because it can substitute for squatting. Testing the argument requires a focus on governments that have made different housing policy choices. The country cases provide such variation: Peru and Colombia have struggled to provide housing for the poor, whereas Chile has made sustained investments in the housing sector and focused on the most vulnerable.

The central empirical challenge is to separate the impact of housing policy from other elements of state performance. States that build housing for the poor also tend to have better police, courts, and bureaucrats to enforce against squatters. They often have fewer poor people. Chile, in particular, is known for its competent police and judicial institutions, and a repressive military dictatorship where squatting was tightly controlled. It is possible, then, that differences in coercive capacity, rather than electoral pressures, drive enforcement.

I separate these explanations in two ways: I pay close attention to the underlying electoral mechanisms, and second, I apply my method of enforcement process tracing to distinguish forbearance from capacity constraints. I used extensive interviews with bureaucrats, politicians, and informal association leaders to identify the electoral mechanisms through which enforcement depends on government housing policy. To corroborate these accounts, I then gathered quantitative indicators about the configuration of societal demands and local politics. These include (1) statistics on the number, type, and aims of interest associations; (2) petitions to local governments and welfare agencies; and (3) local campaign platforms.

Figure 3.1 summarizes the channels through which housing policy changes the electoral costs of enforcement and their observable implications. First, substitutive housing policy directly crowds out the need to occupy land illegally. But, even with generous housing policies, countries rarely sop up all land claims and squatting can remain attractive compared to state housing projects. The second mechanism concerns the target of mass demands. Substitutive policy concentrates demands and organizing on national housing authorities. In contrast, the insufficiency of housing policy leads citizens to expect little from formal housing programs and displaces demands to local politicians who control enforcement, as well as service and titling bureaucracies. I use data on organizational density, petitioning, and interviews with neighborhood leaders to confirm differences in the targets and substance of the poor's demands. Third, housing policy changes the electoral signals conveyed by enforcement, as tested in the previous chapter through a survey experiment in Bogotá. I draw on my interviews with neighborhood leaders and politicians, as well as a structured survey of bureaucrats, to extend the experimental results and demonstrate how voters and state agents view enforcement when the state provides housing alternatives. I find that actors see forbearance as an illegitimate reward to those trying to "cheat" the state housing system when alternatives are available. In contrast, forbearance is viewed as a justifiable attempt to assist poor constituents when housing programs are inadequate.

Establishing that politicians face different incentives does not mean that they have scope for choice in their enforcement actions. The second

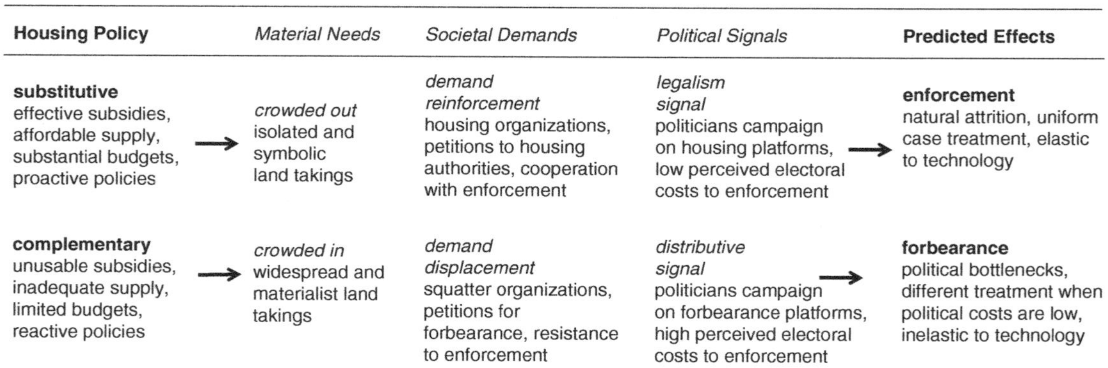

| **Housing Policy** | *Material Needs* | *Societal Demands* | *Political Signals* | **Predicted Effects** |
|---|---|---|---|---|
| **substitutive** effective subsidies, affordable supply, substantial budgets, proactive policies → | *crowded out* isolated and symbolic land takings | *demand reinforcement* housing organizations, petitions to housing authorities, cooperation with enforcement | *legalism signal* politicians campaign on housing platforms, low perceived electoral costs to enforcement → | **enforcement** natural attrition, uniform case treatment, elastic to technology |
| **complementary** unusable subsidies, inadequate supply, limited budgets, reactive policies → | *crowded in* widespread and materialist land takings | *demand displacement* squatter organizations, petitions for forbearance, resistance to enforcement | *distributive signal* politicians campaign on forbearance platforms, high perceived electoral costs to enforcement → | **forbearance** political bottlenecks, different treatment when political costs are low, inelastic to technology |

FIGURE 3.1 The Effects of Housing Policy on Enforcement Incentives

goal of this chapter is to isolate forbearance from a more standard view of weak enforcement. To do so, I gathered statistical data from government agencies, local housing inspectors, and court documents on when and what type of enforcement takes place in each city. These data allow me to apply the methods in Chapter 1's discussion to identify forbearance. In particular, I look for several types of observations consistent with forbearance: *political bottlenecks* in which enforcement breaks down when politicians intervene, *selective attrition* in which more politically sensitive legal cases receive lax treatment, and *inelastic enforcement* in which politicians do not respond to changes in the resources or technology available. I also explore the patterns of sanctions to determine whether forbearance is allocated in a clientelistic or welfarist manner. Sanctions that target specific individuals or groups suggest clientelistic exchanges. Generalized shifts by political administration, and especially periods of no enforcement, are more consistent with an informal welfare policy.

The chapter is divided into two main parts. The first part provides essential information on housing policy in each country. I also clarify what squatting entails, how it is sanctioned, and the legal tensions that arise in countries that recognize a constitutional right to housing. The second part of the chapter traces variation in enforcement outcomes to the electoral incentives created by housing policy, working through each case sequentially. To preview, close to half of all new urban development in Bogotá and Lima since 1990 has occurred through illegal construction. The urban poor organize around forbearance and improvements to squatter settlements. Sanctions are rare. Although the cities have the same enforcement outcome, squatting persists due to a combination of strategic electoral choice and capacity constraints in Lima, or a more traditional case of weak enforcement. I suggest, however, that many of the bureaucratic difficulties in Lima reflect political choices to maintain an informal housing policy. Bogotá is a clearer case of forbearance, in which politicians direct a capable bureaucracy to stop enforcement. Social rights and a larger electoral district give forbearance a more programmatic flavor in Bogotá than in Lima. Santiago forms a sharp contrast. Only in Santiago do citizens organize around state housing provision and collaborate with enforcement efforts when land invasions occur. The Chilean government's decision to house the poor has been the lynchpin of its control of squatters, not strong courts or police.

## 3.1 A COMPARISON OF HOUSING POLICY

Social interest housing, meaning government housing targeted at low-income households, saw its heyday in the 1960s in Latin America. Most governments then retreated from housing policy during the state and market reforms of the 1980s and 1990s. Even as Latin American governments expanded social policy to the informal-sector poor in the 2000s, housing budgets continued to shrink and remained focused on middle-income households able to afford commercial mortgages (Szalachman and Collinao 2010: 11). Nevertheless, there is substantial variation in government efforts to house their citizens, and their poorest citizens in particular. In this section, I sketch the differences in housing programs across Chile, Colombia, and Peru. I address the question of why these housing policies have taken distinct turns in Chapter 6.

The most straightforward way to measure a country's housing effort is through expenditures as a fraction of GDP (see Appendix B for details). The cases reveal clear variation. From 2000 to 2010, Peru spent less than 0.1 percent of GDP on average on housing programs, which stands among the lowest percentages in Latin America. Colombia spent a touch more, 0.2 percent of GDP.[1] In contrast, Chile averaged around 1 percent of GDP for the same decade, surpassing even the OECD average of 0.6 percent of GDP. Other indicators of scale, such as the share of government-sponsored housing lending, reinforce these contrasts. Peru and Colombia play minor roles in mortgage financing. For instance, the Colombian state provides just 0.4 percent of all residential mortgage credit, whereas the Chilean state accounts for more than 25 percent (Bouillon 2012: 189).

Although expenditures and lending are useful to evaluate the overall scale of housing investments, additional indicators are necessary to assess targeting. There are two basic approaches to housing policy, one focused on supply-side interventions and the other on demand-side tools. The clearest supply-side intervention is construction of affordable housing. Direct housing construction lost favor as part of broader public-sector privatizations and state retrenchment in the 1980s and 1990s (Mayo and Angel 1993; Pierson 1993: chapter 4). But states still play a central role in housing supply through a number of other tools – tax incentives, land grants, expedited construction licenses, and so on. The best summary statistic of supply-side

[1] Housing expenditures have been on the rise in Peru and Colombia: in 2014, Peru spent 0.45 percent of GDP on housing and urban expenses, and Colombia spent more than 1 percent of GDP (MVCT 2014: 79).

TABLE 3.1 *Descriptive Statistics on Housing Policy*

| | Peru *skeletal* | | Colombia *truncated* | | Chile *substitutive* | |
|---|---|---|---|---|---|---|
| | Capital | Nation | Capital | Nation | Capital | Nation |
| Housing Expenditures as % GDP | | 0.09 | | 0.19 | | 1.1 |
| Social Interest Housing as % Construction | 2 | | | 33 | | 65 |
| Subsidies Approved for Lower Class | 217 | 5,991 | 2,473 | 31,601 | 26,488 | 34,853 |
| Subsidies Used by Lower Class as % Granted | | 0.6 | | 14.7 | | 82.0 |

*Notes:* Budget statistics calculated as an average from 2000 to 2010, from the Ministry of Economics and Finance (MEF) in Peru, the Finance Ministry (Minhacienda) in Colombia, and the Budget Office (Dipres) in Chile. Housing construction and subsidy use statistics are for 2010 and come from the construction chambers in each country (Capeco, Camaco, and CChC). Appendix B provides additional details.

interventions comes from the number of social interest housing projects initiated as a share of all new construction. Whether social interest housing exists on the market gives a sense of how effectively states promote affordable housing, regardless of the way that they do it.

Again, we see dramatic contrasts across the cases: almost no social interest housing is on offer in Peru, while Chile and Colombia make substantial efforts. In 2010, 90 percent of housing supply in Lima was built for the richest quintile of families, and 69 percent of Lima households could not afford any housing on the market (Bouillon 2012: 69).[2] Colombia is an intermediate case. The government has made important, but erratic, efforts to ramp up housing construction. Since 1990, 76,000 social interest housing units have been built. Most state housing projects, however, have aided the middle or lower-middle class. The challenge of assisting the poor is particularly acute in the largest and most expensive cities like Bogotá. Almost no housing was built for the poorest tranche of the market in Bogotá for much of the 2000s (Camacol 2009).

Social interest housing, in contrast, constitutes the majority of new construction in Chile. The pace of construction has been astounding – Chile

[2] Of 21,577 houses sold in Lima in 2011, lower-class groups purchased only 2.6 percent and the lower-middle class purchased 6.7 percent. See "Se venderán más de 21 mil viviendas en Lima este año," *El Comercio* November 8, 2011.

promoted the construction of 1.9 million houses between 1990 and 2006, or roughly 100,000 new houses per year (Rodríguez et al. 2006: 22). To put this in perspective, the Chilean government generates more affordable housing in a single year than Peru or Colombia have generated in two decades. As we will see, unique historical circumstances, namely, fear about renewed land invasions that could destabilize the democratic regime just as they did Allende's government, contributed to the extraordinary pace of construction.

States also can intervene to improve the ability of the poor to purchase housing through demand subsidies. In so doing, the state limits its role to "enabling" the housing market. The Chilean military regime pioneered a demand-side subsidy approach, which has been replicated throughout much of the developing world (Gilbert 2004). All three cases examined here use variants of Chile's "ABC" model that encourages the poor to save (*Ahorro*), provides a government subsidy (*Bono*), and requires access to mortgage credit (*Crédito*) to purchase a house. Latin American governments rarely use rent subsidies due to weak rental markets (in part attributable to the difficulty evicting tenants) (Bouillon 2012: chapter 4).[3]

To judge how much countries do to help the poor through demand-side assistance, I include statistics on both the number of housing subsidies assigned to the poor and the share of these subsidies put to use by recipients. Although governments advertise the quantity of subsidies allocated, the latter measure of usage is more revealing of housing access. A majority of housing subsidies goes unused in Peru and Colombia because the poor cannot find affordable housing on the market or meet program requirements.[4] In Chile, the poor almost always make use of housing subsidies.

Descriptive statistics thus make clear that Chile has the largest and most targeted housing policy of the three cases. I consider it a case of substitutive housing policy. Colombia struggles with the targeting of its housing programs, which often fail to benefit the poor – the definition of a truncated housing policy. Peru simply does little, a skeletal housing policy. Housing policies in Colombia and Peru are complementary to squatting in the sense that they leave housing needs unmet, and the poor

[3] One exception is Chile, which introduced the first major rent subsidy program in the region for young couples in 2013, "Goodbye Mother-in-Law" (*Chao Suegra*).

[4] An exception to the use of subsidies in Colombia is the treatment of households displaced by the civil war, as I elaborate on in Chapter 6.

turn to squatting to find affordable options. I now turn to the types of property law violations that the poor engage in to find housing, and explain what enforcement entails against squatters.

## 3.2 SQUATTING AND THE LAW

Squatting involves the physical occupation of a plot of land by an individual or group with either an absent or defective property right. Although lumping full and partial property takings together glosses over some important distinctions, I coincide with state officials and other scholars in thinking of these activities as a single broad category of legal violations (e.g., Alvarez Rivadulla 2012; Caldeira 2000; Camargo and Hurtado 2011; Fischer 2008, 2014; Holston 2008). Both acts allow the poor to access land at below-market prices and leave them vulnerable to eviction.

Let us begin with the case in which squatters have no property rights claim, often referred to as a land taking, land seizure, or land invasion. Squatters begin with no property rights to the land that they occupy and acquire rights through their continued possession of the land. In the 1960s and 1970s, many land takings took an organized form, headed by political parties, community leaders, or even church officials.[5] Although organized invasions still occur, their scale and links to political actors have diminished. Most land takings have organizers, either a professional known as a "land trafficker" (*traficante del terreno* or *terrero*) or a local leader who has links to an existing squatter settlement. Households generally pay intermediaries to take part in an invasion.[6]

Another form of squatting involves individuals with partial property rights. These often are known as informal or illegal land occupations. Property rights often are described as a "bundle of sticks," composed of many individual rights, such as the right to exploit the resources on the

[5] Land takings can occur through an organized invasion in which households unite to occupy land together, an accretion invasion in which households gradually encroach on land or an intermediary brings households separately to an area, or an isolated invasion in which a household takes land apart from a broader process. For a description of different settlement types, see Collier (1976: chapter 3).

[6] Traffickers tend to find out about "safe" plots (public land or private land whose owners are unlikely to react in an opportune fashion) and then recruit households to pay to take part in the invasion. In the case of local leaders, they tend to negotiate with existing squatter settlements to take nearby land. They recruit family and friends to take part in the invasion. Occupants may pay, but generally less, to take part in the invasion. These invasion types can lead to organizational and tactical differences, as detailed in Dosh (2010: 16–20).

land, to build a house on the land, to transfer the land, and so on. In a common case, individuals buy rural or environmental conservation land, but the title excludes the right to build housing on the land. The informal "occupation" then involves a regulatory taking rather than a physical taking. The occupant needs to convince the government to change the zoning (if possible) to permit urban development and service extensions.[7] Sometimes the line between land invasions and informal occupations is blurry. For instance, individuals may purchase land from a trafficker who pretends to have legitimate title, but who does not own the land, and effectively engage in a land invasion.[8]

A comparison of the distributive incidence of land invasions and informal occupations in Lima and Bogotá reinforces their similarities. In Lima, squatting tends to involve the invasion of public (and occasionally private) land. The costs fall on the public at large in the form of a lost state resource (land) and additional public services (water, garbage collection, roads, environmental protections, and sewage) that are expensive to extend to precarious settlements. To get a rough estimate of how much the land is worth, I consider how much squatters would accept in rent for their houses (subtracting any construction and improvement costs). Squatters estimate that their houses would rent for an average of $60 per month, about $45 of which comes from the land itself.[9] Some squatters also pay fees to intermediaries who organize and sometimes occupy (but tend not to own) the land. Local leaders report that intermediaries charge fees that range from $50 to $2,000 depending on the quality of the land, the probability of a successful invasion, and the relationship to the intermediary.[10] I amortize these costs over the time that a squatter spends on a piece of land. Thus, even an extractive land trafficker leaves squatters with a benefit of roughly $30 per month from land ownership over a decade.

In Bogotá, the poor tend to purchase private land that is inappropriate for housing construction. These are, thus, illegal land occupations, not

[7] These land occupations often are called "irregular" or "informal" subdivisions because the occupants have rights to the land itself. In contrast, land occupations in which the occupants have no rights to the land tend to be called squatter settlements, land invasions, or "fraudulent" subdivisions (Holston 2008: 206–07).

[8] These often are known as "fraudulent" subdivisions, which are different from "irregular" or "informal" subdivisions in which the occupants have rights to the land itself (Holston 2008: 206–07).

[9] See Appendix B for details on this calculation.

[10] Focus group with leaders of squatter settlements in Villa María del Triunfo, June 12, 2011.

land invasions.[11] The most common illegal land occupations have occurred on environmental conservation land. The government does not own the conservation land that rings the city; rather, it was rezoned as conservation land despite private ownership. Given that the landowners cannot legally build on conservation land, many have sold their plots, or land traffickers have sold them with questionable authorization. The poor buy or occupy lots from intermediaries for a cost generally between \$1,000 and \$2,000, often paid in installments.[12] What, then, do the poor gain from this transaction? One piece of the distributive transfer comes in the change of zoning. Eventually, the government faces pressure to transform previously uninhabitable land into urban real estate. Urban land sells for much higher prices than rural or conservation land – almost \$10,000 if sold with the appropriate zoning and service access – so those in possession of the land gain the difference. But the primary transfer to the poor comes in the provision of basic services. When the poor purchase land in an informal settlement, they do not pay the costs of service infrastructure. The government provides this infrastructure after settlement occurs. Extending piped water, electricity, sewage, transportation, and roads to an informal settlement – particularly one on precarious land – is enormously expensive. It costs the Bogotá city government an average of \$1,900 per lot, and can be assumed to raise the land value at least in equal measure (Maldonado Copello 2009: 332). Were land transactions fully legal and services provided at their real cost, the poor would be unable to access land markets at all.[13]

I consider land invasions and informal occupations as a single category because the sanction for both activities is an eviction. The occupant is removed from the land and prevented from returning, usually through police presence. Or, in the case in which the individual has bought a defective title to the land, the construction is demolished and the occupant is prevented from building on the land. Both actions leave families homeless. Evictions are very severe punishments, but many governments

[11] Fads for referring to informal settlements vary over time, so these also have been called pirate urbanizations, pirate subdivisions, and illegal subdivisions. Historically, open land invasions largely were repressed in Bogotá (Doebele 1977; Gilbert 1981; Gilbert and Ward 1985; Torres Tovar 2009).

[12] Maldonado Copello (2009: 339) calculates that traffickers sell land for between \$19 and \$27 per $m^2$ and plots tend to be around $48m^2$ to $72m^2$ in recent years, leading to my estimates of \$1,000 and \$2,000 for plots.

[13] Holston (2008: 206–07) nicely underscores the distributive impact of this process: "The very illegality of house lots in the peripheries makes land accessible to those who cannot afford the higher sale or rental prices of legal residences."

do conduct them, as we will see in the case of Turkey in Chapter 7. Given their severity, many governments try to avoid evictions and protect the occupant's due process rights. Police evictions in Colombia and Peru, for instance, can occur only within the first twenty-four to forty-eight hours of an illegal land occupation. The idea is that the police must catch squatters in the act (*en flagrante*). After this point, governments must use the civil or criminal court system to balance the owner and occupant's rights. Land invasions are both civil and criminal offenses in Chile, Colombia, and Peru, although they rarely have been prosecuted through the criminal system.[14]

Some may wonder whether evictions themselves are legal, especially in countries that recognize a right to housing through constitutional or international law.[15] Although a full discussion of the legal issues at stake would require a book of its own, a few clarifications are necessary. First, few governments view the right to housing as encompassing the right to seize land or property in its pursuit. The Constitutional Court of Colombia, for instance, has upheld provisions to remove squatters and punish the organizers of illegal land occupations. Although the Court has recognized that many illegal land occupations "have as a cause the extreme necessity and poverty of squatters," it also has upheld a government obligation to protect private property rights and public land (for instance, to avoid construction in high-risk areas, conservation areas, or land reserved for public works).[16]

Second, not all evictions are prohibited under domestic and international human rights law. The central requirement is that evictions protect the affected parties' rights to due process and social protection. Governments differ in when they determine that squatters acquire rights over the property that they occupy. For instance, Peru long was seen to

[14] See Código Penal de la República de Chile, *usurpación* Art. 457–62; Código Penal de Colombia (*invasión de tierras o edificaciones*, Art. 263, 367). Sanctions can fall on both the organizer and the occupant of the invasion (Ley 308 de 1996, Ley 1453 de 2011, Art. 23). Land invasions were considered crimes in Peru (Código Penal de 1991, *usurpación*, Art. 202), but the penalties and procedures recently were modified to make evictions easier (Ley 30076 de 2013).

[15] The International Covenant on Economic, Social and Cultural Rights recognizes a right to housing. A host of Latin American constitutions give this covenant the weight of law, and the majority of countries also include a right to housing within their domestic constitutions (e.g., Argentina, Bolivia, Brazil, Colombia, Ecuador, Mexico, Venezuela, Uruguay). Some, such as Bolivia and Uruguay, even specify that governments have a responsibility to promote access to housing.

[16] See Constitutional Court of Colombia, Sentence C-157, 1997.

have permissive laws toward squatting because the police could intervene only for forty-eight hours after an invasion. Squatters simply waited for long weekends or moments when the police were understaffed to invade land. In 2013, the legislature extended the time period in which the police can act to thirty days. Evictions became easier.[17]

What guarantees are required in an eviction process also has been the subject of substantial litigation, especially in countries that recognize constitutional rights to housing. Most relevant here, the Constitutional Court of Colombia has required the government to take steps to protect the fundamental rights of poor and vulnerable individuals. One of the most famous Colombian movies, *The Snail Strategy* (1993), mocks the ways that squatters strategically use children, pregnant women, and the elderly to stall evictions. These protections can, but do not always, require the relocation of those affected. They may instead include the provision of temporary relief (like rent assistance), access to social assistance services, and so on.[18] Bogotá has an office that coordinates the social services surrounding eviction proceedings. Officials insist that mayors have to prevent illegal land occupations, which means conducting evictions even when they cannot find another place for squatters to live.[19]

Third, substantial legal debate exists on the proper interpretation and enforcement of social rights. In countries like Colombia that recognize social rights, judges, bureaucrats, and politicians sometimes see themselves as favoring one law (social rights) over another law (property rights), rather than engaging in forbearance. But many governments view the right to housing as an "aspirational" or "second-generation" right in the sense that its positive fulfillment depends on the programmatic choices and resources available to legislators. Governments commit to work progressively toward their fulfillment, but do not necessarily see social rights obligations as trumping private property rights. Colombian citizens, for instance, could not file constitutional claims (*tutelas*) to protect social rights, such as the right to housing, until

[17] See Law 30076 of 2013 (Ley sobre el delito de usurpación). For an excellent review of the changes to the legal proceedings and continuing debate surrounding their application, see "Acciones del Estado frente a las invasiones," *Jurídica* 536, February 3, 2015.

[18] See T-309 of 1995, T-958 of 2001, T-585 and T-754 of 2006, T-601 of 2007, T-527 of 2011, T-239 of 2013. Some of the most complex legal cases involve the relocation of squatters from high-risk zones like Altos de Estancia in Bogotá; see T-585 of 2008. For a comprehensive analysis of the politics of protecting the poor against risk in Colombia, see Zeiderman (2016, esp. 64–5, 202–10).

[19] Author interview with Inés Esteban Parra, lawyer, Secretaria de Gobierno de Bogotá, July 16, 2010.

2008.[20] Lower courts have privileged private property rights, as well as collective rights like the environment, when they conflict with individual rights claims to housing. The city of Bogotá, for example, has a major court ruling against it for permitting illegal construction in the forest preserve around the city. An administrative court required the city to remove squatter settlements and demolish any new construction in the conservation zone.[21] Evictions thus are possible.

There are few more palatable enforcement alternatives to evictions for squatters. Governments can impose fines, but squatters' precarious economic situations mean that they often are judgment proof.[22] Other than evictions, the main lever for governments to control illegal land occupations comes from the pace of basic service provision and legal recognition. Governments can make life so nasty that only the most desperate will occupy land. This tactic, however, raises similar legal and political complications to evictions.[23] When asked whether squatters should receive basic services, most politicians reply along the lines that they cannot "prejudice new settlements"[24] or "condemn them for years without land titles or services worrying about some future contingency."[25] Politicians claim to support existing settlements and to be "enemies" of new ones.[26]

[20] Claimants instead needed to show that a state action posed a concrete threat to the fulfillment of fundamental rights. For the early housing jurisprudence, see Constitutional Court of Colombia, T-251 of 1995, T-258 of 1997, T-203 and 383 of 1999. Over time, court justices created a fundamental right to a vital minimum living standard that claimants could say was threatened by eviction proceedings, and then the Court broke down distinctions between first- and second-generation rights entirely in T-585 of 2008.

[21] Environmental groups brought a lawsuit (Acción Popular No. 2005–00662) against the Bogotá government for its failure to protect the forest preserve from urbanization. They won in the lower court (Tribunal Administrativo de Cundinamarca), and the judge ordered the city to remove all constructions from the preserve and protect the area from future land occupations. The removal of existing constructions – if it relocated or compensated poor residents – would cost more than the city's entire budget, and does not account for the new building occurring.

[22] If fines were calibrated to the poor's ability to pay, it is unclear that they could deter squatting, given the benefits at stake.

[23] Cutting off or denying services to individuals to make it untenable for them to remain in their home violates the right to housing under international law, as well as constitutional rights to basic services like water and electricity (UN-Habitat 2014).

[24] Author interview with Erasmo Segundo Cardenas Obregon, local councilor, District of Ate, Lima, Peru, November 23, 2011.

[25] Author interview with Ivan Coronado, local councilor, District of Comas, Lima, Peru, November 25, 2011.

[26] Author interview with Victoria Andrade, local councilor, District of Usaquén, Bogotá, Colombia, August 4, 2011.

But this position still requires enforcement against new squatter settlements, which few politicians are willing to conduct.

Forbearance is very hard to revoke in the case of squatters due to the legal difficulties of evictions. It can take months or years to remove squatters through the court system, by which time expressions of political disloyalty often are forgotten and squatters form alliances with local politicians. The severity of the sanction also generates heavy political costs, as we will see below, because other voters observe and condemn politicians who are willing to remove the poor from their homes. Therefore, forbearance tends to be extended as an informal welfare policy to build support from direct beneficiaries and create affective ties with non-beneficiaries. Informal welfare appeals are especially common in Bogotá due to the large district size and incorporation of social rights. Even in Lima, most clientelism occurs around local legal recognition and service provision after land invasions have occurred, rather than through threats or protection against evictions.

In sum, I focus on two forms of squatting, land invasions and informal occupations. Enforcement against these legal violations involves evictions, which are strong deterrents given the investments at stake and displacement of poor households. The potential legal complications require special attention to how eviction proceedings fail, especially in Colombia. I trace four steps in the enforcement process – the detection of an offense, the opening of an administrative case or police action, the eviction ruling, and the execution of the sanction – to separate whether enforcement stops at police, judicial, or political decision points. The next section examines how inadequate housing policy leads Peruvian politicians to prefer forbearance toward squatter settlements.

## 3.3 SKELETAL HOUSING POLICY AND WEAK ENFORCEMENT IN LIMA

Inadequate formal housing provision is at the heart of squatting's persistence in Peru. Skeletal housing policy set in motion a pattern that has led the poor to access housing through land invasions and subsequently to demand legal recognition and services to improve their living conditions. I show that, given skeletal housing policies and common knowledge that land invasions end in legalization, district politicians face few incentives to enforce. Capacity constraints in Lima are substantial, making it harder to distinguish forbearance from weak enforcement.

However, I show that the government decided not to fund or create procedures to improve enforcement due to the inadequacy of housing alternatives. The demonstrated ability to legalize and monitor certain types of land invasions suggests that state weakness does not fully explain enforcement outcomes.

### 3.3.1 Crowding In Squatting

Squatting is ubiquitous in Lima.[27] About half of Lima's population lives on land originally settled through invasions (Calderón Cockburn 2006: 75), and 10 percent currently lives in houses acquired through land invasion (ENAHO 2011). Although land invasions tend to be associated with Peru's rapid urban migration in the mid-twentieth century or the debt crisis of the 1980s, squatting continued apace throughout the 1990s and 2000s. Nationwide, the government identified 3,003 informal settlements in 1993, 7,419 in 2002, and more than 10,000 by 2012 (Calderón Cockburn 2013b: 46–7; also Chapter 6). These statistics must be interpreted with caution, given that the average size of a settlement fell over time as squatters seized more precarious and marginal urban land (Ramírez Corzo and Riofrío 2006). But what is clear is that land invasions have not stopped.

To what extent has the government actively encouraged squatting? Direct political involvement in land invasions has been relatively rare, although major exceptions did occur under the competitive authoritarian regime of Alberto Fujimori. For instance, in the run-up to the 2000 presidential elections, Fujimori gave a speech in which he identified open land in Lima. Massive invasions followed. One invasion involved more than 10,000 people; another named itself "Perú 2000" after Fujimori's political party. Government ministers appeared to provide water and food to squatters, and also promised to prevent police action (at least until they located alternative land for squatters).[28] Such bald political involvement

[27] Numerous studies have noted the city's extensive, sustained informal growth (e.g., Calderón Cockburn 2006; Collier 1976; De Soto, Ghersi, and Ghibellini 1986; De Soto 2000; Dietz 1985, 1989, 1998; Dosh 2010; Driant 1991; Ramírez Corzo and Riofrío 2006; Riofrío 1991; Stepan 1978; Stokes 1995).

[28] These invasions included Chancherías and Nueva Rinconada in San Juan de Miraflores, as well as land reserved for a hospital and agricultural use in Villa El Salvador; *Caretas*, No. 164, February 3, 2000; "La situación en Villa El Salvador sigue tensa," *El Comercio* January 31, 2000.

has been the exception. Politicians generally prefer to intervene in squatter settlements after they have formed.[29]

More indirectly, the Peruvian government has incentivized land invasions by raising the expected benefits through easy procedures to gain legal security, public services, and eventually property title. At the local level, district mayors approve the boundaries of squatter settlements, known as the "perimeter map" (*plano perimétrico*), as well as the legal clearance of land (*saneamiento físico legal*) and a local authorization process (*prehabilitación urbana*) in which squatters become eligible to receive services.[30] For instance, eligibility for national water programs hinges on local district approval of the squatter settlement association and its perimeter maps.[31] Mayors therefore have a number of ways in which they can ease, or complicate, life for squatters after a land invasion occurs.

At the national level, presidents have simplified the process to grant individual property titles, as I expand on in Chapter 6. Although property titling was intended as a one-off measure to legalize existing constructions and create formal land markets, every single president since the return of full democracy has extended eligibility for property titles.[32] Knowing that a land invasion ends in a transfer raises the expected value of a taking and reinforces societal beliefs that invasions are the way to secure housing. In this way, the Peruvian government has encouraged the poor to invade land, build housing, and then request services and property titles.

In addition, Peru's capacity and willingness to provide services to squatter settlements has improved, perversely making invasions more attractive. The Fujimori period marked a shift in government willingness to invest in informal settlements. As with other projects run by the

[29] Author interview with Paulo Hinostroza, mayor (2003–2006), District of San Juan de Miraflores, June 24, 2011; Author interview with housing director, District of San Juan de Miraflores, May 17, 2011.

[30] For a description of the process of urban authorization, see Webb, Beuermann, and Carla (2006: 54–6). The pre-urban authorization process does not require property title to the land, but demands some of the same requirements, such as the registration of perimeter and lot maps and legal clearance. Mayors and their bureaucrats often ignore these requirements.

[31] See Sedapal, "Requisitos para tramita factibilidad de servicios de agua potable y alcantarillado para nuevas habilitaciones: Asentamientos humanos y similares," 2014.

[32] Measures to extend the date at which informal occupations could receive property title were passed under Alejandro Toledo 2006 (Law 28687), under Alan García in 2009 (Law 29320), and under Ollanta Humala in 2015 (Legislative Decree No. 1202).

Ministry of the Presidency, housing improvement funds and local public goods were allocated in politicized ways to advance Fujimori's electoral aims (Roberts and Arce 1998; Schady 2000). Nonetheless, local infrastructure investments improved the quality of life and demonstrated a preoccupation with Lima's vast squatter settlements, which previously had been excluded from many infrastructure projects due to their illegal status. Interviews with settlement leaders revealed a sense of gratitude for Fujimori's investments in roads, schools, water, and so on. Leaders praised Fujimori as the first politician to "put things in the hills"[33] where squatter settlements are located, and who did "not ignore the informal settlements."[34]

With the transition back to full democracy in 2001, presidents, along with Lima's mayors, largely continued the initiatives to boost services and infrastructure in squatter settlements.[35] This focus can be seen in the government's budget allocations: programs to provide water and services to squatter settlements receive two times more funding than programs to provide affordable housing. Access to services has improved. While only 45 percent of squatters had access to public water infrastructure in 2004, 76 percent did a decade later (INEI 2004–2014).

In sum, the poor's housing demands in Lima continue to be met through illegal land occupations followed by legalization and service provision. State housing provision plays a negligible role. Commentators often joke that Peruvians think they have a "right to land," not a "right to housing." Now I turn to how skeletal housing policies create strong incentives for district mayors to tolerate land invasions.

### 3.3.2 Demand Displacement

Inadequate housing policies have sculpted popular sector organizing, attitudes, and cooperation with enforcement. To assess the demands of the urban poor, I gathered data on participation in interest associations

[33] Author interviews with informal settlement leaders, District of Ventanilla, Callao, Peru, May 30, 2011.

[34] Author interview with Adolfo Diez Vargas, leader, AAHH Felipe Las Casas, May 30, 2011; Author interview with leader, Villa María del Triunfo, June 12, 2011.

[35] Some of these programs include construction credits on existing lots like Mi Barrio, parts of Techo Propio, and Mi Construcción, as well as the city's program to build stairs to informal settlements (*Escaleras de Solidaridad*). The biggest presidential initiative has been a push to universalize water coverage (*Agua para Todos*).

and personally interviewed leaders to understand their housing demands and reactions to evictions.[36] Observations that citizens organize for service extensions and legalization of their informal properties, rather than housing programs, and hesitate to cooperate in eviction proceedings support my theory of demand displacement.

First, squatter settlements in Peru must register as neighborhood associations through national and district offices.[37] These procedures have their origins in corporatist attempts to incorporate squatter settlements into the state in the mid-twentieth century.[38] Registration helps squatter settlements prove the date of their foundation, and is required to apply for many public programs, such as water and property titles. Registered squatter settlement associations thus are ubiquitous. Take the case of Puente Piedra, a poor district in Lima's northern cone with 230,000 residents and around 25,000 people in illegal land occupations without property titles. The Citizen Participation Office registered 268 informal settlement associations, around 60 of which have received urban authorizations but do not have title. In contrast, not a single civic association is registered in Puente Piedra to pressure the district for formal housing provision. The distribution of organizations thus suggests that the urban poor's demands center on forbearance and post-hoc policies. This pattern extends across Lima: there were 3,181 registered informal settlement associations across the city, and hundreds in districts known for land invasions (SUNARP 2014).

Although some scholars see squatting as a way for the poor to opt out of the state, the activities of squatter associations suggest the opposite. Squatter leaders emphasize that land invasions are a necessary way to make distributive claims. As one leader captures the logic, a land invasion is "the only way to start the process to get the politicians

[36] The interviews were conducted primarily in government offices where association leaders come to speak with politicians and bureaucrats about issues in their neighborhoods.

[37] Registration occurs through the National Superintendency of Public Registries (*Superintendencia Nacional de los Registros Públicos*, SUNARP); district registration occurs through offices of citizen participation (*Gerencia de Participación Ciudadana*).

[38] The military government of General Manuel Odría (1948–1956) encouraged the formation of dwellers' associations, which he used to undercut political organizing by the populist party, APRA. The left-wing military dictatorship focused their efforts on monitoring association leaders to prevent radical leftist movements through the National System for the Support of Social Mobilization (SINAMOS) (Collier 1976: 60–3, 106, 112; Stepan 1978).

involved."[39] Once a land invasion occurs, squatter settlement associations can pressure for public services and land rights, which otherwise are inaccessible. Associational life tends to be most vibrant prior to the receipt of property titles and services; members often demobilize once their needs are met (Dosh 2010). This process still results in extensive civic engagement. Unlike in many other Latin American cities, lower-class groups in Lima participate in associations at rates equal to those of other class groups. Even more pertinent, past participation in a land invasion is associated with a significant increase in the probability of being a member of any civic association (Dunning 2009: 124).

A second way to observe the urban poor's attitudes toward squatting is through their cooperation with law enforcement. The quick turnaround time for police to evict squatters means that enforcement actions depend on information from residents about when illegal construction is occurring. If the poor prefer enforcement, then they should assist the state in this process by telling the mayor and police about new invasions. Squatter leaders, however, report on invasions in a narrow set of circumstances: when new squatters pose direct threats to their settlements, when they occupy land intended for community projects (such as schools and parks), and when they are violent.[40] Otherwise, most leaders refuse to report on squatter settlements. This silence in part reflects the frequent involvement of existing squatter settlements in new land invasions; leaders often organize new land invasions and recruit family and friends to participate. Even when residents want to stop land invasions, many also see evictions as illegitimate. Because "people need somewhere to live, they are not seen as committing a crime," explained one local official.[41]

Government agencies consider societal acceptance of land invasions an impediment to enforcement. The Housing Ministry emphasizes that land invasions are "a socially accepted form to access land in peripheral zones" (MVCS 2006). The director of the main agency in charge of state land, the Superintendency for State Goods (*Superintendencia Nacional de Bienes Estatales*, SBN), traces the lack of citizen cooperation with enforcement back to the country's housing policies:

[39] Author interview with settlement founder, Villas de Ancón, District of Ancón, Lima, Peru, November 8, 2011.

[40] Focus group with settlement leaders, Villa El Salvador, November 12, 2011.

[41] Author interview with sub-director of Cadaster, District of Ventanilla, Callao, Peru, November 23, 2011.

> We need better police support to stop land invasions, but we also need to develop better housing plans like they have in Chile. We need to be able to tell people when they invade land, "Hold on, no, you can't just take this piece of land because we have housing projects for people who need housing that you can access." Then there wouldn't be so much support for invaders so *people would help us when they saw something happening*.[42]

The poor resist enforcement, but they do not want land invasions. Most settlement leaders were frustrated about the disorderly growth and strain on public services caused by new land invasions. The limited public opinion data available from Peru reinforces this view: only 21 percent of poor respondents approve of land invasions, compared to 5 percent of nonpoor respondents (AmericasBarometer 1997). Thus, as found in the previous chapter, most voters prefer to live without squatter settlements. Nevertheless, evictions are seen as excessively harsh.

### 3.3.3 Distributive Signals

Politicians face high electoral costs when they choose to enforce against squatters. Beyond the loss of support from squatters themselves, there are indirect reputational costs in which the public at large comes to see politicians as "anti-poor." I turn to my survey of housing bureaucrats to measure the perceived electoral repercussions. I asked bureaucrats whether the mayor in their district tends to lose or gain electoral support if he enforces against squatters. Bureaucrats are ideally situated to judge because they both advise the mayor on enforcement actions and receive complaints from citizens. Two-thirds of bureaucrats in Lima answered that the mayor loses political support by evicting squatters. Only one bureaucrat believed that the mayor would gain political support by evicting squatters; the rest saw the public as divided.

An additional way to understand the electoral incentives for forbearance comes from campaign platforms. If politicians believe that they will win votes through forbearance, then they should make promises of forbearance and legalization in their campaign statements, especially when they run for office in majority poor districts. State housing provision, in contrast, should be a minor campaign issue. Analyzing campaign platforms also allows me to focus on political intentions to enforce the law apart from the capacity to do so. Politicians who want to enforce should

[42] Author interview with Sonia Cordero, superintendent, SBN, Lima, Peru, November 24, 2011. Emphasis added.

promise control measures on the campaign trail, even if they struggle to complete them in office.

To test these hypotheses, I compiled and coded a database of political platforms for the 2010 district elections in Lima (see Appendix B for details). In Peru, all mayors and their council list must file a platform (*Plan de Gobierno*) with national election authorities to run for office. Presumably a minority of motivated citizens read these written platforms, but the documents do give a sense for the general topics of discussion in local campaigns. Local leaders also regularly ask candidates to incorporate their promises into campaign platforms as a written record of their commitments.

I compare platforms between districts with a majority of low-income residents (fourteen poor districts) and those with a plurality of upper-income residents (nine nonpoor districts), for a total of 306 platforms. Issues of housing and squatting are salient issues in local campaigns: they show up in more than four-fifths of platforms in poor districts, and about half in nonpoor districts.[43]

To get a sense of the differences by district, I first identified platforms with clear enforcement promises. These include platforms that mention (1) police actions (evictions of squatters, monitoring of open lands, and so on), (2) commitments to improve enforcement capabilities (additional police or bureaucrats), or (3) promises to apply existing laws with respect to squatting. Consider a few typical enforcement platforms: mayors promise to put "a stop to the degradation of agricultural areas promoted by informal developers,"[44] "preserve hillside zones exclusively for forestry and preservation, not urbanization,"[45] or create a "green band" to avoid "still more land invasions."[46] Second, I analyzed whether platforms included statements in favor of forbearance and post-hoc policies. These fell into three broad categories: (1) calls to refrain from police action, (2) promises to support squatter settlements through the legal recognition and titling of their claims, and (3) language that prioritizes squatters' housing needs over the law.[47] For instance, platforms offered "massive

[43] In nonpoor districts, discussion of informal construction tends to refer to problems of buildings without licenses (or improper ones). The construction of new informal settlements is a very rare event.

[44] Cambio Radical, Plan de Gobierno Municipal 2011–2014, District of Puente Piedra.

[45] Juntos por la Molina, Plan de Gobierno Municipal 2011–2014, District of La Molina.

[46] Despertar Nacional, Plan de Gobierno Municipal 2011–2014, District of San Juan de Lurigancho.

[47] I exclude promises of basic service provision, given that they are ubiquitous.

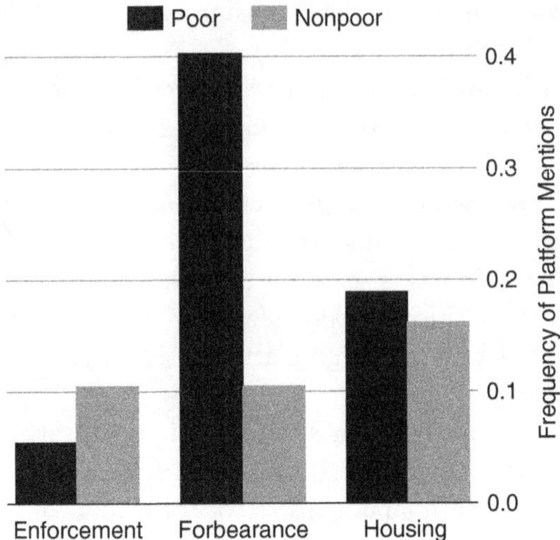


FIGURE 3.2 Campaign Platforms by Topic and District Poverty
Source: Author's Coding of District Campaign Platforms from the National Electoral Authority, Governance Observatory, 2010.

titling and property regularization,"[48] "the defense of urban authorizations in ALL of our district,"[49] and commitments that squatters "should not be viewed as exiles but rather given even more assistance."[50] Lastly I looked for whether a politician mentioned formal housing policy. While most housing investments are made by the central government, district mayors sometimes promise to work with the private sector to improve housing access and cooperate with national initiatives.[51]

Figure 3.2 presents the frequency of each platform type in poor and nonpoor districts. Consistent with my theory, enforcement platforms are more common in nonpoor districts. While just 5 percent of platforms proposed enforcement actions in poor districts, 11 percent did in nonpoor districts. This difference is small, but it is important to bear in mind that squatting tends to be a rare occurrence in nonpoor districts and thus unlikely to make it into platforms. Crucially, these ratios reverse for

[48] Perú Posible, Plan de Gobierno Municipal, 2011–2014, District of Ate.

[49] Cambio 90, Plan de Gobierno Municipal, 2011–2014, District of Villa María del Triunfo.

[50] Partido Aprista Peruano, Plan de Gobierno Municipal, 2011–2014, District of Villa María Del Triunfo, Lima, Peru.

[51] For examples, see Perú Posible, Plan de Gobierno Municipal 2011–2014, District of Comas; Partido Democratico Somos Peru, Plan de Gobierno Municipal 2011–2014, District of Villa María El Triunfo.

forbearance platforms. In poor districts, 40 percent of all platforms proposed some form of forbearance. Only 10 percent of platforms in nonpoor districts made similar promises, and they usually focused on the need to regularize the property titles and zoning of older buildings. The platforms also confirm the irrelevance of housing provision in poor and nonpoor districts: less than a fifth of platforms in poor and nonpoor districts mentioned housing policy at all and almost none offered specific proposals.

The platforms reinforce the second-best nature of forbearance. More than a third of platforms include remarks of frustration about informal housing construction. Some focus on the declining land supply that makes informal housing policies less effective and therefore threatens what is colloquially referred to as the "occupy to then urbanize" (*ocupar para luego habilitar*) model.[52] Others note that informal growth has multiplied demands for complementary goods, such as "roads, sidewalks, retaining walls, stairs, and so on, to which municipal authorities cannot respond effectively."[53] Due to Lima's decentralization, district governments shoulder many of the costs of illegal land occupations. As one mayor elaborated in an interview, "There are huge economic consequences to letting invasions occur because [district governments] assume all the service costs, but there also is such strong social and political reaction to evictions that we are stuck until the central government chooses to build housing."[54] Like voters, mayors prefer an end to land invasions, yet they are unwilling to enforce against new invasions or to withdraw support from those that exist. This brings us to the next issue, whether mayors choose not to enforce or cannot enforce.

### 3.3.4 Forbearance Decisions and Endogenous State Capacity

Enforcement process tracing separates the relative role of political calculations and capacity constraints in a comparatively weak state like Peru. I look for three types of causal process observations – whether political bottlenecks arise, how enforcement responds to additional resources, and whether politicians enforce more in cases where the

[52] Perú Posible, Plan de Gobierno Municipal 2011–2014, District of Villa María del Triunfo.

[53] Somos Acción Vecinal, Plan de Gobierno Municipal, 2011–2014, District of Carabayllo.

[54] Author interview with John Barrera, mayor, District of Ancón, Lima, Peru, December 1, 2011.

political costs are lower. To analyze how enforcement proceeds, I first need to establish a baseline for the universe of cases against which authorities could possibly act. I rely on household surveys, which suggest that 89,980 households have acquired housing through an invasion and have not received a property title in 2011 (INEI 2011). It can be assumed that most of these land invasions occurred after the titling deadline in 2004 (otherwise households would have applied to the titling program).

In Lima, the most politically charged step in the enforcement process is the detection of a land invasion. Calculating how many land invasions are detected is challenging and necessarily approximate because no single authority monitors invasions, as we will see in Bogotá. The state also "sees" land invasions for different purposes. The Lima city government is supposed to report illegal land occupations to the state agency that owns the land. Yet, it does not maintain procedures to track or aggregate information on illegal occupations, nor is a single city inspector assigned to monitor illegal land occupations.[55]

Three additional agencies are involved in detection depending on the type of land at stake: the Ministry of Defense, the SBN, and district governments. The Ministry of Defense leaves most of its land unmonitored, unless it is used by the military or serves strategic purposes.[56] The SBN, which manages state property, also has no monitoring process or even database of the land that it owns. The SBN can take months to determine if invaded land belongs to the state, let alone act on the case. Likewise, only a handful of district governments reported any type of proactive monitoring of land invasions. Combined across district, city, and state institutions, I found 5,920 cases, or just 6 percent of all illegal land occupations uncovered from household surveys, were detected by state institutions and sent to state attorneys to take action.

The low rate of detection results primarily from failures to pass information about land invasions to enforcement authorities, not a lack of underlying information. As described earlier, squatters register their associations with the government; they also apply for services, urban

[55] The designated city authority, the Metropolitan Planning Institute (*Instituto Metropolitano de Planificación*, IMP), keeps track of newspaper reports on land invasions, but has no policy to contact the police or its own staff assigned to prevent their occurrence. Author interview with Carlos Escalante, executive director, IMP, Lima, Peru, June 23, 2011.

[56] Author interview with bureaucrat, Office of Patrimonial Management (*Dirección de Gestión Patrimonial*), Ministry of Defense, December 6, 2011.

authorizations, and police certificates to verify their land possession. Mayors use this information to report invasions to authorities when cases involve valuable resources (land reserved for public goods, archeological sites, and so on). In the majority of cases, however, politicians do not pass information about squatter settlements along to enforcement authorities.

Politicians cite the lack of housing programs and associated reputational costs as the reasons that they suppress information. One mayor, who has been elected multiple times in a poor district, complained about rampant squatting only to conclude, "We can't stop land invasions when there is no policy from the central government to offer housing to people."[57] Another politician expressed a common view that local enforcement decisions hinge on national housing policy investments, explaining that, "We're not isolated in how we deal with these themes because, even though there are clear legal norms that people can't invade the land and that the government should act, there's no clear option for what to do with people."[58]

Beyond the direct social effects, almost half of the politicians that I interviewed in Lima stressed that evictions were impossible because of the impression they created in the community. One politician was indignant when I asked about reporting on squatter settlements: "How can I say that I support the poor and then go behind their back to try to get people who need housing taken off their land?"[59] Bureaucrats admitted that the district knew about land invasions, but mayors told them not to act. As one put it, "Of course, we knew the invasions occurred, but what was a mayor who supported the poor going to do, throw people out and pretend that there's another way to get housing in this country?"[60]

Conversely, politicians saw electoral benefits from forbearance. One politician emphasized that working with new invasions bolstered his reputation among the poor residents of the district: "People look for politicians who can empathize with their problems, and when you work for communities that are just getting off the ground it shows that you understand how

[57] Author interview with Washington Ipenza, mayor, District of Villa María del Triunfo (1984–1986, 1999–2006), June 18, 2011.

[58] Author interview with local councilor, District of San Agustino, Lima, Peru, November 18, 2011.

[59] Author interview with Ivan Coronado, local councilor, District of Comas, Lima, Peru, November 25, 2011.

[60] Author interview with housing director, District of San Juan de Miraflores, May 17, 2011.

hard things are and what people need to do to find housing."[61] I accompanied politicians on their visits to several recent land invasions. One politician nicely summarizes the importance of visiting and assisting land invasions to build a reputation and goodwill in the community:

> Democracy creates more demands on the local governments because we are closer to the people and absorb the social problems. My support comes from the poor, so when there is a land invasion, I visit *to show my sympathy*. If you bring in the police, then it's clear to everyone that *the mayor does not really fight for the social needs of people* and isn't really looking for ways to help.[62]

The scope for political choice to enforce should not be overstated in Lima. Once local authorities provide information on where illegal land occupations have occurred, state attorneys struggle to prosecute cases. The number of reported land occupations that result in legal action is tiny. I found 180 cases open across all state entities, involving roughly 4,500 claimants for the period examined.[63] Most legal cases end with judicial resolutions to expropriate the land in favor of the squatters. Because legal cases drag on, courts find it impractical to order evictions. Official statistics on the number of court cases that end with an eviction order are unavailable, but the Attorney General's Office estimates that 212 evictions occurred.

Figure 3.3 plots the enforcement chain. On the vertical axis, I log the number of cases so the change can be interpreted as the percent decline at each step. The straight dotted line represents a constant percent change in the cases lost at each step, or constant institutional weakness. It shows a uniform rate of institutional weakness of a third, meaning that one-third of all cases advance to the next enforcement stage. This seems like a relatively low bar to meet.

[61] Author interview with César Augusto Lerzundi, local councilor, District of Villa El Salvador, November 4, 2011.

[62] Author interview with Erasmo Segundo Cardenas Obregon, local councilor, Municipality of Ate, Lima, Peru, November 23, 2011. Emphasis added.

[63] Each case can involve multiple claimants. Attorneys estimate that a case involves twenty-five households on average, which is how I arrive at the figure of 4,500 proceedings total. Another way to follow the process would be to use statistics on the number of "usurpations" (the category of crime used to describe squatting). In 2006, for instance, there were 1,348 usurpations denounced to attorneys in Lima. In 2011, the Congressional Commission of Justice and Human Rights found that the northern cone of Lima (Corte de Lima Norte) had 2,888 cases of usurpation registered. However, these cases can involve a wide variety of property situations and do not isolate squatter settlement formations. See Sesión de la Comisión de Justicia y Derechos Humanos, Congreso de la República, Lima, Peru, January 17, 2011.

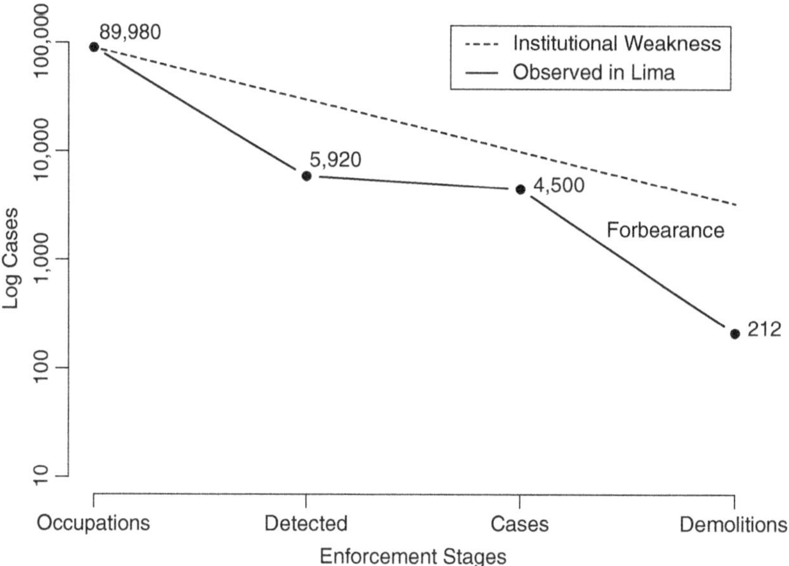


FIGURE 3.3 Enforcement against Illegal Land Occupations, Lima, 2006–2011
Sources: National Household Surveys (ENAHO) (occupations); Author's Survey of District Housing Offices, Metropolitan Planning Institute, Ministry of Defense, Superintendence of State Goods (detection); Lima Attorney General's Office (cases, evictions).

The most important thing to notice is that a sharp drop-off occurs in the number of cases that enter the legal system in the first place. Local mayors have a strong impact on detection because they report on land takings. They see no political benefits in doing so. The second plunge comes from court cases opened to evictions, as judges and politicians prefer to avoid the political costs of evicting squatters. Both of these moments represent political bottlenecks in the enforcement process.

Another way to understand political intent is to observe how behavior changes when the costs of enforcement drop, or the elasticity of enforcement. If politicians want to enforce the law, but are constrained by resources or administrative capacity, then they will increase enforcement as additional money or technology makes it easier to enforce. If politicians prefer not to enforce, then they do not react to such "price" changes. The rise of new technology – namely drones that take aerial photographs – to monitor land invasions helps to separate these scenarios. For decades, local and national authorities have tried to prevent squatting on archeological sites with limited success. With the increasing availability of drones, the government is able to monitor encroachments. Evictions of squatters on archeological land have increased.[64] This change in enforcement activity in response to a reduction in the cost of monitoring shows that the government wants to enforce on archeological sites and previously faced constraints. Yet, the same technology has not been used to control squatting in peripheral urban areas where the poor tend to occupy vacant state land for housing purposes. Bureaucrats reported that mayors followed a split approach in which they allowed the poor to take "empty land" for housing purposes, but collaborated with national authorities to enforce when archeological land was at stake.[65] Hence, Peru's incomplete adoption of a new technology that reduces the costs of enforcement suggests that administrative constraints are not the full story.

Additionally, there are several reasons to believe that weak enforcement capacity is an endogenous choice. That is to say, incoherent and underfunded enforcement procedures are a result of the state's insufficient housing policy rather than an underlying inability to muster the police or bureaucrats to enforce. This logic comes out in the case of the national property-titling agency, the Committee for the Formalization of Informal Property (*Organismo de Formalización de la Propiedad Informal*, COFOPRI). In order to title land, COFOPRI needed to establish detailed maps of local districts and unify land registries. These maps could have been helpful to bureaucrats and police attempting to track new land invasions. But COFOPRI did not share its database of titled properties because, as the director of COFOPRI explained, sharing information would "undermine COFOPRI's efforts to maximize the number of titles provided and popular appreciation for the presidential initiative."[66] Resources, skills, and property registries from a vast titling bureaucracy were not being applied to enforcement efforts. More generally, relatively simple reorganizations of the bureaucracy, such as the assignment of monitoring responsibilities to a single authority, or investments, such as the creation of a database of state property, could vastly improve Peru's administrative capacity.

[64] See "Ministerio de Cultura evitó invasión de zona arqueológica de Matabuey," Press Release, Dirección General de Defensa del Patrimonio, January 13, 2014.

[65] Author interview with housing bureaucrats, District of Lurín, May 24, 2011; District of Ventanilla, June 1, 2011; District of Ate, May 31, 2011; Villa El Salvador, May 23, 2011.

[66] COFOPRI legalized the land, not the constructions, and used its own map technology separate from local cadasters required for property tax collection. Author interview with Ais Jesus Tarabay Yaya, executive director, COFOPRI, Lima, Peru, November 17, 2011; Also see "Proliferación de viviendas ilegales crea problemas de recaudación," *El Comercio* August 19, 2000.

City and national officials also could pressure district mayors to exert more enforcement effort. They do not. Some reports even suggest that mayors reported land invasions but central authorities never responded.[67] Apathy is surprising, given that land invasions often occur on state land over which central authorities have jurisdiction. The director of the city planning agency emphasized that national housing policies drove the city's choice not to do more against land invasions: "We understand that in a poor country, market mechanisms are insufficient to result in an orderly occupation of land, but we can't repress invasions until there are other housing options."[68]

Thus, fine-grained process tracing of enforcement outcomes and qualitative interviews help to distinguish the role of institutional capacity and electoral incentives. Observations that mayors are resistant to adopting new technology and sharing information to improve enforcement confirms that capacity constraints are not decisive, even in contexts of substantial constraints. Electoral politics provides greater leverage to understand why politicians let illegal land occupations persist.

### 3.3.5 Political Decentralization and Clientelism

Do politicians negotiate quid pro quo agreements in which squatters can stay only if they engage in particular political behaviors, or do they make broad promises to all poor voters? In my interviews with more than two dozen local politicians in Lima, the vast majority saw targeted enforcement as "impossible" because it risked a political backlash. To see why enforcement is not part of clientelistic exchanges, I consider two off-the-line cases where enforcement threats occurred. I then show that clientelistic negotiations are far more common around post-hoc policies than around enforcement decisions.

First, the example of a mayor who proposed to enforce the law against squatters for ideological reasons underscores the affective ties at stake. Michel Azcueta, one of the founding figures of the iconic district of Villa El Salvador, has a strong commitment to urban planning to promote the long-run development of the district. As mayor in the late 1990s, he created a zoning plan and reserved land for a university and a hospital. He again ran for mayor in 2006 and told residents that he would not permit land invasions or grant authorizations to existing squatter

[67] For example, see "Invasores vuelven a San Antonio de Cañete," *La República* July 27, 2010.
[68] Author interview with Carlos Escalante, executive director, IMP, Lima, Peru, June 23, 2011.

settlements in order to conserve the district's remaining space. Instead, Azcueta pushed for the district's inclusion in national housing plans and "orderly growth" in the district.[69]

Azcueta's opponent, Jaime Zea, disagreed with urban control measures. Zea promised to provide basic services and legal recognition to squatter settlements (*saneamiento físico legal*) and to "diminish" (but not eliminate) informal construction.[70] Because Azcueta threatened enforcement, Zea informally reassured squatters that he would not evict them if he were mayor so, as a local councilor recounted, "they came to all the rallies and meetings."[71] Zea won the election by less than 1,500 votes in a district of about 300,000 voters. The consensus among observers, as well as Azcueta himself, was that Zea's promise of forbearance swung the election.[72]

Squatters voted based on the candidates' enforcement platforms, much as they would vote for a candidate's social policy or investment promises. Forbearance was not provided in a contingent way. For instance, local leaders of squatter settlements doubted that Zea would have evicted squatters if they did not campaign for him. He made no moves to evict squatter settlements that supported Azcueta. As one local leader explained, "[Zea] would have looked terrible to the rest of us."[73] The motivation to support Zea, according to local leaders, came from Azcueta, who was a competitive candidate with an ideological commitment to orderly urban development. Monitoring votes or political behavior was not necessary because "we knew to pick the candidate who would cause us fewer problems and who understood our situation."[74] Squatters participated in Zea's campaign and continued to attend government meetings after his election to guarantee that they received priority in the allocation of public goods, particularly sidewalks. Thus, the mechanisms by which

69 Confianza Peru, Plan de Gobierno Municipal 2007–2011, District of Villa El Salvador.

70 Restauración Nacional, Plan de Gobierno Municipal 2007–2011, District of Villa El Salvador.

71 Author interview with Walter Quispe, local councilor, Villa El Salvador, November 4, 2011.

72 Author interview with Ramiro García, head of urban program, DESCO, May 23, 2011; Author interview with Walter Quispe and Cesar Augusto Lerzundi, local councilors, District of Villa El Salvador, November 10, 2011; Author interview with Paula Gamboa Perez, local councilor, District of Villa El Salvador, November 4, 2011; Author interview with Michel Azcueta, mayor (1984–1990, 1996–1998), District of Villa El Salvador, Lima, Peru, July 6, 2011.

73 Focus group with association leaders, District of Villa El Salvador, May 23, 2011.

74 Author interview with squatter settlement leader, District of Villa El Salvador, May 25, 2011.

forbearance is converted into votes – direct material benefits from a broad enforcement position, affective ties to a politician, and attendance at government events to secure public investments – differ substantially from clientelistic enforcement threats deployed against political detractors.

Second, observing a case in which a politician promised clientelistic forbearance shows the strategy's pitfalls. In the thirty-four districts that I visited, I found only one clear case in which a politician offered forbearance to his supporters and threatened to evict those who failed to support him. It is telling that the case occurred in one of the smallest districts in the city, Santa Rosa, where politicians can win with the votes of squatters alone. In 2010, mayoral candidate and land trafficker Carlos Arce Arias (known as *La Metralleta*, "The Machine Gun") allegedly organized the invasion of more than 1.5 square miles of state land. He sold plots of land to approximately 5,000 households, which was equivalent to the number of registered voters in Santa Rosa. A voice recording captured Arce threatening to evict squatters if he did not win the election:

> If I don't win the election it's because you betrayed me and that's not pardonable, because with 2,800 votes I will have won the mayoralty of Santa Rosa and I will win against the poor devils that are running, and if one of you fails me everyone will pay and you can all forget about your shacks. Is that understood?[75]

This message was clear electoral coercion: squatters' ability to stay in their homes would be contingent on how they voted as a group. This clientelistic strategy, I suggest, works best in small districts in which politicians can discount broad reputational effects (and with substantial private violence). Strikingly, Arce even emphasized the fact that he could win the election exclusively with squatters' votes. Yet, even in the most propitious case, enforcement threats backfired. Voters outside of the squatter settlements mobilized in huge numbers to oppose Arce. Even leaders of squatter settlements opposed Arce and complained that he was a "trickster," a "mafia boss," and "doesn't care about the community's welfare."[76] Arce lost the 2010 election. He indeed retaliated against squatters, allegedly throwing a grenade at one local leader's house.[77] This off-the-line case in

[75] "Traficante de terreno por la negligencia de la ONPE podría ser alcalde en Santa Rosa," *Noticias Lima Norte*, October 19, 2010.

[76] Author interview with local leaders, District of Santa Rosa, November 8, 2011.

[77] See "Lanzan granada a vivienda de dirigente de balneario Santa Rosa," *RPP* November 4, 2011. Arce's tactics ultimately were successful in the 2014 election in Santa Rosa because

which a politician used forbearance and threats of selective enforcement in a clientelistic fashion reinforces the reputational concerns of the majority of politicians that I interviewed in Lima.

Relations between squatter settlements and politicians nevertheless do involve clientelistic exchanges, just not around the threat of evictions. The glue that ties informal settlements to district politicians tends to be the access to local legal authorizations and the accompanying goods and services that mayors can control. Mayors shape the extent of legal security for squatter settlements by granting local legal recognition (*prehabilitación urbana*). Such recognition does not grant individual property rights. Still, 89 percent of possessors feel secure in their property when recognized by the local government (compared to 93 percent with individual property titles and just 47 percent of those who lack documents) (Webb, Beuermann, and Carla 2006: 15). Squatter settlements also are ripe arenas for political clientelism because public investment often is prohibited in untitled areas. Mayors extend local public goods as personal favors prior to the legal incorporation of squatter settlements.

Leaders of squatter settlements confirm that politicians affect their development by deciding whether to ignore their neighborhoods' legal problems when deciding where to provide services and public investments. They believe that their political support affects their chances of gaining legal security. A typical description of the legal hassle created when squatters do not support the mayor comes from the president of a squatter settlement association on a precarious piece of land:

> During the last election, we didn't support the candidate who won and so we had a lot of problems. We couldn't get the mayor's approval for our projects, and they would delay our paperwork for as long as possible or *tell us that we didn't meet the legal requirements* – but who does here! So we couldn't do anything during four years … this election we all discussed to back the winning candidate and showed up at all his rallies and now we have all the facilities possible to get our projects approved … There isn't always money but *the mayor always approves our profile* and then we can go to the central government to ask for projects.[78]

Politicians monitor group, but not individual, behavior to reward supporters. It is important to remember that Peru's party system has collapsed

he continued to change the electorate. The voting population of Santa Rosa doubled from 5,800 voters to 11,000 by the 2014 election due to the growth of squatter settlements and voter fraud. Arce was accused of changing voters' registration numbers. See "PPC denuncia presunto fraude electoral en Santa Rosa," *El Comercio* September 6, 2014.

[78] Author interview with anonymous settlement leader, District of Puente Piedra, Lima, Peru, November 9, 2011. Emphasis added.

so there are no well-organized political machines to monitor vote choice. Electoral authorities assign voters to polling stations randomly by their identification numbers, making it difficult to monitor polling station–level results. Voting is compulsory and fines are enforced, diminishing the value of turnout buying. Thus, rather than monitor individual vote choice or turnout, politicians have a general sense of whether association leaders "did their part" in the campaign. They also look to associations to continue to demonstrate their support by attending project openings and local government meetings, and, in the worst-case scenario, blocking recall attempts.[79] As found by Muñoz (2014), the politicians that I interviewed provided small rewards for associations to show up at campaign events or to organize meetings with members.

Hence, the taproot of weak enforcement against land invasions at all levels of government is a calculation about the positive material benefits and the goodwill that it generates. Mayors can offer forbearance as a way to signal support for squatters, especially when their competitors make credible threats to enforce, as in the case of Villa El Salvador. But they generally try to avoid the reputational costs of enforcement, as in the case of the mayor's losing campaign in Santa Rosa. Limited housing policy investments help explain why politicians have been unwilling to enforce even when they have the information to do so and technological developments make it easier to control squatting. Although forbearance does not hinge on individual or group political behaviors, mayors do manipulate the provision of local public goods and legal recognition to build clientelistic ties in an inchoate party system. The next section, on Bogotá, further reinforces the centrality of housing policy choices in enforcement outcomes, but reveals a less clientelistic electoral logic due to the large district size and constitutional structure.

## 3.4 TRUNCATED HOUSING POLICY AND FORBEARANCE IN BOGOTÁ

Bogotá has a capable bureaucracy and police, which would lead us to expect enforcement against illegal land occupations under dominant capacity-based theories. Nonetheless, with few exceptions, housing programs do not reach low-income groups. In this section, I show how truncated housing policy elevates the political costs of enforcement.

[79] Popular recall referenda are a common occurrence in Peru in which citizens gather signatures to remove the mayor from office (see Tuesta Soldevilla 2014).

Mayors block enforcement against squatters even after bureaucrats have completed lengthy administrative and court proceedings to enforce. The facts that enforcement has occurred against nonpoor squatters and that the adoption of satellite technology has not changed enforcement behavior provide disconfirming evidence of capacity-based theories. I suggest that mayors have invested in "excess" capacity, meaning the ability to act against invasions, as a way to deter squatting without incurring the political costs of coercive sanctions. Given Bogotá's political centralization and Colombia's constitutional structure, forbearance (as well as accompanying property titles and services) is less likely to be tied to squatters' political behaviors. Instead, mayors alter enforcement levels depending on the core constituencies that they support.

### 3.4.1 Crowding In Squatting

Illegal land occupations have been a common route for the poor to access housing in Bogotá. More than 2.1 million people, or about a quarter of the city's population, have acquired their houses through illegal land occupations (SDP 2011). As in Lima, informal construction has been associated with the rapid migration and unequal rewards from industrialization in the mid-twentieth century. But the pace of squatting has not ceased and has possibly even accelerated in the 1990s and 2000s. Unlike in Lima, squatting in Bogotá primarily involves the purchase of irregular land, such as land zoned for environmental conservation, environmental-risk zones, or agricultural areas (Camargo and Hurtado 2011; Torres Tovar 2009).[80] What makes these transactions informal is that construction is prohibited on the land purchased.

City mayors do not intervene directly to promote illegal land occupations. As in Lima, they indirectly support informal settlement through their decisions not to call the police, and their investments in policies that legalize and provide services to existing settlements. Because most squatting occurs through land sales that provide some form of receipt or title, squatters want their neighborhoods to be "regularized" so they can access public infrastructure and investment funds. In 2008, the Constitutional Court ruled that local governments could not deny individuals access to water or electricity based on the legal status of the land where they live.

[80] Of all informal settlements in Bogotá, 61 percent have formed through informal sales, 31 percent can be traced to a land invasion, and the others cannot be identified (SDP 2011).

Service denials violate the right to a minimum living standard.[81] As a result, the time that settlements wait to receive basic services has dropped from an average of five years in the 1980s to months in 2010. Chapter 6 develops in more detail how legalization and servicing has encouraged illegal land occupations.

### 3.4.2 Demand Displacement

Chapter 2 provided survey evidence on the interdependence of formal and informal housing demands. I found that individuals who believe that housing programs are inadequate are more supportive of squatting. Of greater analytic importance than this aggregate result is whether poor voters actually mobilize around forbearance and post-hoc goods when housing programs fail. I examine two implications of my theory. First, I expect that demand displacement has been less consistent in Bogotá than in Lima, given that the Colombian state has on occasion invested in housing programs for the poor. I expect popular organizing to shift toward housing programs during periods in which the government invests in state alternatives. Second, I examine whether popular sectors want forbearance and post-hoc goods from the government using a rich archive of petitions from informal settlements.

First, poor citizens did organize around state housing policies in the 1980s, when Colombia attempted to pursue a substitutive housing policy. As I will explain in Chapter 6, Belisario Betancur attempted to implement housing policies to reach the poor and crowd out squatter settlements. Major housing organizations, such as the National Federation of Popular Housing Organizations (*Federación Nacional de Organizaciones de Vivienda Popular*, Fedevivienda) and another organization closely tied to the Betancur administration, *Construyamos*, worked with the state to organize the poor in housing cooperatives and to pressure for more housing assistance (Florian 1991). These organizations lost much of their strength as the Colombian state moved to a model of demand subsidies and eliminated state housing banks in the 1990s. As the director of Fedevivienda emphasizes, the poor now are skeptical that government housing programs will reach them and see little reason to push for them.[82] Only a

[81] See Colombian Constitutional Court. Sentence C-1189/08, *Gaceta Corte Constitucional* December 3, 2008.

[82] Author interview with Alejandro Florian, director, Fedevivienda, Bogotá, Colombia, June 23, 2010.

handful of organizations dedicated to state housing provision still exist. Even among housing subsidy beneficiaries, who we would expect to mobilize to make use of their allocated benefits, there has been little citizen pressure in the 1990s and 2000s. Complaints to the Housing Ministry about the inability to use housing subsidies were so insignificant that ministry employees instead had to call beneficiaries to understand why subsidies went unused.[83]

Second, informal settlements organize collectively. Bogotá's Department of Planning houses a vast archive on the city's more than 2,000 squatter settlements (SDP 2011). In hopes of gaining legal recognition, each settlement submits records that trace its correspondence with city and national authorities since founding. Roughly half of settlements have a "communal action council" (*Juntas de Acción Comunal*, JAC). JACs are local organizations created with corporatist purposes during the National Front but they now serve as a central channel of communication between popular neighborhoods and city officials (Jaramillo, Alfonso, and Hataya 1996: 9–10).[84] I reviewed a sample of correspondence to understand the demands that squatter associations make on city officials.

Much of the correspondence involves petitions to mayors, congressmen, and city councilors for help when legal problems arose with the land that squatters purchased or for the extension of basic services. It is clear from the archive that many poor individuals understood that they purchased land at below-market prices because it lacked full documentation or property title. But they also differentiated between types of illegality, with land invasions of private property being clearly "worse" than other violations (like the use of public land or purchases of defective land). The emergence of absentee landlords was a major complaint. For instance, one association recoiled at the idea that they willingly invaded private land: "We paid less to live without the amenities that others more accustomed to city life and with more resources enjoy, but we paid a price through great personal effort sufficient for the land to be ours ... we did not usurp it from another person."[85] Beyond requests for legal assistance in the case of disputes, the archive includes correspondence asking politicians to incorporate their neighborhoods into the city's

[83] "Call center del viceministerio de Vivienda," *El Tiempo* June 25, 2004.

[84] Of the 2,000 settlements, the Informal Land Observatory matched 893 to a JAC, but this probably underestimates the number of JACs due to the problems matching names across databases (Camargo and Hurtado 2013).

[85] Letter from Junta de Acción Comunal to Mayor Julio César Sánchez, Barrio Andalucia, 1987.

official perimeter, which would give them access to public electricity, sanitation, and water services. What comes out of these petitions is that the poor did not want to escape the state's radar. Rather, the urban poor were in intense communication with state authorities, but around issues like protection against evictions, zoning changes, and public services. Strikingly, not a single petition that I reviewed was addressed to the Ministry of Housing.

Finally, societal support for forbearance can be observed in the lack of collaboration with state enforcement agencies. As in Lima, citizens play a central role in the detection of new illegal land occupations, given the short window in which the police can evict squatters without a court order. Citizen reports of new land occupations are rare. Community resistance is easiest to observe in the district with the most active new land occupations, Ciudad Bolívar. As I explain subsequently, most of the city's information about squatting comes from satellite images. In a typical month, there are 500 new land occupations detected by the city through satellite imagery. Authorities, in contrast, receive an average of two complaints from residents living in the district.[86] Bureaucrats explained to me that no one reported the occupations because residents were in "solidarity" based on squatters' economic position[87] or "because they think the state will come for them next" if they report on new occupations.[88]

Further, given that Colombia recognizes a constitutional right to housing, many bureaucrats, politicians, and squatter associations justified their support for invasions in social rights terms. A common belief is that squatters cannot legally be removed until the state protects squatters' housing rights.[89] Even when a land occupation is actively occurring (in which case the police legally can conduct evictions), enforcement is perceived as illegitimate without greater effort to provide housing. A director of the city's housing program expressed a common sentiment: "The social

86 Author interview with judicial coordinator, District of Ciudad Bolívar, October 14, 2011.

87 Author interview with housing inspector, District of Chapinero, Bogotá, Colombia, July 6, 2010; author interview with housing inspector, District of Rafael Uribe Uribe, September 16, 2011.

88 Author interview with housing inspector, District of San Cristóbal, Bogotá, Colombia, July 10, 2010.

89 Author interview with housing inspector, District of Santa Fe, Bogotá, Colombia, July 8, 2010; author interview with district mayor, District of Engativá, Bogotá, Colombia, July 21, 2010; author interview with Inés Esteban Parra, lawyer, Secretary of Government, Bogotá, Colombia, July 16, 2010; author interview with housing inspector, District of Ciudad Bolivar, July 28, 2010.

problem [of not having housing to offer] means that neighbors believe that the state hasn't done its job to provide housing so they don't tell us about illegal occupations."[90]

On balance, then, the poor's housing demands only centered on welfare bureaucracies when the state provided housing alternatives. In the absence of state housing provision, the poor take land informally, and then turn to politicians for forbearance, public services, and ultimately legal recognition. Enforcement garners little support from poor residents and, as we will see next, it can have significant electoral costs.

### 3.4.3 Distributive Signals

Politicians risk a substantial electoral backlash if they evict squatters due to the structure of popular demands. Data from my survey of housing bureaucrats confirm the heavy electoral costs of evictions. Figure 3.4 illustrates the responses of bureaucrats in Lima and Bogotá to several questions that probed the electoral environment. I asked bureaucrats whether mayors lose or gain political support if they evict squatters (*Loses Votes*). I graph

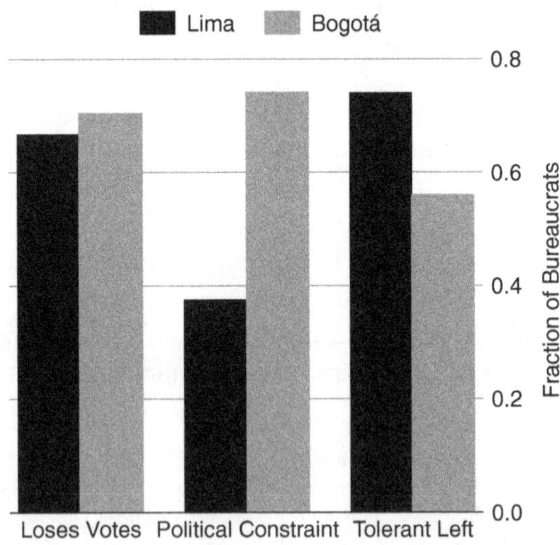


FIGURE 3.4 Bureaucratic Perceptions of Political Bottlenecks in Lima and Bogotá

[90] Author interview with Francisco Álvarez, director of control and director of projects, Metrovivienda, Bogotá, Colombia, July 10, 2010.

the fraction that answered that the mayor loses support (less than a five on a ten-point scale, see Appendix C for question wording). In both cities, about two-thirds of bureaucrats believe that mayors lose political support if they enforce the law. Typical sentiments in Bogotá were that "Any politician who dares to do [evictions] dies politically."[91]

Other questions reinforce the political obstacles to enforcement. For instance, I asked bureaucrats whether political interference or institutional resources (like budgets, cars, and personnel) constitutes a greater obstacle to enforcement (*Political Constraint*). Responses were divided in Lima; both resources and politics played a role, as I detailed earlier. But Figure 3.4 shows that three-quarters of bureaucrats in Bogotá saw political interference as a more significant impediment. Further, I asked bureaucrats whether politicians from the Left or Right were more likely to tolerate illegal land occupations (*Tolerant Left*). Interestingly, although many bureaucrats thought that all politicians engaged in forbearance, the majority thought those who represented the Left were "more willing to tolerate squatters due to their social sympathies."

No database of political platforms exists to study forbearance promises in Bogotá. Instead, I reviewed campaign statements and interviewed local politicians to understand how they evaluate the poor's housing demands. Local and city councilors, who play a key role as intermediaries between citizens and state offices, told me that they almost never assist with housing subsidy applications. A shared sense of skepticism about housing programs came out in the comments of politicians with remarks like, "People know that you need to have savings and credit [to access government housing], and people here don't even have enough money for the bus,"[92] and "Helping someone with a housing application doesn't cause anyone to win or lose votes because demand is met through other forms."[93]

In contrast, politicians respond to the poor through constituency service to help informal settlements access public services and legal titles. Local councilors view their jobs in terms of a responsibility to "orient" squatters to receive public services and legalization (*orientador* or *tramitador*). The platform of a city councilor trying to distinguish himself from

[91] Author interview with judicial advisor, District of Rafael Uribe Uribe, Bogotá, Colombia, July 7, 2010.

[92] Author interview with Heidi Luz Quiroga, local councilor, District of San Cristóbal, Bogotá, Colombia, October 13, 2011.

[93] Author interview with Alfredo Díaz, local councilor, District of Ciudad Bolívar, Bogotá, Colombia, October 14, 2011.

"traditional" politicians perhaps best captures the way that forbearance is used to show a commitment to the poor: "In unequal and clientelistic societies, people think that it is more important to promote social justice rather than to apply the law. Traditional political leaders make the negotiation of the law a rhetorical instrument to support the poorest, in other words to evade the law to benefit those most in need."[94]

### 3.4.4 Forbearance Decisions and Excess State Capacity

To separate whether politicians *will not* or *cannot* control illegal land occupations, I repeat the enforcement process tracing exercise. Institutional investments that do not go to use ("excess capacity") make it is easier to pinpoint where enforcement breaks down in Bogotá than in Lima.

A single agency in Bogotá has monitored illegal land occupations using satellite imagery and teams of inspectors since 2003.[95] City authorities have registered 13,931 illegal land occupations from 2006 to 2011. Of course, it is unclear if the detected occupations match the underlying level of offenses. A plausible measure of the wider universe of illegal land occupations comes from the number of new "provisional" water connections registered in the city. Informal settlements almost immediately apply to receive services, and the city's water company acquiesces to avoid service theft and to comply with the Constitutional Court's mandate. These statistics suggest that there were 23,024 new "provisional" connections in Bogotá during the period studied (Camargo and Hurtado 2011: 13). Water connections could overstate informal land occupations because they can be granted to legal constructions too, and the city water company sometimes services areas outside of the city limits. Even assuming that all provisional water connections are made to informal constructions in Bogotá, the city would spot 60 percent of informal land occupations.

The second step in the enforcement process is to open an administrative case against an illegal land occupation. Detection is the responsibility of the city government, but districts headed by appointed mayors take responsibility for subsequent administrative proceedings. District

[94] Campaign website of Felipe Ríos, city councilor, Cambio Radical, accessed July 6, 2015.

[95] The Subsecretary for Inspection, Oversight, and Control (*Subsecretaria de Inspección, Vigilancia y Control*) within the District Housing Secretary tracks illegal land occupations. There were important changes in the areas that they monitored in 2006, so data from previous years are not comparable.

governments face a number of obstacles on top of limited staff and resources that I observed as I shadowed bureaucrats opening legal cases. For one, informal settlements lack addresses so all legal procedures require hand-delivered notifications. City officials identify illegal land occupations using geographic coordinates. Local officials often do not have access to GPS units, or choose not to carry them due to high crime rates in peripheral districts. Relying on photographs and approximate locations, local officials struggle to identify land occupations because physical appearances change rapidly. Between visits by officials, an isolated tin shack may suddenly be surrounded by other homes. The identification process needs to be repeated multiple times during the course of legal proceedings. In addition, given the high stakes of land claims, residents in illegal settlements are savvy about property laws and can outsmart bureaucrats. Squatters claim to be renters (administrative sanctions must be filed against the owner of the construction) or to have occupied the land for three years (past the statute of limitations). The unique challenges of enforcement in low-income settings, combined with limited personnel and equipment, mean that only 20 percent of illegal land occupations result in administrative actions.

Third, once the local government opens an administrative case, a court must review the case and issue a demolition approval. Cases can drag on if the occupants file constitutional rights claims to protect their right to housing. But administrative courts do order demolitions and fines. About 39 percent of administrative actions make it through judicial review to end in a demolition order.

The final part of the enforcement process is the execution of the sanction. Mayors must sign and schedule the removal of an illegal land occupation. But mayors largely refuse to do so. They postpone demolitions through foot-dragging until the orders must be archived. Only 4 percent of court orders result in a sanction being imposed, which is the lowest rate of efficacy in the entire enforcement process. In Ciudad Bolívar, where land invasions continue apace, bureaucrats explained that mayors would not sign demolition orders because "the community does not think that evictions are the solution – they just want housing, and the mayor serves the community."[96] Another district mayor signed eviction orders, but allocated no resources to the demolitions because of

[96] Author interview with housing inspector, District of Ciudad Bolívar, Bogotá, Colombia, July 28, 2010.

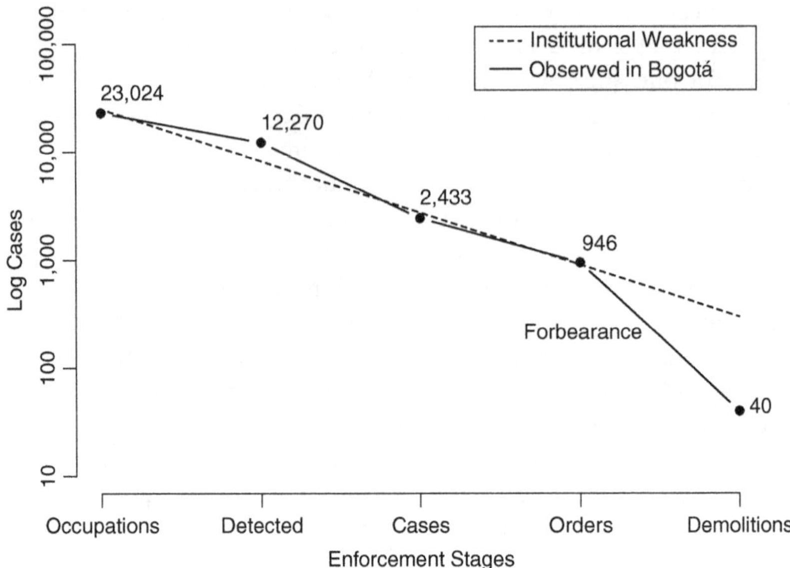


FIGURE 3.5 Enforcement against Illegal Land Occupations, Bogotá, 2006–2011
Sources: Bogotá Water Company (*Empresa de Acueducto, Alcantarillado y Aseo de Bogotá*, EAAB) (occupations); District Housing Secretary (*Secretaría Distrital del Hábitat*, SDH) (detection); Author's Survey of District Housing Offices (cases, orders, and demolitions).

concerns that they would alienate the community and hurt the administration's image.[97]

Figure 3.5 visually summarizes the "leakage" at each step of the enforcement process to produce almost no enforcement. The vertical axis again represents the log of the number of cases so the change can be interpreted as the percent decline at each step; the dotted line shows a constant rate of institutional weakness. In Bogotá, the rate of institutional leakage is about a third, which is higher than observed in Lima. This observation is consistent with evidence that the bureaucracy is stronger in Bogotá (Chapter 1). A sharp deviation occurs from the log linear trend when mayors have to sign eviction orders. This drop reflects a political bottleneck.

It may seem that weak state capacity is the major explanation for enforcement outcomes, given that so few cases even make it to the stage when enforcement orders are issued. However, evictions have a very

[97] Author interview with mayor, District of San Cristóbal, Bogotá, Colombia, July 10, 2010.

strong deterrent effect if executed due to the severity of sanction involved. If the thousand cases that proceeded through the bureaucracy actually ended in evictions, squatters would have a roughly one in twenty-five chance of losing their house and investments. The harshness of the sanction is part of what makes enforcement so repulsive to elected officials, but it also means that even infrequent actions produce substantial deterrence.

Probing further, the demolitions that do occur are designed to minimize the impact on low-income squatters. Roughly half of demolitions resulted from pressure from the Comptroller, which monitors the city's compliance with a court order to protect the forest preserve. Pressure from horizontal accountability authorities has led some mayors to conduct demolitions. One housing bureaucrat explained that the district created the impression of action for the Comptroller without affecting poor voters:

> We did a few easy demolitions of abandoned constructions because technically the mayor is insubordinate if he does not execute the court's orders. But we didn't want a social drama, and *we can't let urban control norms become more important than the need for housing*, so we just did enough to satisfy the Comptroller.[98]

Demolitions also have occurred against upper-class homeowners. The hills surrounding Bogotá are beautiful spots for the wealthy to build weekend homes. Demolitions of these luxury houses are surprising under capacity-based theories because it is cheaper to demolish the homes of the poor (due to their size) and less complicated administratively (due to the poor's inferior access to lawyers and bribes). Yet mayors were willing to evict the wealthy due to the lower social and political costs. The political logic of targeting the nonpoor comes out in the comments of bureaucrats:

> The city mayor doesn't want to disrupt things, where are you going to move all these poor people to? What good would it serve to take away their homes? There is no other place for them to go so you just can't do it ... *It's different when wealthy people decide to build* weekend chalets in the forest preserve. We took down 16 elegant homes last year *because there is no reason that they should be there.*[99]

[98] Author interview with construction and zoning administrator, District of Ciudad Bolívar, Bogotá, Colombia, September 7, 2011, emphasis added.

[99] Author interview with construction and housing director, District of Santa Fe, Bogotá, Colombia, September 7, 2011, emphasis added.

It is useful to pause to consider just how unique these observations are compared to dominant capacity-based explanations. The common view is that states are unable to sanction illegal land occupations, or deliberately unaware of their occurrence. My days spent with bureaucrats giving legal notice to squatters and locating their houses reinforced that enforcement against illegal land occupations is complicated and costly. But process tracing reveals that Bogotá actually maintains substantial knowledge and infrastructure to control illegal land occupations. The city introduced a sophisticated system to monitor land invasions based on satellite imagery and teams of engineers. Still, when the city manages to detect and prosecute illegal occupations, mayors block sanctions when they arrive at their desk. Behavior therefore is inelastic to improvements in the enforcement process. Further evidence that enforcement choices are politically motivated comes from the patterns of selective enforcement in which the poor – who garner greater public sympathy – are less likely to experience evictions than the nonpoor.

Some may ask, why bother with these administrative proceedings at all? The idea of an entire enforcement process that almost never results in a sanction seems Orwellian. The administrative arrangement appears even more bizarre when one considers the political centralization of Bogotá – this is not a circumstance of multiple agents where a central mayor wants to enforce and local elected politicians or bureaucrats act differently. Although I did not receive a simple answer to this puzzle, the choice to invest in an enforcement apparatus makes sense in light of the dynamics of public opinion established in Chapter 2: most citizens (as well as politicians) do not want squatting, but they also object to enforcement and increasingly see it in tension with the right to housing. Building the bureaucratic infrastructure to enforce acts as a deterrent. Just as industrial firms sometimes maintain "excess" production capacity to produce enough goods to drive out potential competitors, governments may invest in enforcement institutions to make it clear to squatters that they can enforce and thus to bolster voluntary societal compliance. Indeed, bureaucrats used this rationalization, or as one told me while reflecting on his fruitless labors: "The idea is to show that the city is watching, and to show that this isn't a no man's land. I can't really stop things, but I can show people that the state exists."[100]

[100] Author interview with housing inspector, District of Ciudad Bolívar, Bogotá, Colombia, July 28, 2010.

### 3.4.5 Political Centralization and Informal Welfare

There is little evidence that politicians in Bogotá use forbearance in a clientelistic manner. The unbiased nature of provision represents a major departure from distributive politics in the twentieth century. Although many things changed with Colombia's political opening, I stress the role of a large electoral district and constitutional reforms. I briefly review the role of these institutional reforms and then sketch the broad differences in enforcement against squatting by mayoral administration. Because squatting largely occurs in poor areas of the city and thus is less visible to the middle class, these shifts are subtler than those in the case of street vending discussed in the next chapter.

Historically, city councilors and legislators exchanged forbearance and public services for votes. City councilors held the most important elected positions in Bogotá and needed few votes to win seats due to high rates of abstention. Land traffickers in the city built political careers by offering squatters access to land for their turnout at the polls. Most famously, former city councilor and senator Alfonso Guerrero Estrada sold 19,000 land plots in more than twenty informal settlements. Guerrero called himself a "revolutionary," who "solved" the housing needs of poor communities and ran for his own "Bread and Roofs" Liberal Party (*Partido Liberal Pan y Techo*). Guerrero engaged in turnout buying, granting lots in exchange for squatters' electoral participation. He also made squatters' lives difficult if they did not support him; for instance, he demanded loan payments or sold occupied homes to other families.[101]

City councilors held immense power over squatters because they sat on the boards of public service companies and could extend services and property titles to their politically favored areas. Petitions from informal settlements promised votes in exchange for services and legal assistance. For instance, an entreaty to a city councilor for the extension of the water system concludes: "Do not doubt that we, in our capacity as voting inhabitants of this city, are willing to help you in whatever you think necessary."[102]

101 On turnout buying more generally, see Nichter (2008). Another example of a Bogotá land trafficker is Rafael Forero Fetecua, who won seats on the City Council and Congress. See "Los dueños del sur," *El Tiempo* November 4, 1999; "A Guerrero Estrada le premiaron," *El Tiempo* February 20, 1999; "Cuando la Cruz decidieron vender Bosa," *El Tiempo* November 5, 1999.

102 Letter from Junta de Acción Comunal, Barrio Unir II to city councilor, June 1992, Bogotá's Department of Planning Archive (*Secretaría Distrital de Planeación*).

This pattern of clientelistic relations broke down with institutional reforms that removed city councilors from the boards of public service companies and gave greater powers to a single elected mayor. City mayors now exercise little discretion over processing squatters' claims for service provision and legal recognition. These tasks are delegated to city bureaucrats, who follow broad directives about enforcement but rarely manipulate outcomes in individual cases (Jaramillo, Alfonso, and Hataya 1996: 39). Unlike in Lima, voters elect one mayor for the entire city of Bogotá. Mayors have incentives to make broad electoral appeals and media coverage of mayoral actions increases the reputational costs of enforcement.

Elected mayors have taken clear stances toward illegal land occupations to advance their core constituencies' interests and their ideological beliefs. For instance, the 1995 election of Antanas Mockus, a former university rector and philosopher, marked an end to clientelistic negotiations with squatter settlements. Mockus was elected on an anti-politics, post-materialist left platform. He considered the tolerance of squatting a "shortcut" in which the consequences for quality of life, shared citizenship rights, and urban planning were discounted (Mockus 2012). Mockus therefore tried to enforce: he ordered one of the largest evictions in Bogotá's history, removing 7,000 people from a newly formed settlement, and conducted 130 housing demolitions throughout the city.[103] Mockus nevertheless recognized the high reputational costs of his choices. As Mockus explained his reaction to a land invasion that occurred early in his term, "I didn't have any interest in my second day as mayor to begin with an eviction and all the media attention that it generated about not caring about the poor" – but he chose to enforce because he "didn't want to create a precedent."[104]

Likewise, Enrique Peñalosa (1998–2000) saw minimal advantages from enforcement against squatting. Peñalosa attracted the support of nonpoor constituents, and as we will see in the next chapter, he enforced strongly against street vendors. But he largely supported a position of social regulation against squatters. In other words, Peñalosa disapproved of illegal land occupations, but saw coercive sanctions as too harsh in the absence of housing alternatives. Peñalosa was the first mayor to invest in

[103] Statistics come from the 2008 locality reports to the District Planning Secretary, but only are available for Mockus's second term and exclude the district of Santa Fe due to differences in reporting.

[104] Author interview with Antanas Mockus, Bogotá, Colombia, July 29, 2013.

social interest housing programs at the city level and he legalized a record number of informal settlements (Chapter 6). However, the small scale of the city's housing projects meant that the city failed to crowd out squatting. Peñalosa was explicit that the constraint on enforcement was housing policy, not police or bureaucratic capacity. In his view, the state's growing coercive capacity actually threatened the poor's welfare: "The problem is that as the city becomes more sophisticated and richer, there are more controls and this is very bad because we are controlling informal construction but we are not offering any alternative."[105]

The election of Luis Garzón (2004–2007), who represented a labor-based left party (*Polo Democrático Alternativo*, Polo), marked a shift in core constituency. Garzón was elected with the overwhelming support of poor voters, and in line with this commitment, he protected illegal settlements by the poor. Tellingly, in the case of illegal land occupations by upper-class groups, Garzón, as well as his successor Samuel Moreno (2008–2011), conducted demolitions.[106] The monitoring of illegal land invasions improved during Moreno's term, partly in response to a court decision that ordered the city to protect the environmental preserve in its eastern hillside. But Moreno also rejected several measures that would have increased sanctions, such as the creation of an environmental police force to monitor encroachments and conduct evictions immediately.[107] The enforcement process tracing exercise was conducted on data primarily from Garzón and Moreno's years in office, and thus reflects the Left's defense of poor squatters against enforcement.

Gustavo Petro (2012–2015), a left-wing mayor who broke with the Polo Party, followed a similar trajectory and defended squatters against enforcement in office. Petro signed a pact to protect all poor households who built in the eastern hillside and to punish wealthy ones. As he told the press, "We only want to protect land in the Forest Preserve that ... *is used by low-income neighborhoods*, we do not want a single square meter more of the hills touched by construction industry interests and to capture

105 Author interview with Enrique Peñalosa, Bogotá, Colombia, September 7, 2011.

106 These land occupations occurred primarily in the nonpoor districts of Chapinero and Usaquén. See, for example, "Se inicia demolición de construcciones sin permisos en zonas forestales de Bogotá," *Caracol* June 20, 2006.

107 The Comptroller has issued a series of reports on the government's compliance and noted the failure of the city to create a new police force as the Court recommended or to conduct permanent operations with the existing police; see Contraloría de Bogotá, "Gestión adelantada por las autoridades distritales en el manejo de los cerros orientales de Bogotá," 2004–2008, p. 37–8.

rents that end up impoverishing the city."[108] Petro thus staked out a general position toward squatter settlements built by the poor, not simply allowing some to stay and removing others. He did so on the basis of a constitutional right to housing, although the court ruling empowered him to clear the forest preserve. As one local politician put it, "The law is there if the mayor wants to enforce it, and the mayor does when the middle class is involved . . . But there's no political will to control construction by the poor because if the mayor ordered evictions, he would become very unpopular. Really no mayor could do it."[109]

In sum, only mayors with nonpoor constituencies have been willing to pay the political costs of evicting the poor. Even these mayors have recognized the electoral repercussions and pushed for improved housing policies as a precondition for enforcement. Mayors with poor core constituencies have tried to enforce against the nonpoor, but have avoided enforcement against the poor. These enforcement positions have affected broad class groups, rather than specific squatter settlements as part of quid pro quo exchanges. These observations cut against theories that view forbearance purely as rent-seeking behavior: it is unlikely that poor squatters can organize and bribe officials to stop enforcement more effectively than the nonpoor. They also provide little support for capacity-based theories centered on the police and bureaucracy. The issue is not whether Colombia can bring in the police to evict squatters; it is whether the poor have anywhere else to live.

## 3.5 SUBSTITUTIVE HOUSING POLICY AND ENFORCEMENT IN SANTIAGO

In contrast to Peru and Colombia, Chile reshaped the electoral politics of enforcement through its housing policy. Although substitutive housing provision ultimately reduced material demands for illegal land occupations, its initial effects were on mass attitudes and political signals. The public held national authorities responsible for housing provision and turned against squatters because they jeopardized state solutions. Whereas politicians are perceived to lose electoral support if they enforce against squatters in Bogotá and Lima, enforcement

[108] "Petro no permitirá construcciones en los Cerros Orientales," *El Espectador*, July 26, 2013.

[109] Author interview with Ramiro Ojeda, local councilor, District of Ciudad Bolívar, Bogotá, Colombia, October 14, 2011.

illustrates a commitment to help the poor through the welfare state and uphold property laws in Santiago. Hence, it is in the electoral interests of local politicians to enforce. Enforcement, in turn, has led voters and mayors to push to improve state housing policies, which further reinforces the role of state housing authorities in meeting demand.

### 3.5.1 Crowding Out Squatting

On the eve of its democratic transition, Chile faced a serious housing shortage. Half a million households, or a fifth of the urban population, lived in overcrowded conditions in urban areas (Arriagada Luco and Moreno Crossley 2006: 29–30). The democratic transition brought an intense focus on how to resolve the poor's housing demand to prevent land invasions. I elaborate on the politics of these programs in Chapter 6, but some stylized facts give a sense for the scale of the investment. About a fifth of Santiago's population lives in state housing. The government produces more social interest housing than the increase in demand, making Chile the only Latin American country to reduce its housing deficit (Arriagada Luco and Moreno Crossley 2006).

Nevertheless, in the early 1990s, most applicants waited five to ten years in the housing queue. The government also struggled with program targeting. The lowest two quintiles received just 25 percent of total housing budget outlays in 1992, and the housing shortage among the poorest quintiles fell by only 12 percent despite massive investments (Marcano and Ruprah 2008: 6, 10). Thus, while housing policies absorbed some demand, it would be a stretch to say that Chile stopped land invasions by offering an immediate resolution to the poor's material demands.

Rather, the Chilean government changed the incentives for land invasions by refraining from post-hoc housing policies, such as property titling and slum upgrading. Because housing programs promised property ownership within a span of years and land invasions were unlikely to end in legal recognition, the attractiveness of land invasions fell. The Housing Ministry maintains a census of informal settlements, according to which the settlement population in Santiago dropped from 10,162 in 1995 to 3,179 in 2006 (MINVU 2013: 104).[110] The few land invasions that have occurred under democracy have aimed to pressure the government to

[110] Nationwide, the squatter settlement numbers were higher, with 972 settlements housing 105,888 people, according to the University of Chile's 1996 Census of Informal Settlements (*Catastro de Asentamientos Informales*).

improve the quality of state housing programs (Chapter 6). State expenditures did not solve all housing problems, but they did shift incentives and, as I turn to next, they concentrated popular demands on the state housing system.

### 3.5.2 Demand Reinforcement

A central goal of housing policy under democracy was to channel popular demands and organizing to state housing authorities so they would not explode in land takings. To do so, the government had citizens create housing committees to apply for state subsidies. Applicants received priority if they applied for housing as a group. Housing committees had to acquire legal status to apply – which they would lose, along with all social benefits, if they attempted to take land illegally. This process inverted the Peruvian and Colombian ones in which squatters first seized land and then were encouraged to register their neighborhood associations with the state. Local housing committees proliferated in Chile. Since the transition, more than 100,000 households have applied for housing subsidies each year (CChC 2011).

In addition to collective applications, the government established a transparent housing queue so applicants knew where they stood in the process. Applicants opened bank accounts and began to save for the deposit on their new home. Accordingly, even if they did not receive a house immediately, they were committed financially to the system. The transparent enrollment process – combined with rapid construction and concrete personal financial investments – helped instill a shared belief that the state would address housing demands with time. The head of the Christian Democratic Party's shantytown unit praised the housing policy design because it "gives people hope and *makes them believe that the government is with them*. If these mechanisms didn't exist, the people would have exploded" (Hipsher 1996: 286, emphasis added). By organizing the poor into housing associations and waiting lists, the government also created a source of social pressure to improve housing programs. Invasions stopped because "the housing queue and credit system were so institutionalized," said one former housing official, and "people bought into the system even when they were dissatisfied so they were invested in fixing it."[111]

[111] Author interview with former housing official, MINVU, Santiago, Chile, June 28, 2012.

Although there were few attempted land invasions, local mayors and bureaucrats said that residents reported those that occurred immediately. Squatting was seen as a threat to public housing programs. Housing committees feared that squatters would occupy state land and undermine their ability to access a house through formal channels.[112] Common impressions of state officials were that land invaders were impatient – they "tried to jump the queue"[113] – or fraudulent and lazy – "they are people who don't qualify for state housing" or "don't want to pay the monthly installments" required in housing projects.[114] To see this difference more systematically, I asked bureaucrats whether they believed that illegal land occupations were justified because the poor had no other means to access housing. In Lima and Bogotá, roughly half of bureaucrats agreed with this statement. Not a single housing official justified land takings in Santiago.

### 3.5.3 Legalism Signals

The electoral costs of enforcement are much lower in a functioning housing system. In my survey of bureaucrats, Chilean mayors were thought to gain political support through enforcement, quite distinct from Lima and Bogotá. Bureaucrats explained that enforcement shows respect for state housing programs and the rule of law. As one bureaucrat clarified, enforcement "just makes clear that the mayor is committed to the state's housing policies."[115] Enforcement does not convey pro-poor sympathies; it conveys pro-state ones.

Cooperation with national authorities to provide housing – not forbearance – signals a mayor's commitment to poor constituents. Local mayors in poor districts believe that they are judged on their willingness to generate housing projects.[116] Consistent with this fact, half of mayoral

[112] Author interview with Pedro Isla, mayor, District of San Ramón, Santiago, Chile, June 21, 2012; Author interview with director of operations, District of Peñalólen, January 11, 2012.

[113] Author interview with head of rents, District of San Bernardo, Santiago, Chile, June 23, 2012.

[114] Author interview with director of inspections, District of Peñalolén, Santiago, Chile, January 11, 2012.

[115] Author interview with director of inspections, District of Peñalolén, Santiago, Chile, January 11, 2012.

[116] Author interview with Pedro Isla, mayor, District of San Ramón, June 21, 2012. This association was particularly true in the 1990s. The role of local mayors was reduced when collective applications were eliminated, and housing subsidies could be used to

campaigns in poor districts in 2008 involved concrete promises to generate housing projects or tried to dispel rumors that they had not done enough. For example, Mayor Claudio Orrego cited as one of the "11 most frequent lies" about his campaign that "he did not support overcrowded residents and refused to change zoning requirements to create new social interest housing."[117] Local councilors in Santiago described their work in terms of constituency service, but unlike in Bogotá, they described assistance in accessing housing projects as one of their tasks. Meanwhile, no mayor or councilor mentioned support for squatters or titling in their campaign platforms. Substitutive housing policy thus displaces demands to the state as the central provider of housing; local politicians function as intermediaries who increase pressure to improve access to national programs.

### 3.5.4 Mayoral Enforcement Decisions

Enforcement process tracing is senseless in Santiago because the government has so thoroughly suppressed land invasions. The best test of my theory instead comes from comparing responses to land invasions before and after housing policy got up to speed. My claim is that Chile struggled to evict squatters prior to investments in housing policy, whereas politicians were willing to do so once they could offer housing alternatives. The police force remained constant across the two periods, given that Chile did not disband or reorganize the police with democratization.

Consider how the government handled one of the first land invasions under democracy. In 1992, 850 families invaded land in Peñalolén forming the Campamento Esperanza Andina. Government officials condemned the invasion. With the election of Christian Democrat Patricio Aylwin as president in 1989, members of Congress, the Cabinet, and party leaders rejected land invasions as a threat to state housing policy and the democratic regime (Hipsher 1996: 283). But the government's housing policy remained in its infancy. Officials faced a tough dilemma: on the one hand, they feared that evicting squatters would be excessively similar to the dictatorship's tactics and generate a backlash among their

purchase existing constructions. In addition, mayors in poor districts have come to be wary of new housing projects given that the compensation to the district is insufficient for the demands placed on local services by increasing the number of low-income residents.

117 "Las 11 mentiras más frecuentes para desprestigiar al Alcalde Orrego y las verdades que debe saber," Campaign Pamphlet for Claudio Orrego, August 8, 2008.

low-income voters and, on the other hand, they worried that forbearance or relocation would encourage further invasions and possibly regime breakdown. Ultimately, the government did not use police force. Officials negotiated the expropriation of the land in favor of the squatters (Figueroa 2003: 563). Hence, before substitutive housing policy was in place in Santiago, politicians faced tensions similar to those observed in Lima and Bogotá.

As housing programs developed and reached poor households in the 1990s and 2000s, mayors committed to the control of land invasions. Mayors report immediately stopping land invasions.[118] This firmness also can be observed in how mayors claim that they would react to hypothetical occupations. Even politicians from the Communist Party, which has a long history of involvement in land invasions in Chile, scoffed at the idea of forbearance: "Obviously, we cannot return to the old system where people invaded land. We now have a housing system to help people who need it."[119]

A potential counterargument is that the threat of a coup, not substitutive housing policies, led Chile to enforce against land invasions. Hipsher (1996), for instance, demonstrates that social actors held back from taking land because they did not want to repeat the radical redistributive claims that led to the breakdown of democracy. It is unclear if substitutive social policies could have controlled land invasions in "normal" political times. I agree that Chile's political history made it easier to thwart land invasions through housing investments. Nonetheless, as I show in Chapter 6, the main effect of the precarious historical moment was a rare political consensus on the need for housing policy to prevent land invasions. The persistence of popular condemnation of squatting as disrespectful of state housing policies after threats to democracy eased attests to the role of substitutive housing policies in shifting public sentiment and mayoral behavior, rather than the military waiting in the wings.

To date, Santiago is the only case of a large city in the region that has eliminated the formation of illegal settlements through social policy mechanisms. The fact that the public condemns land invasions as a form of cheating suggests that state capacity plays a role in enforcement, although not the one conventionally discussed. Popular rejection

118 Author interview with Pedro Isla, mayor, District of San Ramón, June 21, 2012.

119 Author interview Tamara Homel Navarro, local councilor, District of Pudahuel, Santiago, Chile, January 17, 2012.

of squatting was aided by a belief that Chile's housing system worked in a fair, transparent way. Were programs riddled with patronage or mere token initiatives, perhaps the poor would have embraced land invasions as a justified response to state dysfunction. Instead, Chile created a sustained and transparent system to allocate housing. It also put money behind it. Mayors therefore could claim that they promoted the poor's well-being through an orderly use of district land for state housing projects. Substitutive housing policies displaced demands to state authorities and shifted the incentives for district mayors to enforce.

## 3.6 CONCLUSION

The idea that squatting is a safety net in contexts where welfare states fail to deliver is well established. The usual logic is a functional one in which the poor search for housing alternatives when the state offers none. This chapter moved beyond this logic to show how national housing policies affect not only material needs but also popular organizing, political signals, and, ultimately, enforcement choices.

Complementary housing policies, such as those in Peru and Colombia, heightened the electoral benefits from forbearance. Inadequate housing policies led the urban poor to seize land and mayors to tolerate invasions in Lima and Bogotá. In a politically decentralized city like Lima, mayors in poor districts provided forbearance to win votes, and often negotiated subsequent service and legal benefits in a clientelistic fashion. In a centralized city like Bogotá, the absence of effective housing policy encouraged mayors, and especially those with poor core constituents, to favor forbearance. The large district size and limited political discretion gave forbearance and post-hoc policies a more programmatic character. The contrast of substitutive housing policy in Chile reinforced how housing policy structures enforcement incentives. Chile's housing policy reflected a deliberate attempt – albeit in very special historical circumstances – to get local mayors and citizens to overcome instincts to permit land takings. Investments in housing policy then encouraged citizens to demand and receive more from the state, while condemning squatting as a threat to state programs.

In many ways, it is unsurprising that a capable state like Chile both builds houses for the poor and prevents land seizures, while a far feebler state like Peru manages neither task. This chapter has taken seriously concerns that weak state capacity determines both a country's social policy expenditures and its enforcement actions, and it has used a rich array of administrative and qualitative data to pull apart different dimensions of state weakness. What is novel in the case study evidence is the role that social policy investments, rather than coercive or administrative capacity, play in shaping politicians' enforcement decisions. Chapter 5 further strengthens the claim that enforcement was not an inevitable result of Chile's capable institutions, legalistic culture, or the legacy of dictatorship. In a context where the Chilean government has been unable to resolve the poor's needs – employment – politicians have pursued forbearance against street vending as an informal welfare policy.

# 4

# When Politicians Choose Forbearance

## *Core Constituencies and Street Vending*

> Street vendors receive a "subsidy" in the form of free rent, public services, and a way to make a living. This is the bare minimum of what a just society owes the poor.
>
> – Yezid García, city councilor, Bogotá, Colombia.[1]

The previous chapter showed how the social policy context results in divergent enforcement incentives and outcomes for squatters. This chapter takes up the challenge of explaining divergent enforcement responses in a context in which social policy substitutes are uniformly unavailable: street vending. If we expect similar responses from cities with comparable political and economic profiles, then we would expect parallel courses of enforcement from governments in Bogotá and Lima. Both cities lack substantial employment programs to substitute for street vending. If anything, Lima confronted street vendors with fewer institutional resources and faced a deeper economic crisis. And yet, Lima responded aggressively to street vendors in the 1990s and largely has defended central city streets since then. Bogotá allowed street vendors to expand throughout the city just as the economy boomed in the 2000s. What can account for these differences?

In this chapter, I highlight the role of core constituencies in explaining when forbearance occurs over time. Citywide electoral districts, such as those in Bogotá and Lima, incorporate many class groups. Mayors can win office by mobilizing the support of divergent core constituencies. I argue that politicians elected by poor core constituencies are more likely

[1] Author interview with Yezid García, city councilor (2011–2015), Progressive Movement, Bogotá, Colombia, September 15, 2011.

to promote forbearance to lift local welfare and signal their commitments to the poor. Politicians may incorporate the interests of the core constituency that elected them because they seek the group's continued electoral support for purposes of reelection or election to higher office. Other politicians select enforcement policies based on their ideological views, which then attract certain class groups. To be consistent with my theory, mayors who enforce against street vendors based on their ideological views should alienate poor voters.

Unlike the previous chapter on squatting, forbearance toward street vending at the city level is an unstable outcome because of the visible changes engendered by different enforcement actions and the fact that vending occurs across city space. Past forbearance inflates the costs imposed on the public and increases vendors' wealth, making vendors appear less deserving. These shifts make it easier for candidates to use enforcement appeals to mobilize nonpoor core constituencies, and even some poor voters, to win office. In a symmetric manner, enforcement builds sympathy with street vendors and spurs the poor (and some segment of the nonpoor) to favor candidates who propose forbearance. These cycles are most pronounced in politically centralized cities, where enforcement results in more uniform foreclosure of work opportunities and where forbearance appeals take on a quasi-programmatic character. In politically decentralized cities, city mayors can control vending in the downtown and allow district mayors to absorb unemployed workers and negotiate with street vendors in a clientelistic manner. Given the complexity of public opinion, putting forward a unidirectional explanation of how electoral preferences influence politicians, though attractively parsimonious, would be unrealistic. But electoral incentives are, once we account for shifts in mass opinion in response to visible enforcement acts, the major precipitant of enforcement outcomes.

The juxtaposition of these city cases highlights that enforcement is largely inelastic to fluctuations in state capacity. State capacity theories cannot explain either forbearance in conditions of institutional strength and substantial revenues, as in Bogotá in the mid-2000s, or enforcement in the context of weak institutions and economic malaise, as in Lima in the mid-1990s. A focus on mayors' core constituencies, in contrast, makes sense of both of these seeming incongruities. Empirically, I rely on a mixture of government documents; interviews with mayors, leaders of street-vending associations, and city officials; and newspaper accounts to reconstruct these swings in enforcement. Given the relative lack of studies of city politics (*c.f.* Davis 1994; Dietz and Myers 2002; Moncada 2016;

Pasotti 2009), this chapter provides substantial detail on the political alignments in city elections. I show that street vending has been a central – although certainly not the only – issue in the rise and fall of city mayors since the introduction of direct elections.

This chapter proceeds in four major parts. I begin by comparing objective facts about street vending, employment policy, and economic conditions in Bogotá and Lima. I also review newspaper coverage of vending to give a sense of its changing centrality to city politics. Second, I show how mayors elected with poor core constituencies in Bogotá have used forbearance to build electoral support among the poor, despite significant institutional improvements. Next, I establish similar enforcement variation with core constituencies in Lima. The election of a mayor who drew on middle-class support explains the unexpected turn to enforcement in the mid-1990s, while the continued election of mayors with mixed-class constituencies led to enforcement continuity in the 2000s. I conclude with a review of why state capacity and interest groups cannot explain the enforcement outcomes.

## 4.1 A COMPARISON OF STREET VENDING

Street vendors exemplify the gap between law and reality in Latin American cities. On paper, cities ban street vendors or restrict their operation to specific hours, zones, and products. In practice, street vendors proliferate. Although the poor work in many informal jobs, I concentrate on street vending because it involves the taking of public property, as with squatting. In this section, I introduce the basic features of street vending, as well as trends in its growth and reception.

### 4.1.1 Street Vending and the Law

Some people become street vendors as a temporary stopgap activity when confronted with unemployment, but many others become street vendors as a more permanent activity due to the lack of better job alternatives. Especially in the latter case, street vending has no clear social policy substitute. Many policies, from tax codes to industrial policy, affect employment levels. I consider only policies that result in active employment, namely, job creation and intermediation programs, as social policy substitutes. By most standard measures, Latin American governments invest little in employment policy. Chile, Colombia, and Peru all spend less than 0.2 percent of GDP on employment policy, compared to

1.7 percent of GDP in an average OECD country.[2] Unemployment insurance is largely nonexistent, or limited to formal-sector workers.[3] So, as I return to in Chapter 6, few government programs exist to offer alternative employment to the urban poor.

Stationary vendors cause a host of negative externalities, including problems with transit, urban planning, noise, garbage, and public health and safety risks. Some vendors also sell goods that compete with licensed businesses. For instance, one study estimates that street vendors in Bogotá reduce commercial sales and formal-sector employment by 14 and 16 percent, respectively (Rocha, Sánchez, and García 2009). As with other forms of informal commerce, most street vendors do not comply with tax or labor laws. Beyond the direct material harms, business and middle-class groups often blame street vendors for the deterioration of public spaces, which they believe to damage a city's image, reduce investment, and increase crime. The idea that signs of minor disorder correlate with serious criminal behavior – or the "broken windows" theory of crime (Kelling and Wilson 1982) – gained popularity in the 1980s and 1990s. From this perspective, the proliferation of street vendors indicates police neglect and encourages harder crime.

The majority of street vendors are poor. The income distribution, however, is skewed, with a small fraction of vendors earning incomes comparable to successful small business owners. For example, a 2001 survey in Bogotá showed that the majority of vendors earned below minimum wage, but 24 percent earned a monthly income between one and three minimum wages, and 13 percent earned more than three minimum wages (Roever 2006: 9). In Lima, household surveys suggest that 78 percent of street vendors earn less than minimum wage, and 15 percent earn below two minimum wages (INEI 2011; Appendix B). Vendors who work in city centers, and particularly those with fixed stands in the streets, tend to be better off than those who work in the urban periphery (Bromley 2000). Incomes also vary over time with government policy. Forbearance

[2] OECD Social Expenditure Statistics Database, 2013, Public Spending on Active Labor Market Policy and Public Unemployment Spending. Statistics on employment spending in Peru and Colombia come from their respective labor ministries. Although these statistics do not factor in government-mandated but employer-provided protection, such measures do not protect workers in the informal sector.

[3] Brazil is an exception that spends substantial sums on unemployment insurance (Holland and Schneider 2017). Unemployed and informal-sector workers also mobilized, and the government responded with a substantial employment program in Argentina (Garay 2007). But even in Europe, unemployment insurance was introduced later than other social welfare policies (Mares 2003).

allows vendors to accumulate wealth and capital, and thus incomes tend to be higher in these periods. Street vendors thus frequently form associations to protect their right to work in lucrative public spaces.[4]

The transfers at stake from forbearance toward street vendors are substantial. Although estimates vary wildly, most observers concur that, at peak, there were more than 300,000 street vendors in Lima and 200,000 in Bogotá. In my survey, one-third of poor respondents in Bogotá have depended on income from street vending at some point. Each vendor receives a benefit in the form of a place to sell their goods or services, rather than needing to rent a space. In central Lima, unlicensed vendors report that they pay an average of $130 in monthly rent when evicted from city sidewalks. Again, I use rent payments, given that vendors often report earning less in formal stands, as a lower-bound estimate of the vendors' willingness to pay to sell on city streets. This calculation translates into a total subsidy of $187 million annually, using my conservative estimate of 117,000 illegal vendors in 2011.[5]

Street vending violates property laws when vendors occupy streets, sidewalks, and parks intended for public use without authorization. In Bogotá, the government is prohibited by the Constitution from licensing or renting public space to vendors. As Article 82 reads, "It is the duty of the state to protect the integrity of public space and its assignment to common use, which has priority over individual interests."[6] City mayors have the responsibility to recover and protect public space. In Lima, the law is more complicated, consisting of both city- and district-level ordinances. Street vending is prohibited unless district governments designate specific areas and licenses for vendors to work.[7] I focus on street vending that occurs without government authorization.

In general, when governments try to control street vending, they use strategies to make it unprofitable to work as a vendor. The police impose

[4] Around half of vendors in central city areas in Lima participate in associations, while rates are likely lower in the urban periphery (Roever 2005). A large-scale survey in Bogotá found that a third of vendors participate in associations (FVP 2004).

[5] Household surveys put the number of street vendors much higher, suggesting that 10 percent of actively employed workers are street vendors, full or part time. But they do not distinguish between licensed and unlicensed vendors, as I attempted to in my survey.

[6] Even before constitutional reforms, Bogotá's 1989 Urban Law recognized public space as collective property that could not be sold or rented, negating licensing agreements previously used. The governing legislation for the city (*Estatuto Orgánico de Bogotá*) reaffirmed the mayor's exclusive control over street vending.

[7] There is wide variation in the licensing practices of local governments. For an excellent study of the overlap of district rules and fee practices, see Roever (2005).

fines, confiscate merchandise and equipment, and dismantle stands to deter vendors. Compared to squatting, it is much easier to revoke forbearance. Politicians can use their control of police and local inspectors to order operations and fines against vendors. Enforcement, of course, is not the only policy option to manage street vendors, but it is an essential complement to alternatives like licensing, relocation, verbal warnings, and small business promotion.

Although the police control vending at the street level, politicians receive the blame and credit for enforcement because sanctions occur in public view. For example, I found in my survey that 77 percent of Bogotá residents name politicians as responsible for the control of street vendors. Only 12 percent hold the police responsible. Likewise, Lima residents associated the control of street vending with city mayors. A third of the public, for instance, names the recovery of the city center from street vendors in the late 1990s as "the greatest public works project of past decades," beating out major mayoral initiatives like highway construction and a public water park (IOP 2008).

### 4.1.2 Objective Trends in Street Vending

Street vending, like the informal economy as a whole, declines as high-quality employment becomes available. Thus, for a comparison of enforcement policy, it is necessary to establish that the aggressiveness of responses cannot be entirely explained by the most obvious economic drivers – that is, that governments respond directly to the business cycle, or even more pointedly, to the number of street vendors. These are tricky tasks given the lack of historical data on enforcement and street vending. I do my best to reconstruct broad trends in enforcement policy and street vending and compare them to economic trends.

First, I classify each administration's enforcement policy based on government and newspaper reports, looking at both "punctuated" operations in which authorities target a geographic area for the removal (and occasional relocation) of street vendors, and "continuous" operations in which authorities try to prevent street vendors from working in the streets through fines, decommission of merchandise or equipment, and blockades. Routine actions are harder to measure, although most authorities consider them essential for the control of street vending. A mayor pursues a forbearance policy if she (1) postpones or avoids punctuated enforcement operations against street vendors, or (2) blocks routine control through the withdrawal of police resources or the suspension of sanctions.

A mayor pursues an enforcement policy if she uses punctuated operations and control procedures to maintain recovered public spaces in at least some segment of the city. This two-part definition thus captures whether a government is willing to impose costs on street vendors to deter their action.[8]

According to this classification, only two mayors in Bogotá and four mayors in Lima have enforced street-vending regulations.[9] They have done so under diverse economic and institutional conditions. Figure 4.1 places vertical lines around the time periods in which city governments enforced against street vendors. To see whether enforcement accompanied improvements in the business cycle, I plot the economic growth rate measured as the percent change in GDP (solid line) and the urban unemployment rate (dashed line).

Economic conditions provide limited leverage to understand enforcement. The first major enforcement episode in Bogotá and Lima occurs in the mid-1990s. As summarized in Chapter 2, Colombia maintained stable, if middling, growth rates throughout Latin America's debt crises. The economy entered its worst recession and urban unemployment rates soared above 20 percent in the late 1990s. Mayors moved to enforce against street vendors as the economy plunged. Peru suffered a profound economic crisis in the late 1980s. Although Peru's economy had begun to recover when enforcement operations started, economic conditions were hardly robust. Growth averaged just 2 percent from 1996 through 2002, and more than half of jobs created were in the informal sector. Yet enforcement peaked.

More puzzling still, Bogotá and Lima have followed divergent enforcement tracks in the 2000s. Both countries saw strong growth thanks to a commodities boom. Urban poverty rates halved during the period. Yet, while Bogotá eased enforcement for most of the 2000s, Lima consistently moved forward with operations. These differences make it hard to believe that governments passively respond to changes in the business cycle. Enforcement, especially in the 2000s, was inelastic to resources.

[8] A more permissive categorization might take occasional crackdowns against street vendors as sufficient evidence of an enforcement policy. However, sporadic operations produce limited deterrence because street vendors return after operations end. A more restrictive categorization might require a certain frequency or spatial coverage of enforcement actions. But determining any minimum threshold is arbitrary and misleading because the population of street vendors varies with time.

[9] A third period of enforcement began in Bogotá after the focus of this study with the return of Peñalosa to the mayor's office in 2016.

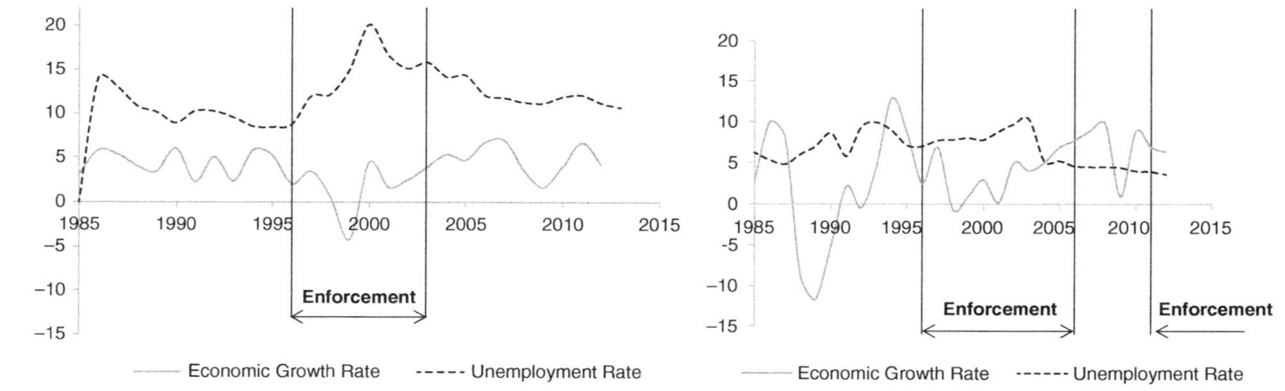


FIGURE 4.1 Economic Growth, Unemployment, and Enforcement in Bogotá (left) and Lima (right), 1985–2013
Sources: Author's classification (enforcement); World Bank (GDP growth); International Labor Organization (urban unemployment rate as percent of total labor force).

The number of street vendors also does not predict government enforcement actions, although data limitations prevent a rigorous evaluation. In the 1990s, the maximum estimates (usually coming from chambers of commerce that advocated enforcement measures) put the numbers around 250,000 for Bogotá, compared to estimates approaching 350,000 for Lima. The modal numbers, often reproduced in newspaper reports in the 1990s, put the estimates closer to 150,000 for Bogotá and 250,000 for Lima. In the 2000s, both cities saw declines in the number of vendors. In my survey, I found just 89,000 vendors in Bogotá and 117,000 in Lima. While the number of vendors has been falling in Lima, it has grown in Bogotá in the 2000s, perhaps ascending as high as 150,000 vendors.[10] Given common improvements in economic growth and the broadly similar trends in street vending, it is hard to understand the divergence in enforcement in Bogotá and Lima.

### 4.1.3 Subjective Perceptions of Street Vending

Subjective perceptions of street vending have changed over time and differ between cities. The survey data presented in Chapter 2 focused on a single moment in time. Yet I suspect that public support for vending varies with economic conditions and past enforcement policies. First, street vendors cause harms that increase with the number of vendors and generate middle-class (and even lower-class) opposition. Economic downturns or past forbearance expand the number of vendors and thus can heighten class conflict around street vending. Second, forbearance allows street vendors to accumulate wealth and form associations. Although this generates economic and organizational resources to push for favorable vending policies, it also can turn the public against vendors. Entrenched street vendors create barriers to entry that reduce the insurance value of vending to the poor; wealth also makes vendors' claims that they will be unable to work or rent storefronts if evicted from city streets less credible. Combined, these two effects make it easier for politicians to build enforcement coalitions in periods of large numbers of street vendors and past forbearance.

I would ideally measure how views toward vending vary through historical poll data. Unfortunately, pollsters have not asked about perceptions of

[10] News reports from 2014 put the number of vendors between 120,000 and 150,000 due to the leniency of Mayor Gustavo Petro. See "Vendedores ambulantes por doquier," *Semana* May 31, 2014.

street vendors. To get a basic sense of the changes in public interest in and sympathy for street vendors in past decades, I examined two national newspapers, *El Tiempo* in Colombia and *El Comercio* in Peru. I chose these papers because they have been published continuously and have the highest circulation over the period studied. News coverage both shapes and responds to readers' preferences, and therefore cannot capture underlying attitudes or a representative sample in the same way that survey data do. But it can provide a rough sense for how preoccupations change, especially among an educated, middle-class readership. In their respective media markets, both papers are situated on the center-right. Given possible differences in editorial slant (*El Comercio* leans farther to the right than *El Tiempo*, but so do Peruvian elites), comparisons can most reliably be drawn over time within each country.

The number of articles on street vending gives us a sense of issue salience. An average of fifty-five and seventeen articles appeared each year in Bogotá and Lima, respectively, between 1990 and 2010. At peak interest, more than a hundred articles a year appeared about street vending in each city. For comparison's sake, consider that Gilens (2000) classic study of welfare politics finds a maximum of twenty-five stories per year about poverty and welfare appearing in all American news magazines. Street vending is an issue of significant discussion in Bogotá and Lima.

Interest in street vending differs over time and across cities. Figure 4.2 shows that concern about street vending peaked in the 1990s, probably due to the large number of vendors. What is most interesting is that street vending remains a salient issue in Bogotá, but it fades from public interest in Lima in the 2000s, despite similar trends in vending. I suspect that the continued debate over street-vending management in Bogotá reflects that mayors have tolerated vendors in central, middle-class parts of the city. Lima has a hybrid political system in which the city mayor controls vending in the downtown and district mayors set local policy. Once downtown and nonpoor districts cleared street vendors in the late 1990s, street vending disappeared from middle-class preoccupations and newspaper discussion.

The shaded bars in Figure 4.2 track whether street vendors are portrayed in a sympathetic or unsympathetic light. Sympathetic portrayals include human-interest stories (sympathetic narratives) focused on a single street vendor's plight, such as a laid-off factory worker or a single mother who tries to put her children through school by working as a street vendor. They also include reports (sympathetic polemics) that tie street vending to external conditions like unemployment, political violence, and

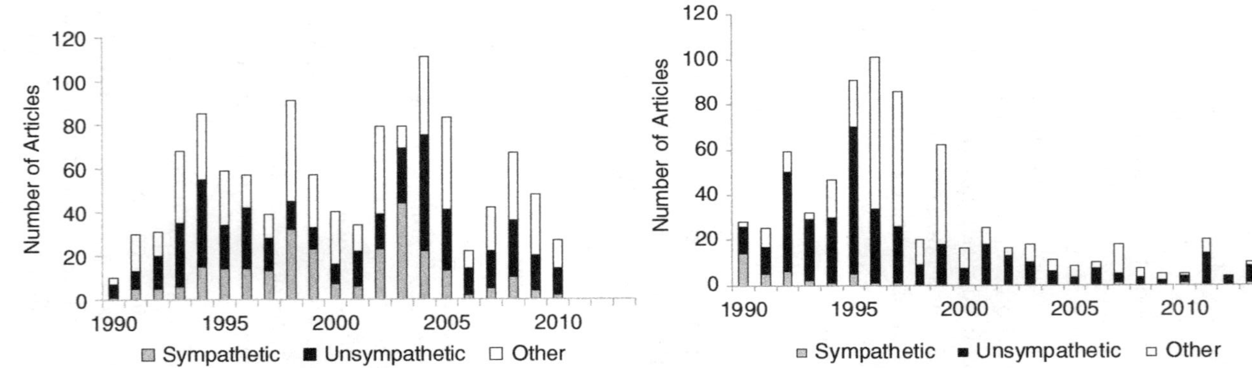


FIGURE 4.2 Newspaper Coverage of Street Vending in Bogotá (left) and Lima (right) by Article Tone, 1990–2010
Sources: Author's compilation from *El Tiempo* and *El Comercio*.

migration, or that defend street vendors as honorable and innocent when faced with enforcement actions. In contrast, unsympathetic narratives include personal interest stories that portray street vendors as exploitative, lazy, or criminal. The more common articles in this broad class are unsympathetic polemics that highlight problems caused by vendors, like jammed traffic or sidewalks, unfair business competition, tax evasion, clandestine electricity connections, and unsanitary or illegal merchandise.

In Bogotá, coverage on street vendors is split. Complaints about the harms caused by street vendors are a dominant theme, constituting 38 percent of all reports on street vending over the time period. Of these articles, about two-fifths are letters to the editor that pillory the "invasion" of city streets. About a third of those complaints concern how street vendors encourage and partake in criminal activities. Other unsympathetic stories concern traffic congestion (15 percent), harm to public space like sidewalks and parks (14 percent), business competition (9 percent), and sanitation (7 percent). Nevertheless, coverage of harms is counterbalanced by compassion for vendors. Roughly a fifth of articles profile street vendors in a positive light, discussing the economic hardships and national conditions that force the poor to work as vendors. After major enforcement operations in the 2000s, more than half of articles and letters to the editor denounced enforcement as a form of "persecution," "repression," and "criminalization of poverty."

In stark contrast, the portrayal of street vending is almost exclusively negative in Lima. Three-quarters of articles in the 1990s relate to vendors' contribution to traffic jams. Pictures of blocked streets and enormous masses of vendors became a favorite trope for front-page photographs. Other common refrains are that vendors sell stolen, unsanitary, and dangerous goods, and undercut formal businesses by marketing the same products. Not a single story sympathizes with street vendors' tough economic situations or labor trajectories in the 2000s. Such minimal sympathetic coverage is astounding given the depth of economic crisis that Peru experienced and continued labor market weakness.

To summarize, street vending continues to be a salient issue in Bogotá, and middle-class newspapers cover both the harms caused and the broader economic injustices that motivate these impositions. Interest and sympathy toward street vending have faded in Lima. Of course, it is possible that this analysis captures editorial choices more than attitudinal differences. But it coincides with the findings of other analysts that the public in Bogotá sees street vending as a structural issue, and after the 1990s, the public in Lima understands street vending as a law enforcement issue (Aliaga Linares 2012; Roever 2005). The next sections provide greater detail on how a range of actors, from nongovernmental organizations to politicians and the Constitutional Court, have defended street vendors in Bogotá, while street vendors lost even their traditional allies in Lima.

## 4.2 FORBEARANCE AND INSTITUTIONAL STRENGTH: BOGOTÁ

Figure 4.3 lays out the empirical puzzle for conventional capacity-based theories of enforcement. The bars show the number of police operations against street vendors from the Colombian National Police's Public Space Unit (*Unidad del Espacio Público*). Operations have dropped off sharply from more than 3,000 per administration in the late 1990s to less than 100 in the 2000s. Institutional capacity has expanded. The security budget more than doubled during the same period, as seen in the solid line.[11]

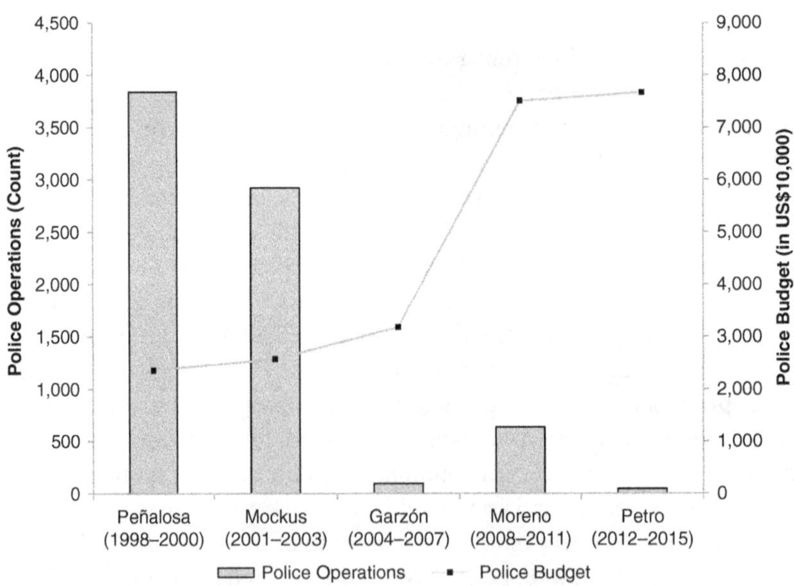


FIGURE 4.3 Coercive Capacity as an Insufficient Explanation of Enforcement in Bogotá

[11] While much of the Colombian National Police's budget comes from the central government, I show changes in the security budget (*Fondo de Vigilancia y Seguridad*) under the discretion of the city mayor reported by the Secretary of Finance (*Secretaría de Hacienda*).

TABLE 4.1 *Core Constituency and Enforcement by Mayor, Bogotá, 1988–2015*

| | Lower | Neutral | Upper |
|---|---|---|---|
| Forbearance | Garzón (2004–2007)<br>Moreno (2008–2011)<br>Petro (2012–2015) | Pastrana (1988–1990)<br>Caicedo (1990–1992)<br>Castro (1992–1994) | |
| Enforcement | | Mockus (1995–1997) | Mockus (2001–2003)<br>Peñalosa (1998–2000) |

Other indicators of state capacity, such as taxes collected, number of police officers, and violent crime rates, show similar improvements. The business cycle also would lead us to expect an uptick in enforcement: unemployment rates fell from a high of 20 percent in 1998 to 10 percent in 2012. What explains the drop in enforcement at a time of state strength?

My argument is that differences in core constituencies help make sense of variation in enforcement. Bogotá has elected mayors with distinct core constituencies since the advent of direct elections in 1988, as laid out in Table 4.1. The columns classify a mayor's class basis of support. Mayors labeled as "lower" receive a higher fraction of their vote share among poor than nonpoor voters; those classified as "upper" gain greater support among nonpoor voters. If the difference in class support is less than 5 percentage points, or the direction of the difference varies by data source, then the mayor is classified as having a "neutral" constituency.[12] Class constituencies differ from political ideology: politicians identified with the Left can repel low-income support, and vice versa. This section divides Bogotá's history into three major periods, which coincide with the core constituencies that mayors attracted, and shows how enforcement tracked different constituency preferences and became more programmatic over time.

### 4.2.1 Neutral Core Constituencies and Clientelistic Forbearance (1988–1994)

Much as in the case of squatting, city councilors negotiated forbearance in a clientelistic manner prior to decentralizing reforms. Vending associations

[12] The ideal way to make these classifications is to use individual-level exit poll or vote intention surveys by class. Unfortunately, survey data are scarce and not available for all city elections. I therefore rely on ecological correlations between district composition and vote share, and supplement these with survey data and polling station-level data when available.

aggregated votes for councilors and received licenses or forbearance in exchange for their support (Nelson 1992). Reforms to elect the city mayor and end licensing practices began to break this cycle in the early 1990s. Mayors needed large numbers of votes to win citywide elections and therefore made broad promises about enforcement (Donovan 2002, 2008). Nevertheless, it took several years to weaken traditional party machines during which time clientelistic forbearance continued.

Running as traditional party candidates, the first three elected mayors – Andrés Pastrana, Juan Martín Caicedo, and Jaime Castro – collected nearly uniform support across the income distribution. Pastrana represented the Conservative Party, which historically had fared badly in Bogotá, and received 40 percent of the vote with marginally weaker backing from the poor. Caicedo and Castro took more than 60 percent of the vote share for the Liberal Party. Large vote margins reflected the institutionalized two-party system. Voters followed the instructions of party bosses and tried to align themselves with the winning mayor to gain access to resources (Pasotti 2009: 87).

Mayors made scattered attempts to enforce against street vendors. Pastrana and Castro concentrated on projects to recuperate one of the city's main avenues, *La Séptima*. Caicedo worked on moving vendors from the downtown plaza. Yet these early mayors were unwilling to conduct continuous control actions or enforce in cases in which the government could not sponsor relocation. City and local councilors complicated attempts at more rigorous enforcement, instead pushing for relocation projects in which they could exchange spots in formal markets for the political support of street-vending associations. But relocation projects were expensive and inefficient. Only a third of the stalls in multimillion-dollar relocation projects were occupied by vendors due to their poor design and location (Castañeda and Bañales 2007: 174–7).

Caicedo was the former head of the national business association (*Federación Nacional de Comerciantes*, Fenalco), which strongly pressured for control of street vending. Caicedo urged the police to decommission merchandise from street vendors, but city councilors from his own Liberal Party scorned the proposal as an attempt to "terminally abolish" the poor and "criminalize" vendors.[13] Caicedo backed off. Only half of district governments reported doing any actions to control street vending, and

[13] See "Viciado de nulidad el reglamento sobre ventas ambulantes," *El Comercio* September 8, 1990.

enforcement efforts concentrated in a handful of nonpoor districts. Oversight authorities sanctioned thirty-three bureaucrats for failing to protect public space from street vending under Caicedo.[14]

Middle-class frustration escalated during the early 1990s. The city's homicide rate steadily increased due to the country's ongoing drug war and local criminal economies. Particularly in the 1990s, street vendors were seen as fronts for the drug trade and part of a general chaos that allowed criminals to operate, as confirmed by the uptick in negative portrayals in Figure 4.2. Business groups spoke out against mayors' passivity and the delegation of authority to city and local councilors who let legal violations occur to win votes. Fenalco's president told the press: "We do not lack laws, what we lack is authority that decides."[15] In 1993, more than 500 business owners in the city center formed an "emergency committee" to pressure for enforcement.[16]

Conflicting social rights claims began to filter into debates over street vending. On the one hand, vendors and advocates of the urban poor began to defend forbearance toward vendors as a way to guarantee the right to work and a minimum standard of living. The poverty rate had increased from 29 percent in 1986 to 40 percent in 1993. Half a million internally displaced people from the civil war flooded into the city in the same period, many finding work as street vendors. One survey showed that most vendors were poor and charges of exploitation by others were overblown: only 10 percent of vendors worked for others or paid rent to sell in city streets.[17] On the other hand, opponents of street vending invoked the constitutional right to public space. They equated street vendors with special-interest groups that damaged the collective rights of citizens to public space. Some market areas were notorious for their powerful vending associations that collected heavy fees from

14 City Ombudsman Antonio Bustos Esguerra complained that in eighty-eight petitions sent to local authorities to act against street vendors, only fifteen district governments even responded (let alone acted to remove vendors). See "En defensa del espacio público," *El Tiempo* December 29, 1993; "Alcaldes locales rinden cuenta," *El Tiempo* November 8, 1993; "Guerra a invasión del espacio público," *El Tiempo* October 16, 1993; "Espacio público, el objectivo," *El Tiempo* May 27, 1994; "Usaquén es el número uno en invasión del espacio público," *El Tiempo* September 15, 1994; "Yo invade, tu invades, él ..." *El Tiempo* February 7, 1993.

15 "Fenalco raja al Alcalde Castro," *El Tiempo* May 28, 1993; on business support for public space clearance, also see Moncada (2016: 136).

16 "Se ahoga San Victorino," *El Tiempo* November 18, 1993; "S.O.S. lanzan comerciantes del centro," *El Tiempo* April 26, 1993.

17 "El rebusque en la calle es buen negocio," *El Tiempo* February 22, 1995.

vendors.[18] As Castro's Secretary of Government described it, "The invasion of public space has converted into a lucrative business for those people who own carts, and has generated a business in renting them to take advantage of the needs of people."[19] Colombia's Constitution thus gave fodder to both sides of the street-vending debate, and revealed sharp disagreement about the prototypical street vendor.

### 4.2.2 Middle-Class Core Constituencies and Enforcement (1995–2003)

The election of mayors with nonpoor core constituencies brought a shift in enforcement policy in the mid-1990s. These eccentric mayors selected their enforcement positions largely on ideological grounds. Although these mayors believed that they were advancing the interests of the have-nots, their enforcement positions attracted nonpoor voters and business groups.

In 1995, Mockus ran as an independent candidate who rejected traditional party politics and advocated a renewal of civic culture. Mockus tied the city's problems, from violent crime to squatting, street vending, and traffic, to a lack of citizen understanding of their collective rights and duties. The attempt to transform civic culture was at the heart of his government's first-term agenda called "Citizen in Formation." Mockus's anti-politics views united voters from different class groups. He won by a large margin, receiving 64 percent of votes cast, against the then-Liberal Party iconoclast Enrique Peñalosa. The unconventional candidates meant that party bosses gave no clear instructions to their clients about how to vote (Pasotti 2009: 81). Abstention reached over 70 percent and even higher among low-income groups.[20]

More than any other mayor, Mockus exemplifies the post-materialist Left. It therefore is worth dwelling on his principles as they relate to enforcement against street vendors. The first core view is that forbearance harms the poor's citizenship rights. It leaves street vendors dependent on the whims of clientelistic politicians, casts them as criminals, and deprives them of labor rights. Given these harms, the goal of the post-materialist

[18] One association leader, Alejandro Barrera, has exercised control over the 20 de Julio market for two decades and is widely criticized for collecting fees and using coercive tactics against vendors.

[19] "El centro de Bogotá: pura carreta," *El Tiempo* July 21, 1993.

[20] "En Bogotá, ir a votar da una pereza," *El Tiempo* October 31, 1994.

Left is enforcement accompanied with social policy for those truly in need. Mockus explains, "My philosophy is apply the law first, and second, if the application of the law results in a precarious social situation, then attend to it through social policies."[21]

Second, connected to the promotion of social equality, the post-materialist Left uses enforcement to promote voluntary compliance. The materialist view of law enforcement is that it changes behavior by affecting the probability that a criminal suffers an economic loss through a fine or lost wages in prison. The post-materialist view is that most sanctions are nonmonetary and people follow the law due to social norms. To Mockus, the problem with legal violations like street vending and squatting is that, although illegal, they are culturally accepted. Social norms therefore are at odds with state enforcement efforts. The goal of the government, then, is to change social norms so that the public reinforces police sanctions (Mockus 2002: 22). Mockus pursued creative techniques to amplify enforcement's pedagogical function: he hired mimes to mock drivers and pedestrians who disrespected traffic laws, tried experiments in self-governance like a day with no police, and used a Chinese ceremonial dragon to accompany the police on operations against street vendors to emphasize the sacred nature of public space.[22] The motivation behind all of these acts was to use coercive sanctions to realign collective norms with the law, not to punish individual offenders.

Last, the post-materialist Left argues that forbearance is not in the poor's economic interests. The idea is that street vending perpetuates poverty and inequality by slowing job growth and private sector investment. Forbearance thus is a shortsighted policy that ignores the consequences for quality of life, urban planning, and economic development. Enforcement serves the poor's long-term interests, even though it removes tangible benefits in the short term. Mockus prioritizes collective goals, explaining, "Street vendors always find a way to survive . . . they do not let others survive."[23]

Guided by these principles, Mockus enforced against street vendors. In his first term, Mockus added 2,500 auxiliary forces to the police, which were responsible for administrative infractions like street vending. Using the expanded police force, decommissions of merchandise and equipment

[21] Author interview with Antanas Mockus, Bogotá, Colombia, July 29, 2013.

[22] Author interview with William Alfonso, Secretary of Planning (*Secretaría Distrital de Planeación*) under Mockus, August 1, 2012.

[23] "El Distrito rindió cuentas," *El Tiempo* August 4, 2003.

accelerated. Vendors staged protests and claimed that they were "persecuted" by the police.[24] But the Mockus administration moved forward with routine and large-scale operations, including a court-ordered removal of street vendors that had been postponed seventeen times by past administrations.[25] Mockus benefited from strong business support and cooperation in his enforcement efforts in downtown business areas (Moncada 2016: 135–6; 142–3).

Strong support from the middle class and business chambers following a period of forbearance, as well as low unemployment rates, reduced the political costs of enforcement. Mockus coordinated with private businesses to offer minimum wage jobs to street vendors. These policies were motivated by a belief that the majority of street vendors were not poor, but substitutive social policies should exist for those who truly needed the work. Politically, it served to attenuate the linkage between enforcement and anti-poor policies. As Mockus describes,

> The rate of unemployment was very low in my first term, and that favored me. If a mother came with children and said to me that she would have no way to feed them, I would say, "Look, this is the minimum wage, and I can offer you a job at that salary. I understand this will be less than you are used to making in the street" ... It eased my conscience about what we were doing and showed to everyone that these were not the very poor because they rejected our options.[26]

Meanwhile, Mockus parted ways from past mayors in rejecting state-sponsored relocations of street vendors on the grounds that they rewarded those who broke the law and provided incentives for others to take to the streets (Castañeda and Bañales 2007: 176).

Enforcement played better with the middle class than the poor. Term limits prevented Mockus from running for a consecutive term in office in 1997. But in 2001, Mockus was reelected with strong support from middle-class voters. The fact that the poor turned against Mockus in his reelection confirms that enforcement had the predicted electoral repercussions.

[24] "El distrito se llena de bachilleres," *El Tiempo* April 6, 1995; "Las protestas callejeros ocasionaron caos vial," *El Tiempo* May 27, 1995; "Mockus entre bueno y regular," *El Tiempo* August 11, 1995.

[25] The operation occurred in Siete de Agosto in Barrios Unidos. "Los beneficios del espacio público," *El Tiempo* August 12, 1996; "El Siete de Agosto, Zona modelo," *El Tiempo* August 9, 1996.

[26] Author interview with Antanas Mockus, mayor, Bogotá, Colombia, July 29, 2013; for a description of vendors' rejection of minimum-wage labor in one project, also see Mockus (2005: 23). The administration also did draw up plans to create a system of rotating street fairs throughout the city, although they never launched.

The campaign brought to the fore the ways in which Mockus's insistence on legal culture threatened the poor's livelihood. As one letter to the editor criticized, "public space is worth more than the life and health of thousands of families in the southeast and Ciudad Bolívar."[27] What is amazing is that these charges were leveled against Mockus, despite the fact that his investments in health, education, and infrastructure prioritized the poor. Because Mockus ran in a citywide electoral district without compulsory voting, he was able to eke out a victory with greater middle-class support and turnout in 2001. Those close to Mockus confirmed that he was motivated by philosophical beliefs and "did not care about losing the poor's support." Nevertheless, it made for "a tough and surprising reelection because so many poor voters hated him."[28]

During his second term, Mockus further intensified enforcement against street vendors.[29] But, unlike during his first term, the economy soured. Underemployment reached 53 percent and open unemployment was estimated at 20 percent. Sympathetic coverage of vendors and discussion of the structural causes of vending multiplied in the press, reaching a high of 55 percent of articles in 2003. A typical editorial, for example, warned of a "social time bomb" caused by enforcing against vendors due to "the explosive combination of unemployment and entrance of displaced people that are fleeing violence."[30] Although Mockus had strong support in the business community for continuing operations against vendors, he could not count on companies to generate alternative employment for street vendors. The charge that vendors "chose" to be in the streets over other paid employment options rang hollow.

Mockus sparked an intense controversy over enforcement against vendors with an attempt to reform the city's police code.[31] The reform

[27] "Testimonio de un desempleado," *El Tiempo* August 24, 2003.

[28] Author interview with Paul Bromberg, advisor to Mockus and appointed interim mayor, Bogotá, Colombia, January 31, 2014.

[29] In 2002, the police reportedly made 9,300 separate seizures of merchandise, dedicated 100 police agents and 70 assistants to daily operations, and used 8 trucks to remove equipment and merchandise. Author interview with major, Public Space Unit, National Police of Colombia, September 8, 2011; also see "La batalla diaria por la calle," *El Tiempo* December 15, 2002.

[30] "La Guerra callejera de Mockus," *El Tiempo* September 23, 2002; Other examples include "Entre la chaza y el cuchillo," *El Tiempo* October 14, 2002; "Qué van a hacer los vendedores," *El Tiempo* November 30, 2002; "Qué hacer con los vendedores ambulantess," *El Tiempo* December 8, 2002; "Tolerancia con los vendedores," *El Tiempo* December 11, 2002.

[31] Agreement 79 and Decree 462 of 2003; "Peluquean el Código de Policía de Bogotá," *El Tiempo* October 4, 2002; "Bloquean vías y Transmilenio," *El Tiempo* October 8, 2002.

package included more than 200 articles to improve citizen culture, such as requiring citizens to form orderly lines for the bus. But it also included fines for individual street vendors and businesses that collaborated with them. City councilor Luis Eduardo Díaz, a former shoeshine, captured the class politics in his opposition to the street-vending measures: "I have the blood of a poor person, and I'm not going against my people."[32] City council members tried to extract bribes from street-vending associations to vote against the measure.[33] Again, Mockus downplayed social concerns and claimed that vending hampered long-term growth.[34] Mockus, in short, was an ideologue. He entered politics because he had a vision of how to improve the city. A major part of his vision to promote social equality consisted of his attitude toward law, not redistribution.

Mockus's terms in office were bracketed by the election of another highly ideological mayor, Enrique Peñalosa. Peñalosa grounded his enforcement against street vending in conservative principles. First, Peñalosa argued that enforcement, particularly in the historical downtown, would improve the city's image. As Peñalosa caricatured, the city center had "lost its majesty and enchantment by the invasion of carts of every brand of soda, ice cream, French fries; with barbeque pits for corn, stands for pork shish-ka-bobs, bathroom slippers and contraband watches." His proposal was to remove street vendors so that Colombians could feel pride in their city and business investors would see economic opportunities (Peñalosa Londoño 2000: 7, 18). Second, the control of street vending was a means to reconstruct the state's broader authority and fight crime. Public space recovery was highly visible and therefore would be "the clearest example of how anything can be accomplished [by the state]," according to Peñalosa (Beccassino 2000: 201; also see Berney 2010). Following a broken-windows theory of crime, a firm approach toward street vendors, and especially street-vending associations or so-called "mafias," was thought to deter other types of crime.[35]

Enforcement again appealed to the middle class and business community. The 1998 election put Peñalosa up against Carlos Moreno de Caro, an independent who had abandoned the Conservative Party to create his

[32] "Así se votaría el Código de Policía," *El Tiempo* December 20, 2002.

[33] City councilors were caught on tape trying to extort $215,000 from a street-vending association with 12,000 members, the *Corporación para el Desarrollo Social de Buhoneros de Colombia*. Courts found the vice-president of the City Council, Judy Consuelo Pinzón, guilty and barred her from public office for twenty years.

[34] "Ni un paso atrás: Mockus," *El Tiempo* December 2, 2002.

[35] Author interview with Enrique Peñalosa, Bogotá, Colombia, September 7, 2011.

own party, Citizen Defense (*Defensa Ciudadana*). In contrast to Peñalosa, Moreno de Caro advocated forbearance toward street vendors for its informal welfare benefits, and showed up at protests by street vendors claiming solidarity with their cause. He explains, "The people who work in the streets have no education, they are displaced, and this is their last response to survive. You can't repress street vending just so the street looks nice, otherwise people resort to crime."[36] Concern about a Moreno de Caro victory, coupled with Peñalosa's promises of efficient management, led to high turnout among middle-income groups. Peñalosa gained more than 50 percent of the vote share in polling stations near upper-class neighborhoods, and less than a quarter in lower-class neighborhoods (Santos 2007: 14).

The Peñalosa administration intensified enforcement against street vendors compared with Mockus's first term. The government reclaimed more than a million square meters of public space and removed an estimated 30,000 street vendors (Donovan 2008: 30). Peñalosa also created new agencies and procedures to institutionalize enforcement. He created a special 200-person unit within the police to seize the goods and equipment of unlicensed street vendors and patrol public spaces (*Unidad del Espacio Público*) and an ombudsman's office for citizens to file complaints against public space invasions (*Defensoría del Espacio Público*, DADEP). To make these procedures effective, Peñalosa coordinated between district governments and city institutions by holding weekly meetings with all authorities involved to plan operations. Appointed district mayors understood that their jobs depended on an increase in enforcement, or, as one bureaucrat related:

> Peñalosa would call and say clean up such and such zone, and the local mayor would issue the order and we'd do it. There was no debate about the situation, or intervention by council members because Peñalosa had such a clear policy of recuperating public space that *all the appointed mayors went along with it or they would lose their jobs*.[37]

Enforcement created a substantial backlash among poor voters. Evictions occurred at a time when the unemployment and poverty rate were on the rise. Peñalosa seemed callous to the economic situation of the poor and grew profoundly unpopular. More than a third had an unfavorable image of Peñalosa because he "caused unemployment" or "did not

[36] Author interview with Carlos Moreno de Caro, Bogotá, Colombia, August 1, 2011.

[37] Author interview with coordinator of legal affairs, District of Suba, Bogotá, Colombia, August 16, 2011, emphasis added.

care about the poor."[38] As one vendor told the press, "He simply got rid of us as if the city wasn't ours too."[39] There indeed was something of a Potemkin village in efforts to rebuild the city's image and authority by removing the poor from public view. Editorials, for instance, referred to "Peñalosa syndrome" as the prioritization of "public works and city aesthetics" over people, and people nicknamed him "Bulldozer."[40] A cartoon from *El Tiempo* best caricatures the class signal that Peñalosa sent to the poor and unemployed. Two men in suits on a park bench ask, "What would the unemployed have done without such a suitable public space?"[41]

A host of politicians and state actors defended forbearance against street vendors due to its employment benefits for the poor. Then-senator Gustavo Petro was a vocal critic of police "repression" of the poor, as were other Liberal Party city councilors.[42] Most notably, as I return to in Chapter 6, the Constitutional Court intervened to require the city government to provide employment alternatives prior to removing street vendors. To be clear, the Court did not prohibit enforcement. The government could proceed with evictions if it implemented unemployment policies or relocation programs to protect street vendors' rights. The Court, however, did not specify the quality or scope of these alternatives, which allowed mayors like Peñalosa and Mockus to continue operations with minimal programs (such as onetime cash payoffs) in place.[43] Moreover, the Court ruled that the government could enforce once it "reset" societal expectations and "recovered" areas.[44] The mandate to

[38] Napoleón Franco & Cía, *Encuesta de Opinión Pública*, October 1999.

[39] "La mano que limpia," *El Espectador* March 21, 1999.

[40] "Síndrome Peñalosa," *El Tiempo* November 27, 2002; "Peñalosa El Buldozer," *Semana* April 5, 1998; "Qué hacer con los vendedores ambulantess," *El Tiempo* December 8, 2002.

[41] "¿Qué hubiéramos hecho los desempleados sin un espacio público tan oportuno?" *El Tiempo* January 10, 2001. Notably, Peñalosa also managed to alienate nonpoor voters through his public space policies. Peñalosa put up bollards to prevent people from parking in the street and attempted to expropriate a private golf course to build a park. A recall referendum against Peñalosa thus united a strange cross-class coalition. The high quorum required to remove a mayor from office in Colombia allowed Peñalosa to survive the recall attempt. Ultimately, he regained nonpoor support through his competent city management.

[42] "Personería y Defensoría piden ver alternativas," *El Espectador*, October 30, 1998; "Peñalosa, al borde del hueco," *El Tiempo* November 22, 1998.

[43] Further litigation clarified the alternatives necessary. See Constitutional Court of Colombia, Sentence T-722, *Gaceta de la Corte Constitucional*, September 4, 2003.

[44] Constitutional Court of Colombia, Sentence SU-360, *Gaceta de la Corte Constitucional*, May 19, 1999.

offer labor alternatives to street vendors forced Peñalosa to compensate vendors, despite his personal distaste for the measures. He then enforced heavily in those areas.

Focusing solely on office-seeking motivations cannot explain the behavior of politicians like Mockus and Peñalosa. Both politicians have been described as idealistic and divorced from popular sentiment. However, in their idealism, they strengthen my claim that enforcement forms part of debates over how to improve social welfare and divides the electorate on class lines. Their support for enforcement communicated a distributive commitment to the middle class and business interests, despite their substantial pro-poor social investments in other policy areas and their self-conceptualization as politicians who prioritized the poor. Peñalosa, for example, perversely boasts that he "did more to advance the cause of equality than any politician since Stalin."[45] Their governments thus empirically illustrate the survey findings that I presented in Chapter 2: voters view politicians who enforce as anti-poor.

### 4.2.3 Lower-Class Core Constituencies and Forbearance (2003–2015)

After almost a decade of mayors who attracted their strongest support from nonpoor voters, a sea change occurred. Voters elected mayors with poor core constituencies. Forbearance toward street vending was used as an explicit campaign appeal to signal a pro-poor commitment. The realignment led to a drop in enforcement, even as state capacity rebounded.

The 2003 elections began the flip in class constituency and enforcement policy. Luis Garzón staked his campaign on representation of the city's poor. He represented a labor-based Left that attempted to build a political party, the Polo Party. His slogan "Bogotá Without Indifference" claimed to prioritize the impoverished and marginalized. Garzón grew up in a poor district of Bogotá and had strong ties to organized labor, eventually becoming the president of the largest Colombian labor confederation (*Central Unitaria de Trabajadores de Colombia*, CUT). In a somewhat unusual decision, the union movement had begun to incorporate informal-sector workers and Garzón promised to extend social welfare benefits beyond the formal sector. Given the previous two mayors' efforts to "clean up" the city, Garzón made forbearance against vendors a central issue and a way to underscore his commitment to the informal-sector

[45] Author interview with Enrique Peñalosa, mayor, Bogotá, Colombia, September 7, 2011.

poor. The campaign folded forbearance into class issues by portraying enforcement as an attempt to ignore poverty – "the city should not be a blank postcard," said Garzón in a campaign debate. Garzón promised to concentrate police resources on wealthy criminals, rather than the "defenseless poor" and to take "into account employment as a social necessity."[46]

The electoral incentive to promote forbearance was clear due to the direct mobilization of street vendors and the indirect social sympathy for their cause. Prior to the election, more than 30,000 of an estimated 110,000 street vendors in the city marched around the slogan "Polo [Garzón's party] or the Police Stick!" (*Polo o Palo!)*.[47] Compassion for street vendors ran high, with more than half of articles offering a sympathetic portrayal of vendors during this period.[48] How to confront employment and poverty dominated the 2003 election due to the magnitude of the economic crisis in Bogotá. More than half of the workforce was in the informal sector, and 45 percent fell below the poverty line (DANE 2012). Four-fifths of city residents named employment as their primary concern (Bogotá Cómo Vamos 2003).

Garzón won decisively among the poor. The election was the first time that the poor turned out at a rate equal to other class groups. The poor overwhelmingly backed the Polo. Garzón received roughly two-thirds of lower-income votes, compared to a quarter of middle-class votes (Bogotá Cómo Vamos 2005).[49] The support for Garzón also was a rejection of continuity with past policies, represented by the losing candidate Juan Lozano, a Liberal Party dissident who received Peñalosa's endorsement. Lozano ran on an enforcement platform, admitting that he would "run the risk of losing votes" and enforce against street vendors because "the law is not negotiable."[50]

46 "Mi lucha es por la inclusión social," *El Tiempo* July 22, 2003; "Agenda de los candidatos," *El Tiempo* August 25, 2003; "Antes que peajes, renegociar la deuda," *El Tiempo* August 6, 2003; "El rebusque, para sobrevivir!" *El Tiempo* August 13, 2003.

47 While the march was organized against the police code reforms proposed by Mockus, it also showed vendors' support for Garzón. "La protesta ambulante," *El Tiempo* July 19, 2003; "Vendedores piden alternativas," *El Tiempo* July 22, 2003.

48 For example, see "Los informales," *El Tiempo* October 14, 2003; "Tolerancia con vendedores ambulantes," *El Tiempo* July 27, 2003; "Peor el remedio que enfermedad," *El Tiempo* August 9, 2003; "El código, una utopía," *El Tiempo* August 21, 2003.

49 Similar trends were found at the polling station level (Santos 2007: 13) and district level (Moncada 2016: 145).

50 "Lozano: Transmilenio no es poesía sino dignidad," *El Tiempo* October 19, 2003; "El ganador fue el debate," *El Tiempo* August 22, 2003; "Lo que dijeron los candidatos," *El Tiempo* August 22, 2003.

In office, Garzón avoided enforcement against street vendors, especially at the start of his administration. Police stopped decommissioning merchandise and equipment from vendors (other than copyrighted and pirated goods) (Jaramillo, Villamil, and Bañales 2008: 80, 128). Garzón reiterated that he intended to enforce sparingly until the government generated job alternatives. As he told the press, "We are not complicit in the illegality, but we also are not going to tell the police to repress."[51] Garzón instead passed a "master plan" that established a joint commission with street-vending associations to manage the use of public space. The commission tried to convince vendors to respect public spaces and reduce negative externalities without the need for police enforcement.[52] Street vendors corroborate police data showing that enforcement operations plummeted. As one street-vending leader put it, "Why do I support the Polo? Because the Polo is the only party that for better or worse has let us work."[53]

Garzón received substantial criticism for easing enforcement. The press attacked the loss of control: 47 percent of news articles were unsympathetic portrayals that berated the government for its leniency. Typical letters denounced the "outrage against ordinary citizens,"[54] and complained about the "populist and permissive strategy" in which "the police themselves say that they have orders not to annoy the vendors."[55] In 2005, 46 percent of the population considered street vendors among the principal problems of the city (Bogotá Como Vamos 2005). Public opinion divided on vending, with a majority (58 percent) in favor of more enforcement and 38 percent opposed to operations.[56] Garzón remained committed to street vendors, although personal attacks and pressure from the business community mounted. As Garzón reflected, "My greatest fault can at the same time be my greatest virtue: I'm a good person, at times things require a hard hand (*mano dura*) and, since I don't have one, others think I'm an imbecile" (Gilbert 2008: 276).

[51] "No voy a arrendar ni a parcelar el espacio público," El *Tiempo* November 12, 2004.

[52] Decree 098 (*Plan Maestro del Espacio Público*). The "master plan" laid out several objectives: (1) to establish a joint commission with street vendors; (2) to restructure the agency in charge of relocation projects, evaluate past projects, and generate alternative labor solutions for vendors; (3) to commission a census of the street-vending population; and (4) to promote the democratic use of public space.

[53] Author interview with anonymous street-vending leader, Bogotá, Colombia, September 20, 2011.

[54] "El centro, invadido," *El Tiempo* February 20, 2004.

[55] "Y la policía?" *El Tiempo* February 1, 2004.

[56] "Debate por el espacio público," *El Tiempo* January 6, 2004.

Why didn't Garzón legalize street vending if he opposed enforcement? Part of the answer is that the city government lacks the authority; the Constitution requires the protection of public space and city authorities cannot allow permanent occupations of public property. Even if legally possible, however, legalization was not the goal. Garzón preferred the revocable nature of forbearance, not for clientelistic ends, but because he saw forbearance as a temporary measure in the context of unemployment and poverty. If employment improved, Garzón would support enforcement. But creating jobs was a tall order. The government spent roughly $20 million each year on job programs for unskilled workers through the Institute for the Popular Economy (*Instituto para la Economía Social*, IPES). Ironically, job creation programs replicated the logic of street vending. For instance, the government invested in kiosks to permit an orderly use of public space and allow the poor to generate capital to then rent a shop. Nevertheless, the city managed to build just 300 kiosks, hardly offering an alternative to thousands of street vendors. As one top city official summarized, "It would have been against the people who voted for the Polo to evict street vendors ... But the Polo still couldn't solve the underlying issue of jobs."[57] Street vendors, and the poor more generally, appeared to reward the Polo's forbearance at the ballot box, even though formal welfare solutions were not forthcoming.

Prioritization of the economic needs of street vendors continued in the subsequent Polo administration of Samuel Moreno. Although Moreno lacked Garzón's working-class background, his family history with the National Popular Alliance (*Alianza Nacional Popular*, ANAPO), which appealed to the informal-sector poor, suggested that he would prioritize the interests of street vendors.[58] Street vendors mobilized for Moreno. Vendors were confident that the Polo would best protect their interests against enforcement, especially when compared with Peñalosa's bid for reelection.[59] Like Garzón, Moreno thus won with the support of lower-class voters (Gilbert 2012: 5).

[57] Author interview with Juan Manuel Roso, Personería, Bogotá, Colombia, September 27, 2011.

[58] Moreno is the grandson of Gustavo Rojas Pinilla, a populist politician who powerfully courted informal-sector voters through his ANAPO opposition party. He narrowly lost the 1970 presidential election (arguably due to fraud). Moreno's mother is María Eugenia Rojas, the former president of ANAPO and a strong advocate of street vendors.

[59] Author's focus group with street-vending leaders, Central Unitaria de Trabajadores de Colombia (CUT), Bogotá, Colombia, September 1, 2011.

Moreno largely continued the Polo's policies of forbearance toward street vendors, even as he invested in police capacity in other areas. Police records show that Moreno did more operations than Garzón, reflecting in part the increasing pressure that the business community put on the Polo administrations to control public space (Moncada 2016: 150–1). Nonetheless, Moreno took a relatively lax approach. A high-ranking official describes, "In private meetings, we're told not to touch the street vendors. Vending regulatory policies aren't meant to work because this is how the Polo Party gains its support base."[60] At the same time, Moreno doubled the police's budget and introduced a number of innovative measures to reduce hard crime, such as a liquor sales ban that the police consistently enforced (Mello, Mejía, and Suárez 2013). These facts suggest that the police had the capacity to act against administrative infractions. Operations against street vendors remained minimal because the Polo needed the poor's electoral support.

Again, forbearance was not the Moreno administration's preferred policy. The ideal option was to employ the poor and enforce against vending. But city authorities struggled to create sufficient employment alternatives and viewed job creation as the national government's responsibility. A report from the authority that receives citizen complaints against street vending underscores how forbearance served as an informal welfare policy to compensate for the national government's failures:

> The focus of public policies implemented in the past two administrations [of Garzón and Moreno] center around the social imperative and citizens' rights to work, which has resulted in that the recovery of invaded public space has not continued at the pace demanded by some public sectors. Nonetheless, it is important to warn that *lasting solutions to the problem of informal sales will not be achieved without the national government's solution of the macroeconomic situations that give rise to the phenomenon. (DADEP 2010, emphasis added)*

Although the Polo's run in office ended in 2011, forbearance remained an attractive means to provide informal welfare to the poor. Moreno left office in disgrace on charges that he took bribes in exchange for public works contracts. But the materialist Left's policies largely continued under a new guise. Gustavo Petro, a former M-19 guerrilla and an ally-turned-critic of the Polo Party, formed a new party, the Progressive Movement (*Movimiento Progresista*). Petro continued to support forbearance toward

[60] Author interview with anonymous official, Personería de Bogotá, September 14, 2011.

street vending as a necessary part of the "popular economy."[61] However, many street-vending leaders saw Petro as a traitor to the labor-based party that the Polo attempted to build. What street vendors did agree on was their opposition to "more bulldozers" under Petro's main rival, Peñalosa.[62] Half of lower-class voters said they would never vote for Peñalosa. Petro won with just 28 percent of the vote, although with a less clear-cut class profile of support due to the fragmentation among moderate candidates.[63]

Petro moved to protect street vendors in two ways. First, going beyond the Polo's position, Petro gutted police capabilities to control street vending. Petro disbanded the unit created to control public space and, according to government officials, ordered the police to suspend control operations and end decommission of merchandise.[64] Operations were suspended. Second, Petro tried to revive legislative proposals to legalize street vending by allowing vendors to rent public spaces subject to restrictions.[65]

Rising middle-class frustration with the deterioration of the city center and the return of street vendors contributed to Peñalosa's successful campaign to take office again in 2016. Peñalosa wasted no time in returning to firm enforcement policies against street vendors. His actions help to separate an electoral account of forbearance from an alternative explanation centered on the intervention of the Constitutional Court. Garzón used the Court's interventions to justify his focus on providing alternatives to vendors (Moncada 2016: 149). However, Peñalosa interpreted the Court as permitting police operations in areas that once had been recovered by the city, and claimed that "no high court would permit that some

[61] "Polémica entre Petro y Araújo por vendedores ambulantes en Bogotá," *El Tiempo* September 15, 2011.

[62] Author interview with Alfredo Machola Rojas, president of the UGTI-CUT (*Unión General de Trabajadores de la Economia Informal*), September 1, 2011; Focus group with street vendors, CUT, Bogotá, September 13, 2011.

[63] Some polls suggest that Petro drew near-even support across class groups, while others give him stronger support among lower and lower-middle sectors (Strata 1, 2, and 3). See "Petro 22%, Peñalosa 19% y Parody 17% de intención de voto, según Ipsos Napoleón," *Semana* October 21, 2011; "Gina Parody es la segunda en Bogotá, según encuesta de Datexco," *Semana* October 27, 2011; "Alianza Gina-Mockus evita polarización, pero la pelea sigue siendo entre Petro y Peñalosa," *La Silla Vacía* October 10, 2011; "Bogotá: la campaña se vuelve seria," *Revista Razón Pública* August 11, 2011.

[64] Author interview with Ricardo María Cañón Prieto, ombudsman (*Personero de Bogotá*), July 31, 2012.

[65] "Reubicación de comerciantes informales, concertada con el distrito," Press Release, Alcaldía Mayor de Bogotá, March 4, 2012; Also see "El polémico decreto de Petro," *Semana* October 17, 2013.

vendors install themselves in the middle of the [main avenues]."[66] Politicians thus have interpreted legal doctrines in ways that support their enforcement positions and core constituencies.

It is worth underscoring the fact that city mayors took programmatic approaches toward street vending. Some mayors embraced a right to work to mobilize street vendors and create affective ties with low-income voters. Mayors did not threaten to enforce if some street vendors failed to vote for them. The incentive to vote came from the prospect that a politician who supported forbearance would be elected. A street-vending leader insisted, "It wouldn't make much sense to pay us or threaten us because we already were loyal to the Polo" (and later, to Petro).[67] Or, as another leader put it, "We don't discuss the candidates or pressure people to vote for a given candidate in this association. We just know that we don't want [Mockus and Peñalosa] because they would bring back coercion (*el palo*) so we can't support them."[68]

In elections for city and local councilors, my interviews with street-vending leaders revealed more clientelistic exchanges. Candidates need fewer votes to win council elections, and receive less media coverage in which they can make broad appeals. In a focus group of twenty-five street-vending leaders, roughly a third reported that city councilors and less well-known mayoral candidates approached them to turn their members out at the polls. Leaders coordinated campaign events, such as small discussion groups between their members and candidates. A minority also brought their members to register at specific polling stations and then tracked their members' turnout. Candidates compensated leaders with small payments in cash or goods for their members, and promised future favors and expenditures, including defending street vendors against police aggression if the mayor turned against them.[69] Politicians kept spreadsheets with the leaders they had paid and their expected returns at each polling station, but did not bother tracking individual-level turnout. For example, one local councilor explains, "I have 318 leaders who are

[66] "Ninguna corte permitiría vendedores ambulantes en mitad de la Séptima: Peñalosa," *Caracol* January 26, 2016; "Comienza la lucha por recuperar el espacio público en Bogotá," *El Tiempo* January 25, 2016.

[67] Author interview with street-vending leader, 20 de Julio Market, September 4, 2011.

[68] Author interview with street-vending leader, Association ASVE Norte, Bogotá, Colombia, August 18, 2011.

[69] Author's focus group with street-vending leaders, CUT, September 11, 2011, Bogotá, Colombia. For further discussion, see Holland and Palmer-Rubin (2015: 20–3).

with me and in my database ... I only know the areas that went well or poorly and so where to focus my efforts in office."[70]

To review, state capacity poorly explains enforcement in Bogotá. Mayors could and did repress street vending at the time when the city's resources were at their nadir. In fact, they enforced the law so effectively that citizens, politicians, and even the Constitutional Court objected. Enforcement instead changed along with the political tides. Mayors proposed enforcement operations that attracted middle-class voters and business support in the 1990s. Even though Mockus and Peñalosa claimed – and in terms of social expenditures even acted – to represent the poor's interests, their enforcement policies alienated poor voters. Rejecting state enforcement, the poor instead voted for mayors who supported forbearance in the 2000s. Garzón, Moreno, and Petro all sought to provide informal welfare and signal their distributive commitments to the poor through their support for street vendors. Their public announcements of support are inconsistent with clientelistic forbearance. Rather, enforcement dropped across the board and quid pro quo exchanges only took place at the district level.

## 4.3 ENFORCEMENT AND INSTITUTIONAL WEAKNESS: LIMA

Peru's notoriously weak institutions, debt crisis, and urban poverty make it an unlikely case for enforcement. But the growth of street vending helped to bring to power a mayor with a middle-class core constituency and support from segments of the lower-middle class. Enforcement followed. To provide a blueprint for my electoral argument, Table 4.2 charts the class basis of support and enforcement policy for each elected mayor in Lima since the reintroduction of direct elections.

### 4.3.1 Lower-Class Core Constituencies and Forbearance (1984–1989)

Social and economic changes, combined with Peru's mandatory voting rules, created a propitious environment for representatives of the poor to win city elections. Millions of previously disenfranchised illiterate voters joined the electorate and more than doubled the voting population in 1981 (Remmer 1985: 258). But, with little time for the Left to organize,

[70] Author interview with Juan Carlos Tavara, local councilor, San Cristóbal, October 12, 2011.

TABLE 4.2 *Core Constituency and Enforcement by Mayor, Lima, 1981–2014*

| | Lower | Neutral | Upper |
|---|---|---|---|
| Forbearance | Barrantes (1984–1986)<br>Del Castillo (1987–1989)<br>Belmont (1990–1995) | Castañeda (2007–2010) | |
| Enforcement | | Castañeda (2003–2006)<br>Villarán (2011–2014) | Orrego (1981–1983)<br>Andrade (1996–2002) |

Eduardo Orrego won the first city election with support from middle- and working-class voters on the centrist Popular Action ticket (Cameron 1991: 299).

An architect by training, Orrego promised to revitalize Lima's downtown in line with middle-class and business interests. But capacity constrained enforcement. The city had just 400 employees to manage all urban tasks, and the decentralization of administrative responsibilities brought no additional budget (Pease Garcia 1989: 51). Orrego thus limited enforcement to a tiny area of the city center, Lima Cuadrada. Although a limited objective, Orrego's enforcement attempt broke with the military government's past tolerance of street vending and put the issue on the city agenda.

In 1983, poor voters overwhelmingly aligned behind the Left, bringing a shift in enforcement. City residents elected Alfonso Barrantes, a popular labor lawyer with Marxist roots who represented the United Left (*Izquierda Unida*, IU) coalition. Barrantes ran against Alfredo Barrenechea from the populist American Popular Revolutionary Alliance (*Alianza Popular Revolucionaria Americana*, APRA). A yawning class gap in preferences emerged. Fifteen of the sixteen poor districts in the capital elected local mayors from the IU (Dietz 1998: 196). Surveys show that 52 percent of the lower class voted for the IU compared to only 23 percent of upper- and middle-class voters. Meanwhile, the urban poor supported APRA in roughly equal proportions to other social groups (Cameron 1991: 297).

On the campaign trail, Barrantes proposed policies and alliances that emphasized his commitment to the urban poor. Barrantes's flagship program "Glass of Milk" (*Vaso de Leche)* provided food assistance to needy children in Lima. He also promoted a "managed" approach to street vending that would be sensitive to employment needs. Orrego's eviction policy had resulted in protests by the largest street-vending association in the city, the Federation of Lima Street Vendors (*Federación Departamental de Vendedores Ambulantes de Lima*, FEDEVAL). The mobilizations highlighted the growing political power of street vendors, totaling around 84,000 at the end of Orrego's term.[71] Some IU legislators and city councilors joined the protests, noting that vendors worked as a means of survival.[72] To make the IU's commitment to street vendors clear, Barrantes incorporated vending leaders on the IU ticket. FEDEVAL head Guillermo Nolasco campaigned alongside Barrantes and won election as a city councilor.

A combination of ideological conviction and strategic calculation led Barrantes to ally with street vendors. Barrantes came from a humble provincial background, worked as a labor lawyer, and understood street vendors as part of an oppressed lower class unable to find work in the industrial sector. Through a Marxist lens, he viewed street vendors as part of a "temporary reserve army of labor" that would be absorbed as Peru industrialized. Nolasco describes how Barrantes saw a common working-class identity in street vendors:

> The consensus was that vendors were a product of economic crisis and migration, and at the core workers who needed to generate a subsistence income ... Maybe we were wrong in not thinking about the harms we imposed on the city, but feeding one's family was seen as more important than beautifying the city to please "traditional" Lima.[73]

The incorporation of street vendors into the IU also had electoral ends. Barrantes had the strategic goal to broaden the IU coalition away from the industrial working class in the hopes to win city and, eventually, national power. Barrantes's attempts to court the informal-sector vote conflicted with hard-left segments of the IU, which dismissed street vendors either as the lumpenproletariat or entrepreneurial capitalists who lacked the necessary working-class identity to become partisans (Cameron 1991: 301; Taylor 1990: 110). Barrantes nevertheless saw the strategic importance

[71] In 1985, De Soto's think tank, Instituto Libertad y Democracia (ILD), counted 84,327 street vendors and an additional 38,897 vendors in informal markets. Head count methodologies, like those used by ILD, tend to undercount street vendors, making this a conservative estimate of their expansion.

[72] "Vendedores ambulantes paralizan el Centro," *El Comercio* April 24, 1981.

[73] Author interview with Guillermo Nolasco, IU city councilor (1984–1987) and FEDEVAL president, Lima, Peru, November 25, 2011.

in incorporating street vendors into the labor movement and the Left. Although FEDEVAL represented only 50,000 street vendors in the mid-1980s, it was the best-organized segment of a much larger contingent of half a million informal-sector workers. The alliance with street vendors signaled a commitment to a more inclusive definition of the working class than offered by traditional parties like APRA.[74]

With direct representation of street vendors in city government, the Barrantes administration passed citywide legislation to improve conditions for street vendors.[75] First, consistent with commitments to organize the working class, the government required street vendors to join an association to work in the streets. These associations would be represented on a sectoral commission including city bureaucrats, police, and politicians. Second, vendors would control their own behavior to reduce the harms imposed on others. Because the IU understood vending as an employment option for the poor, the government also capped street vendors to the sale of $2,675 worth of merchandise (although there was no way to police the limit). Presciently, the IU worried that public sympathy toward street vendors would fray if they earned substantial profits. Third, the legislation established provisions for social benefits to be administered by district governments. Vendors would occupy public space in exchange for the payment of an excise tax (*sisa*). Half of the revenue would support health, pension, and emergency coverage for vendors. The legislation thus provided a legal option to work as a street vendor subject to restrictions, or what Roever (2005: 57–60) describes as an attempt at "cooperative governance."

The city government ceased retentions of merchandise. As the then-head of street-vending affairs for the city government puts it, "The priority was social assistance and attention, not removal, so we did not invest police resources in control."[76] Some middle-class districts, such as La Molina and San Isidro, issued a restricted number of licenses and tried to enforce the restrictions. In contrast, poor districts attracted thousands of vendors (De Soto 1989: 68–9). IU mayors, who governed most poor districts, defended street vending, or as one relates:

[74] Author interview with Guillermo Nolasco, November 25, 2011.

[75] Metropolitan Ordinance 002, *El Peruano*, April 17, 1985.

[76] Barrantes tried to reduce negative externalities by moving vendors to fairgrounds, closing off certain segments of streets to create rotating markets, and licenses to reduce entry. Author interview with Elsie Guerrero, former director of Commercialization (*Comercialización*), Lima Metropolitan Government, Lima, Peru, June 7, 2011.

I couldn't touch street vendors because of the IU and the relationship that we had with the poor. In those days, vendors were seen as poor and this was a way to assist them, while we had little else to offer the popular sectors. We were with the poor so there was no way that I could remove or even control vendors and ever be reelected in the district.[77]

The absence of social policy made forbearance the government's preferred approach, but it was a second-best policy for the IU for two reasons. First, Barrantes understood that his administration was a test of whether the IU could govern the city effectively (Schönwälder 2002: 119). The growing number of street vendors compromised the IU's reputation for efficient management, which helps explain why the administration prodded street vendors to control their own behavior and public image. Second, the government viewed street vending as a temporary employment solution. Its preferred approach – to move vendors into industrial employment and associated labor unions – required national economic transformations. Short of taking national power, options to employ the poor were minimal. The city budget in 1985 was a mere $42 million, or roughly $8 per capita (Dietz 1998: 70). Revolutionary factions of the IU questioned the logic of investing in city government at all, given that it deflected the demands of popular sectors away from the national economic system where real power and resources were concentrated (Chirinos 1980). But forbearance was a way for the IU to offer labor alternatives at the level of city government while awaiting the chance to make more fundamental changes. The party platform made this logic explicit:

The city cannot resolve the tough problems of employment that, given their character and magnitude, correspond to other entities ... Here we can develop *special initiatives at the scale of what a local government can do*. These initiatives include the sector to which we have given preferential attention: street vending. Not to eradicate street vending, as some sectors still hope ... but to recognize and put value in self-employment as *a mechanism for low-income groups to improve their socioeconomic situation. (IU 1986: 65–6, emphasis added)*

Thus, the Barrantes administration pushed as far as possible toward the incorporation of street vending in the city's employment plans. The inferiority of forbearance to state employment solutions, however, became clear in the 1986 election. President Alan García masterminded APRA's transition from a centrist party to a populist movement that could appeal to informal-sector workers. In 1986, APRA's mayoral candidate, Jorge

[77] Author interview with Washington Ipenza, mayor (1984–1987, 1999–2006), District of Villa María del Triunfo, Lima, Peru, June 18, 2011.

Del Castillo, rode on García's coattails to win election against Barrantes. Del Castillo proposed to "manage" street vending through many of the same tactics used by the IU. But he also offered access to temporary job creation programs. Ties to a spendthrift national government made these promises credible. Enrollment in temporary employment programs run by the national government surged just prior to city elections (Graham 1991: 104). Polls show that the urban poor preferred Barrantes by a narrow margin (47 to 43 percent). This split reflects the division between poor voters with more clientelistic and conservative orientations toward politics and those with more ideological and leftist views that Stokes (1991, 1995) captures in her analysis of Lima's shanytowns in the mid-1980s.

Nonetheless, APRA's plan to crowd out street vending through social policy substitutes was short-lived. Resources evaporated as García's heterodox economic reforms resulted in economic tumult. The number of street vendors swelled, reaching 300,000 in 1990 according to city officials.[78] National social expenditures fell to a fifth of their 1980 values, or just $12 per capita (Graham 1994: 92). The APRA-aligned city government had no response to the poor's distributive demands beyond forbearance. City officials saw no other choice but to allow vendors to take over city streets during the economic crisis, even calling it a "moral imperative."[79]

These sketches illustrate how elected mayors used forbearance to seek the electoral support of poor voters, who primarily worked in the informal sector. While a left-wing ideology shaped Barrantes's decisions, forbearance also was the strategy of a vote-seeking party. Continued forbearance under a populist – and next, a neopopulist – government shows how an electoral logic provides greater analytic leverage to understand enforcement than ideology alone.

### 4.3.2 Lower-Class Core Constituencies and Weak Enforcement (1990–1995)

The rise of neoliberal proposals for the informal sector led to a new type of appeal to street vendors in the 1990s. De Soto, Ghersi, and Ghibellini's

[78] Author interview with Elsie Guerrero, former director of Commercialization (*Comercialización*), Lima Metropolitan Government, Lima, Peru, June 7, 2011.

[79] Author interview with former sub-director of Commercialization (1986–1987), May 23, 2011.

treatise on informality, *The Other Path*, sparked debate about street-vending policy in Peru. The book concludes that no enforcement is required to end street vending, only support for entrepreneurship through credits and efficient business registration. The authors write, "If, instead of overregulating the street vendors, the authorities had removed the obstacles to their activities and made it easier for them to form business organizations and obtain formal credit so that they could build more markets, by 1993 all of today's street vendors would be off the streets" (De Soto 1989: 240).[80]

The Peruvian brand of neoliberalism recast class conflict as the informal-sector poor pitted against all groups that benefit from state regulations. To De Soto, Ghersi, and Ghibellini street vendors were capitalists creatively responding to byzantine business regulations, not workers shut out of industrial employment. This reasoning confirmed the suspicions of segments of the hard Left: it positioned informal-sector workers as part of a petty bourgeoisie. IU leader Rolando Breña, for instance, explained that neoliberalism constituted an ideological defeat of the Left because "from the small business owner to the street vendor, all of them were made businessmen" (Adrianzén 2012: 269). De Soto, Ghersi, and Ghibellini offered a prescription for a popular right party that could follow the "other path" of appealing to voters in the informal sector by eschewing regulation and enforcement, rather than a traditional route of aligning with the wealthy and alienating poor voters. This anti-elite rhetoric gave rise to an electorally successful form of "neopopulism" that linked libertarian elites with the informal-sector poor (Roberts 1995; Weyland 1996b).

The neoliberal Right attempted to build a political party, but it failed to recognize the anti-elite message of De Soto, Ghersi, and Ghibellini's work. The neoliberal Right aligned with Peru's traditional Right to form a coalition, the Democratic Front (*Frente Democrático*, Fredemo). This alignment, not to mention the choice to put a prototypical elite, the novelist Mario Vargas Llosa at its helm, diluted the anti-elite message. Fredemo fielded a candidate for city mayor, Juan Incáustegui, who offered to reduce barriers to help informal-sector workers start businesses and access credit. Incáustegui ran against Ricardo Belmont,

[80] The book initially was published in Spanish with three authors (De Soto, Ghersi, and Ghibellini). De Soto then published a sole-authored English edition, although Ghersi and Ghibellini won a lawsuit that recognized their authorship. I therefore recognize their joint authorship in the text, but cite the English edition published under De Soto's name.

a popular television personality with no political experience who captured the anti-establishment moment. Belmont created his own "independent movement" called Works (*Obras*) with a simple platform: to build infrastructure in the city. Belmont admitted that he shared many ideas with Fredemo, including proposals to help informal-sector workers start businesses. He only opposed "the parties that are all burned out" (Vargas Llosa 2011: 73–4). Belmont's victory became a harbinger for Peru's collapsing party system, and he secured much the same anti-party vote that would take Fujimori to presidential power the following year (Seawright 2012: 138–9). Incáustegui maintained relatively narrow support among nonpoor voters, while Belmont drew almost double the level of support from poor than from nonpoor voters (Cameron 1991: 85).

In office, Belmont avoided enforcement. It is unclear that Belmont had a choice, given the severity of Peru's economic crisis and Fujimori's hostility. An estimated 1,700 new vendors took to Lima's streets each month in the early 1990s, and only 11 percent of the population had adequate employment (Webb and Fernández Baca 1999). The country's economic situation aside, Fujimori viewed Belmont as a political rival and therefore tried to emasculate the city government, taking away 80 percent of the city's revenue in a 1993 decree (Delgado Silva 1994; Tanaka 2002: 13). The cuts decimated Belmont's ability to execute public works, pay city employees, and provide basic services. For instance, only 300 city police officers patrolled all of Lima's downtown.[81]

Several observations nevertheless suggest that Belmont did not want to enforce against street vendors. First, if resources were the major constraint, we would expect a discontinuity with Fujimori's budget cuts. Yet, the government made little enforcement effort pre- or post-cuts. Second, reports suggest that Belmont refused police support even for "essential" actions to control street vendors, such as operations to reduce fire and emergency hazards in street markets. The director of the National Civil Defense Institute (*Instituto Nacional de Defensa Civil*, Indeci), which proposed the measures to reduce public risks, lamented that Belmont "does not care about genuinely solving the problem" and instead proposed an independent commission to circumvent the "political

[81] "Se necesitan más policías ediles para controlar a tricicleros," *El Comercio* March 17, 1994.

obstacles" to enforcement.[82] Third, city politicians expressed concern that enforcement would alienate voters: the employment situation meant that it would have been "social and political suicide to take any stronger actions," according to one city councilor.[83] A structural interpretation of street vending prevailed and high-ranking officials blamed its expansion on "the inexistence of industrial policy to increase employment."[84]

Although the focus of this chapter is city politics, it bears mentioning that Fujimori's election in 1990 involved clear promises of forbearance toward street vendors. On the campaign trail, Fujimori went beyond neoliberal recommendations to cut state bureaucracy and proposed legislation to provide social assistance to street vendors. Street-vending leaders offered their support to Fujimori because of his promises of forbearance and social support. FEDEVAL leader Nolasco distinguishes Fujimori's broad insistence on forbearance and sectoral policies from more clientelistic tactics attempted by other politicians:

> Around fifty vending-association leaders went to Fujimori's house during the campaign. He didn't pay the leaders or even offer personal benefits like jobs like [Fredemo]. Instead, he made an offer to the group. Fujimori offered to develop a bank for low-interest loans, medical insurance, and to let us work in the street ... All along the agreement was that he would let us work in the street but also expand the benefits that the state offered us.[85]

Fujimori won by a large margin, with more than 75 percent of the second-round vote in Lima's poorest districts (Panfichi 1997: 228). Chapter 6 expands on how Fujimori used support for street vending, as well as small business promotion, as part of his employment policy once elected. What is clear is that both Belmont and Fujimori understood that forbearance toward street vendors could generate votes among the informal-sector poor.

[82] See "Urge el reordenamiento de ambulantes en Mercado Castilla," *El Comercio* September 26, 1995; "La Parada afronta descontrolado aumento de vendedores informales," *El Comercio* August 19, 1994; "Estéril resulta esfuerzo por reordenar informales en el ex Mercado Central," *El Comercio* September 22, 1994; "Por falta de apoyo fracasó el reordenamiento del Mercado Central," *El Comercio* October 26, 1994.

[83] "Municipio de Lima iniciará recuperación de 'Las Malvinas'," *El Comercio* March 19, 1994.

[84] "En el centro hay unos 60 mil ambulantes," *El Comercio* June 17, 1994.

[85] Author interview with Guillermo Nolasco, FEDEVAL head and former city councilor, Municipality of Lima, Lima, Peru, November 25, 2011.

### 4.3.3 Middle-Class Core Constituencies and Enforcement (1996–2002)

Enforcement occurred at an unlikely political moment in Lima according to conventional theories. Budgets were depleted. Fujimori's increasingly authoritarian government withheld police and funds. Nonetheless, Mayor Alberto Andrade united a nonpoor core constituency and increased enforcement.

Understanding the rise of an enforcement coalition requires a look at the shifts in public opinion engendered by forbearance toward street vendors. Segments of the public turned against street vending due to the increasing wealth and nuisance associated with it. First, the lack of enforcement – combined with economic liberalization that gave street vendors access to tax-free goods – helped some street vendors flourish economically. Peruvian officials love to use the maxim "In a choppy river, the fisherman benefits" to describe how vendors leveraged the state's absence during the economic crisis for profit. News reports homed in on vendors' wealth, claiming that some vendors owned enormous stands and charged others monthly rent to work in city streets.[86] "Attitudes toward street vendors changed in the 1990s," explains one street-vending leader, "because of street vendors' own development and accumulation due to the stability and permissiveness of the authorities."[87] Second, growing negative externalities hardened attitudes against vendors. Street vendors spread from sidewalks into the main downtown streets, causing congestion. Vendors also were seen as a threat to city authority and international investment, with newspaper headlines like "Who governs this city?" and invectives like "Where authority is the only one who doesn't have a place."[88] Thus, previous forbearance eroded social sympathy and generated frustration.

In 1995, Alberto Andrade brought these frustrations to the fore to build a winning electoral coalition. As a three-time mayor of the affluent

86 "Hay que contener a los ambulantes," *El Comercio* June 7, 1995; "El 60% de los desalojados posee tiendas," *El Comercio* February 19, 1999. In La Parada, the price for a stand was reported as 150 soles each month (or about $35) for a 1–6 meter square stand; in Garmarra the price was 120 soles. "Alto! La Parada no va más … sus días están contados," *El Comercio* April 21, 1999; "Desalojados venden pistas y veredas de Jr. América," *El Comercio* March 23, 1999.

87 Author interview with street-vending leader, District of San Martín de Porres, Lima, Peru, November 25, 2011.

88 "¿Quién manda en esta ciudad?" *El Comercio* August 22, 1994; "Puestos callejeros bloquean avenidas Caquetá y Zarumilla," *El Comercio* November 5, 1995.

Miraflores district, Andrade had earned a reputation for modern management principles and control of street vending. But Miraflores did not reflect the demographic composition of the Lima electorate. Andrade also was a white businessman and a longtime member of the center-right Christian Democratic Party (*Partido Popular Cristiano*, PPC). He easily could be pinned as part of Lima's traditional elite, which voters had rejected in past election cycles. Andrade's campaign managers recognized the strategic importance of the lower-middle-class vote. This vote is known as "Class C" in an alphabetic ranking of socioeconomic groups from the highest "A" to the lowest "E." As one campaign advisor put it, "In metropolitan Lima, the public was divided [on street vending]: about half wanted an end to the disorder, and another half lived off the chaos ... we needed to make sure that Class C voted for their frustration and not for social sympathy with vendors."[89]

Much like Peñalosa, Andrade used popular appeals rooted in urban subnationalism, law and order, and state authority to build support for enforcement.[90] First, Andrade cultivated support based on appeals to urban pride. Although a longtime member of the PPC, Andrade detected the antiparty mood and created an independent political movement, We Are Lima (*Somos Lima*). The name accentuated that Andrade represented the collective interest in restoring order against a minority that benefited from the city's deterioration. Andrade and his allies spoke of the "rebirth" of Lima's historic center as a symbol of Peru's greatness (Ronda 2000: 91).

Second, to expand his electoral appeal, Andrade separated the "true" poor from street vendors who violated property laws. As Andrade's advisor continues, "The first political question we asked ourselves was how do you convince the public that street vending is a problem of 'property,' rather than social injustice?"[91] To do so, Andrade distinguished between vendors who walk through the city to earn subsistence income, and stationary, "speculating" street vendors, who "only harm the city and have to go."[92] More than a decade of tolerance, as well as the neoliberal Right's emphasis on vendors as "hidden capitalists," made possible this distinction, or, as Andrade stated in a speech:

[89] Author interview with Oswaldo Carpio Villegas, June 1, 2011.

[90] Andrade actually inspired many of Peñalosa's tactics, not vice versa.

[91] Author interview with Oswaldo Carpio Villegas, Lima, Peru, June 1, 2011.

[92] "Comercio informal solo perjudica a la ciudad," *El Comercio* March 6, 1996.

> One has to remember that these vendors for more than 15 years have occupied a public space, that belongs to all citizens, and after these 15 years, they no longer are little poor street vendors that walk with their little box selling gum and chocolate. These are people with capital that can easily incorporate themselves into the formal sector.[93]

Andrade did not subscribe to the neoliberal Right's policy prescription that the state should extricate itself from commercial regulation to reduce street vending. Neoliberals viewed the state's regulations as illegitimate and driven by middle-class interests. Andrade believed that vendors violated legitimate city regulations. Hence, Andrade favored enforcement, not regulatory dilution.

The final related piece of Andrade's campaign was a focus on the reconstruction of state authority. Andrade viewed street vending as a visible manifestation of the state's loss of power and he committed to restore order in a mayoral debate: "There is a generalized crisis and authority has been supremely deteriorated for more than 20 years; here everyone does what they want, and that is not governing."[94] Unlike past mayors who advocated the "reordering" (*reordenamiento*) of street vendors, Andrade used strong terms to describe his enforcement actions. He proposed "eradications," "liberations," and "clean-ups." The neoliberal Right believed that shifting business incentives would change behavior, whereas Andrade was a liberal who emphasized the need for state authority to protect property rights.[95] Welfare needs were brushed aside as the responsibility of the national government. As one Somos Lima district mayor expressed it, "Informal workers need to be oriented and trained, given the skills so they can compete. But this is the role of the Peruvian state."[96]

Andrade's liberal appeals to authority and property law contrasted with those of the government-backed candidate and perceived successor to Fujimori, Jaime Yoshiyama. Yoshiyama's campaign portrayed Andrade as "the mayor of the rich," who viewed vendors as criminals and ignored unemployment.[97] Yoshiyama proposed that "the solution is

93 "Habían sido notificados y no cumplieron, explicó Andrade," *El Comercio* November 27, 1996.

94 "Dos propuestas para un problema: Lima," *El Comercio* October 22, 1995.

95 "Habían sido notificados y no cumplieron, explicó Andrade," *El Comercio* November 27, 1996.

96 Statement by Ramón Gastón Barúa Lecaros, mayor of San Isidro. "La opinión de los alcaldes," *El Comercio* July 23, 1996.

97 There was some truth in their claims of Andrade's paternalistic view of vendors. Andrade often spoke of vendors in a condescending fashion where he insisted that reordering

to work hand in hand with [street vendors], to come to agreements."[98] Because of his promises of support, street-vending associations backed Yoshiyama, but with little enthusiasm. The economic shock, labor code reforms, and Fujimori's decision to shelve a legalization project had soured many street vendors on Fujimori. Nevertheless, the electorate divided along class lines. Yoshiyama fared well among the urban poor. Andrade captured the middle- and lower-middle-class vote to win. Somos Lima mayors, for instance, won in all but one nonpoor district, while Fujimori's party (*Cambio 90-Nueva Mayoría*, NM) took all but one poor district.

In line with the preferences of nonpoor core constituents, Andrade pursued a clear enforcement policy that included major operations and continuous control actions. The city carried out more than twenty large-scale operations in the historic center between 1996 and 1999, each involving from 90 to 1,200 police officers (Egusquiza 2000). By 1997, the government claimed that it had removed 20,000 street vendors just from the historic center.[99] To maintain control, the government expanded the city police, the "Blue Helmets" (*Cascos Azules*), from 200 to 1,000 agents. The Blue Helmets engaged in regular patrols and decommission of merchandise.[100]

Civil society offered a weak defense of street vendors, particularly compared to the reaction to vendor removals in Bogotá. Labor unions, which had been decimated during the economic crisis, offered minimal support to street vendors.[101] Evicted vendors appealed to the courts to

would be for their own good. For example, he would say that operations against street vendors are "not something that one does, sadly, with love, shooing them: 'move away from here, child.' This has to be done with a little push, because if not, [street vendors] will never leave." "Habían sido notificados y no cumplieron, explicó Andrade," *El Comercio* November 27, 1996.

98 "Dos propuestas para un problema: Lima," *El Comercio* October 22, 1995.

99 The Andrade administration did work to relocate vendors to indoor markets. But the government insisted that enforcement would proceed whether or not vendors managed to find spots to relocate, and the projects were designed after removal operations began.

100 "Comuna limeña sí puede decomisar," *El Comercio* February 23, 1996; "Policías ediles sólo son preparados para la defensa," *El Comercio* March 26, 1997.

101 Peru's largest labor confederation during the period, the Peruvian Workers' Confederation (*Confederación de Trabajadores Peruanos*, CTP), was notably absent from street-vending issues. CTP historically was affiliated with APRA and focused on formal-sector workers. Peru's other labor confederation, the Unitary Confederation of Workers, (*Confederación Unitaria de Trabajadores del Perú*, CUT), circulated fliers that denounced Andrade "for trying to resolve a social problem in an irrational and inhumane manner, with clubs, arms, etc." (Roever 2005: 125).

protect their right to work, but unlike in Colombia, they found no allies (Aliaga Linares 2012: 39). Vendors' own organizing power also was compromised, as FEDEVAL fragmented due to disagreements over Fujimori's economic policies and violence by Shining Path against popular-sector leaders (Roever 2005: 63–4, 122–3). The National Confederation of Street-Vending Organizations (*Confederación Nacional de Trabajadores Ambulantes del Perú*, Conatap) presented an alternative legislative project to formalize and relocate vendors to state-funded commercial centers. It went nowhere. The main defenders of street vendors, if somewhat inconsistent in their support, were Fujimori and his allies.

Fujimori used his control over police and fiscal resources to create obstacles to Andrade's enforcement initiatives. The city government had a limited number of its own police officers, and they were unarmed and required national police protection to conduct operations that could result in confrontations. Accordingly, the large-scale operations against street vendors that Andrade planned required the cooperation of the National Police, which is under the direction of the executive branch. Support was not forthcoming. In one operation to remove 2,000 of the most entrenched street vendors in historic Lima, the National Police – whose regional command in Lima included 35,000 agents – sent just twenty-four officers.[102] In another operation, the National Police received an order to abandon a major vendor-removal operation at the last minute. An angry Andrade personally charged ahead with the operation. The National Police then joined forces with street vendors and hurled metal barricades at the city forces. Television footage shows street vendors chanting, "Fujimori, Fujimori!" as the city police retreated.[103] National Police Director Fernando Dianderas explained that the operation stopped "to avoid a social cost that afterwards we would come to regret." Andrade, in contrast, blamed Fujimori and said that the operation was suspended due to "a political hand that harms the capital, that harms the city of Lima."[104] Andrade proceeded to strengthen the city and district police forces.

[102] One cannot be certain that Fujimori himself was responsible for the lack of police cooperation. The police told the press that the regional commander had orders to provide "full support" to Andrade, but had faced conflicting security requirements on the day of the operation. See "Alto mando de PNP dispuso el apoyo requerido por Andrade," *El Comercio* March 29, 1996; "La opinión de los alcaldes," *El Comercio*, July 23, 1996.

[103] "Batalle campal entre policías y comerciantes," *ATV*, May 14, 1997, video www.youtube.com/watch?v=Rkn_1hcTbzk.

[104] "Batalle campal entre policías y comerciantes," *ATV*, May 14, 1997.

Fujimori also tried to stop enforcement through financial channels. Fujimori had slashed the city budget to $128 million, or $19 per capita, in 1996. By comparison, Bogotá's budget during the same period was $284 million, or $45 per capita for a similar population. In order to finance the removal of street vendors and renovate the city center, therefore, Andrade drew up plans to apply for a $20 million loan from the Inter-American Development Bank. But the city needed central government approval to borrow money. The finance minister, Jorge Camet, disqualified the loan as a "useless expense" that exacerbated poverty, and did not constitute an "investment" eligible for international lending. Andrade again accused Fujimori of blocking his plans.[105]

Why did Fujimori go to such lengths to block enforcement? On the one hand, Fujimori sought to discredit Andrade as a presidential candidate. Although Andrade was far from a vocal opponent of the Fujimori regime, his popularity ratings and defeat of Yoshiyama made him an electoral threat. Just a year out from the 2000 presidential election, 64 percent of poll respondents approved of Andrade's work as mayor, and 31 percent said they would vote for him in a presidential election (Apoyo 1999). On the other hand, Fujimori and his supporters used forbearance as a tactic to rebuild popularity among low-income voters. Fujimori hit a nadir in popular support after economic liberalization and a constitutional referendum. He then began to boost social spending and target poor communities for expenditures to restore his base (Graham and Kane 1998; Roberts and Arce 1998; Schady 2000). Fujimori revived his defense of street vendors as another tactic to rebuild popular-sector support.

Despite Fujimori's opposition, Andrade won reelection as city mayor in 1998. Andrade's party – renamed We are Peru (*Somos Perú*) in anticipation of his 2000 presidential bid – again won almost every middle-income district in the city and only a handful of poor districts. Much of the public gave Andrade high marks for restoring order to the city center, but opinion divided along class lines. Roughly a third of low-income voters said that they did not support Andrade's reelection because he "has been abusive with street vendors" and "does not care about the poor." Only 5 percent of middle-class voters shared these beliefs (Apoyo 2002).

[105] "Municipio no detendrá gestiones para recuperar Centro Histórico," *El Comercio* November 6, 1996; "Andrade confía en que algún día podrá dialogar con Fujimori," *El Comercio* October 16, 1996; "Proyectos de Lima presentados al BID," *El Comercio* August 18, 1996.

Class divisions also were reflected in the adoption of enforcement policies by district governments. Recall that Lima is a politically decentralized city, so district mayors can control enforcement. Of twenty-two nonpoor districts in the city, twenty undertook major enforcement actions in tandem with Andrade. Most of these mayors represented Andrade's party and viewed enforcement as a central dimension of his political platform. In the nonpoor district of Jesús María, for example, the mayor believed she had a mandate to enforce: "I have been chosen to impose order and recover the city, not to make the street vendors happy or those who infringe the law, which is what voters consider to be correct."[106] In contrast, poor districts in the city pursued less consistent enforcement policies. Of fourteen majority-poor districts, only two (Ate and Villa El Salvador) reported enforcement operations.

District demographics tended to be more important than party in determining enforcement policy. Mayors aligned with Fujimori's party (Cambio 90-NM) enforced when they governed nonpoor districts. The most notable example is the mayor of San Martín de Porres, Javier Kanashiro, who undertook major enforcement actions around the Caquetá market, despite his ties to Fujimori. Conversely, mayors aligned with Andrade's party (Somos Perú) who won in poor districts followed their electorate's preferences and chose not to enforce. For example, the Somos Perú mayor of San Juan de Miraflores, Paulo Hinostroza, justified forbearance as in line with the poverty of his district and the need for support among street-vending associations:

> I didn't receive any advice from Andrade about what to do with street vendors, although obviously I knew what he had done in the center of Lima. I didn't want to fight vendors because this is a poor district and street vending is an honorable profession, and good jobs are hard to come by in this country ... if you try too much to impose order, vendors threaten with marches and spread bad rumors, and they have a lot of force because they are a huge group. Both disorder and order have support in this district and you can't make both groups happy.[107]

In sum, the mere election of Andrade was remarkable: he was a white, conservative, uncharismatic politician elected at a time when the public clearly had rejected traditional elites. But he rightly calculated that he could extend his appeal among middle- and lower-middle-class voters through an enforcement platform; growing frustration with better-off

106 "Reordenarán a ambulantes en Jesús María," *El Comercio* April 24, 1996.

107 Author interview with Paulo Hinostroza, mayor (2003–2006), District of San Juan de Miraflores, Lima, Peru, June 24, 2011.

vendors added to the appeal. Second, the fact that Andrade mustered the capacity to enforce with minimal financial or police assistance from the central government provides disconfirming evidence of arguments that focus on state capacity. Instead, the events support the interpretation that changing political tides drove enforcement. Third, the main legacy of Andrade's administration was a generalized perception that street vending could be controlled, at least in the city center. Urban political decentralization, however, allowed district mayors to continue to pursue forbearance.

### 4.3.4 Neutral Core Constituencies and Enforcement (2002–2014)

Quite different from the polarized citywide debates in Bogotá, much of the controversy in Lima over street vending shifted to poor districts where vendors lived and voted in the 2000s. Vending lost issue salience among the middle class, as seen through the newspaper coverage in Figure 4.2. Electoral incentives thus played a more muted role in the enforcement choices of city mayors. The centrist administration of Luis Castañeda, in particular, altered enforcement along with the electoral cycle. The leftist administration of Susana Villarán used forbearance appeals to mobilize street vendors in her campaign, but ultimately enforced, following post-materialist ideological convictions and losing support among the poor.

In 2002, Andrade lost a tight race to Castañeda, a former head of the Social Security Institute. Castañeda's platform echoed the infrastructure-based approach of Belmont. Castañeda tried to portray Andrade as a mayor of the rich, but the accusations did not stick. In one debate, for example, Castañeda claimed that Andrade never visited the squatter settlements in Lima. Andrade took off his boots and showed them to the crowd, saying that the mud on them proved that he had marched to poor neighborhoods and back, and not just prior to the elections.[108] Both mayors, moreover, agreed on the need to maintain order in central Lima. Castañeda complained, "People do whatever they feel like here … and when I call attention to it, they say that I am authoritarian. If that is authoritarian, then I am."[109] Castañeda eked out a victory largely

[108] "Castañeda y Andrade protagonizaron acalorado debate," *AgenciaPeru* November 10, 2002; "Andrade reta a Castañeda a un nuevo debate," *AgenciaPeru* November 7, 2002.

[109] "Luis Castañeda, un político reservado," *Terra* June 26, 2013.

based on voters' exhaustion with the Andrade administration (Apoyo 2002).[110]

Castañeda straddled class preferences on street vending. Particularly in his first term, he recognized that the majority of voters preferred order in downtown Lima, and he took a zero-tolerance approach. But he also recognized Andrade's error in ignoring the employment issues that caused street vending. Castañeda noted:

> In contrast to Andrade, I knew that we couldn't tolerate such extreme inequality and expel the poor in an improvised fashion . . . But if you say, "oh poor thing" and only recognize the poor's need to work, that's a perspective of weakness and resignation that most people no longer support. I was firm with what needed to happen, that first, street vendors had to leave the city center but, second, they would not leave without work.[111]

Castañeda undertook operations against street vendors and relocated them or offered them slots in his temporary licensing program (*Capitalizando*) to address employment concerns. Unlike Andrade, Castañeda avoided any personal association with enforcement operations and told his bureaucrats to answer any press questions with the line: "This is not an eviction, this is not an eradication, this is a relocation in which vendors will now work elsewhere."[112] The apolitical approach neither won nor lost him support among voters. Castañeda instead focused on construction projects in the city and maintained even support across class groups in his reelection in 2006.

Castañeda proved less consistent in his enforcement policies as he geared up for a presidential run. He engaged in forbearance by gutting the city's coercive capacity. He transferred control of street vending from the city police to an inspections office (*Fiscalización*). Just forty-five inspectors covered all economic infractions in central Lima, compared to more than 1,000 police under Andrade. The government also slowed decommissions of merchandise by the agents that remained. Although the Peruvian economy did dip with the global financial crisis, there is no evidence that budget cuts motivated these drawdowns.[113] Castañeda also expanded the number of licensed vendors from 300 to upward of

[110] Castañeda won with roughly 30 percent support across class groups (IMA October 20, 2002; IMA October 30, 2002).

[111] Author interview with Luis Castañeda, Lima, Peru, July 12, 2011.

[112] Author interview with Luis Castañeda, July 12, 2011.

[113] Author interview with Álvaro Anicama González, head of inspections (*Gerente de Fiscalización y Control*) under Villarán, Metropolitan Municipality of Lima (*Municipalidad Metropolitana de Lima*, MML), November 30, 2011.

5,000 to reward his supporters.[114] One official in charge of street-vending management describes:

It was a political theme: sometimes [the Inspections Department] wanted to take a hard line in certain areas, but then suddenly we'd receive calls from congressmen, city councilors, or advisors to the mayor asking us to "not abuse" the vendors, and then the mayor's office would tell us to take a softer approach ... Andrade had a lot of support for the control of vending, but by the time Castañeda took office, there was more sympathy for the vendors ... and more politicians wanted to get involved.[115]

In addition to reducing continuous control operations, Castañeda put major enforcement projects on hold, especially the relocation of Lima's wholesale market from La Parada to a new site. More than 3,000 street vendors surrounded La Parada, and well-organized associations opposed the move. As the mayor of La Victoria, where La Parada is located, speculates, "With elections, there is a lot of fear of using coercive force to accomplish something big."[116] Castañeda therefore left his successor to absorb the political costs of removing vendors in the market's move.

In 2010, citizens elected Susana Villarán, a human-rights activist who represented a new left-wing party, Social Force (*Fuerza Social*). It was the first time that the Left had won in the capital since 1983. The election gave Villarán a narrow victory over Lourdes Flores, a conservative from the PPC. Two months before the election, more than half of upper-class voters said that they would support Flores compared to a quarter of lower-class voters (IOP 2010). But support for Flores slipped amid a scandal and Villarán surged, gaining among middle-class voters. Many voters turned to Villarán with little sense of her platform. Just prior to the election, there were minimal differences in vote intention by socioeconomic group.[117]

Given that Villarán was an unknown candidate identified with the Left, street vendors hoped for a permissive approach as under the IU. Vending leaders claim that Villarán promised to work with them and mobilized as

[114] Author interview with Luis Valer, city councilor (2011–2013), Lima, Peru, November 28, 2011; "Unos 5.000 vendedores saldrán del Cercado," *El Comercio* February 4, 2011.

[115] Sub-director of inspections (*Fiscalización*), MML (2003–2009), Lima, Peru, December 2, 2011.

[116] Author interview with Alberto Sánchez Aizcorbe, mayor, District of La Victoria, June 15, 2011.

[117] Ecological correlations suggest that Fuerza Social attracted a larger vote share in poor districts (Sulmont and Gordillo 2011: 61), but individual-level polls do not confirm these results (IOP 2010).

part of her campaign.[118] Business and middle-class groups feared that Villarán would "backslide" into the IU's permissive policies.[119] Castañeda stoked these popular fears by granting temporary permits to vendors before the transfer of power. The increase in vendors forced Villarán into an awkward position in which she needed to remove vendors, abandoning her supporters, or confirm business fears.

Nonetheless, the Left's return brought back a very different ideology and orientation toward street vending. Villarán drew inspiration from the post-materialist Left, and looked to Mockus in particular. Villarán emphasized that enforcement serves the poor's long-term interests, or what observers called a position of "progress through force" (*progreso a palos*). In this spirit, the Villarán government pushed ahead with the postponed relocation of the wholesale market, although it required substantial coercive force, upset vendors, and left four people dead. In addition, Villarán improved the government's routine enforcement capacity. She canceled temporary authorizations, revived decommissions of merchandise, and doubled the numbers of city police and inspectors dedicated to commercial violations. Consistent with the beliefs of the post-materialist Left, these actions were intended to change social norms. City inspectors even wore vests with the slogan "If you change, Lima changes. Follow the law."[120]

Villarán had an ideological commitment to enforcement, but she also (perhaps wrongly) judged the political costs of enforcement to be low due to Lima's decentralization. Vice-Mayor Hernán Núñez, for example, emphasized that "one has to understand street vending as a social necessity."[121] But enforcement in the city center, as pursued by Villarán, would not infringe on vendors' ability to work in the local districts where they live. City Councilor Luis Valer elaborates on the logic:

> We took out 5,000–6,000 street vendors from the city center. There was little protest by the vendors or outcry that vendors were "poor things" because they went back to the districts where they live, and mayors in poor districts aren't confronting the vendors ... The idea is to progressively eliminate vendors and let each district do it at its own pace because there is a lack of work and business opportunities.[122]

[118] Author interview with street-vending leaders, CUT, Informal Sector Division, Lima, Peru, May 16, 2011.

[119] "Deambulando," *El Comercio* December 18, 2013.

[120] Author interview with Álvaro Anicama González, head of inspections under Villarán, MML, Lima, Peru, November 30, 2011.

[121] "Una necesidad social," *El Comercio* December 12, 2013.

[122] Interview with Luis Valer, city councilor and president of Commercialization Commission, Lima, Peru, November 28, 2011.

Although urban decentralization cushioned the electoral blow, the post-materialist Left tends to be unpopular with the poor and Villarán proved no exception. Only 15 percent of poor voters, compared to 34 percent of nonpoor voters, approved of her administration. Inaction and crime were the most common criticisms of her government (17 percent of respondents). But the use of fines by city inspectors and relocation of street vendors were cited almost as often (16 percent) (CPI 2013). Enforcement eroded what support Villarán initially had among the poor.

I found more evidence of clientelistic forbearance in district elections than at the city level, and in the case of street vending than squatting. Although few politicians admitted to clientelistic forbearance, about a quarter pointed the finger at other mayors who "condition" vendors' ability to stay in the streets on their political behaviors, such as attending rallies and government events. The terms of the clientelistic exchange became clearest when under threat. For instance, one mayor planned to evict street vendors to expand a highway. Street vendors wrote to President García explaining, "The mayor does not want to recognize local norms and that when he was a candidate he offered to support us as long as we inclined our votes to his candidacy."[123] Nevertheless, many politicians avoided enforcement entirely due to the political costs. A common sentiment came from one politician who explained, "You have to express solidarity with vendors and get them behind you in the campaign because they can spread the word about you to their customers and bring their people to your rallies."[124] A street-vending leader echoed that associations participate in politics to demonstrate their clout: "You have to participate in the campaigns to show that you have the numbers and will cause the mayor a big headache if he tries to evict your people."[125] Thus, at the district level, some politicians do punish associations that fail to support their campaigns, but they also risk their reputations for supporting the poor.

In sum, an examination of street vending in Lima showcases the electoral dynamics of enforcement in a context of weak institutions. I have demonstrated how enforcement varies with the core constituency of

[123] Letter from Mesa de Trabajo para la Formalización Comercial de Ceres to President Alan García, "Solicitamos expropriación y/o adjudicación en venta del terreno que administra SUNAT (Ex ECASA)," District of Ate, Lima, Peru, March 24, 2011.

[124] Author interview with Walter Quispe, local councilor, District of Villa El Salvador, Lima, Peru, November 4, 2011.

[125] Author interview with leader, Red de las Mujeres, Lima, Peru, May 16, 2011.

a mayor and serves as a form of informal welfare provision. Politicians who courted poor voters, from ideologues like Barrantes to outsiders like Belmont, preferred forbearance to demonstrate their commitments to the poor and to guarantee some form of employment. In contrast, mayors who promoted enforcement, such as Andrade and Villarán, alienated poor voters.

I should be careful not to overstate politicians' scope for choice in Lima. Institutional and fiscal capacity certainly limited the *extent* of enforcement, particularly during the economic tumult of the late 1980s and presidential conflict in the 1990s. In broad terms, enforcement increased as state capacity improved in Lima. But a focus on institutional capacity provides limited leverage to understand rapid shifts in enforcement. Andrade and Belmont inherited similar institutional resources. Andrade insisted on enforcement because he had an electoral mandate to remove vendors. Castañeda, in contrast, scaled back on enforcement when Peru's commodities boom was in full swing in order to gain an electoral edge. Hence, the evidence is more consistent with the claim that politicians faced variable electoral incentives to enforce depending on the constituencies that they courted and past enforcement choices.

## 4.4 CONCLUSIONS

This chapter has explored how a mayor's core constituency accounts for when enforcement occurs at the city level. Basic correlations confirmed that mayors with poor core constituents enforced less than those with nonpoor constituents. Mayors, state officials, and street vendors understood forbearance as a policy choice with welfare and electoral repercussions. Politicians traded the costs of enforcement in the form of lost support among the poor against the benefits in support from the nonpoor. Strategic incentives encouraged mayors with poor core supporters to forgo enforcement and employ the poor through informal means.

The comparative analysis of enforcement in Lima and Bogotá yielded multiple empirical observations that are inconsistent with rival explanations rooted in state capacity. Bogotá mayors enforced during the city's worse downturn in decades, when capacity presumably hit a nadir. More puzzling from capacity-based perspectives, mayors tolerated street vendors, and quite openly, as the economy rebounded. Lima, which suffered a profound economic crisis, moved to enforce during a period of high underemployment, paltry budgets, and central government opposition. An explanation rooted in electoral dynamics resolves these anomalies.

Can alternative political explanations account for these patterns? Partisan ideology provided limited leverage. The historical analysis showed that forbearance often is rooted in ideological debates, but these debates do not fall neatly along the conventional left–right divisions. The neoliberal Right favored forbearance to protect street vendors' economic freedom; the conservative Right pushed enforcement to guarantee respect for property rights and state authority. The materialist Left defended forbearance to improve the material welfare of the poor, while the post-materialist Left – as well as the old Communist Left – wanted to enforce and rely on formal welfare policies. Left–right labels thus tell us little about enforcement policy. Nonetheless, enforcement positions often are driven by philosophical views about how to help the poor.

A pluralist model, focused on the strength of either street-vending or business associations, may seem to account for these enforcement outcomes. Indeed, street-vending associations declined in membership and cohesion in the mid-1990s, when enforcement peaked in Lima and Bogotá. In Lima, the vending association FEDEVAL collapsed due to internal divisions as well as attacks on leaders by Shining Path. Associations in Bogotá experienced a similar fragmentation. Changes in labor law led to a proliferation of vending groups, which diluted their organizational power. Leaders from the radical vending association SINUCROM also were victims of political violence in the 1980s due to their support of the guerillas' political arm (Donovan 2008: 37–8). In opposition, market liberalization arguably strengthened business groups through their alliances with international capitalists. Frustration with street vendors also mounted as the business community tried to attract foreign investment and strengthen city "brands." Business associations were active participants in plans to remove street vendors from central city areas (Moncada 2016). Thus, in broad strokes, a decline in the power of street-vending associations and a rise in business power does coincide with enforcement operations.

However, the timing and distribution of enforcement expose flaws in pluralist accounts. In both Lima and Bogotá, declines in vendors' organizational power were most dramatic on the urban periphery. Vendors were well organized in central city areas and continued to aggregate votes and financial resources throughout the period. Street-vending associations in historic Lima, for example, pooled more than a million dollars to move to formal commercial centers in the mid-1990s; they petitioned Congress and wrote to Fujimori to prevent their removal. Vending associations in downtown Bogotá likewise sued for their right to work and bribed city councilors to vote against changes in the police code. If organizational power prevents enforcement, then we should have observed limited enforcement in the city center compared to the urban periphery. The opposite occurred. Andrade, Peñalosa, and Mockus all enforced against the street-vending associations that were best organized, railing against the "mafias" that controlled public space in downtown areas. This anomaly makes sense in my electoral account in which associational strength perversely makes vendors seem less needy and thereby reduces the political costs of enforcement.

Business associations, likewise, cannot readily account for the ebb and flow of enforcement. Although globalization brought new urgency to the recovery of downtown areas, business's opposition to street vending had peaked years earlier. In Lima, major hotels and banks threatened to leave the central city if Belmont did not act against street vendors. He did not budge. In Bogotá, business leaders also planned strikes and donated funds to remove vendors in the early 1990s. But even Caicedo, who once headed the main business confederation, ignored their complaints. When enforcement occurred, it also did not take place in ways that necessarily aligned with business interests. For example, business groups threatened to strike when Mockus came to power in 1995 if he did not control street vending. Mockus enforced and cooperated with business groups (Moncada 2016: 137–40). But Mockus also deviated from their preferences and levied fines on companies that sponsored street vendors, as was a common practice by major candy and soda companies. Yet it is the divergence in outcomes between Lima and Bogotá that best shows the limitations of purely business-based accounts. Both cities have followed open-market policies, tried to build up their city brands, and seen major international investment, but only Lima has maintained a hard line against street vendors. Understanding when business groups and nonpoor interests are part of winning electoral coalitions thus provides greater leverage to understand enforcement politics. Business groups have played an important role in shaping enforcement, but as one former mayor put it, "they aren't the ones who will bring you votes."[126]

[126] Author interview with Paul Bromberg, interim mayor, Bogotá, Colombia, January 31, 2014.

# 5

# Where Forbearance Occurs

## *The Role of Electoral Institutions*

> We realize that this is arbitrary legal discrimination, but to win elections in this district, you have to appear like you care about the poor ... Things would be different if you wanted to be mayor in a rich district, or if you were Pinochet, then you could enforce the law just as they give it to you.
>
> – Head of Inspections, District of Conchalí, Santiago, Chile

Do electoral incentives shape enforcement? The qualitative evidence presented in Chapters 3 and 4 suggest that politicians use forbearance to provide informal welfare benefits and signal their representation of poor voters. This chapter provides an additional test of my argument by exploiting differences in the electoral structure of cities. The intuition is simple: if electoral incentives influence enforcement, then cities with different electoral institutions should have different enforcement patterns, all else being equal. I add the case of Santiago as a "hard" test of the theory: high levels of institutional capacity and police centralization make it unlikely to observe weak enforcement under conventional theories. Yet under my theory, urban political decentralization – combined with inadequate employment policy – creates strong incentives for some mayors in Santiago to prefer forbearance.

More concretely, I argue that the extent of political decentralization in a city produces differences in *electoral geography*. The boundaries of electoral districts make the votes of the urban poor more or less useful for office-seeking politicians. Due to residential segregation, some districts overwhelmingly concentrate poor or nonpoor voters. Others mix different class groups, as we saw in the case of citywide electoral districts in Chapter 4. The political costs of enforcement vary with the share of poor voters in an electoral district. In districts with high concentrations of poor residents, politicians are more likely to forbear and attract more offenders due to their lax enforcement policies. In districts with few poor voters, the most viable strategy is to enforce, following the median voter's preference and displacing offenses to poor districts.

Of course, poor districts differ in a host of other ways from nonpoor districts: they often collect fewer taxes, receive worse police attention, and employ less well-trained and remunerated bureaucrats. The distinguishing empirical observations of my theory are twofold: first, I expect enforcement to vary with district poverty *only in cities that hold local elections*, and not to respond to demographics in cities that centrally determine enforcement policy. Second, I expect district demographics to predict enforcement *only for offenses where classes differ in their preferences over enforcement*, and not more broadly for offenses like violent crime that almost all voters want to control.

As I noted in Chapter 1, I deliberately study cities with different electoral institutions: Santiago is a politically decentralized city, meaning that residents elect a local mayor for their district, while Bogotá is a politically centralized city, meaning that residents elect a city mayor who appoints administrators for their district. Lima is a hybrid that elects both types of mayors, but allows local mayors to determine enforcement policy. Empirically, then, I expect enforcement to vary with district poverty in the cities that hold local elections, Lima and Santiago. District demographics should not predict enforcement in cities that centrally determine enforcement policy, as in Bogotá. An additional test of my theory comes from looking at the causal mechanisms: the perceived electoral costs of enforcement should vary with district poverty in Lima and Santiago, but not in Bogotá.

In this chapter, I concentrate on street vending because it occurs across urban space and thus electoral geography is more likely to matter. But, a focus on electoral geography also brings into relief why enforcement against squatting is so minimal and stable over time. The electoral costs of enforcement are high in districts where squatting occurs and housing policy is absent. The co-occurrence of district poverty and squatting thus helps make sense of why forbearance is a stable outcome in the case of squatting (Chapter 3) and a volatile one in the case of street vending (Chapter 4).

The rest of this chapter is organized as follows. I begin by discussing my empirical strategy and measures of key variables: enforcement, street vending, and state capacity. Second, I present the empirical analysis, showing both simple bivariate plots and fitting statistical models. Third, I show that the perceived political costs of enforcement increase with district poverty in politically decentralized cities, and that these political costs can explain the differences in enforcement toward squatting and street vending presented in the preceding chapters. Fourth, I elaborate on the mechanisms that connect district demographics and enforcement through qualitative interviews from the unlikely case of Santiago. I conclude with a discussion of whether capacity limitations, such as corruption or shirking, drive the results.

## 5.1 MEASUREMENT STRATEGY

As noted in Chapter 1, studies of enforcement face a measurement and an identification challenge. A count of sanctions alone cannot distinguish between perfect control of a small number of offenses and limited control of numerous offenses. What I want to measure is enforcement effort, where forbearance implies limited effort given the magnitude of the problem. In Chapter 3, I relied on process tracing to separate the portion of enforcement explained by political choice versus administrative constraints. In Chapter 4, I used a threshold definition of whether governments exerted any effort to conduct operations and continuous police control. This dichotomous operationalization ignored variation in how much effort a government exerts and, as with any categorical definition, could be criticized as an arbitrary standard. More systematic comparisons, however, were impossible due to the lack of data on both enforcement and offenses over time.

The empirical test of the theory developed here tries to surmount these problems by relying on my original survey of district governments to develop comparable measures of both offenses and enforcement across space. This feature allows me to expand the number of predictions that I should observe if my theory holds. As I suggested in Chapter 1, it is natural to think of enforcement as an equilibrium outcome determined by sanctions and offenses. Forbearance represents an outward shift in the enforcement supply curve, where a government decreases enforcement and thus increases the number of vendors. Thus, there is a *negative* relationship between sanctions and street vendors across space. Critically, this approach distinguishes alternative means through which a reduction in enforcement can be observed, such as a demand shifter that decreases the number of street vendors and thus enforcement. If most of the variation in enforcement comes in the level of offenses,

I expect to see a *positive* relationship between sanctions and street vending across space.

I examine whether electoral politics leads politicians to shift the supply of enforcement by selecting cities that differ in their electoral structure. Political decentralization changes the distribution of class groups within electoral districts and the level at which enforcement policy is determined. The intuitive idea is that political decentralization produces uneven enforcement across districts, as politicians tailor enforcement to the poverty level in their electoral district and disregard spillover effects. Poor electoral districts should conduct fewer enforcement actions and attract *more* vendors. Districts therefore should trace out a downward-sloping curve in the cross-sectional data. Politically centralized cities constitute a single electoral district with a mayor who sets enforcement policy for the city. A mayor who represents an entire city internalizes both the benefits and costs imposed on others. As such, most variation in enforcement across districts comes from differences in the number of violations, resulting in an upward-sloping curve in the cross-sectional data under political centralization.

While bivariate correlations provide an initial test of my theory, I further examine the relationship between district poverty and enforcement using a Poisson regression and controlling for other important district characteristics.[1] My first hypothesis is that enforcement operations drop off with the fraction of poor residents in an electoral district. So, district poverty should be a negative and significant predictor of enforcement, but only in politically decentralized cities. Poverty should have no relationship with enforcement in politically centralized cities once controlling for the number of vendors.

I include the number of vendors as a covariate for the limited purpose of observing the difference depending on whether enforcement policy is locally or centrally determined. In politically centralized cities, I expect that enforcement is a positive function of the number of vendors. But this relationship should be much attenuated or reversed in politically decentralized cities. There is no clean prediction because my theory implies reverse causality: districts have more vendors because they enforce less.

My second hypothesis is that competition shapes politicians' responsiveness to enforcement preferences. In addition to differences across cities due to political decentralization, I look at a mayor's margin of victory.

[1] Holland (2015) provides additional details on the Poisson specification and robustness checks using other distributions.

Mayors who win by larger margins enjoy greater office security and may be less sensitive to the political costs of enforcement.

Third, I expect that a politician's core constituency predicts enforcement. I test this hypothesis in a crude way, given that I do not have measures of the class gradient of support at the district level, as in the previous chapter. Instead, I use partisan affiliation to operationalize core support; loosely, politicians from the Right may attract a wealthier core constituency and thus favor more enforcement. But, as stressed in Chapter 1, ideology is an imperfect proxy for core constituency.

I distinguish my theory from capacity-based alternatives in several ways. First, if state authorities are generally less capable or less attentive in poor districts, then demographics should shape enforcement irrespective of electoral rules. Under my theory, in contrast, district poverty predicts enforcement *only* when elections occur at the local level. Additionally, while I expect that officials in centralized cities respond to the number of offenses, elected politicians manipulate enforcement so that it bears no relationship to offense levels.

I also compare enforcement across cities with different electoral institutions. While capacity constraints play a larger role in administratively decentralized cities (and especially those with local police forces), I still expect political pressures to be a substantively more important explanation for enforcement. The critical case for theory testing, however, is a politically decentralized city with a single police force. Capacity-based theories suggest minimal variation when a single institution manages enforcement. My theory instead posits that politicians choose how to deploy common police resources in response to electoral pressure, such that demographics still predict enforcement variation.

Of course, the same formal institutions do not necessarily translate into the same informal access to policing. To rule out that difference in the responsiveness of police to poor communities accounts for the observed patterns, I compare enforcement against violent crime to street vending. Violent crime is a classic valence issue; the poor and nonpoor reward politicians for improved control. Less criminal law enforcement in poor districts would suggest that institutional debilities or neglectful policing accounts for class-based variation in enforcement. A "placebo" test of my theory is that poverty should explain enforcement against street vending, but it should not more broadly explain enforcement against crime with weaker distributive implications.

To test these hypotheses, I draw on the structured survey that I personally administered to the director or sub-director of the district office in charge of street commerce and inspections in all urban districts in Lima, Santiago, and Bogotá. Appendix C provides additional information on the survey implementation and summary statistics.

The dependent variable is the average number of enforcement operations conducted per month by a district (*Operations*). A challenge is to determine a consistent definition of an enforcement operation. I use the involvement of the national police as a standard in Bogotá and Santiago. Because only the national police can require vendors to identify themselves, which allows authorities to impose fines and decommission goods, police assistance implies an operation of a certain scale. The measure of an operation must be adjusted in Lima because national police only supplement local district forces to protect them in large-scale actions. Local police take primary responsibility for the control of public space. As such, in Lima, I use the retention of merchandise or equipment from a group of vendors as the threshold for an operation because it indicates willingness to impose costs on vendors. As one police director explains, "If I apply the law as written and take away [vendors'] merchandise, I take away their work, so I don't do it."[2] I therefore ask officials how many operations the district has requested with the national police, or have involved decommission, in each of the last three months. I average the monthly reports and verify the director's report with district records and police logs whenever possible. The measurement difference (operations in Lima are on a smaller scale) requires caution in drawing level comparisons across cities. Accordingly, all results are expressed in percent terms.

I also measure the number of unlicensed street vendors in thousands (*Vendors*). I ask each director for the district's estimates and records on unlicensed vendors. In about half of cases, these records come from local street-vending censuses, and in the other half, they come from inspection team estimates.

The main explanatory variable of theoretical interest is the district's class composition. I code the portion of lower-class residents (*Lower*). These measures come from government stratifications in Colombia, and polling firm stratifications in Peru and Chile. Stratification measures often aggregate information on consumption patterns, housing prices, and service access. While I check an alternative measure of poverty based on unsatisfied basic needs, class stratifications better capture district characteristics.

[2] Author interview with director of citizen security and inspections, District of Puente Piedra, Lima, Peru, June 20, 2011.

Given that the dominant alternative explanation focuses on resource constraints, I include the district budget per capita as a control variable (*Budget*). Budgets are an imperfect proxy for capacity so I check alternatives, including the number and salary of bureaucrats, police stations, and local tax collection. Population likely affects the amount of enforcement, as well as the number of street vendors, and therefore is included as a control (*Population*).

To operationalize competitive threats, I calculate the mayor's margin of victory (*Margin*) as the percentage of votes for the winning candidate less the percentage won by the second-place candidate. A wide margin suggests greater office security.

Of the cases, only Chile has an identifiable political spectrum to test the role of partisan constituencies in the cross-sectional data. I include an indicator variable (*Right*) that takes on the value of "1" if the district mayor represents a party that forms part of the right-leaning Alianza coalition, which is the case for half the districts.

To examine enforcement patterns in the absence of distributive incentives, I use arrests for hard crimes as a dependent variable (*Arrests*). Arrests indicate that the police have taken action in a case beyond arriving at the scene of a crime. I measure the underlying level of violations using citizen crime reports (*Reports*). I conduct this placebo test in Santiago, given that it is a politically decentralized city with a national police force.

## 5.2 SPATIAL PATTERNS OF STREET VENDING AND ENFORCEMENT

I first explore the bivariate relationship between enforcement and street vending in the raw data. Figure 5.1 reveals a negative relationship in the politically decentralized cities, Lima and Santiago, as predicted if some mayors do fewer enforcement operations and attract more street vendors. The opposite relationship emerges in the politically centralized case, Bogotá. Districts do more operations when they face more street vendors. Similarly, enforcement against hard crimes increases roughly in proportion with the number of offenses in Santiago. The observed positive correlation between offenses and enforcement suggests that political supply-side distortions are likely at work to generate a negative relationship in politically decentralized cities.

To visually examine the role of district demographics, poor districts, defined as those with more than half lower-class households, are

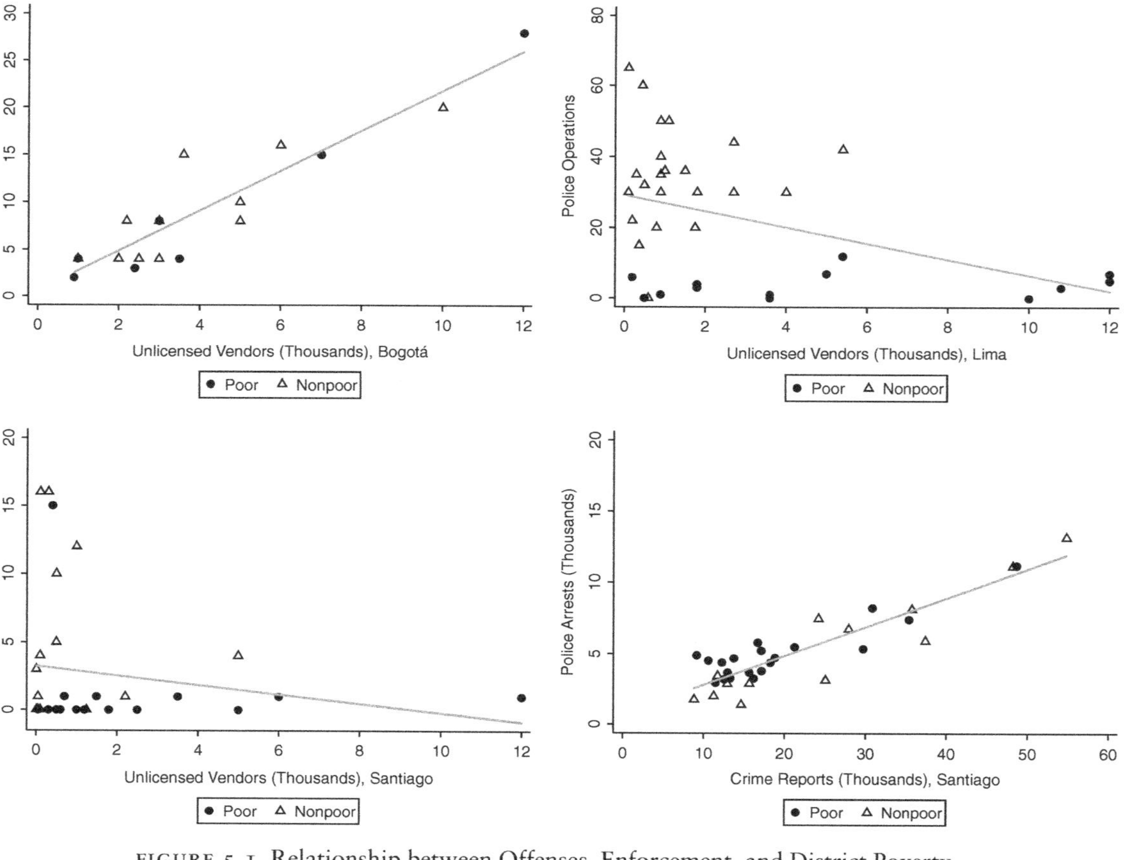


FIGURE 5.1 Relationship between Offenses, Enforcement, and District Poverty

represented as black circles in the figure. Nonpoor districts are open triangles. Again, the cities follow distinct patterns based on their electoral structures. In Bogotá, poor and nonpoor districts alike enforce in proportion to the number of street vendors. In Lima and Santiago, poor districts have more vendors and conduct fewer police operations. Valence crime occurs in all types of districts in Santiago, and enforcement is proportional to the extent of violations. These patterns are consistent with my theory that the combination of elections and district poverty drives enforcement toward street vending.

I next use a Poisson regression to probe the relationships of interest.[3] Given the small dataset, the asymptotic standard errors are large and may be overstated if the Poisson assumptions are in fact satisfied. I therefore note where results are significant under the Poisson assumptions but lose significance with robust standard errors. To make the results readily interpretable, Table 5.1 reports the standardized coefficients, or the average percent change in enforcement for a standard deviation change in the covariate.[4] The size of a standard deviation differs by city, so I describe the results for uniform covariate changes.[5]

Model 1 tests and confirms the core argument. Moving from a typical district that is 10 percent lower class to one that is 50 percent lower class (roughly two standard deviations) reduces enforcement by 71 and 78 percent in Lima and Santiago, respectively. District demographics have no significant impact on enforcement in Bogotá, as expected given a centrally determined enforcement policy.

In contrast, the coefficient on the number of street vendors is positive and significant in Bogotá. For a typical district, an increase of 3,000 street vendors (a standard deviation) is associated with 75 percent more enforcement. The number of street vendors has no relationship with enforcement in Lima and Santiago. These findings are consistent with the theory that politically centralized cities determine enforcement policy primarily based on the magnitude of violations.

[3] The Poisson fits reasonably (the goodness-of-fit chi-squared test is not statistically significant), but the assumption is frequently violated by over-dispersion and/or excess zeros. I report the Poisson regression results using the Sandwich linearized estimator of variance to relax the assumption of equal mean and variance.

[4] I standardize the coefficient and then use the Stata command nlcom to calculate the exponentiated coefficients and standard errors using the Delta method.

[5] The Poisson regression has an exponential structure, so, for an $x$ unit change in a covariate, the percent change in the response variable is $e^{(\hat{\beta}*x)} - 1$. Due to the nonlinearity, the standardized coefficients cannot simply be multiplied to calculate the predicted changes.

TABLE 5.1 *Cross-Sectional Analysis of Enforcement*

| | Bogotá | Lima | | | Santiago | | | | |
|---|---|---|---|---|---|---|---|---|---|
| | (1) | (1) | (2) | (3) | (1) | (2) | (3) | (4) | (5) |
| *Lower* | −0.052 | −0.500* | −0.473* | −0.623* | −0.507* | −0.490* | −0.535* | −0.361 | 0.048 |
| | (0.074) | (0.069) | (0.070) | (0.089) | (0.237) | (0.221) | (0.243) | (0.259) | (0.111) |
| *Vendors* | 0.770* | −0.166 | −0.150 | −0.086 | −0.410 | −0.495 | −0.529 | −0.391 | |
| | (0.091) | (0.113) | (0.100) | (0.131) | (0.306) | (0.333) | (0.324) | (0.202) | |
| *Budget* | 0.039 | 0.062 | 0.127* | 0.090 | −0.138 | 0.100 | 0.148 | −0.163 | −0.628 |
| | (0.051) | (0.037) | (0.049) | (0.060) | (0.297) | (0.353) | (0.371) | (0.240) | (0.124) |
| *Population* | 0.230* | 0.597* | 0.595* | 0.445* | 0.312 | 0.797 | 0.886 | 0.500 | 0.101* |
| | (0.076) | (0.200) | (0.170) | (0.172) | (0.355) | (0.634) | (0.695) | (0.528) | (0.029) |
| *Margin* | | | 0.180 | −0.172 | | −0.493* | −0.580* | | |
| | | | (0.099) | (0.171) | | (0.192) | (0.227) | | |
| *Margin**Lower* | | | | 0.530 | | | 0.339 | | |
| | | | | (0.325) | | | (0.777) | | |
| *Right* | | | | | | | | 7.028 | 0.096 |
| | | | | | | | | (4.670) | (0.093) |
| *Reports* | | | | | | | | | 0.492* |
| | | | | | | | | | (0.070) |
| *N* | 19 | 36 | 36 | 36 | 34 | 34 | 34 | 34 | 34 |
| $R^2$ | 0.467 | 0.413 | 0.441 | 0.473 | 0.213 | 0.294 | 0.295 | 0.354 | 0.388 |

*Notes:* *$p < 0.05$; standardized Poisson coefficients with robust standard errors in parentheses; two-tailed tests. The indicator variable for "Right" is not standardized for ease of interpretation. Model 5 uses *Arrests* as the dependent variable.

Among the other variables of interest, an increase of $800 in the budget per capita (two standard deviations) is associated with 13 percent more enforcement in Lima. This finding likely reflects the fact that Lima relies on local police, so resources play a larger role in enforcement. Nonetheless, even in Lima, the budget falls just shy of statistical significance and district poverty remains a substantively more important predictor of enforcement. Resources explain just 0.6 percent of the variation in enforcement in Lima, while district poverty accounts for 26 percent.

Models 2 and 3 analyze the second hypothesis on the role of political competition. The margin of victory on its own has an inconsistent relationship with enforcement, but the interaction with district poverty points in the predicted direction (although failing to reach statistical significance using robust standard errors). In a typical nonpoor district, a mayor who wins by 30 percentage points does 42 and 38 percent less enforcement in Lima and Santiago, compared to one who wins by a hair. Meanwhile, a mayor in a poor uncompetitive district does 35 and 11 percent *more* enforcement in Lima and Santiago, respectively. A natural confounder may explain the fragility of these results: a mayor who dominates politics may gain freedom and enforce, but a mayor also may win by wide margins by catering to his constituents' interests.

Model 4 shows that a mayor's core constituency – measured loosely by party affiliation – has a substantial relationship with enforcement. Mayors from right-leaning parties do seven times more enforcement than left-leaning mayors. However, the result is only significant at the 10 percent level.

Finally, Model 5 compares enforcement against valence crime in Santiago. When crime data are used, the number of offenses is strongly predictive of enforcement as expected. Reassuringly, consistent with my theory, poverty and partisan affiliation do not more broadly predict enforcement against non-redistributive crime.

The regression results confirm that poor districts pursue less enforcement and, contrary to competing theories, this relationship only holds for cities that elect district mayors and distributive offenses. The differences by the electoral structure of a city become even clearer when illustrated with a graph. Figure 5.2 plots the predicted number of operations relative to the corresponding city average and the 95 percent confidence intervals. The left panel shows the predicted relative operations as the share of lower-class residents in a district changes. As the figure makes clear, when the share of lower-class residents is low in Lima and Santiago, districts do more than double the usual operations. When the share is

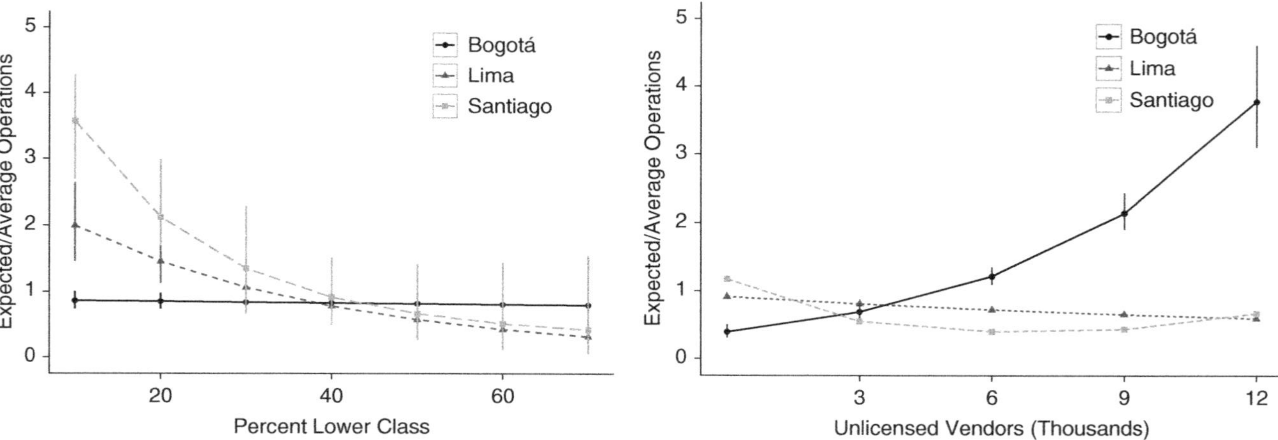


FIGURE 5.2 Predicted Enforcement Operations Relative to City Average by District Poverty (left) and Street Vending (right)

high, districts execute less than half the average. The flat line at the city mean reinforces that the irrelevance of district demographics in centralized cities like Bogotá. Instead, the enforcement logic in Bogotá becomes clear in the right panel, which illustrates the predicted enforcement operations as the number of street vendors changes. More vendors are strongly associated with more operations in Bogotá, but not in the politically decentralized cities.[6]

The regression results thus demonstrate that poor districts are less likely to enforce, but contrary to capacity-based alternatives, this relationship only holds in cities that elect local mayors and in enforcement against distributive crime. These findings also differentiate my explanation from interest-group based theories, which see little role for formal electoral rules in driving enforcement outcomes.

## 5.3 THE ELECTORAL COSTS OF ENFORCEMENT

The cross-sectional results suggest that when politicians run for office in poor districts, they are less likely to enforce against street vendors. But do politicians actually choose to enforce less due to the electoral repercussions, as my theory suggests, or is some other mechanism at work? To evaluate the mechanism – variation in electoral incentives – through which district poverty affects enforcement, I measure bureaucrats' perceptions of the electoral costs of enforcement. Chapter 3 presented similar descriptive findings by city for squatting. Here, I elaborate on the city differences in electoral costs by looking across different types of districts and offenses. I show that (1) the electoral costs of enforcement vary with district type only in politically decentralized cities, and (2) the main variation in electoral costs occurs across districts for street vending and across cities for squatting. This latter difference stems from the offense geographies: street vending occurs throughout the city, whereas squatting occurs almost exclusively in poor districts where attitudes turn on the national housing alternatives on offer.

I test the electoral mechanism by looking at whether the mayor is perceived to lose (coded as a "1") or gain (coded as a "10") electoral support if he enforces the law (*Electoral Costs*). Admittedly, it might be the case that bureaucrats and politicians have different perceptions of the electoral consequences, or that bureaucrats do not accurately report their

[6] The large 95 percent confidence intervals are suppressed for Lima and Santiago on the right panel of Figure 5.3 to highlight the Bogotá result.

perceptions on a survey where the stakes are low. But there are compelling reasons to be interested in the patterns that bureaucrats' subjective perceptions reveal. Street-level actors often have intimate knowledge of enforcement politics. Local politicians rarely have poll information. Accordingly, it is not uncommon for politicians to consult bureaucrats on how the community will respond to enforcement.

Politically decentralized cities should have a strong negative relationship between district poverty and electoral costs of enforcement. Indeed, the left side of Figure 5.3 shows a clear connection in the case of street vending. Mayors in nonpoor districts are perceived to gain electoral support from enforcement, while mayors in poor districts are expected to lose support in Lima and Santiago.

The right-column of Figure 5.3 repeats the exercise for squatting. The first thing to note is a selection effect: mainly poor districts contend with squatters. Other than in hypothetical scenarios, it is impossible to measure the electoral costs in nonpoor districts. Bureaucrats do not know how to answer the questions. Focusing on poor districts where squatting actually occurs, the comparison of cities supports my argument that the political costs of enforcement are high where social policy substitutes are absent, as in Peru, but that they fall where the state develops alternative solutions, as in Chile.

In contrast, my expectation is that electoral costs vary little across urban space in politically centralized cities because any support gained locally must be weighed against the broader urban effects. Figure 5.4 repeats the same plot for the politically centralized city of Bogotá. The relationship between the perceived electoral costs and district poverty is much weaker. This helps us make sense of why district poverty did not predict enforcement in the statistical models for Bogotá. The results do show a negative correlation between political costs and district type for squatting, but this relationship is weak. As expected given Colombia's truncated housing programs, most bureaucrats believed that the city mayor would lose political support if he enforced against squatters.

In sum, I compared the perceived electoral costs of enforcement across cities and legal violations to provide a more systematic assessment of the mechanism linking district demographics and enforcement. Consistent with the statistical findings, perceived electoral costs vary by district type only in politically decentralized cities. The contrast between squatting and street vending also hammers home why enforcement against squatters is minimal in the absence of housing policy. The electoral costs

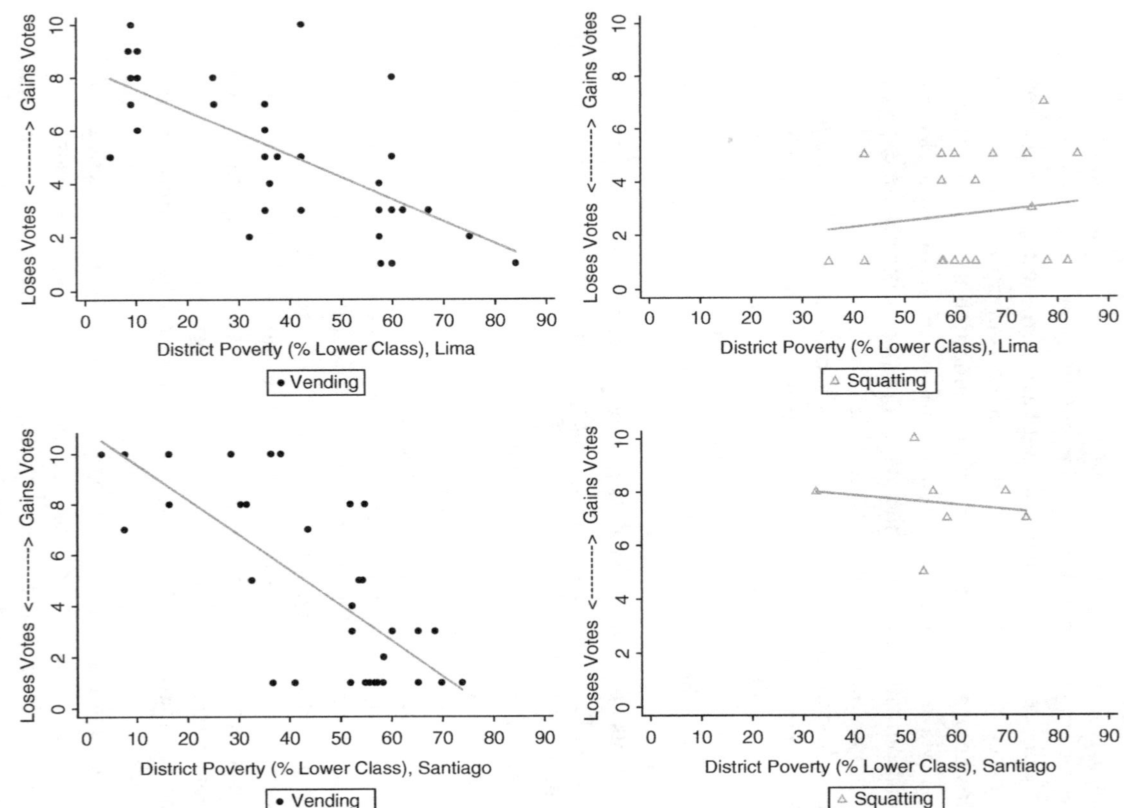


FIGURE 5.3 Electoral Costs of Enforcement by District Poverty, Decentralized Cities

Source: Author's survey, see Appendix C.

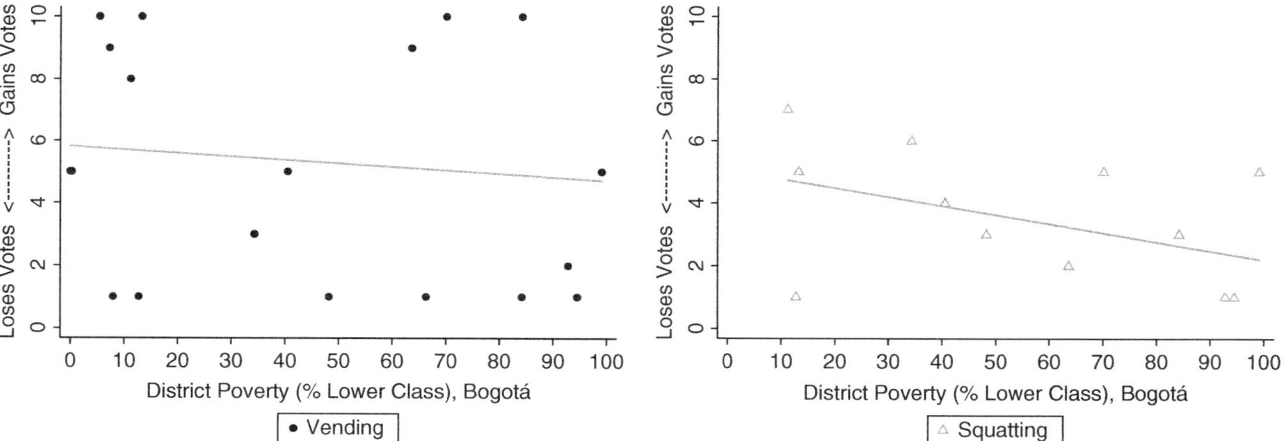


FIGURE 5.4 Electoral Costs of Enforcement by District Poverty, Centralized Cities

of enforcement are uniformly high in the poor areas of the city where squatting occurs.

## 5.4 ILLUSTRATING THE MECHANISM IN A LEAST-LIKELY CASE: SANTIAGO

The number of street vendors is particularly surprising in Santiago, given that Chile boasts one of the region's strongest economies, a capable police force, and targeted poverty reduction programs. I now draw on qualitative interviews from Santiago to flesh out the electoral logic that motivates mayors to pursue forbearance. Although Chile has the administrative capacity to control street vending, its employment policies are weak. It lacks unemployment insurance for unskilled workers, and job intermediation programs depend on mayors' links with the business community. The Achilles' heel of recent administrations has been employment.

I use my qualitative fieldwork to detail the more specific ways in which employment needs are used to justify forbearance. I conducted interviews with mayors, bureaucrats, police officers, and street vendors in both poor and nonpoor districts to understand how actors thought about the electoral policies of enforcement. First, it is almost universal that politicians reference employment problems when discussing their enforcement choices against street vendors. Politicians in poor districts saw forbearance as expanding the jobs that they could offer their constituents. They emphasized that they did not discriminate among political supporters or opponents because, either way, forbearance created gratitude among recipients. In contrast, politicians in nonpoor districts denied responsibility to solve employment problems for the poor and for people who do not live in their districts.

Second, although a forbearance strategy understandably is most effective with direct beneficiaries, politicians also worried about their reputations. Local elections are low-information environments, where even strong party brands lose meaning and personal loyalties matter (Luna 2015). In poor districts, politicians saw forbearance as a way to project a sympathetic image to constituents. They visited street markets, invited street vendors to local council meetings, and saw street vendors as channels of communication to a broader community of voters. In nonpoor districts, mayors promoted enforcement as an efficient way to demonstrate their commitment to order, modern values, and efficient management.

Here, I try to give a sense for these mechanisms and their variation across district types in Santiago. I also compare the behavior of mayors who switched electoral districts to explore whether district demographics, rather than political ideology, explain the enforcement logic.

### 5.4.1 Informal Welfare Provision

Elected officials differ in their beliefs that forbearance toward street vending is a necessary form of informal employment provision. In poor districts, politicians emphasized that forbearance offers distributive benefits to the poor, and that enforcement was inappropriate absent job alternatives. Even in a comparatively strong economy like Chile's, officials lamented that jobs were unstable and poorly remunerated, leading to temporary periods when the poor needed to work as street vendors. Politicians' observations that street vending is a "palliative for macro problems"[7] and a visible "reflection of labor market flexibility and declining industrialization"[8] were typical of the links made between forbearance and unemployment. Officials also discussed the employment problems of specific groups, such as the elderly, unskilled workers, single mothers, and the disabled.[9] Forbearance toward street vending offered a way to integrate workers who struggle in more traditional workplaces.

Some mayors voiced indignation about economic and spatial inequalities in Santiago that contribute to poor districts' need to rely on forbearance. Each district must run an employment office that matches job seekers with employers (*Oficina Municipal de Intermediación Laboral*, OMIL). Districts receive no national support to fund employment offices. Decentralization thus results in substantial variation in the quality of employment programs, especially based on the mayor's business connections (Pribble 2015). Mayors stress that unemployment and "hidden" underemployment rates are much higher in poor districts. Nevertheless, poor districts have smaller budgets and a tougher time building connections to private employers. The richest districts in Santiago have budgets that exceed $1,100 per capita; the poorest districts have budgets under $200 per capita. Businesses tend to sponsor jobs in the districts where they are located and where they feel an obligation to participate in labor

7 Author interview with Tamara Homel Navarro, councilor, District of Pudahuel, Santiago, Chile, January 17, 2012.

8 Author interview with anonymous councilor, District of Quinta Normal, Santiago, Chile, January 10, 2012.

9 Author interviews with director of inspections, District of Quinta Normal, Santiago, Chile, January 10, 2012; director of normalization and inspections, District of La Pintana, Santiago, Chile, June 15, 2012.

intermediation activities. But many poor districts have lower commercial densities and smaller businesses, limiting linkages to the private sector.[10] A councilor in a poor district captured how this inadequacy led her to support forbearance:

> The municipality has its office of labor intermediation, but it can't deal with the number of people who need jobs in this district and so [street vending] is a way to help poor people from the district. We can't have more police or resources to clean up the markets until this district solves the unemployment issue, so at this time, I think that the disorder is necessary for people to work.[11]

Politicians in poor districts were quite explicit that they used forbearance toward street vending to assist constituents. Claudia Lange, a local councilor from a conservative party, the Independent Democratic Union (*Unión Demócrata Independiente*, UDI), provides a typical example. She described how people came to her office asking for help with a job, food, or money to help them get through a period of unemployment. Although she works with a congressman on policy initiatives, she has been unsuccessful in finding private sector or government jobs for her constituents. Instead, Lange helps the unemployed set up as street vendors by buying them raw materials like ingredients to make Chilean snacks (*sopapillas*) or having friends donate used clothes to sell in rotating street fairs (as an unlicensed *colero*, or vendor at the end of a market). When asked if encouraging vendors to work without permits fomented illegality, Lange replies,

> What are the other possibilities? The poor want things immediately that day, but I help them to get the tools they need to generate income in the longer term. It isn't clientelism because I'm not just giving them things or making them vote for me, this is a way to help them get started and people are always grateful for the opportunity to work.[12]

Other politicians were less direct in the assistance that they provided to street vendors. As one put it, "We never tell people to go to work as street vendors, but they'll ask the mayor what to do when out of work and whether they can join the unlicensed vendors at the end of the market [*la cola*]. And [the mayor] will say that no one will stop you."[13]

[10] Author interview with Pedro Isla, mayor, District of San Ramón, Santiago, Chile, June 21, 2012.

[11] Author interview with councilor, District of Puente Alto, Santiago, Chile, June 20, 2012.

[12] Author interview with Claudia Lange, councilor, District of San Ramón, Santiago, Chile, June 19, 2012.

[13] Author interview with local councilor, District of San Bernardo, Santiago, Chile, June 23, 2013.

Politicians in poor districts like the one that Lange represents responded to questions about why they avoided enforcement in two ways. First, they emphasize that the median voter in their district did not demand enforcement. Residents tolerated unlicensed street vendors as long as the negative externalities, such as noise, garbage, or direct competition with local businesses, were contained. As one bureaucrat put it, most poor residents "took the point of view of the poor" given that "many people have suffered poverty."[14] Another bureaucrat made a direct comparison with nonpoor districts,

> If this were a rich district, then you'd have to protect the sidewalk of rich people because they don't like seeing poor people in the streets. But in this district, everyone has a modest economic level and if some people with a little bit less are working in the streets, the other residents don't get annoyed ... they put themselves in the position of the vendors and understand their needs.[15]

Second, politicians and bureaucrats commonly discussed the "social cost" of enforcement, by which they meant the dislocations caused by denying the poor the income achieved through forbearance. Mayors objected that the police could not discriminate between vendors who needed to be in the streets and those with other income sources. Complaints of the police as a "blunt instrument"[16] and "bringing the law in too harsh a form"[17] are indicative of these concerns.

Mayors in nonpoor districts, in contrast, rejected forbearance as a form of employment and stressed that their constituents demanded enforcement. Officials remarked that social agencies, not law enforcement, address employment issues. The director of operations in Las Condes, a nonpoor district, for example, spoke about a separation of responsibilities, "Our job is not to solve the country's social problems, there are all types of program for that ... If lawmakers want to change the law so that some can stay, then I'll change how to do my job."[18] Other officials stressed that the mayor received a mandate from constituents to enforce.

[14] Author interview with head of inspections, District of La Pintana, Santiago, Chile, June 15, 2012.

[15] Author interview with head of judicial affairs, District of Renca, Santiago, Chile, June 27, 2012.

[16] Author interview with head of rents, District of San Bernardo, Santiago, Chile, June 23, 2012.

[17] Author interview with head of rents and inspections, District of Quilicura, Santiago, Chile, June 25, 2012.

[18] Author interview with director of inspections, District of Las Condes, Santiago, Chile, June 29, 2012.

As one bureaucrat bothered by the social costs of enforcement put it, "We don't want to be a punishment entity, but here all the neighbors want to live in a clean neighborhood and the mayor made a clear promise to control vending."[19]

This interview evidence thus suggests that the weight put on informal welfare concerns differs depending on the type of constituency that politicians represent. Officials in poor districts thought that the public showed solidarity with vendors and opposed enforcement. In nonpoor districts, officials stressed that unemployment and poverty were not "their" jobs and that voters supported enforcement. The next section examines how politicians convert the provision of forbearance to direct beneficiaries into a broader reputation for serving the poor.

### 5.4.2 Signaling

Politicians fret about the impact of enforcement on their reputation. As I demonstrated in an experiment in Chapter 2, politicians can use forbearance or enforcement to signal their distributive commitments, namely, whether they are with the poor or not. Because enforcement toward street vending is publicly observable, mayors risked their reputation for understanding the poor if they enforced against street vending. One bureaucrat captured the sentiment:

> If you bring the police, you are worse than Pinochet ... The mayor tries to be part of the community, always trying to help the community, so he can't go against them in this public way. The day we try to force an unemployed man to stop selling things in the streets, the cameras will come out to the district and poor people will denounce the mayor as a traitor.[20]

Mayors in nonpoor districts, by comparison, projected a "modern" image and "efficiency"[21] through enforcement. Although the public was not uniformly supportive of enforcement, there were gains from appearing to respect the rule of law. As one politician commented on the signaling calculation in a nonpoor district:

[19] Author interview with director of inspections, District of Vitacura, Santiago, Chile, July 4, 2012.

[20] Author interview with director of inspections, District of Pedro Aguirre Cerda, Santiago, Chile, June 26, 2012.

[21] Author interview with director of citizen security, District of Las Condes, Santiago, Chile, July 4, 2012.

> From a human perspective, these are people who support families and it is viewed as an abuse to repress their activity and there are always people who take up the common cause. But at some point, the mayor realized that more people in this district applauded control . . . and that it made him seem decisive, like he respected the residents' desire for cleanliness and clear streets.[22]

It is plausible that the signals around forbearance are particularly strong in Chile due to the country's authoritarian legacies. Indeed, I witnessed many comparisons of enforcement under Pinochet, especially when shadowing long-serving bureaucrats on their jobs. Some bureaucrats remembered the Pinochet period with nostalgia, recalling that they could "walk with ease" and recounting major coercive operations. The military would spray the sidewalks with fire hoses to force street vendors to pick up their wares and scatter. As one bureaucrat lamented, "Now politicians only want to get reelected . . . so no one does unpopular and dirty things . . . but sometimes you have to do those things for the general good."[23] Other politicians, primarily from the Left, contrasted forbearance against street vending to Pinochet's disregard for the poor. One bureaucrat spoke at length about democracy "being different" and "not permitting the same abuses of the poor."[24]

Although memories of the military government impact how Chilean actors think about enforcement, political legacies of the dictatorship cannot explain variation in enforcement across districts, sectors, or cities. As I show subsequently, politicians from conservative parties take a lax approach against street vending when they govern poor districts. Concerns about replicating authoritarian tactics also did not lead to forbearance against squatting, as detailed in Chapter 3. Moreover, I found similar reputational concerns about enforcement in Lima, despite a very different authoritarian legacy. More than a third of politicians interviewed in Lima said that they viewed enforcement as a signal of their class commitments. A mayor in a mixed-income district in Lima best captures the analogous logic:

> Politicians use the support of street vending as a way to show that they are with the poor. But now [this district] is doing better and there's a significant group of people who want order that I brought together. I tell people that we shouldn't

[22] Author interview with councilor, District of Providencia, Santiago, Chile, January 6, 2012.

[23] Author interview with director of inspections, District of Conchalí, Santiago, Chile, June 27, 2012.

[24] Author interview with director of inspections, District of Pudahuel, Santiago, Chile, January 17, 2012.

always be a popular district that allows people to do what they want and violate the law because they are poor; we should invest in culture, public parks, sidewalks, and cleanliness like [wealthy districts].[25]

To summarize, both concerns about constituent welfare and political reputation reinforce a view of forbearance as a tool to tailor welfare policy to citizens' demands. Whether politicians genuinely care about the poor's welfare, or whether they just want to appear that they care, the electoral incentives not to enforce in poor districts are strong.

### 5.4.3 Mayors Who Move Districts

A logical question in the case of Chile, given a coherent left–right party spectrum, is whether political ideology drives enforcement. It could be the case that forbearance is motivated by a shared left-leaning ideology that the poor are deserving and that forbearance advances their material welfare. My claim is that concerns about the welfare costs and signals conveyed by enforcement transcend ideological divisions. Ideology may motivate mayors, but their primary concern is to retain popular support by responding to their district's interests. One way to separate these accounts is to examine mayors who run for office in different electoral districts. My theory predicts that politicians should shift their enforcement behavior depending on a district's demographic composition, whereas enforcement should remain constant regardless of constituency if political ideology drives behavior.

A notable illustration of the weak impact of partisan ideology comes from the career of a mayor of Santiago, Pablo Zalaquett (2008–2011). Zalaquett represents the conservative party, the UDI. Zalaquett began his career in politics as the mayor of a poor district, La Florida. La Florida conducts minimal enforcement operations against street vendors because forbearance elicits public sympathy and votes. Prior to the 2012 municipal elections, for example, the mayor appointed a special advisor to manage street vending. The head of inspections explains that the appointment was a way to boost forbearance: "The mayor has appointed someone who thinks that a person's income changes the legality of what he is doing ... This is a poor district so the mayor thinks that [letting vendors stay] shows that he understands the

[25] Author interview with Leonor Chumbimune, mayor, District of Santa Anita, Lima, Peru, October 26, 2011.

people."[26] Licensed vendors protested that unlicensed street vending should not be a way to address unemployment.[27] Photos released to the press show that Zalaquett similarly allowed street vendors to work unchecked in La Florida.[28] This finding confirms past studies that show the UDI takes a "segmented approach" in which it unites an upper-class core constituency on ideological grounds with targeted distributive appeals to poor voters (Luna 2010, 2015).

In 2008, Zalaquett ran for mayor of Santiago, a middle-income district and business center. Still representing the UDI, Zalaquett promised frequent control operations against street vendors and emphasized order in his "I Want a Clean Santiago" campaign. Zalaquett's opponents tried to shame him for his inability to control street vending in La Florida. Nonetheless, fulfilling his promise, Zalaquett has conducted frequent street vending control operations in Santiago center. The change in behavior – the same politician with the same party pursued radically different enforcement operations as he moved districts – is one example of how constituency interests overwhelm partisan ideology.

## 5.5 ALTERNATIVE EXPLANATIONS

Much of the existing literature treats limited enforcement as an undesirable consequence of weak state capacity. It is possible that district poverty captures understaffed and underfunded bureaucracies that *cannot* enforce state regulations, rather than differences in political choices to enforce. To summarize my findings on the relative importance of resources and politics, I return to my survey of bureaucrats. I asked bureaucrats what they consider to be the main constraint on their ability to enforce – political intervention or resources (*Constraint*). Table 5.2 shows the fraction of bureaucrats that named each constraint by sector and city. The question was asked on a ten-point scale, so I interpret intermediate responses (i.e., "5") as reflecting that both politics and resources played a role. Bureaucrats divide in what they consider the primary constraint.

[26] Author interview with head of inspections, District of La Florida, Santiago, Chile, June 20, 2012.

[27] "Comerciantes de las ferias libres de La Florida agudizan su lucha contra los coleros," November 15, 2010, *El Paradiario 14*.

[28] "Ravinet acusa a Zalaquett de fomenter el comercio ambulante en La Florida," *El Mercurio* October 14, 2008.

TABLE 5.2 *Perceived Primary Constraint on Enforcement by City and Sector*

| | Bogotá | | Lima | | Santiago | |
|---|---|---|---|---|---|---|
| | squatting | vending | squatting | vending | squatting | vending |
| *Intervention* | 0.67 | 0.63 | 0.46 | 0.43 | 0.80 | 0.50 |
| *Resources* | 0.27 | 0.21 | 0.42 | 0.32 | 0.20 | 0.42 |
| *Both* | 0.07 | 0.16 | 0.13 | 0.24 | 0.00 | 0.08 |

TABLE 5.3 *Perceived Corruption in Enforcement by City and Sector*

| | Bogotá | | Lima | | Santiago | |
|---|---|---|---|---|---|---|
| | squatting | vending | squatting | vending | squatting | vending |
| *Common* | 0.17 | 0.04 | 0.45 | 0.42 | 0.00 | 0.00 |
| *Uncommon* | 0.75 | 0.85 | 0.45 | 0.54 | 1.00 | 0.97 |
| *Unsure* | 0.08 | 0.11 | 0.09 | 0.03 | 0.00 | 0.03 |

In my extensive unstructured conversations, many did discuss resource constraints, including the availability of cars, staff, storage space (for decommissioned merchandise), and legal aid. But in every case, political interference is at least as important as resources, if not more so.

Another explanation for enforcement patterns centers on the corruption of street-level bureaucrats. Principal–agent theories expect a gap between the way that politicians want to enforce laws and how bureaucrats implement their directives. The way that I evaluate the importance of corruption is by asking bureaucrats whether they believe that squatters and street vendors bribe the police to prevent enforcement (*Corruption*). Although some bureaucrats avoided answering this question due to its potential implications about local government, many were happy to shift blame to police agencies. Table 5.3 reports bureaucrats' corruption perceptions. Consistent with most evaluations of Peru's bureaucracy, bribery is perceived to play a much larger role in the case of Lima. About half of bureaucrats admitted that street vendors and squatters often paid off the police. However, corruption is considered to be uncommon in Bogotá and Santiago. Not a single bureaucrat reported that street vendors or squatters bribed the police in Santiago. Leaders of street-vending associations corroborated the results. None of the street-vending leaders that I interviewed in Bogotá and Santiago reported paying bribes to the police, while about half did in Lima. We can thus conclude that corruption is not a necessary condition for forbearance, although it can be an important part of the story. Forbearance occurs even in Santiago, where there is overwhelming evidence that the police are clean and bribes are rare.

Principal–agent models often assume that bureaucrats shirk on the job, even if not exposed to corruption. Politicians are the ones who hold their agents to account and make them enforce written regulations. Yet, my qualitative research revealed the opposite: many politicians give orders to bureaucrats not to enforce the law, and bureaucrats are the ones who try to convince politicians otherwise. For example, bureaucrats in all three cities knew to avoid enforcement in election years. They alluded to political directives to take a "softer" approach to enforcement.[29] Perhaps most surprising is the number of bureaucrats who acknowledged risking their jobs in order to enforce the law as written. For instance, one bureaucrat in a poor district in Santiago refused to follow the mayor's requests and was transferred to another office. He described a principled rejection of the electoral uses of forbearance:

> [Street vending] is a black and white problem, and I'm not willing to put intermediate colors as to whether to let one person stay and another one leave ... The mayor thinks that these are poor people who don't have jobs and who will vote for him, but I'm unwilling to mix up the criteria of poverty and legality ... so [the mayor] put his own person in charge of street vending.[30]

In sum, a variety of evidence runs counter to capacity-based theories. The regression results controlled for resources at the sub-city level. District demographics remained a significant predictor of enforcement even after accounting for resource disparities. Enforcement against hard crime occurs evenly across city space. I also reinforced the statistical findings with qualitative evidence showing that mayors worry about the political consequences of enforcement, and bureaucrats find political intervention to be a more important constraint on their actions than resources or corruption. Of course, state capacity is not irrelevant. In particular, greater administrative and fiscal decentralization resulted in more reports of resource shortages and corruption in Lima. Nonetheless, these observations are more consistent with an explanation in which political calculations motivate enforcement decisions, rather than coercive or administrative capacity alone.

[29] Author interview with head of inspections, District of Conchalí, Santiago, Chile, June 27, 2012.

[30] Author interview with head of inspections, District of La Florida, Santiago, Chile, June 20, 2012.

## 5.6 CONCLUSIONS

This chapter asks why some politicians opt *not* to enforce the law against the poor. To answer this question, I shift the analysis away from the traditional focus on fiscal and institutional constraints and consider enforcement's distributive effects. Forbearance can help a politician gain votes among the poor, but it may cost a politician support from the middle class. The statistical results are consistent with the claim that enforcement follows an electoral logic in which politicians choose enforcement levels to serve their constituents. Poverty decreases enforcement when elections occur at the local level, while having little effect on enforcement in less competitive settings or against hard crime that angers all class groups. These relationships hold even in a context of institutional strength like Santiago.

A focus on electoral geography also helps make sense of the limited enforcement against squatting. The overlap between district poverty and illegal land occupations means that mayors rarely have incentives to enforce. Only in Chile, where housing programs address the poor's demands, are there few perceived electoral costs of enforcement. Thus, the social policy environment primarily shapes enforcement incentives against squatting, while district demographics create variable incentives for mayors to enforce against street vending. Taken together, these multiple tests of my theoretical expectations – within and across cities and sectors – provide robust and wide-ranging support for the electoral logic of forbearance.

# 6

# Why Forbearance Continues

## *Path Dependencies in the Informal Welfare State*

There is nothing as permanent as a temporary solution.

– Israeli proverb

Thus far, I have focused on how national social policies affect electoral incentives to enforce at the local level where urban property law violations occur. Having shown that forbearance can serve to make transfers to the poor and court poor voters, this chapter now turns to the national level, where presidents and their parties have the authority to change social policy. It asks a broader question about Latin American welfare states: Why have national governments come to rely so heavily on informal welfare in certain policy areas? Do national politicians favor forbearance to tax-based instruments of redistribution?

My answer hinges on the observation that informal welfare benefits, like public social programs, have policy feedback effects on institutions and societal demands that alter subsequent political choices. First, as recognized in work on path dependencies, efforts to implement social policies expand administrative capacities and change the options for future initiatives (Pierson 1993: 603–5; Skocpol 1995: 58). Reversing the logic, reliance on informal welfare policies mean that states never develop the administrative procedures and organizations that enable later policy implementation. To be clear, issues of state capacity transcend those caused by forbearance. Housing and employment programs are expensive and complicated for any government to pursue. But the scarcity of bureaucratic expertise and private sector alliances makes it even harder to launch and sustain welfare initiatives following informal welfare provision.

Second, societal demands shift in response to social policy investments. Once a segment of the population has violated the law and secured forbearance, it is less likely to demand state welfare solutions. Instead, individuals in violation of the law want forbearance followed by post-hoc measures to improve their property claims. After decades of informal welfare policies, critical parts of the electorate – the typical beneficiaries – become less interested in programmatic welfare solutions. At the same time, nonpoor sectors may warm to the informal welfare model. After all, they do not have to fund a "real" welfare state. Informal welfare policies also alleviate some of the worst negative externalities of poverty (such as crime, social unrest, and homelessness) that in other contexts lead to instrumental or altruistic support for social policy expansions among the nonpoor (e.g., Rueda and Stegmueller 2016; Piven and Cloward 1971).

Third, post-hoc policies encourage individuals to behave in ways that further reinforce the informal welfare model. Presidents, as well as international financial institutions, advocated the provision of property rights to squatters and credits to street vendors as a way to eliminate legal violations. This did not occur. Post-hoc policies create perverse incentives: they raise expectations that illegal activities will end in legalization or compensation. The result is a vicious cycle of further legal violations, local forbearance, and more post-hoc policies, producing a collectively suboptimal outcome that I call a *forbearance trap*.

Despite the "stickiness" of an informal welfare model, a major theme in this chapter is that presidents and their parties often want to transition away from it. The desire to crowd out legal violations has been the main justification for increased national investments in housing and employment policy in the countries studied. Take housing as an example. National politicians blame many of Latin America's urban problems – land shortages, excess infrastructure costs, vulnerabilities to natural disaster, shortage of green spaces, class segregation, incomplete citizenship rights, sluggish growth, etc. – on unplanned, informal sprawl. Although housing programs have high up-front costs, many national actors understand that they are cheaper in the long run than upgrading illegal settlements (Bouillon 2012: 145).[1]

[1] As early as the 1960s, international development reports emphasized that it would be more efficient to build housing or provide serviced lots to the poor than to improve squatter settlements after they formed (Mangin 1967: 88).

Why don't national politicians invest in substitutive social policy? I emphasize the role of policy legacies and time horizons. The first factor that presidents consider when deciding how to spend resources is the number of voters who will benefit in the short run. If large numbers of voters already have violated the law, presidents are more likely to favor post-hoc policies. Conversely, if fewer individuals violate the law, due either to an exogenous shock (like a repressive dictatorship) or endogenous changes (like the scarcity of urban land), politicians have stronger reasons to invest in substitutive social policy. Second, most presidents simply want to win the next election. For politicians who expect to leave office quickly, post-hoc policies are a great way to win votes. They can be provided at lower cost and faster to more people, especially compared to cumbersome and slow government programs to create jobs and housing. Politicians discount any long-term savings from implementing social welfare programs. Leaders from strong political parties or authoritarian systems are more likely to care about the end game and shift to a formal welfare model. Thus, legacies of forbearance and short time horizons explain both the widespread frustration with informal welfare policies and their long half-life.

My key empirical prediction is that countries with fewer legal violations are more likely to invest in substitutive social policies, all else being equal. The bulk of my analysis focuses on housing policy because the country cases vary in their starting conditions. Peru and Colombia confronted a stock of squatters in violation of the law when they entered the democratic period, whereas a repressive military government eliminated squatting in Chile. I show that, consistent with my theory, presidents in Peru and Colombia have aimed to crowd out squatting. However, they were dogged by strong demands for post-hoc policies and inadequate welfare bureaucracies that led them to scale back housing policy efforts. In contrast, Chilean presidents inherited few squatter settlements and citizens expected repression. It was easier to eschew post-hoc policies and retrofit preexisting bureaucracies to resolve the poor's housing demands. The Chilean housing model, especially in its early years, had many flaws. But it centered popular demands on the state housing system, and governments gradually built better, less segregated housing.

A secondary prediction is that a decline in the informal welfare system increases popular pressure for substitutive social policy. I concentrate on how local decisions to enforce affect national social policy debates. In particular, enforcement against street vendors in Bogotá foreclosed an instrument of informal employment policy (by contrast, urban decentralization in Lima and Santiago meant that enforcement scattered vendors to more peripheral districts). Such enforcement led to an important expansion in public employment policy in Colombia, and even a court decision to force social policy to progress in tandem with enforcement. More speculatively, urban land constraints (and rising land prices during a commodities boom) have started to compromise the ability of squatting to meet housing needs. Presidents in Peru and Colombia thus have begun to put more resources into state housing alternatives.

This chapter's focus on path dependencies created by informal welfare substitutes contrasts with the theoretical variables that are considered important determinants of social policy, such as the strength of left-wing partisanship, policy diffusion, and the organizational density of business and labor, which I evaluate at the chapter's end. It also presents a different path-dependent story than common in the literature: rather than just "insiders" who create pressure to maintain their welfare benefits and exclude others, I stress that informal welfare policies reorganize the demands of "outsiders."

Given the focus on the macro level, the empirical evidence is necessarily looser and more suggestive in this chapter. I draw on evidence from legislative debates, ministry reports, newspapers, and interviews with policymakers. The rest of the chapter proceeds by country case to highlight the contrasts that grow out of their different starting points.

## 6.1 THE FORBEARANCE TRAP: PERU

No country better illustrates the ways that forbearance has shaped social policy than Peru. At the end of Fujimori's period of authoritarian rule, large populations of squatters and self-employed workers created electoral incentives for presidents to extend post-hoc policies. The ease of providing post-hoc policies, particularly when contrasted with the challenges of running social policies in areas where they never have existed, turned several presidents away from substitutive social policy investments. In this section, I start with the case of housing policy, where the perverse incentives of property titling have been strongest, and then I briefly apply the argument to employment policy.

### 6.1.1 Housing Policy

The Fujimori regime gutted what existed of Peruvian housing policy. Fujimori closed more than fifteen housing agencies and planning authorities, and struck the right to housing from the Constitution.[2] In Fujimori's view, housing institutions catered to middle-class groups, exemplifying the state inefficiency and resource capture that his government claimed to combat. Instead, Fujimori proclaimed that property titling is a "payment of the social debt to the poor" and made it the center of Peru's approach to housing (Calderón Cockburn 2013b: 52).

The main intellectual advocate of property titling was Fujimori's advisor, Hernando De Soto. De Soto's core thesis was that secure title would allow households to use their possessions as collateral to access loans, sell and rent their property, and thus "unleash" capitalism. Property titling also offered a more abstract promise to end "legal apartheid," and build societal inclusion by permitting full access to the legal system (De Soto 1989: 241).

While the provision of property titles had long been a response to squatting – the revolutionary military regime, as well as democratically elected city governments, distributed thousands of property titles in the 1960s through 1980s – it gained popularity and international support with market reforms in the 1990s. The Washington Consensus, a series of standard market reforms, included property titling as one of its ten core recommendations (Williamson 2003). Property titling appealed to the spirit of the times with its promises to reduce poverty, strengthen the legal system, and expand the tax base with minimal state intervention. There is substantial debate on whether titling achieved its promises to open credit markets, economic opportunities, and legal protections to the poor.[3]

Even when property titling was first proposed, some observers noticed the deep irony in assigning property title to those who invaded land as the lynchpin of a functional system of property rights (for example, see Woodruff 2001). Providing an easy way to legalize property makes land takings all the more attractive to those in search of affordable housing. But

[2] These included the housing bank (*Banco Nacional de la Vivienda*), state credit agency (*Banco Central Hipotecario*), the savings agencies (*Sistema Mutual de Vivienda*), and site and service lot programs (*Fondo Nacional de Vivienda*). Other programs, including the previous housing ministry, were merged into the Ministry of the Presidency under Decree No. 25490.

[3] Research shows a limited ability to use land as collateral for credit (Deininger and Feder 2009; Gilbert 2002; Webb, Beuermann, and Carla 2006), but other studies find positive effects on labor market participation (Field 2007) and increased physical and human capital investment (Galiani and Schargrodsky 2010). Some of the value may be symbolic, but the effects on citizenship rights have been harder to disentangle empirically. One study does find stronger market beliefs among households quasi-randomly assigned property titles (DiTella, Galiani, and Schargrodsky 2007).

advocates of property titling downplayed these possible incentive effects. First, they argued that property titling was the only logical response. Evictions were unrealistic, given that roughly a third of Lima's population lived in informal settlements in 1990 and the majority lacked property titles (Riofrío 2003: 9). Second, many believed that the main constraint on the poor's access to legal property was the bureaucracy associated with registering property, rather than the funds to purchase land or housing. From this vantage point, the poor who did not already occupy land would be able to access it on the private market once a more efficient bureaucracy and land registry formed.

Fujimori shifted authority for property titling from city to national authorities and massively increased the pace of titling through a new institution, COFOPRI. Its charter made COFOPRI an independent national entity. The old process of acquiring a land title was cumbersome, and also made local politicians the key political brokers.[4] In 1996, COFOPRI started a free and centralized process in which claimants only had to verify residence on an eligible property, which was broadly defined to include private property and even environmental-risk zones.[5] The sheer number of titles distributed – more than a million under Fujimori – underscores the past prevalence of squatting.

Property titling was a political boon. According to De Soto's think tank, polls showed that between 80 and 90 percent of Peruvians supported formalization.[6] Fujimori and his ministers only assigned property titles in public ceremonies to maximize the program's electoral effects (COFOPRI 2004: 87). Feierherd (2014) estimates that areas that received property titles had roughly 7 percentage points more support for Fujimori in the subsequent period. Although it is unclear that property titles increased credit access or legal security (relative to local government recognition), titles permitted additional government investments. Fujimori also doled out credits from a construction bank and local infrastructure projects to upgrade newly titled informal settlements and, as I return to below, employ local workers.

4 Part of the reason to nationalize control was that Fujimori did not control key local governments, especially Lima (Chapter 4).

5 Excluded properties included archeological sites and flood plains; even private property could be negotiated under the 1999 Law of Prescriptions, which allowed COFOPRI to extinguish existing property claims after ten years if the squatters were shown to have acted in good faith.

6 ILD, "Bringing Extralegal Property into the Legal System," www.ild.org.pe/index.php/en/introduction, accessed February 8, 2015.

Fujimori dabbled with the creation of housing programs beyond the provision of property titles. Prior to the 2000 elections, as Fujimori started to fear a loss of political support, he created a housing program to provide state land to poor families, the Family Lot Program (*Programa de Lotes Familiares*, Profam). More than 60 percent of survey respondents believed that the program was a vote-buying measure prior to the election. Nonetheless, it was a hugely popular one among the poor: 86 percent of low-income survey respondents supported Profam, compared to 45 percent of upper-income respondents (Carrión 2006: 143–4). More than 15,000 people applied for a free lot through Profam in Lima just on the first day the program was announced, and more than 700,000 people applied nationwide by the closure deadline.[7]

The wild popularity of Profam came from the fact that the program replicated the logic of land invasions. Families were to occupy empty lots (albeit with state authorization) without services, permits, or zoning approvals. City authorities, rather than the national government that launched the program, would bear the costs of providing infrastructure after households built their homes. Minister of the Presidency Juan Incháustegui explained that the government did not have the funds to provide more than the land because "there we are talking about a budget that exceeds all economic and fiscal possibilities of the Government."[8] Profam drew sharp criticism from city politicians who saw it as a burden-shifting political maneuver; one top city official called it "useless" and questioned, "why an outgoing government has put in a place a housing policy to be implemented in the medium term."[9] The lots never were distributed.

The perverse incentive effects of property titling, coupled with no housing policy to absorb future demand, soon became apparent. As Figure 6.1 shows, the number of informal settlements formed in Peru accelerated in the 1990s, more than doubling between the 1993 and 2001 census and growing at the fastest rate in Peruvian history (MVCS 2005). Changes in methodology may account for some of the increase: the government data from the

7 "Se inscribieron veinte mil personas en el primer día," *El Comercio* February 16, 2000; "Aumentan en Lima locales de inscripción para el Profam," *El Comercio* February 29, 2000; "Falta de presupuesto haría imposible habilitar Profam," *El Comercio* November 30, 2000.

8 "Falta de presupuesto haría imposible habilitar Profam," *El Comercio* November 30, 2000.

9 "Una parte de las áreas para lotes del Profam estaría en Ancón," *El Comercio* October 19, 2000.

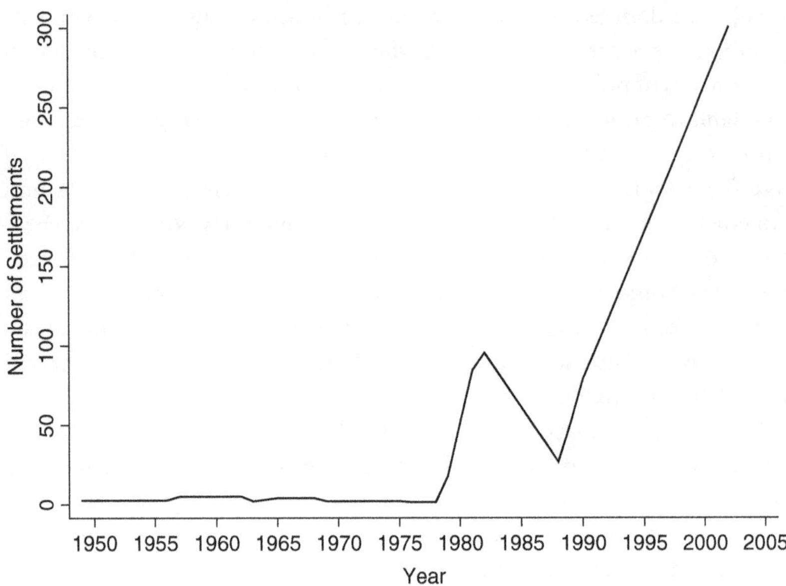


FIGURE 6.1 Annual Informal Settlement Formation, Lima, 1950–2001
Source and Notes: Data come from Collier (1976: 151) for the period 1948–1972, and from MVCS (2005).

1980s onward capture more settlements than newspaper accounts used to track invasions in earlier periods. The average size of a settlement also decreased with time. There is little doubt, however, that land invasions continued apace. By 2001, there were an estimated 50,000 lots in squatter settlements in Lima and 700,000 nationwide that formed after COFOPRI's creation. These new settlements were ineligible to receive property title under the program's rules (COFOPRI 2004).

Rampant land invasions contributed to the reemergence of substitutive housing policies as a goal with the return to full democracy and the election of Alejandro Toledo in 2001. Toledo reinstated a housing ministry (*Ministerio de Vivienda, Construcción y Saneamiento*, MVCS) and appointed technocratic urban planners who pushed for housing investments to stop land invasions. With an implicit dig at Fujimori's government, Vice-Minister of Housing Miguel Romero Sotelo embraced the catchphrase "growth by investment, not invasion" to promote Toledo's housing programs.[10] The Ministry viewed substitutive housing policy as

[10] "Ciudades deben crecer por inversión no por invasión," *Gestión* January 14, 2014; "Crecimiento por inversión," *Gestión* October 26, 2010.

part of a broader transformation in which Peru would reap lower service costs and higher taxes. In a speech, Romero declared a "democratic goal of housing for all" and made the explicit connection between housing programs and squatting dynamics:

> Given the sluggishness of the State, it was foreseeable that to solve housing needs, families appealed to the pernicious process of invasion-self-construction-tax evasion generating an informal society. What our administration is promoting is a virtuous chain to produce a city: investment-construction industrialization-taxation with which we would pass from an informal to a formal society.[11]

At first, Toledo seemed poised to make the necessary investments to implement this vision of substitutive housing policy. He proposed to put into action a program modeled on Chile's demand-side approach: applicants would receive a subsidy, provide a 10 percent down payment, and seek a commercial bank loan for the remaining cost of a new house. One housing program, *Techo Propio*, assisted the poor, while another, *Mi Vivienda*, focused on the middle class.[12] Toledo set a goal of building 800,000 houses, and claimed that housing programs would generate 300,000 construction jobs.[13] The comeback of Alan García as president in 2006 brought similarly ambitious promises to build 250,000 houses, generate jobs, and start a "responsible change to rebuild the state."[14]

Despite grand promises to crowd out land invasions and build massive quantities of housing, a model of a minimalist state "enabling" the market failed to reach the poor. On the demand side, few poor families could access commercial credit to use housing subsidies. A study found that 62 percent of households that bought houses with Techo Propio subsidies were employed in the formal sector, often as police and teachers. Only 5 percent came from lower-income brackets, the group that is prone to invade land (Calderón Cockburn 2013a: 18). On the supply side, there were major problems with the availability of affordable housing. Just 3,000 subsidies provided to low-income households were put to use

11 Romero, Miguel. "La meta democrática de una vivienda para todos," *La República* February 4, 2001. Also see "La mitad de Lima vive en pueblos jóvenes: Plan Nacional Vivienda para Todos busca revertir la situación," *Construcción e Industria* July 2003.

12 Fujimori passed the initial legislation to create the Fondo MiVivienda in 1998, but it did not begin until Toledo took up the project (Calderón Cockburn 2009: 110).

13 "Edificación de viviendas generaría 300 mil puestos de trabajo," *El Comercio* April 6, 2000.

14 Juan Sarmiento Soto, "Vivienda para los más pobres," *La República* July 2, 2011.

under Toledo, leading one housing expert to describe Techo Propio as a "sample size program."[15]

The García administration did little better in the targeting and use of subsidies. Although the middle class constitutes 17 percent of households in Lima, it received more than 90 percent of housing credits (Calderón Cockburn 2013a: 8–9). Housing supply for the poor was dismal. Incredibly, there were only 800 houses that cost less than $30,000 – double the standard benchmark for social interest housing in Latin America (Bouillon 2012: 62) – on the Lima market in 2011.[16] One Lima city councilor put it bluntly: "For the truly poor – say the bottom third of the income distribution – there is no housing to be purchased and no housing policy beyond legalizing land invasions."[17] Public opinion data confirm that lower-class respondents saw housing prospects deteriorate under García, while the middle class saw improvements (Lima Cómo Vamos 2011).

Rapid economic growth during the commodities boom and a nominally center-left president did not change housing policy. President Ollanta Humala (2011–2016) increased the budget dedicated to housing programs. Nevertheless, only 21,000 credits were provided for new housing acquisition to low-income households nationwide. The middle class received triple that number of credits. A housing bubble also made it even harder for low-income households to find a house in the required price range.[18]

Why did housing programs fail? Part of the challenge came from the Peruvian state's limitations. Toledo, in particular, had to build a housing ministry from scratch. Top housing officials emphasize that there was little experience in the management and contracting of housing projects; instead, most of the Ministry's expertise came in the provision of credit, sanitation, and construction loans.[19] Toledo needed to compel the

[15] Author interview with Ramiro García, head of urban programs, Centro de Estudios y Promoción del Desarrollo (DESCO), Lima, Peru, May 23, 2011.

[16] "Oferta de vivienda varía entre US$15,000 y US$2.8 millones," *El Comercio* December 2, 2011.

[17] Author interview with Sigifredo Velásquez Ramos, city councilor (2011–2013), Lima, Peru, November 7, 2011.

[18] "Las viviendas de menor precio mantienen una oferta reducida," *El Comercio* September 18, 2015; "Capeco: Ya tocamos fondo en el 2014 y no podemos vender menos," *El Comercio* July 3, 2015.

[19] Author interview with technical coordinator, Office of Policy and Regulation for Housing and Urbanism (*Dirección General de Políticas y Regulación en Vivienda y Urbanismo*), MINVU, Lima, Peru, December 15, 2014.

construction industry to build affordable housing, but industry heads claimed that they had little expertise in low-cost construction and could not build for the poor without transfers of state land or heavy subsidization. Construction companies preferred for the government to subsidize demand among the solvent middle class, who could purchase higher-quality units that generated greater profits (Calderón Cockburn 2009: 113).

Anti-statist ideological views compounded Peru's preexisting institutional weakness. Since the return of full democracy, Peruvian presidents governed largely from the center-right and avoided the state-heavy interventions necessary to make housing programs work for the poor. Housing finance makes this most obvious. As Toledo began to invest in housing policy, ministry studies showed that the poor could not access the commercial mortgage credits required to supplement government subsidies. Many other governments run state banks, as we will see in Chile, or serve as guarantors of last resort to make mortgages accessible. Peru resisted these approaches. Toledo said that it would be "excessively statist" to create a public bank to target the poor.[20] He then did an about-face: he abandoned his "growth by investment" strategy and focused subsidies on "emerging" middle-class sectors that could access commercial credit through private banks. Toledo's housing minister Carlos Bruce shelved criticisms from those who wanted to see alternatives and credit for the poor, saying, "The problem of poverty cannot be solved by the Ministry of Housing."[21]

Beyond the institutional constraints and ideological resistance to overcoming them, Peruvian presidents ignored housing provision for the poor because social demands were structured around the provision of property titles and upgrading projects. Toledo initially rejected granting property titles as a "populist" measure, and followed the advice of technocrats in the Housing Ministry to avoid the long-run costs of informal construction. But there were three-quarters of a million squatters who could benefit from the extension of titling deadlines. Toledo thus made squatters who took land between 1996 and 2001 eligible to receive property titles, and announced that he "would travel up and down the country to provide property titles to those excluded from ownership."[22] Public ceremonies

[20] "En Techo Propio se subsidia el 90% del costo de una casa," *El Comercio* August 11, 2002.

[21] "Créditos para Mivivienda se triplican en primer trimester," *El Comercio* April 3, 2003.

[22] See "Darían títulos a ocupantes de 700 mil lotes," *El Comercio* June 16, 2002.

allocating property titles – often presided over by Toledo and local mayors – continued (COFOPRI 2004: 88). The Toledo administration thus pursued a segmented strategy in which the state concentrated scarce public housing benefits on the middle class, and allowed land invasions and property titles to address the poor's housing demands.

García likewise saw the electoral attraction of providing property titles to the poor. He again extended the deadline for squatters to receive property title.[23] He touted the provision of more than a million property titles nationwide to claim that his government had "favored the poorest."[24] Meanwhile, the only housing programs available for the poor assumed that households already had access to land, which mainly was secured through land invasions.[25] Housing Minister Juan Sarmiento Soto explicitly pitched the state's housing policy in terms of "diverse products destined to finance housing for each socioeconomic level," in which assistance to purchase housing was reserved for the middle class. Property titles and construction credits helped the poor who already had seized land.[26]

It is common knowledge in Peru that the provision of property titles is good politics and bad urban planning. Land titling initiatives met a genuine demand of the poor once they violated property laws. They continued because they cost little to the central government and reached large numbers of citizens. But they also normalized land invasions as a way to acquire housing. Of more than two dozen local politicians that I interviewed in Lima, every single one believed that mass property titling had increased the pace of land invasions. As one mayor put it, "If the president wanted me to stop land invasions, then he would stop legalizing them every three years."[27] Although some top officials insist that property titling does not encourage land invasions due to the clear end dates after which squatters cannot receive title,[28] many others, including COFOPRI's

[23] Law 29320 (formalización de predios invadidos), published in *El Peruano* February 11, 2009.

[24] "Alan García: "Mi gobierno ha sido para los más pobres," *El Comercio* February 19, 2011; "Mensaje a la nación del Presidente Constitucional de la República Doctor Alan García Pérez," *President's Office Press Release* July 28, 2009; Also see MVCS (2011).

[25] These programs (*Sitio Propio* and *Mejorando MiVivienda*) offered construction credits and loans to improve the quality of housing on existing land.

[26] Juan Sarmiento Soto, "Vivienda para los más pobres," *La República* July 2, 2011.

[27] Author interview with John Barrera, mayor, District of Ancón, Lima, Peru, December 1, 2011.

[28] See "En 30 días estará listo reglamento de Ley de Expropiaciones, afirma ministra Vílchez," *Diario Gestión* February 18, 2009; "Cofopri no formalizará invasiones," *RPP* January 30, 2009.

director, acknowledge the perverse incentives created: "Institutionally, the idea of COFOPRI in the past was just to formalize for formalization's sake. If there was more to formalize, then all the better! It's just like a factory where the more orders you have, the better that you do."[29]

The short time horizons of Peruvian politicians increased the attraction of post-hoc policies. Perhaps if Toledo had expected to hold power for multiple terms, or came from a political party with a chance to stay in power, he would have followed through on his housing plans. But Toledo was a political novice who created his party, *Perú Posible*, for no other objective than his presidential candidacy. Toledo allegedly abandoned efforts to build housing for the poor after he learned that his first major housing project would not be completed until after he left office.[30] Likewise, García's party APRA did not even field a candidate following his presidential term. García cared little about the costs from tolerating land invasions because they would be borne by future presidents and local governments. For instance, García visited new land invasions in Lima and vowed to provide property titles, while telling squatters, "You should bring [the city mayor] to build public works here."[31]

There is some evidence that the informal housing model is changing due to the costs and continued proliferation of land invasions. First, squatters build on increasingly precarious and marginal land, such as environmental risk zones, archeological reserves, and conservation areas (Ramírez Corzo and Riofrío 2006). These new constructions leave populations at risk in the case of natural disasters. Rising real estate prices also have made peripheral land more valuable. Second, national policymakers do not want to replicate Lima's unplanned sprawl in Peru's growing secondary cities. These smaller cities, such as Arequipa and Trujillo, have become the epicenter of squatting activity. For instance, roughly 40,000 new illegal lots arranged in 400 squatter settlements, or enough to house approximately a fifth of the city's residents, formed between 2004 and 2009 in Arequipa.[32]

[29] Author interview with Ais Jesus Tarabay Yaya, executive director, COFOPRI, Lima, Peru, November 17, 2011.

[30] Author interview with former program director, Techo Propio, MINVU, November 17, 2011.

[31] "Alan García se lanza a la conquista de votos en asentamientos humanos," *La República* January 26, 2006.

[32] "COFOPRI no titular más invasiones en Arequipa," COFOPRI Press Release, April 13, 2009; "Informe sobre la Problemática de las Invasiones de Terrenos en la Región Arequipa," *Sesión Descentralizada de Coordinación de la Función Congresal entre Congresistas de la República por Arequipa y el Consejo Regional* February 17, 2014 and April 21, 2014.

The Office for the Prevention of Conflicts in Arequipa, an internationally funded institution created to manage conflicts around the mining industry, proposed new legal measures to control land invasions.[33]

The Humala administration tried to intervene in land invasions due to the rising costs and pressure from officials in secondary cities. The government proposed a national planning authority, which Fujimori had eliminated.[34] It also extended the time period in which the police can evict squatters without a court order.[35] In explaining the law's rationale, the legislative record emphasizes the need to break with past practices: "Invasions form part of a social stage that has concluded," and reflect a "communitarian philosophy incommensurate with free markets." Stronger criminal sanctions are justified because "a wide variety of investments in housing programs mean that the State no longer can continue to be permissive and tolerant of land invasions."[36]

Nevertheless, limited housing alternatives and a stock of squatters in need of property title mean the government has not escaped the forbearance trap. In Arequipa, for instance, the inspector general attempted to rely on the new legislation to evict squatters.[37] The governor then intervened to stop evictions; she met with the squatters and opened an investigation into the legality of the inspector general's actions.[38] She requested that squatters remain until housing alternatives are located. But that seems far off – the government granted only 1,750 housing subsidies in Arequipa from 2008 to 2014, far short of the 40,000 households who acquired housing through land invasions.[39] More generally, just 7 percent of the total housing budget went to housing subsidies for poor households who did not already have land (compared to 70 percent for upgrading projects

[33] Author interview with César Angel Huamantuma Alarcón, director, Office for the Prevention of Conflicts in the Regional Government of Arequipa, October 13, 2015.

[34] MINVU, *Reglamento de acondicionamiento territorial y desarrollo urbanos sostenible* December 3, 2014.

[35] Law 30076 of 2013 (Ley sobre el delito de usurpación).

[36] Exposición de motivos, Oficio No. 009–2013-PR, Proyecto de Ley No. 1898 (Que modifica artículos del código penal y código procesal penal; e, incorpora medidas de lucha para proteger la propiedad pública y privada de las usurpaciones).

[37] "Arequipa: gobierno regional desalojó a mil 200 invasores de sus terrenos," *RPP* June 9, 2015; "Arequipa: Otras 20 asociaciones en proceso de desalojo," *Correo* June 11, 2015.

[38] "Yamila Osorio cuestiona desalojo de invasores del Cono Norte de Arequipa," *La República* June 12, 2015; "Yamila Osorio ordena investigar a procuradores por desalojar a invasores del Cono Norte," *La República* June 26, 2015.

[39] Fondo MiVivienda, "Techo Propio: No. bonos familiares habitacionales desembolsados, Vivienda nueva, por regiones, Enero 2008 al 31 Diciembre 2014"; also see "Solo 250 bonos del Fondo Mi Vivienda en Arequipa," *Diario Correo* November 17, 2014.

in existing informal settlements).[40] In the run-up to elections, Congress also extended the deadline to allow COFOPRI to provide property titles to invasions formed prior to 2010.[41]

To summarize, Peru illustrates a cycle of inadequate housing provision, squatting, and legalization. The weight of thousands of squatters who expect property titles makes it hard for national governments to transition to a system of substitutive housing provision. While property titling was pitched as a one-off attempt to recognize the reality of past land invasions, it became a recurrent policy. Presidents lacked the institutional resources to make effective housing investments – bureaucracies and construction companies able to build affordable housing never developed – but they also understood that post-hoc policies reached more people and more quickly. The forbearance trap thus continues.

### 6.1.2 Employment Policy

Similar to the focus on property titling, Peruvian presidents have viewed support for those who start informal businesses, whether in the streets or their homes, as a centerpiece of employment policy. Forbearance and assistance to existing self-employed workers have taken precedence over substitutive employment policies.

As with most Latin American governments, employment programs in Peru largely have focused on creating jobs through quick-dispensing local public works projects. In the 1980s, García implemented a temporary jobs program that hired the urban poor to collect trash and build public works on three-month contracts.[42] But the program was cut just as the economic crisis deepened.

Fujimori similarly created a workfare program through the Peruvian Social Fund (*Fondo Nacional de Compensación y Desarrollo Social*, FONCODES). FONCODES prioritized the construction of labor-intensive public works for populations in extreme poverty, including basic sanitation, roads, schools, medical posts, and so on. Program expenditures were substantial: spending accounted for 0.5 percent of GDP in 1991, and rose in the late 1990s (Graham and Kane 1998: 72). Most projects targeted rural

[40] See "Ministerio de Vivienda peruano destinará el 88% de su presupuesto a obras el 2014," *Agencia Peruana de Noticias* October 15, 2013.

[41] Legislative Decree No. 1202, Published in *El Peruano* No. 561975, September 23, 2015.

[42] Accusations abound that the program, the Temporary Employment Assistance Program (PAIT), was manipulated to build political support (Graham 1991). Indeed, party identification with APRA peaked at 53 percent in 1986 (Seawright 2012: 93).

districts, where Fujimori sought to rebuild his electoral support and court swing voters (Roberts and Arce 1998; Schady 2000).

In urban areas, the cornerstone of Fujimori's employment policy consisted of support for the informal sector. Fujimori contemplated legalizing street vending outright during the depths of the economic crisis. He passed a decree that described street vending as a "social reality generated by the economic crisis that the country had suffered for several years."[43] The decree prohibited decommissions of merchandise and therefore threatened to remove enforcement powers from city authorities. The catch was that the law suspended decommissions based on a corresponding regulation that would establish alternative sanctions and requirements for street vending. Fujimori never drafted the accompanying regulations (Roever 2005: 65–70). Whether city officials could enforce against street vendors therefore was ambiguous as a point of law. Street vendors viewed the decree as recognition of their rights to remain in the streets, but mayors interpreted sanctions as permissible under city regulations.[44]

Unlike in the case of squatters, Fujimori stopped short of legalizing street vending. Instead, he drew on De Soto's view of street vendors as entrepreneurs struggling against the state. The goal was to get them to become storeowners, not to promote their permanence. Cutting bureaucracy around small business registration and expanding credit access would allow street vendors to shift into the formal economy. Fujimori thus adopted the neoliberal Right's vision of small business promotion in crafting his response to surging unemployment and rampant street vending. As he announced to Congress, the way out of Peru's employment crisis was to promote "family businesses where people can become self-employed."[45] On this basis, Fujimori's employment generation bill in 1991 granted "administrative amnesty" to micro- and small-business owners, as well as credit to help grow existing informal businesses.[46]

Credit access is a post-hoc policy in the sense that it presumes that workers already have created their own jobs. A focus on credit to micro-businesses sends the message that the unemployed first need to invent jobs,

43 Supreme Decree 005–91-TR, published in *El Peruano* January 26, 1991; also see Ministerial Resolution 022, published in *El Peruano* February 7, 1991.

44 "Ambulantes consideran que pago de 'sisa' les da derecho a trabajar en la vía pública," *El Comercio* March 5, 1995; "Comerciantes se defienden," *La República* June 24, 1995.

45 "Mensaje del Presidente Constitucional del Perú, Ingeniero Alberto Fujimori Fujimori ante el Congreso Nacional," July 28, 1990.

46 Ley de Fomento de Empleo, Legislative Decree No. 728, Published in *El Peruano* November 12, 1991, Art. 143.

including as vendors in city streets, and then seek government assistance to improve them. In the words of one mayor:

> The closest thing that the national government has [to an employment policy] is a program that offers tiny loans to people who start a business. So what's the message? What do I tell someone who loses their job? Well, try working in the street or opening a store in your house and maybe someone will help you a little once your street business gets bigger.[47]

In contrast to the provision of property title to squatters, however, street vendors never end up "owning" anything through credit assistance and individuals can access credits without violating the law. Everyone from computer programmers to domestic workers can be eligible for government credits. Thus, the reinforcing effects of microcredit programs are weaker. They cement the informal welfare state by leaving job needs unaddressed and by creating the perception that the logical response to job loss is to seek informal employment through activities like street vending and then to apply for state credits.

The stress on workfare and credit to the self-employed continued under democracy. Most Latin American governments rolled back workfare programs due to their inefficiencies and embraced cash transfers during the 1990s and 2000s (Pagés, Pierre, and Scarpetta 2009: 386–9). But Toledo and García were resistant to the "dependency" and moral hazard problems associated with cash transfers (MEF 2003: 7, 22). García, for example, praised workfare as the "best program against poverty."[48] Both presidents created their own workfare programs, *A Trabajar* and *Construyendo Perú*, respectively. Only under Humala did Peru's cash transfer program (*Juntos*) expand beyond rural areas. All three presidents strengthened programs to promote micro- and small-businesses by expanding credit and reducing their legal and tax obligations (Aliaga Linares 2010: 14–17).

Nevertheless, workfare programs have been an incomplete substitute for street vending. The programs are relatively small, but the more serious problem is that the quality of jobs does not surpass those in the informal sector. Public works projects paid less than minimum wage so as to deter those who did not need the benefits from seeking employment. Given the low salaries, a third of participants reported having secondary jobs, including as street vendors (MEF 2003). A job also is a three- to six-

[47] Author interview with Alberto Sánchez Aizcorbe, mayor, District of La Victoria, June 15, 2011.

[48] Discurso del Presidente, doctor Alan García Pérez, en la Reunión Plenaria de Alto Nivel de la ONU sobre los Objetivos de Desarrollo del Milenio, September 22, 2010.

month position, which raises the question of what workers do at the end. Due to these inadequacies, local politicians view microcredit policies and short-term workfare programs as complementary with street vending. City and district officials laughed at the idea that temporary workfare projects could crowd out street vending. Instead, street vending, illegal taxi driving, and informal shops were viewed as the "de facto employment policy."[49] The inadequacy of workfare can be seen in workers' reliance on informal income generation: for instance, following a downturn linked to the Asian financial crisis in 1999, the main response of workers who lost their jobs was to "work more" in the informal sector (MEF 2003: 6).

In sum, the Peruvian government has seen forbearance toward street vending as a de facto employment policy. Public works projects served this role in rural areas, and complemented informal employment in cities. Credit policies and tax exemptions benefit large numbers of workers already in the informal sector and therefore have been the government's favored post-hoc policy.

## 6.2 A RIGHT TO FORBEARANCE: COLOMBIA

Much as in Peru, the weight of past legal violations has shaped social policy in Colombia. Widespread informal land occupations and street vending shifted popular demands to post-hoc policies. However, compared to Peru, Colombian presidents invested more in substitutive social policy due to the greater development of welfare bureaucracies, an activist Constitutional Court that forced presidents to pay the costs of forbearance in the short run, and subnational enforcement decisions. In particular, enforcement against street vendors in a politically centralized city created social and political pressure on national policymakers to reform employment policy. Colombia thus is an intermediate case, which illustrates how a decline in informal welfare provision and institutions that lead politicians to bear the costs of forbearance while in office can spark social policy investments.

### 6.2.1 Housing Policy

Colombia has a longer tradition of housing provision than Peru, although investments historically focused on the middle class. During the 1950s and 1960s, Colombia developed generous housing policies for formal-sector

[49] Author interview with Elsi Guerrero, director of economic development, Municipality of Lima, November 23, 2011.

workers, largely run through social insurance funds (CCFs) and sponsored by a US foreign aid initiative, the Alliance for Progress. The Colombian government believed that construction focused on the middle class eventually would produce a stock of used housing that would trickle down to those with fewer resources (MVCT 2014: 36).

In the 1980s, Colombia tried to reorient its housing efforts to the poor as a way to stop informal settlement formation and increase redistribution as the country edged toward peace talks. President Belisario Betancur understood the truncation that plagued Colombian social policy. As he diagnosed, "Our problem is not the lack of resources, but the use of resources ... our country has been guiding housing subsidies to middle and upper-income groups." Betancur instead proposed a program of "housing without a down payment" (*vivienda sin cuota inicial*). Construction for the poor, in Betancur's words, would "provide lower-income families a realistic alternative within the law to spontaneous solutions such as clandestine developments, land invasions and the like."[50]

The targeting of housing programs remained a thorny issue due to the traditional use of public housing as a source of patronage. Contention over the diversion of housing resources from politically favored middle-class groups to the poor became most notable under Betancur's successor, Virgilio Barco (1986–1990). Congress passed legislation that blocked workers without formal labor contracts from access to the state mortgage loan system and thus effectively from housing programs. The move allowed legislators to continue to use slots in housing programs to reward their political brokers (Gilbert 1997: 156). The state housing authority teetered on the edge of bankruptcy with the expense of trying to maintain political perquisites and serve the poor (Cuervo and Jaramillo 2009: 7–8). Forbearance toward illegal land occupations continued. By the end of the 1980s, a housing ministry report summarized "those who actually developed what would be considered social interest housing were illegal and informal" developers (MVCT 2014: 39).

As part of Colombia's democratic opening, President César Gaviria revamped Colombia's housing policy in response to two different impulses. On the one hand, Colombia drafted a new constitution that introduced a right to housing. In this spirit, the Gaviria government created a new social interest housing authority (*Instituto Nacional de*

[50] Palabras del Presidente Betancur en la posesión de la Señora María Eugenia Rojas de Moreno Díaz como Directora del ICT y del Doctor Javier Soto Ramírez como Consejero Presidencial de la Vivienda, August 31, 1982.

*Vivienda de Interés Social y Reforma Urbana*, INURBE) and required that part of payroll taxes on formal-sector workers be earmarked for low-income housing projects. On the other hand, Gaviria reformed housing policy as part of a broad packet of market reforms. The state abandoned tools like housing banks that had helped to reach the poor under Betancur, and replaced them with a demand-subsidy program modeled on the Chilean experience. The results were welfare policies "with a neoliberal spine and a social democratic heart" (Brinks and Forbath 2014: 225). Betancur proclaimed that whether Gaviria's housing program reached the poor following electoral reforms would be "the best test" of whether representative democracy "has come to life in Colombia."[51] By this rubric, Colombia failed its democratic test.

The use of housing subsidies by the poor is dismal. In the 1990s, households from the top third of the income distribution used 42 percent of subsidies. Most households that manage to use subsidies are lower-middle class, rather than the poorest "priority" segment that the government hoped to target.[52] The fundamental problem, as in Peru, is that demand subsidies do not cover the full cost of a home, so they must be supplemented with savings and commercial credit. Less than half of Colombian households have the capacity to save. Even if a family meets the savings requirements, 70 percent do not have formal (or stable) labor contracts. Being able to document income is a prerequisite to access most commercial mortgages, which means that informal-sector workers generally cannot receive commercial credit (Gaviria and Tovar 2011: 5). A builder explains the paradox, "To receive a subsidy, you have to show that you are poor, and to receive a credit, you have to show that you are rich."[53]

The supply of housing also is an obstacle. The Colombian state retreated from the business of direct housing provision, but it struggled to compel private-sector construction companies to build affordable housing. For instance, there were only 3,290 units intended for the poorest half of the income distribution available in Bogotá in 2009, and not a single unit in

[51] Belisario Betancur, "El plan Gaviria de vivienda popular," *El Tiempo* November 19, 1990.

[52] Colombia provides subsidies to two tranches of the income distribution: a "priority" category for approximately half the population that earns below two minimum wages (*vivienda de interés prioritario*, VIP), as well as a separate "social" category for lower-middle-class families who earn below four minimum wages (*vivienda de interés social*, VIS). To be consistent with the other country cases, I refer to Colombia's VIS as housing for the lower-middle class, and VIP as social interest housing built for the poor.

[53] "Planeación y vivienda en Bogotá fue tema de discusión en el debate de CityTV," *CityTV* October 27, 2011.

2011 (Alfonso 2012: 32). Mortgage payments were beyond the poor's reach: the only housing on the market for a family in the bottom third of the income distribution required mortgage payments equivalent to 92 percent of their monthly income in the 1990s, and more than half in the 2000s (Gilbert 1997: 164–6; MVCT 2014: 56, 87).

Beyond the institutional challenges, politicians saw little incentive to focus on housing provision. Housing reforms allocated mayors and presidents shared responsibility. City mayors were to designate land and organize housing projects, and the national government was to allocate subsidies. Elected mayors instead have preferred to use limited resources to regularize and upgrade informal settlements. A huge spike in legalization in Bogotá occurred soon after the introduction of direct elections for mayors in 1988, as seen in Figure 6.2. In the 1950s, it took an average of twenty years to legalize an informal settlement; in the 2000s, it took four years (Camargo and Hurtado 2013: 98). City officials now call the housing model one of "ex-post planning."[54] A top national housing official

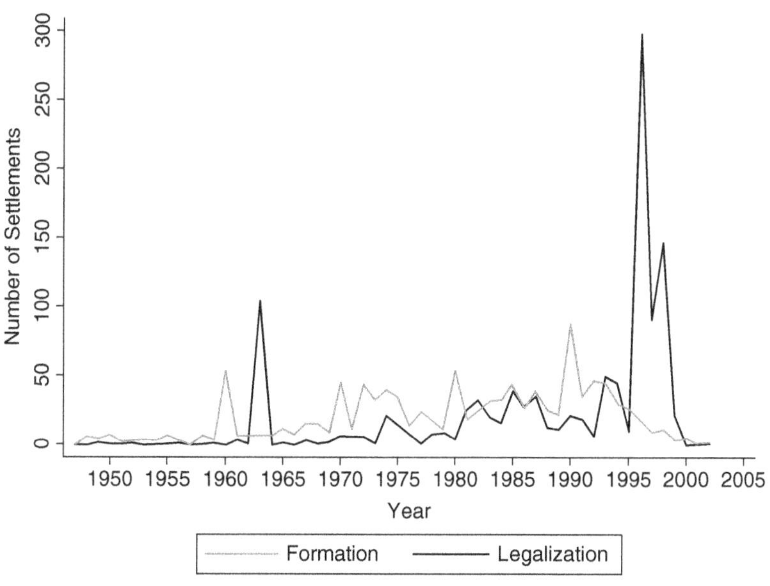


FIGURE 6.2 Annual Informal Settlement Formation and Legalization, Bogotá, 1945–2001
Sources: SDP and Informal Land Market Observatory.

[54] Author interview with Glenda Luna, director, Office of Barrio Legalization, Department of Planning, Bogotá, Colombia, August 2, 2011.

lamented that "cities concentrate their resources entirely on programs to address what has happened and not what will happen" yet national policy "lacks the teeth to confront informal settlement growth."[55]

Informal settlement growth arguably has accelerated along with post-hoc policies. A common methodology to measure informal construction calculates the difference between the number of dwellings registered in the household census and the number recorded in the city's building census (Caldeira 2000: 267; Holston 2008: 210). By this measure, illegal land occupations fell in Bogotá in the 1980s, when Betancur invested in housing for the poor (and legalization and services depended on political connections). Meanwhile, Bogotá experienced its fastest rate of informal settlement formation in the 1990s when the government transitioned to a demand-subsidy model that struggled to reach the poor. Informal construction accounted for almost 300,000 homes or 44 percent of all new construction in the intercensal period from 1993 to 2005, the highest share since the 1970s (Cuervo and Jaramillo 2009: 21). Of course, the data must be taken with a grain of salt due to measurement error, as well as demand-side changes such as internal displacement from the civil war.

Colombian politicians are aware of the trade-offs between the electoral benefits and the incentive effects of legalizing informal settlements. City mayors can regularize settlements, but they also must pay the costs of servicing them. On the one hand, legalization and post-hoc policies are popular: in my survey, 74 percent of poor and 48 percent of nonpoor respondents agree that the government should provide property titles to the poor. In contrast, 52 percent of poor and 42 percent of nonpoor respondents supported more housing expenditures. On the other hand, post-hoc policies encourage further informal construction and require expensive city interventions. The director of the Office for Settlement Legalization explains, "Cities fear that there would be more land invasions if we extend the deadline [to regularize settlements], and it would require investments in all sorts of issues at the same time like more housing and control for future demand."[56] Officials also complain that post-hoc policies empower land traffickers who can credibly promise that informal

55 Author interview with Jorge Alexander Vargas Mesa, sub-director of housing and urban development, MVCT, July 14, 2010.

56 Author interview with Glenda Luna, director, Office of Barrio Legalization, Department of Planning, Bogotá, Colombia, August 2, 2011.

settlements will be serviced and regularized by city authorities and therefore sell land at higher prices.[57]

City and national authorities have attempted to improve housing alternatives, although their efforts have been insufficient to crowd out squatting. In part, these state investments reflect the fact that the exhaustion of urban land has been more complete in Bogotá than in Lima. The difference is clear in the housing deficit: three-quarters of the total housing deficit in Bogotá is quantitative – people need more housing (DANE 2005). In contrast, four-fifths of the Peruvian housing deficit is qualitative – people need better housing (Calderón Cockburn 2013a: 6). Thus, more households stand to benefit from government housing provision in Colombia than in Peru.

Most notably, Peñalosa proposed an ambitious housing policy when he was elected mayor in 1998. His government platform explicitly advocated a "substitution policy" to "stop the process of growth through illegal urbanization and elevate the quantity and quality of the housing offering for the poorest strata."[58] Peñalosa created a new city institution, Metrovivienda, to expedite land purchasing and social interest housing development. But decades of informal construction and a focus on regularization complicated substitutive policy: land was scarce, construction companies had little experience in affordable housing provision, and legal procedures to acquire land were cumbersome. Peñalosa had projected that the city should acquire 5,330 acres to crowd out informal land development; the city acquired just 250 acres.[59] On the land that it did acquire, the government provided the necessary permits and services and then resold the plots to private constructors to build housing for the poor. But construction companies claimed that they could not turn a profit on housing projects for the poor, so they built houses for the lower-middle class.[60] Metrovivienda built 12,000 houses for the lower-middle class during its most active period from 1998 until 2005 (Casasfranco and Arcos 2007).

57 Author interview with judicial advisor, District of Rafael Uribe, Bogotá, Colombia, July 7, 2010; author interview with housing inspector, District of San Cristóbal, Bogotá, Colombia, September 6, 2011; author interview with housing inspector, District of Chapinero, Bogotá, Colombia, July 6, 2010.

58 Plan de Desarrollo 1998–2001, Acuerdo No. 6 of 1998, "Por la Bogotá Que Queremos," Article 210, p. 20.

59 "Por la Bogotá que Queremos," Article 230(a).

60 Author interview with Maria Mercedes Maldonado, housing secretary under Gustavo Petro, Bogotá, July 29, 2010.

Subsequent mayors largely abandoned the idea of land acquisition and housing construction for the poor. Again, post-hoc policies were cheaper, easier, and more popular. Even Peñalosa spent more than half of city housing funds on programs to regularize existing informal settlements, not on housing development.[61] Peñalosa accepts that housing investments require long time horizons and do not bring immediate electoral rewards: "No one will judge the mayor of Bogotá if he [makes housing available for the poor] or not, but it is so painful [not to do it] because it is something that affects many generations."[62]

At the national level, Colombian presidents also have made efforts to invest in housing, tapping into conservative values around homeownership and the rule of law. In particular, President Álvaro Uribe (2002–2010), a right-wing populist, favored massive housing construction to grow the economy, "create a country of homeowners," and "avoid the formation of new precarious settlements" (DNP 2007: 177). Uribe tried to circumvent mayors, who tended to favor post-hoc policies and had limited institutional capacity. He created a new national housing authority to build "macroprojects" (*macroproyectos*).[63] By having the central government purchase land and contract projects at scale, Uribe believed he could solve the bottleneck in Colombia's housing system. The government also tried to deter further squatter settlement formation by banning public investment and private-sector service provision in untitled settlements.[64]

Mayors objected that macroprojects interfered with their planning authority, and they sued the government. Politically, the housing battle was part of a broader pushback against Uribe's attempts to recentralize power. The Constitutional Court agreed with mayors' legal claims and blocked the central government from imposing housing projects on subnational governments.[65] In a separate decision, the Court also required the government to provide basic services to households regardless of the status of the land (Chapter 3). Thus, the government could not use service denials to force a slowdown in settlement growth.

While the Constitutional Court threw a wrench in Uribe's housing plans, it simultaneously prodded the national government to invest more in housing projects, especially for populations displaced by the civil war.

[61] Plan Acuerdo No 6 1998–2001, "Por la Bogotá que queremos," Anexo 4–5, p. 20–4

[62] Author interview with Enrique Peñalosa, Bogotá, Colombia, September 7, 2011.

[63] Law 1151 of 2007, Art. 79 (*Macroproyectos de Interés Social Nacional*).

[64] See Law 812 of 2003, Art. 99.

[65] See Constitutional Court of Colombia, Sentence C-149/10, *Gaceta Corte Constitucional*, March 4, 2010.

In 2004, the Constitutional Court issued a landmark structural injunction, meaning a measure that requires other government agencies to take actions, to protect the rights of internally displaced people, including their right to housing.[66] The government responded to the ruling by increasing the share of the budget allocated to housing for the displaced (to 42 percent) (Gaviria and Tovar 2011: 16). Performance nevertheless was dismal, especially in Bogotá, where affordable housing is hardest to construct. Monitoring reports from 2011 suggest that only 11 percent of displaced people live in conditions that fulfill basic housing standards (Rodríguez-Garavito and Rodríguez-Franco 2015: 148, 158).

Following poor performance reports and public outrage after a series of mudslides that killed several squatters, the center-right administration of Juan Manuel Santos (2010–) further intensified state housing efforts. The administration directly linked continued squatting to the lack of affordable housing. For example, when Santos's housing minister and later vice-president, Germán Vargas Lleras, was asked in an interview why two-thirds of construction in Colombia occurred informally "within the view of local and national authorities," he cited the lack of housing projects: "Because in this country the poorest families could not access a house, the only response that they had for decades was to turn to informal procedures, which explains the slums, the land invasions, and the pirate urbanizations. And that was a disgrace."[67]

The Santos government recognized that the state must play a more active role for housing to reach the poor (MVCT 2014: 44, 79). To this end, Santos gave away 100,000 houses for free, eliminating mortgage credit requirements and contracting housing projects directly. Vargas Lleras used a heavy hand to guarantee that the state reached its goals, such as refusing to pay contractors until they turned over houses at government specifications. Housing expenditures increased to more than 1 percent of GDP in 2014, on par with countries like Chile that invest substantial resources in housing. The government plans to continue the program after reaching its goal of distributing 100,000 free houses.[68]

Thus, the picture that emerges from the Colombian case is one in which past forbearance structured social demands around post-hoc policies like

[66] For a detailed discussion of the ruling (T-025 of 2004), see Rodríguez-Garavito and Rodríguez-Franco (2015).

[67] "Entrevista: Germán Vargas Lleras revela detalles de la vivienda en Colombia," *El País* December 22, 2012.

[68] Minvivienda, "Minvivienda amplía convocatoria para presentación de proyectos de la segunda fase del Programa de Vivienda Gratuita," Press Release, January 2015.

regularization and service provision. City mayors could not increase housing provision without greater national assistance, especially given limited land availability and weak housing bureaucracies. They also saw immediate rewards from legalization and upgrading programs. But unlike in Peru, presidents gained little from the informal housing process because they did not take charge of post-hoc provision, and they faced judicial pressure to shift to a formal housing model. Both Uribe and Santos thus tried to crowd out land invasions. The success of their efforts will depend on scaling up and sustaining housing investments.

### 6.2.2 Employment Policy

Similar to housing policy, Colombia has made more progress toward substitutive employment policy than Peru. For our purposes, what is most interesting is the national employment policy debate following the removal of street vendors in the late 1990s. This moment allows for an examination of the hypothesis that enforcement creates pressure for formal welfare investments (while forbearance alleviates it). It also illustrates how the Constitutional Court linked enforcement to social policy alternatives.

The turn to enforce against street vendors in the late 1990s prompted severe criticism from the national government, which saw street vending as an essential buffer against unemployment. President Ernesto Samper (1994–1998), who represented the Liberal Party, emphasized social equality in his development plan, the Social Leap (*El Salto Social*). But as the economy nosedived, the national government had little response to those who lost their jobs. Minister of Labor Carlos Bula told Peñalosa to avoid evictions because "street vendors are people who for necessity, not caprice or taste, undertake their subsistence activities in plazas, parks, and streets."[69]

The strongest defense of forbearance as employment policy came from the Constitutional Court. Early constitutional jurisprudence encouraged city governments to balance the collective right to public space and the right to work.[70] But in 1999, the Court underscored that

[69] "No desalojar, pide ministro de Trabajo," *El Tiempo* July 4, 1998.

[70] One of the first cases that the Court heard involved a dispute in Ibagué between business owners, defending the right to public space, and street vendors, defending their right to work. See Constitutional Court of Colombia, Sentence T-225, *Gaceta de la Corte Constitucional*, February 12, 1992. Also, "Vendedor ambulante, primer favorecido por la tutela," *El Tiempo* December 15, 1991.

the country's economic conditions required a recalibration of rights in favor of employment needs. The Court denounced Peñalosa's insistence on enforcement at a time of high unemployment: "[I]t would be nonsensical to increase unemployment without presenting alternatives that mitigate it, and as such, a judge cannot support that force is used precisely to augment the crisis." More than bluster, the Court issued a negative injunction to support street vendors' claims. The logic was that the positive aspect of the right to work (the provision of employment or income) could not be realized immediately. But the government could implement the negative aspect of the right and refrain from actions that interfere with the poor's need for subsistence work.[71] The Court's powerful language is perhaps one of the most explicit philosophical defenses of forbearance as informal welfare provision and thus is worth quoting at length:

> One cannot deny that, in the context of poverty as extreme as that affecting the capital, there are not dozens but thousands of people who opt to work for subsistence and, *in the absence of formal-sector opportunities, they should use the streets, plazas, and public parks* to market their diverse articles in order to satisfy their own basic needs and those of their families ... To deny someone who tries to escape from poverty *the only means of work* that they have at their disposal, in order to clear urban public space, *without offering them a dignified subsistence alternative*, is equivalent to requiring the individual to sacrifice disproportionately before a general interest formulated in terms of abstract ideals, which openly denies whatever type of social solidarity.[72]

The Court rooted vendors' rights to relocation or social policy not only in their vulnerability, but also in their expectations – or "legitimate confidence" (*confianza légitima*) – that they could generate their income in the streets due to past "tacit or express acquiescence of the state."[73] If the government changed these expectations through enforcement, then vendors would lose their claims. The interpretation that vendors deserved compensation conflicted with that of politicians who reasoned that vendors *already* had received distributive benefits from forbearance, and that the government would be rewarding illegality. Mockus, for instance, mocked the Court's position by posing the following hypothetical:

71 For a discussion of negative injunctions as a way to enforce social rights, see Landau (2012: 444–7).

72 Constitutional Court of Colombia, Sentence SU-360, *Gaceta de la Corte Constitucional*, May 19, 1999, emphasis added.

73 Constitutional Court of Colombia, Sentence SU-360.

A group of attackers comes here and introduces themselves to us and they say that they also want to become legal (a type of early pension), they offer that we give them a pension and they stop attacking ... I can see the advantages and up to a point I can negotiate. But this model shocks us and makes us laugh. The Court has been managing very subtly and very skillfully this [reasoning] through the use of legitimate confidence. *(Mockus 2005: 25)*

If central to employment policy, why didn't the national government legalize street vending? In 2001, the Colombian legislature did debate whether to permit street vending as a form of unemployment relief. The bill's proponents, the Liberal Party senators José Ignasio Mesa and Flora Sierra de Lara, argued that street vending would guarantee work for thousands of Colombians. The business chamber estimated the number of street vendors, and by their calculations, street vending reduced the national unemployment rate by 2 percent. Supporters used this fact to bolster the case for permitting street vending. Reducing unemployment by 2 percent was far more than most government programs could muster.

Opposition to legalization came from business groups, the executive branch, and city mayors. Business groups lobbied against legalization on the grounds that it was an ineffective way to restart the economy.[74] They calculated that economic growth could reduce unemployment by 10 percent, but argued that street vending undermined investment and respect for property rights. President Andrés Pastrana (1998–2002), a Conservative Party member, rejected legalization as a violation of the Constitution's guarantee to public space, a drain on growth, and interference in municipal authority. Mockus likewise warned against using street vending as an employment policy due to the effects on growth: "There is a deep discussion: if I sell cellphone cards on the corner, stores, drug stores, supermarkets sell fewer. No book recommends, as a temporary strategy to confront an economic crisis, to let street vendors invade."[75] The law passed in the House, but failed in the Senate. Thus, when confronted with the choice to incorporate street vending as

[74] The legislative project was Law 289 of 2001, and involved vigorous lobbying by the business community (Moncada 2016: 142–3). Also see "Frente común contra ventas ambulantes," *El Tiempo* June 5, 2001; "A punto de hundirse ley de ambulantes," *El Tiempo* 15 June 2001; "Ley contra el espacio público," *El Tiempo* June 15, 2001; "No al proyecto de vendedores," *El Tiempo* June 27, 2001; "No, a ley de ambulantes," *El Tiempo* June 21, 2001.

[75] "Alcalde: Sí han servido mis shows," *El Tiempo* September 21, 2003.

a formal employment policy, the executive and legislative branches refused it on the grounds that it would harm long-run social welfare.

Pastrana instead attempted to bolster employment policy. He introduced a packet of measures as part of the Employment Promotion and Unemployment Protection Fund (*Fondo para el Fomento del Empleo y Protección al Desempleado*, Fonede).[76] Given the large informal sector, including street vendors, the initiative emphasized measures to boost the income of self-employed workers. In particular, 35 percent of the budget for employment policies was earmarked for the provision of credit to micro- and small businesses, including street vendors. The measures were intended to help move vendors out of streets, but as in Peru, they also encouraged reliance on informal entrepreneurship to surmount unemployment. The other components of the employment bill, namely a workfare program (*Empleo en Acción*) and a youth training program (*Jovenes en Acción*), generated just 300,000 jobs between 2001 and 2003 nationwide, falling well short of those needed or supplied through the informal economy.[77] Other measures included tax incentives for companies that employed vulnerable groups, such as low-income heads of household, former guerrillas, and youths. The government thus did more to assist the poor to find jobs as informal alternatives were foreclosed, consistent with my substitution hypothesis. This is a relatively weak test, however, given that the economic downturn also pushed the national government to respond.

The takeaway is that street vending has been folded into a broader policy debate about how an unequal country guarantees a right to work and subsistence. The importance of street vending as an informal welfare policy came to the fore when threatened by Peñalosa (and evictions by mayors across Colombian cities). Although legislators ultimately were unwilling to recognize street vending as a way to employ the poor, politicians and court justices made it clear that forbearance was necessary until the state could do a better job of providing alternatives. Neither city nor national officials have been able to generate employment alternatives at scale. Instead, post-hoc policies, such as credits from the national government, cement societal expectations that street vending buffers unemployment.

[76] Law 789 of 2002; Decree 2340 of 2003.

[77] Speech by President Andrés Pastrana, "Alocución sobre el programa Empleos en Acción," Presidential Library, www.andrespastrana.org/biblioteca/alocucion-sobre-el-programa-empleo-en-accion/, accessed January 18, 2015.

## 6.3 EXIT FROM THE FORBEARANCE TRAP: CHILE

Chile started from a different point than Peru and Colombia, and thus offers the clearest observation of how enforcement reshapes social policy. Repression under a military regime broke the cycle of squatting, opening a window for democratic authorities to reset societal expectations about access to basic social goods. An intense fear of renewed land invasions under democracy elevated the costs of an informal housing model and made them tangible to presidents in the short run. The government's substantial institutional capacity, in part developed through housing policies under the dictatorship, and ties to local politicians eased the transition to state housing for the poor. The same did not occur with employment policy. Street vending and other forms of informal employment were less thoroughly repressed during the dictatorship. Elected presidents therefore concentrated on post-hoc measures to improve the quality of informal jobs, and left district governments to rely on forbearance toward street vending to employ the poor.

### 6.3.1 Housing Policy

The role of squatting in Chile's democratic breakdown colored its housing policy. In the run-up to the election and early years in office of Socialist president Allende, more than 400,000 people acquired housing through land takings, often in quite central areas of Santiago (Castells 1971: 8). As Figure 6.3 shows, the scale of informal housing growth was unprecedented in Santiago. As the leader of a "government of the people," Allende refused to repress squatters. He aspired to build massive quantities of social interest housing, although in the end he built less than his predecessors (Portes and Walton 1976: 83). Rampant and visible urban land invasions contributed to the sense of social chaos and redistributive threat that provoked the military to overthrow Allende. When the military took power in a coup in 1973, it abruptly ended the use of land invasions as an informal housing policy.

The military government initiated a demand-based subsidy program run by a technocratic housing ministry (*Ministerio de Vivienda y Urbanismo*, MINVU). In theory, the ABC program targeted the poor and assigned priority to those households in greater need. The housing program design was influenced by Arnold Harberger, a Chicago economist who supported in-kind transfers on the basis that the public derives utility from others'

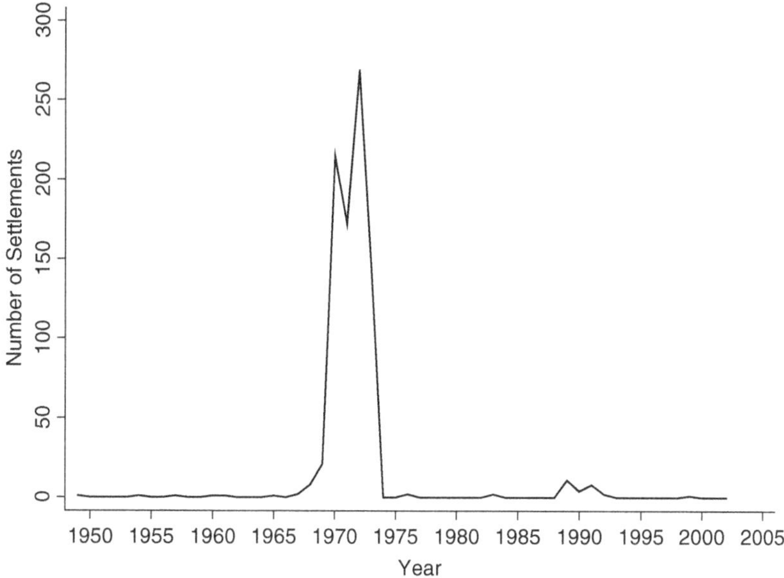


FIGURE 6.3 Annual Informal Settlement Formation, Santiago, 1950–2001
Sources and Notes: Author's compilation from Castells (1971); Klaarhamer (1989); Schneider (1995); and *El Mercurio* 1990–2001.

consumption of particular goods or services. Harberger (1978, 1984) modeled this idea as a social demand curve, where public demand exceeds the private demand curve for specific goods like housing and education. Avoiding homelessness among the poorest thus became the stated goal of housing authorities.

Despite the stated aims, most housing benefits during the dictatorship went to military and state employees. About two-thirds of all new housing construction concentrated in wealthy, central districts of Santiago (Kusnetzoff 1987: 165–6). To free up land in central city neighborhoods, Pinochet relocated at least 50,000 poor families to barracks on the urban periphery (Schneider 1995: 99–101). As a memorandum from Pinochet's chief of staff put it, squatter removals were needed to improve the city's "environmental and aesthetic quality" (Murphy 2015: 164). Construction companies that agreed to build low-income housing to relocate removed populations were given property rights to central city lands in exchange, making the deals quite lucrative. For informal settlements on the city's periphery, the government provided post-hoc policies, including property titles and sanitation infrastructure. Much as advocated by De Soto, the military's goal was to integrate squatters into financial and state institutions (Kusnetzoff 1987: 165). In contrast to Peru, repression ensured that no new land invasions took hold.[78]

With little possibility to enter housing programs or invade new land, many poor families crowded into whatever spaces they could afford. "Overcrowded" residents (*allegados*) in apartments and existing settlements organized politically as part of the Movement of Shantydwellers (*Movimiento de Pobladores*, MPL). They played a central role in protests against the dictatorship, and drew attention to the plight of the poor (Oxhorn 1995; Schneider 1995).

At the democratic transition, Chile's elected government inherited a mobilized population in need of housing, an established housing bureaucracy, and a powerful construction sector. Repression meant that the poor needed more houses, not just post-hoc policies to title and upgrade existing ones. Housing also was a highly salient issue due to the military government's repressive tactics. A fifth of the population nationwide named the lack of housing as one of the country's principal problems (CEP 1991). Less than 1 percent of the public named housing as one of the main problems in Peru and Colombia throughout the 1990s and 2000s, possibly because informal solutions provided alternatives (Latinobarometer 1995–2000). Those in need of housing were politically organized from their mobilization against the dictatorship and therefore able to pressure the new democratic government for housing alternatives.

President Patricio Aylwin (1990–1994), a member of the Christian Democratic Party, which was part of a bloc of center-left parties (*Concertación*), designed Chile's housing policy to stymie invasions. The goal was to accelerate the number of housing units that the state produced, largely irrespective of quality or surrounding urban features. Aylwin's director of housing relations explains that the government prioritized resetting societal expectations about the state's ability to house the poor:

> The key pragmatic question was how in a short period of time could the government signal that it was possible to absorb a housing deficit of this magnitude through the State? We had to recover the confidence of the poor that

[78] The one major exception proves the rule: some 8,000 families undertook a major land invasion in September 1983. The government did not evict the massive invasion, but it purposely attempted to deter any further attempts by harassing the leaders and patrolling the invasion (Klaarhamer 1989: 186; Oxhorn 1995).

the State would build housing – not all in one term – but that under democracy it would happen, so that we would make land takings unnecessary.[79]

The government's ability to draw on a competent bureaucracy like MINVU and create a transparent housing cue helped convince citizens to participate in the state system (Chapter 3). But capacity and targeting issues also plagued state housing programs. A state bank provided mortgages to poor families who did not qualify on standard markets. But after receiving a loan, low-income households struggled to meet mortgage requirements and even middle-class households refused to pay knowing that they would not be evicted. Massive defaults on state loans in the 1990s made the housing program more generous than intended and risked making the state bank insolvent.

Rather than leave the poor to their own devices as complaints about the quality of housing projects and the state's shaky mortgage portfolio accumulated, President Ricardo Lagos (2000–2006) decided to reform the housing policy to become even more bottom-targeted. Lagos understood that there was a trade-off between savings and loan requirements and coverage of the poorest. He opted for the latter and eliminated mortgage requirements. Debt-free housing required a major ideological shift. One of the reasons that the political Right (including the military regime) supported housing programs was the insistence that housing required contributions from families that kept the poor "focused" on keeping a house (Murphy 2015: 183–4). Debt-free houses, or the *Casas Lagos* as they were colloquially known, rejected these requirements as unrealistic.[80] They proved immensely popular. Demand outstripped the large supply of 100,000 houses built each year (Lagos 2012: 188). A testament to the relaxed savings and loan requirements, the share of public expenditures going to the bottom quarter of the income distribution climbed from 56 percent in 1996 to 75 percent in 2006 (Rodríguez et al. 2006: 14). The effectiveness of Chile's housing model can be seen in the fact that roughly three-quarters of recipients used their assigned subsidies (CChC 2008).

Beyond increases in the pace of housing production, presidents sharply limited post-hoc policies to prevent perverse incentive effects. Only in

79 Author interview with Paulina Saball, director (1990–1994), Unit of Diffusion and Promotion, MINVU, and subsecretary of housing and urbanism (2006–2010), Santiago, Chile, July 4, 2012.

80 Officially, this program was called Dynamic Social Housing without Debt (*Vivienda Social Dinámica sin Deuda*).

1996 did President Eduardo Frei (1994–2000) institute a post-hoc housing policy called *Chile Barrio* to improve conditions in existing informal settlements. The program had a firm end date. As the program's assistant director explained, "Chile Barrio will not incorporate new settlements, by definition; from its creation, we did not want to signal that we are going to solve the social housing problem through land takings" (Carvallo 2000: 61). This promise was credible in large part because the government continued to ramp up housing expenditures and evict land invasions. The government also deterred squatting by making those who attempted a land invasion ineligible for housing programs.[81] Contrast this single reactive program, penalties for property takings, and a major push to create formal housing solutions with Peru's near-constant legalization of informal settlements and Colombia's rules that those who take land must receive services. Chile's national government created the right institutional environment to thwart property takings and center societal demands on the state.

Not to idolize Chile's housing policy, the downside of an emphasis on housing quantity has been quality. Projects were built on the urban periphery with few surrounding services, exacerbating spatial segregation (Sabatini et al. 2009). Analysts began to discuss the problems of those "with housing," rather than those without it (Rodríguez and Sugranyes 2005). That said, the state housing system gradually improved. Poor households pressured for higher quality housing in better locations. Most notably, one group that attempted a land taking in Peñalolén in 2006 asserted a "right to stay," meaning the ability for low-income groups to access housing in central city districts rather than in far-flung peripheral areas (Guzmán et al. 2009). In her first administration, President Michelle Bachelet (2006–2010) responded by increasing the average up-front subsidy so that the poor could purchase houses in better locations (Razmilic 2010: 9).

The final feature that helped Chile to transition to a formal housing model is the party system. Unlike Peru and Colombia, Chile has an institutionalized party system, which can lengthen presidents' time horizons and create ties across levels of government. Aylwin perceived the main threat of forbearance to come from district mayors aligned with the *Concertación*, as well as far-left parties, many of whom had ties to squatter and overcrowded movements and a history of involvement in land invasions. Officials in the Housing Ministry therefore met extensively

[81] Author interview with Paulina Saball, Santiago, Chile, July 4, 2012.

with district mayors and shantytown leaders to secure their cooperation.[82] Elites in both the Christian Democratic Party and Socialist Party were very explicit that state housing programs for the poor, not illegal land occupations, were critical to their parties' programmatic initiatives and the country's democratic stability. For instance, as the Socialist Party secretary explained, "It would be easy to occupy the piece of land near the airport and to encourage a big land seizure to solve the problem but that would be irresponsible on our part. We don't want to provoke the police or our opponents" (Hipsher 1996: 284).

Stepping back, the Chilean housing system is often erroneously viewed as a neoliberal model where the state provides subsidies and credits to correct market failures and then backs off. Indeed, these are the design elements that Peru and Colombia copied. But Chile's housing system blends state intervention with market-based elements. Unlike in Colombia and Peru, for example, the Chilean government developed construction projects to match the subsidies provided, contracted the private sector to build the number of housing units required, and then assigned subsidy recipients to units. At the democratic transition, center-left presidents invested substantially in housing provision and drew on their party and local alliances to avoid land invasions. State provision in turn funneled societal demands toward housing authorities. Thus, Chile developed self-reinforcing dynamics in housing provision in which citizens expect more out of the state and disavow informal housing options. The provision of housing to the poor has been one of Chile's most important social policy investments. Unlike most of Latin America, as former president Lagos puts it, Chile "can truthfully say that it has almost eliminated informal settlements."[83]

### 6.3.2 Employment Policy

Why has Chile been unable to develop substitutive employment policy, as in the case of housing? My explanation centers on the fact that it was impossible to repress street vending (and informal employment) to the same degree as squatting under the dictatorship. Street vendors were in constant conflict with local authorities over the right to stay in city streets

[82] Author interview with Paulina Saball, Santiago, Chile, July 4, 2012. Some of the government's tactics were more coercive, such as trying to replace the leaders of the Unitary Congress of Pobladores (CUP) with more moderate party loyalists after the CUP attempted to go on a hunger march in 1988 (Oxhorn 1995: 60).

[83] Author interview with Ricardo Lagos, Cambridge, Massachusetts, October 8, 2013.

under Pinochet. Police would arrest and detain street vendors overnight (Contreras 1988: 38–40). When enforcement occurred, it pushed vendors out of public spaces, but never eliminated self-employment as a means to generate income. This difference in starting conditions made it more attractive for democratic leaders to resolve employment demands through post-hoc policies.

The difference in social policy approach can be observed most clearly at the democratic transition. Whereas renewed squatting threatened the regime, Aylwin saw no comparable threat from street vendors. In 1990, Aylwin created a fund (*Fondo de Solidaridad e Inversión Social*, Fosis) to provide credits and technical assistance to help individuals grow their own microenterprises. The program viewed self-employment as a central response to unemployment, with credits intended "so that [the unemployed] can generate income that will allow them to overcome the situation that they find themselves in, by developing independent work."[84]

Presidents Frei and Lagos concentrated Fosis's projects even more heavily on financial intermediation to provide credit to self-employed workers and microenterprises. They expanded the number of programs to offer seed capital and training to microenterprises. But given that credit, as well as training programs, provided no location for the poor to sell their products, the credit-as-employment model complemented street vending, much as in Peru. A bureaucrat nicely captures the frustration that many expressed toward the national government's employment policy: "The state has encouraged illegal vending because it creates these programs for small-scale entrepreneurship, which give people the skills to produce something but no market or store to sell it, so then people think that they have a right to sell in the streets because the state wants them to generate their own employment."[85]

The other important cause of government inaction was the devolution of authority over employment policy to local governments. As I noted in Chapter 5, local governments bear the primary responsibility for assisting the unemployed. Mayors often struggle to generate business connections and match unskilled workers with stable employment. They instead use schemes that encourage self-employment, ranging from the authorization of street fairs (*ferias*) to tolerance of unlicensed vendors in public spaces

[84] Fosis, Apoyo al Microemprendimiento, Mission Statement. Also see Law 18989, Article 6, July 13, 1990.

[85] Author interview with director of inspections, District of Peñalolén, Santiago, Chile, January 11, 2012.

and licensed markets. Presidents wash their hands of responsibility and blame mayors for any "disorder" caused by street vendors.

Thus, while presidents designed housing policy to provide an alternative to squatting, no comparable efforts were made for employment policy. The military regime did not end informal employment. Post-hoc policies to provide credit and training to low-income groups thus were politically attractive. National politicians cared little about the incentive effects given that street vending was not "their" problem. Squatting, in contrast, threatened the regime and the success of national housing initiatives, and therefore sparked a very different social policy response.

## 6.4 CONCLUSION

It has become commonplace to argue that public welfare programs generate policy feedback effects through the reorganization of societal demands and institutions. In this chapter, I suggested that informal welfare policies can "produce politics" too – that is, they shape the interests, actors, and ideas in a policy area. In countries with a legacy of widespread legal violations, such as Colombia and Peru, policymakers responded to societal demands to improve and secure informal welfare policies through the provision of property titles and services to squatters and credit to street vendors. These actions to strengthen informal welfare came at a price: welfare bureaucracies capable of implementing in-kind social policies never developed. Although housing and employment are expensive and complicated goods for any government to provide, the state's historic absence from these policy areas left presidents without the administrative apparatus to easily change course.

The contrast with housing policy in Chile was dramatic. Because the military regime repressed and relocated squatters, the poor had less land to title and improve. Democratic governments avoided post-hoc policies, instead channeling societal demands to state housing institutions. The housing bureaucracy developed managerial and financial expertise. There is much to criticize about Chile's housing programs, but presidents and bureaucrats have tackled many shortcomings and learned with time.

It is useful to close this chapter by discussing other explanations for these social policy trajectories, by way of contrast with the argument developed here. I take up three alternatives focused on policy diffusion, partisan ideology, and power resource theory. First, it is tempting to see the lack of investment in housing and employment programs as simply another feature in the regional wave of market-oriented reforms in the

1980s and 1990s. In moving toward subsidies for housing consumption, rather than construction, Latin American governments were part of an international trend in conservative governance that took hold under Margaret Thatcher and Ronald Reagan, not to mention Pinochet (Pierson 1993: chapter 4).

The diffusion of "neoliberal" ideas is an incomplete explanation of social policy development. Colombia and Peru both claimed to follow Chile's housing model (as did many other developing economies, like South Africa, Mexico, and Brazil). Yet, governments were terrible copies. They grabbed on to the idea of demand subsidies, but with none of the instruments that made them work for the poor, such as state mortgage assistance, low savings requirements, and direct contracting of affordable housing projects. Ideas for a different housing policy were more than just in the air; they were available from the very country that inspired market-based housing policy across the region, Chile. Moreover, the retreat from in-kind provision dovetailed with the recognition of social rights in many constitutions. Colombia recognized constitutional rights to housing and work at the same time that the state shuttered agencies responsible for their fulfillment. Diffusion tells us little about why certain ideas about state responsibility to house and employ the poor won out.

Partisan ideology, of course, could be the lurking variable to explain differences in policy adoption. Presidents from left-of-center parties held executive power in Chile through the 2000s, while Peru and Colombia never really caught Latin America's left turn. Right-leaning presidents in Peru and Colombia indeed resisted "statist" interventions in housing policy, especially with regard to mortgage banks and state involvement in construction. The center-left coalition that ruled Chile preserved the consumption-based housing policy that it inherited from the dictatorship, but was far more willing to intervene in ways that enabled the market to work for the poor.

Nevertheless, housing policy fits uncomfortably in the usual partisan spectrum. The Right often has emerged as the strongest advocate of housing investments. Colombia, for instance, advanced toward substitutive housing policy with presidents that governed from the popular Right (Uribe) and the center-Right (Santos). Chile's housing policy attracted broad support in part because it appealed to conservative ideas about homeownership and financial responsibility. While the shift further to the left deepened housing policy to make it more targeted and equitable, the choice to invest in mass housing policy had been made soon after democracy was restored and conservative lawmakers still held veto power. In this sense, housing is an exception to the general pattern of Chilean social policy. Social spending was paltry in most areas during the 1990s and then deepened in the 2000s as Lagos and Bachelet won on more left-wing platforms and stripped away authoritarian remnants. An emphasis on partisan ideology also struggles to explain why employment policy remains underdeveloped in Chile. Colombia, a country that has never come close to having the Left in power, has the least-bad employment programs, though that is not saying much in Latin America.

A final approach to social policy reform looks at the relative power of business and labor groups. The stronger unions are, the argument goes, the more likely it is that left-leaning governments will come to power and pursue social policies to benefit the working class (Korpi 1983). The issue is how to adapt this framework to a setting in which workers are split between the formal and informal economy. There is limited evidence of a coherent socioeconomic class identity among workers or unified organizing at the heart of power-resource approaches developed in the context of Western Europe (e.g., Haggard, Kaufman, and Long 2013; Roberts 2002; Weyland 1996a). In Latin America, labor power may result in more spending, but much of this spending still goes to social insurance schemes to protect insiders (Hunter and Sugiyama 2009; Wibbels Forthcoming; Wibbels and Alqhuist 2011). Other scholars do see all good things going together, with stronger unions and institutionalized left parties translating into commitments to inequality reduction (Carnes and Mares 2015; Huber and Stephens 2012; Pribble 2013).

There is little evidence that labor has acted as a protagonist to expand substitutive policy in the specific policy areas studied. Legislators protected housing benefits centered on the organized middle class in Colombia. Unions played little role in housing program expansions in Chile. Informal-sector organizing has been used to explain the pace and form of social policy extensions (Garay 2017), but it largely has centered on post-hoc policies in countries with legacies of squatting. On employment policy, unions even may have retarded the extension of employment benefits. Although not a focus here, Chilean unions blocked efforts to reform severance pay and introduce public unemployment insurance that would protect informal and subcontracted workers (Holland and Schneider 2017).

It also does not seem that housing policies were built on the shoulders of an unwilling capitalist class. Construction lobbies, in particular, have been eager for governments to invest more in housing, although their interests do not neatly align with those of the poor. As seen in Peru and

Colombia, construction companies used state housing subsidies to serve more profitable, middle-income segments of the market. In Chile, the construction sector was the most powerful and organized. Yet, the government still managed to convince construction companies to adopt the government's housing agenda, by providing the necessary price supports and risk-sharing agreements. Business groups were most active in their attempts to end street vending, which makes its continuation all the more puzzling. Labor and business groups certainly play a role in how social policy is designed, but we cannot assume that labor pushes for substitutive social policy and business against it, especially when the absence of social policy can result in legal violations to secure the same goods.

In short, the system of informal welfare benefits that emerged in housing and employment has been hard to change, just like many formal welfare programs. The paradox is that many actors, from citizens to presidents and bureaucrats, are genuinely dissatisfied with informal welfare policies. Multiple presidents rejected the costs imposed by unplanned squatter settlements and street vendors, and promised better alternatives. Some presidents and legislatures contemplated the legalization of street vending as an unemployment strategy, but ultimately declared it counterproductive and a drain on economic growth. The informal welfare state continues, not because it is efficient or just, but because a stock of squatters and street vendors and a bureaucracy set up to improve their lot pose challenges to reform.

# 7

# How Forbearance Ends

## *Lessons from Turkey*

The very nature of the topic studied – legal violations by the urban poor – means that the theory developed potentially is applicable to a range of countries and offenses. A full quantitative test of the generalizability of the electoral model would require detailed statistics on offenses, sanctions, electoral rules, and social policy in many countries. Such data do not exist. My goals in this chapter therefore are more limited. I explore the portability of my argument through a single qualitative case study. This approach allows for more accurate measurement of a tricky dependent variable and a closer analysis of the theoretical mechanisms at work.[1] Looking beyond Latin America, a region of uniformly high levels of income inequality, also allows me to explore the role that poverty and inequality play in sustaining forbearance. My aim is to identify a city with a similar growth trajectory but a more equal income distribution so that local politicians depend less on poor voters to win elections. When the lower-middle class expands, do local politicians respond with enforcement? Put otherwise, is there a developmental path away from forbearance?

Empirically, I focus on comparing the Latin American capitals studied to Istanbul, Turkey. I selected Istanbul for a controlled comparison because it shares key commonalities with the Latin American cities studied. First, Turkey has a similar development level to Chile, as seen in the left panel of Figure 7.1. Second, as in Latin America, ISI policies gave rise to a segmented labor market and truncated welfare state. Third, Turkey is a unitary system that undertook a major process of political and urban

[1] On the use of controlled case comparisons to establish external validity, see Slater and Ziblatt (2013).

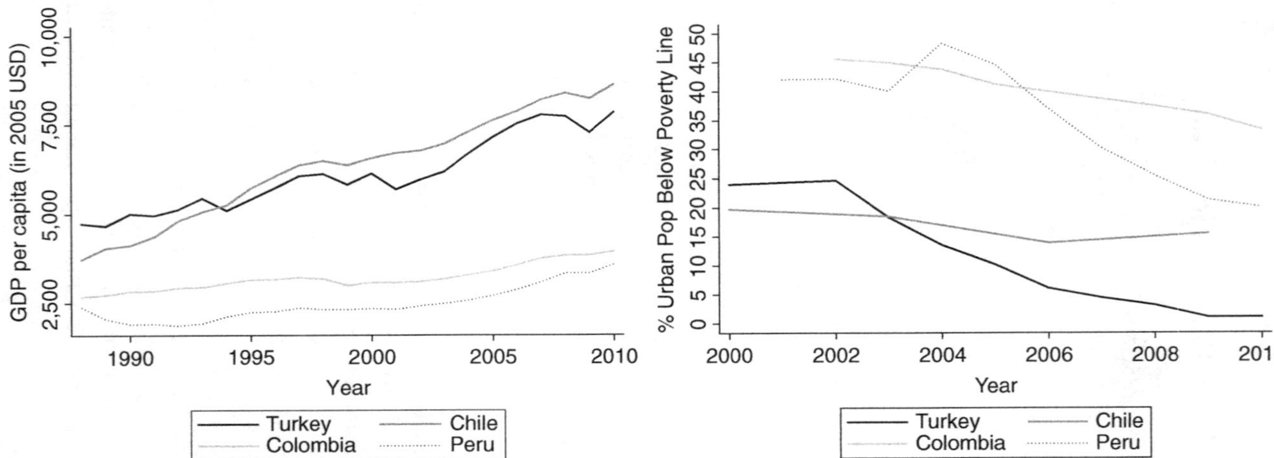


FIGURE 7.1 Economic Development (left) and Urban Poverty (right)

Source: World Bank Development Indicators.

decentralization in 1984, right after its third-wave democratic transition. Fourth, under capacity-based theories, Turkey is another "least-likely" case for forbearance given its well-trained bureaucracy. Common indicators of state capacity, such as income tax collection and bureaucratic effectiveness, put Turkey on a par with Chile.[2] Turkey's strong bureaucracy often is dated back to the rule of Mustafa Kemal Atatürk (1923–1938). Perhaps most famously, Atatürk's Turkey jailed people for wearing the wrong type of hat. Last, I study Istanbul because it is the largest city in Turkey and its city mayors have tended to go on to national politics. The best example of this career path is Recep Tayyip Erdoğan, who has spent more than two decades in power, from 1994 as Istanbul's mayor, from 2003 as Turkey's prime minister, and from 2014 on as its president.

While a focus on Istanbul allows for me to hold constant important characteristics, the city differs from the Latin American cases studied in theoretically interesting ways. First, crucially, the income distribution in Turkey is more equal than that in any Latin American country. Inequality, as measured by the Gini coefficient, is one-fifth lower than in Chile, for instance. Urban poverty, in particular, declined dramatically over the 2000s, as seen in the right panel of Figure 7.1. No district in Istanbul has a majority of poor voters. Istanbul thus allows me to explore whether the growth of a lower-middle class can push countries away from forbearance.

Second, Turkey has sharp ethnic and religious cleavages that may affect the electoral incentives to enforce. Directly, politicians may calculate a lower chance of winning over minority voters who work as street vendors or live in squatter settlements and therefore see greater latitude to enforce against them. Indirectly, ethnic divisions can alter the signals conveyed by enforcement. The previous chapters showed that forbearance functions as a signal of social affinities in the absence of welfare policies. Ethnic and religious cleavages may attenuate this association, as politicians portray those who violate the law as undeserving, criminal, or simply the "other." This argument parallels a large scholarship that emphasizes how social heterogeneity reduces popular support for taxation and redistribution (e.g., Alesina and Glaeser 2004; Gilens 2000; Lieberman 2003; Luttmer 2001; Shayo 2009).

[2] Turkey collects more income tax than Chile, yielding 6.3 percent compared to 3.8 percent of GDP (Lieberman 2003: 65). Both Chile and Turkey score in the top third of the World Bank's measures of government effectiveness (although Chile has the edge in the 84th versus the 67th percentile, see World Bank Governance Indicators 2014).

My central argument is that the expansion of the lower-middle class reduced the electoral costs of enforcement in Istanbul. The dominant conservative party, the Justice and Development Party (*Adalet ve Kalkınma Partisi*, AKP), capitalized on these shifting income demographics to expand support for enforcement. It also linked legal violations to Kurdish, Roma, and Alevi minorities, targeting the largest enforcement operations to minority areas and playing on popular prejudices to reduce the reputational costs of enforcement. Social policy did not provide effective substitutes for the urban poor, although increased investment in housing programs for the nonpoor in the 2000s was used to create the impression of state alternatives.

To develop the argument, I track enforcement politics over time and space in Istanbul, using original interviews and secondary sources. I conducted interviews in a stratified sample of about a third of Istanbul's thirty-nine district governments (*belediye*) and applied the same local government questionnaire developed for the Latin American cases. Before proceeding with my analysis, I first describe the social policy and economic context. I then sketch two major periods of enforcement politics: first, a period during the twentieth century in which politicians of all stripes used forbearance and post-hoc policies to win the votes of the urban poor; and second, a contemporary period in which the AKP has used enforcement to court a growing middle-class vote and signal pro-Sunni majority positions. Many Latin American countries also are ethnically diverse, and this discussion provides a chance to rethink the cases presented and extensions within the region in the last part of the chapter.

## 7.1 COMPARING THE SOCIAL POLICY CONTEXT

As in most of Latin America, Turkey developed a truncated welfare state in the mid-twentieth century. In the 1960s, Turkey embarked on a model of state-led industrialization. The focus on accelerating industrialization unleashed substantial rural migration, leading Istanbul to triple in size between 1950 and 1970 (Keyder 1999: 146). Welfare state expansion went hand in hand with industrial development. Yet, as in Latin America, welfare benefits were reserved for the salaried workforce, which was a minority.[3] Turkey often is considered a Southern European welfare regime, meaning that it combines social insurance benefits for formal-

[3] For instance, only half a million workers qualified for state pension benefits in a country with a working population of 14.5 million (Buğra 2007: 42).

sector workers with reliance on family aid, clientelism, and, as I return to below, forbearance toward legal violations by the poor (Buğra and Keyder 2006; Ferrera 1996).[4]

Housing policy exemplifies the truncated welfare system that developed and persisted through economic liberalization. After an economic crash and a controlled transition to multiparty elections in 1983, the conservative government of the Motherland Party (*Anavatan Partisi*, ANAP) initiated a set of market reforms, including privatizations and greater export-oriented development. Prime Minister Turgut Özal viewed construction as a major engine of growth in the newly liberalized economy and created the Mass Housing Authority (*Toplu Konut İdaresi Mudurluğu*, TOKİ) to spur development. Like other Turkish welfare programs, TOKİ largely built housing for organized formal-sector workers. TOKİ required households to save 20–25 percent of housing costs through cooperatives. Such requirements meant that housing went to people who were "not in need of subsidies" (Özdemir 2011: 1103). Not much housing was available even for those who could afford it. From 1984 to 2002, TOKİ only produced around 43,000 housing units (Marschall, Aydogan, and Bulut 2016: 205). Most squatters were unaware of the existence of state housing supports (Buğra 1998: 308–9).

Housing policy began to shift with the election of the AKP in 2003. To provide a bit of background, the AKP is a nominally secular party with roots in the National Outlook Movement (*Milli Görüş*, NOM) and the National Order Party (MNP). Founded in 1970, the MNP was the first party with clear Islamic credentials. But state officials and military generals wanted Turkey to remain a secular state as envisioned by Atatürk and enshrined in the Constitution. The Constitutional Court therefore banned the MNP and continued to exclude other political parties associated with the NOM in the 1980s and 1990s. The Welfare Party (*Refah Partisi*) made substantial inroads in local politics and even formed part of the national ruling coalition before it was banned in 1997. Party members regrouped as the Virtue Party (*Fazilet Partisi*) only to split after the Court banned the Islamists once again in 2001. Erdoğan represented the modernizing faction that broke from a more traditionalist wing to form the AKP.

The AKP inherited much of the grassroots organization and party structure from the Welfare Party. However, it adopted a more pro-Western

[4] Turkey differs somewhat from its welfare state family in a heavy (and increasing) role for religious and charitable organizations in social assistance (Buğra 2007; Eder 2010: 177–81; Göçmen 2014).

agenda, supporting Turkish economic integration and membership in the European Union. It also courted the business community and, most relevant for our purposes, found close allies in a growing domestic construction industry.

Although Turkey has taken a competitive authoritarian tilt in recent years, it is worth emphasizing that the AKP won free and fair elections in the 2000s. The AKP's popularity rested in part on Erdoğan's personal appeal as an outsider and a "common" (and pious) man, in contrast to the secular elite establishment (Aytaç and Öni 2014). But the AKP also oversaw an important economic turnaround. Turkey went through an economic crash in 2001, which discredited the previous government and propelled the AKP to power. Construction was the cornerstone of the AKP's economic growth strategy and arguably also its early electoral success.

The AKP overhauled housing policy to help pull the economy out of recession. TOKİ was transformed into a state real estate corporation under direct control of the prime minister. Moving far beyond its initial mandate of social interest housing, the agency gained the authority to develop for-profit projects, expropriate land, and forgo public budgeting requirements (Buğra and Savaskan 2014: 85). Most controversially, TOKİ began to undertake urban renewal (often translated as "urban transformation projects"). These projects relocated low-income groups from central areas – some of which formed through informal settlement processes decades earlier – to housing on the urban periphery so that prime real estate could be redeveloped, generally as luxury housing or commercial real estate. Neighborhood clearances unleashed intense popular resistance (Arslanalp 2015; El-Kazaz 2014; Karaman 2014; Kuyucu and Unsal 2010).

Turkey has a housing program of scale, but still provides limited housing options to the urban poor. Invested with new powers and funds, the public sector's share of housing construction jumped from less than 1 percent in 1984 to almost 25 percent in 2004 (Candan and Kolluoglu 2008: 17). TOKİ constructed roughly 432,000 housing units and invested $11 billion between 2003 and 2014 (Marschall, Aydogan, and Bulut 2016: 202). Of TOKİ projects, 40 percent have been directed to middle-income groups and 26 percent to social interest housing (with the rest involving urban renewal and public works projects) (Sarica 2012: 31). Although the quantity of housing construction is not trivial, it falls short of a substitutive program due to its targeting. Turkey has built in a decade roughly the same number of social interest housing units that Chile builds in two years for a population a quarter of the size. Complaints abound that TOKİ focuses on lucrative projects, especially in Istanbul where land is most valuable, and that even "social interest" housing projects are out of reach of low-income households (Kuyucu and Unsal 2010). Not a single housing bureaucrat that I interviewed believed that TOKİ provides housing alternatives for low-income groups in Istanbul.[5] Thus, Turkey's housing policy is best characterized as truncated: it spends substantial sums on housing development but favors the lower-middle and middle class in its programs.

Housing investments involve not only subsidized housing, but also construction contracts and jobs that have helped the AKP to consolidate its electoral strength. The distribution of housing brings electoral returns. Marschall, Aydogan, and Bulut (2016) show that the AKP has won more local elections in districts where it invests more in housing projects, all else being equal. TOKİ also contracts the building of housing units to private firms, most of which have strong ties to the AKP and provide crucial financing for the party and associated charitable foundations (Buğra and Savaskan 2014: 93).

In contrast to increasing expenditures on housing, employment policy remains limited in Turkey. Like the Latin American cases examined, Turkey reports no expenditures on active labor market policies, and spends just 0.1 percent of GDP on public unemployment insurance for formal-sector workers (OECD 2011). District governments are responsible for employment programs. Their efforts vary widely. Although many districts employ unskilled workers as drivers, gardeners, cleaners, or construction workers on housing projects, few have institutionalized or large-scale jobs programs or labor intermediation services. More generally, Turkey introduced a conditional cash transfer program and extended health care and schooling coverage in the 2000s. However, social expenditures have remained at modest levels overall, climbing to a peak of 14 percent of GDP in 2009 (Dorlach 2015: 522). This spending still does little to redistribute income. Tax and transfer policies reduce the Gini coefficient by only 11 percent, which is far off the OECD average of 25 percent and closer to the Latin American median (İnan 2011).

Finally, the demand for social policy is different in Turkey. As shown in Figure 7.1, GDP per capita increased substantially over the course of the

[5] Some emphasized that TOKİ abandoned its focus on affordable projects with time, or that it worked better in secondary cities. Author interview with director of housing, District of Sultangazi, Istanbul, Turkey, June 6, 2014.

1990s and 2000s, growing at an average rate of 4 percent per year and hitting rates of 7 percent per year during the first five years of AKP rule. Unlike Latin America's largely commodity-driven growth, Turkey expanded its exports and benefited from a surge of capital inflows to emerging economies. Due to its dependence on foreign financing and real estate investment, the economy took a hard hit in the 2008 financial crisis (Rodrik 2012). But inequality has remained low. Turkey's Gini coefficient peaked at 0.49 in 1994, before steadily dropping to 0.41 in 2011. For comparison's sake, Chile's Gini coefficient only dropped to 0.50 in 2011 after a decade of social investments.

Turkey's reduction in inequality enhanced the impact of economic growth on poverty. In the 2000s, rates of extreme and moderate poverty in Turkey fell by more than half, and the middle class doubled in size. Almost all of the improvement came from growth and more equal distribution of labor income, rather than government transfers (Azevedo and Atamanov 2014). More specifically, urban poverty declined. In the poorest district in Istanbul, only one-fifth of residents would be considered poor by the definition used in the Latin American cases.[6] Politicians can win elections without the support of the poor in Istanbul.

This brief summary has revealed that the origins of truncated social policy in Turkey are similar to those in Latin America. Housing policy initially focused on formal-sector workers, and even as expenditures took off under the AKP, investments favored the middle (and lower-middle) class. Employment policy is minimal. But there also is a striking divergence from Latin American cities in the level of inequality. Fewer voters in Istanbul are poor, which makes it easier for politicians to win elections without the support of those who are. I now turn to how the absence of housing policy made forbearance central to the Turkish welfare regime in the 1980s and 1990s. I then show how the rising wealth of voters, combined with steps to expand housing programs and politicize ethnic cleavages, reduced the electoral costs of enforcement and allowed the AKP to shift away from forbearance toward squatters and street vendors in the 2000s.

[6] Household surveys confirm that just 3 percent of Turkey's poor live in Istanbul (Konda 2006: 17). District income is notoriously hard to measure in Turkey. I use receipt of noncontributory health insurance as a proxy for district poverty, given that recipients must have a per capita household income of less than two minimum wages to receive subsidies from the program. By way of contrast, the poorest district in Bogotá has 52 percent of the population that is classified as the highest priority for social assistance, and 91 percent qualify for targeted social benefits that require income levels below the Turkish threshold of two minimum wages.

## 7.2 INFORMAL WELFARE IN TURKEY

During the twentieth century, informal welfare provision was central to electoral politics and the social safety net in urban Turkey. In particular, I focus on how inadequate housing policy created incentives for local politicians to favor forbearance in the 1980s and 1990s. Following the same logic developed in Chapter 3, I trace how truncated housing policy raised the electoral costs of enforcement through three mechanisms: (1) crowding in legal violations, (2) demand displacement to local politicians and post-hoc policies, and (3) an association between enforcement and anti-poor distributive positions. I draw on a rich secondary source literature, as well as interviews with long-serving bureaucrats. In my interviews, I asked questions about capacity constraints and political intervention in the enforcement process. Reports of political constraints on enforcement, as well as the rapid changes in enforcement to which I turn in the next section, confirm that politicians had the ability to enforce but chose not to act in order to win votes.

### 7.2.1 Crowding In Squatters

The inadequacy of Turkey's housing policies in the twentieth century resulted in widespread informal construction. As in Latin America, squatter settlements grew at their fastest pace in the post–World War II period and then persisted through changes in economic models. Nationwide, squatter settlements housed 5 percent of Turkey's urban population in 1955 and 26 percent in 1980 (Keleş 2010: 493–4). Agricultural liberalization, war in the Kurdish regions, and urban job opportunities continued to spur migration to Istanbul throughout the 1980s and 1990s. By the 1990s, about half of all housing stock in Istanbul was built illegally (Keyder 1999: 143). About three-quarters of squatter settlements formed through coordinated invasions of state land, leading to their nickname *gecekondu* ("built overnight"). The remainder involved illegal construction on agricultural land (Buğra 1998: 309).[7]

Politicians rarely organized land invasions or promoted squatting directly. As in Lima and Bogotá, they crowded in squatting through their forbearance and decisions to invest in and formalize informal settlements. Evictions were rare. Mayors also used their discretion to

[7] As in Lima, most land in Istanbul belonged to the state, making land invasions more common than illegal land sales (Keyder 2005: 126).

alter the pace through which settlements received urban amenities. They chose whether to approve a map and "improvement plan" for squatter settlements, granting access to urban services. They also provided local land deeds ("title assignation documents," *tapu tahsis*). Land deeds recognize the occupant's right to inhabit the land, but stop short of formal property title. Much as in Lima, squatters mobilized for mayors' campaigns in exchange for support in accessing land deeds and services (Güneş-Ayata 1987: 239–40; Keyder 1999: 147–78). Politicians tied positive inducements to squatters' political participation, but rarely evicted those who did not support them. The exchange of services and land deeds thus cemented clientelistic linkages to voters in urban areas.

At the national level, legislators issued more than nineteen "amnesties" to legalize informal housing. The cartoon in Figure 7.2 ridicules this process with a little boy asking his parents, "What is our crime that they declared amnesty for?" Squatting was so common in Istanbul that the idea of "amnesty" seemed absurd. Political parties across the ideological spectrum promised to assign land deeds and pass amnesties prior to elections. For instance, the Republican People's Party (*Cumhuriyet Halk Partisi*, CHP) – the statist, secular party founded by Atatürk – secured electoral victory in 1973 up until the 1980 military coup in part thanks to offers of land deeds in exchange for squatters' votes (Karpat 1976: 65; Özler 2000: 44–5). So too did the conservative Justice Party (AP). AP prime minister Süleyman Demirel emphasized that "demolition of *gecekondu* without providing alternative shelter for squatters was totally out of the question." His statement unleashed a wave of new land invasions (Buğra 1998: 308). The electoral benefits stemming from amnesties can be seen in their timing: all major amnesties were issued the year prior to an election (Arslanalp 2015: 70–1).

The transfers that occurred through forbearance and post-hoc policies toward informal settlements were substantial. In 1996, the state land occupied by squatters was valued at \$75 billion and encompassed 600,000 households in Istanbul alone (Özler 2000: 41). Başlevent and Dayıoğlu (2005: 37) use household surveys to impute rent payments in squatter settlements – much as I did in Peru in Chapter 4. They calculate that the transfers to the poor through forbearance toward informal construction constitute 1.2 percent of annual household income in urban Turkey. In comparison, benefits from social assistance programs amount to only 0.4 percent of household income. Thus, much as in Latin America, the benefits from forbearance rival state welfare programs. The

FIGURE 7.2 The Normalcy of Squatting
Source: Tan Oral, "What is our crime that they declared amnesty for?" *Cumhuriyet*, April 1983.

government's own accounting also makes clear the importance of forbearance. The Turkish undersecretary of housing calculated that there was sufficient housing in all Turkish cities if both legal and informal housing were counted. If informal housing were excluded, the country faced an acute housing shortage (Çanga 2002). Scholars thus have considered forbearance toward squatter settlements to be a central feature of the Turkish welfare regime (e.g., Buğra and Keyder 2006; Buğra 1998; Eder 2010; Dorlach 2015; Keyder 1999).

The perverse incentive effects of the informal housing system did not go unnoticed. The controversy is best seen in debates over amnesty in 1996. When part of the ruling coalition, the Welfare Party (from which the AKP splintered) proposed another amnesty to recognize existing constructions. Mayors complained that it would encourage further illegal land occupations and place a heavy burden on them to provide infrastructure and services to legalized areas. The Chamber of City Planners in Istanbul, a powerful professional association, denounced the Welfare Party for trying to reward its voters through property transfers.[8] Much as in Latin America, national politicians recognized the short-term electoral rewards of forbearance and post-hoc policies, and discounted the objections of overburdened local governments and bureaucrats interested in long-term planning. As Kuyucu and Unsal (2010: 1484) put it, "No political party dared to terminate such a vibrant channel of vote-seeking and wealth redistribution."

### 7.2.2 Demand Displacement

Forbearance toward informal settlements reshaped popular demands. Arslanalp (2015) documents the connections between "legal exemptions" and the type of collective organizing. Only in the 1950s, when the state tried to carry out demolitions did neighborhood associations form a federation to make collective claims for state housing assistance. From the 1960s through the 1990s, the government's permissive policies instead channeled organizing toward local authorities and post-hoc policies. Informal settlement associations (known as "beautification" associations) developed to pressure local mayors for services and legal deeds (Karpat 1976; Şenyapılı 2004). Forbearance and post-hoc goods thus stunted the development of collective movements for housing provision, property law changes, or more inclusive citizenship policies.

Politics in poor districts came to center around the right to occupy land and then gain recognition and services. The tolerance of squatter settlements was the primary "subsidy" provided to win the votes of Istanbul's poor in the 1980s and 1990s (Keyder 1999: 147). In some cases, squatter settlements constituted such an important voting block that they elected their own representatives to municipal councils and mayors' offices, who then managed the informal construction process (Arslanalp 2015: 77). In one district in which most residents lived in informal settlements (Ümraniye), for example, local councilors said that the formalization of squatter settlements was the main priority of the district government (Erder 1996: 136).

[8] "Rent Wars for Squatter Houses Cause Misery and Controversy," *Hurriyet* August 30, 1996.

### 7.2.3 Distributive Signals

The electoral costs of enforcement were high in the 1980s and early 1990s. As in Lima and Bogotá, the absence of housing programs generated popular sympathy for squatters. As Buğra (1998: 307) explains, "Since [housing] projects have rarely materialized in an effective way, the demolition of existing [squatter settlements], whenever it was attempted, was regarded as an act of cruelty against helpless individuals and represented in the media with the aid of heartbreaking pictures of human misery."

Forbearance played a key role in how politicians signaled their representation of the urban poor. This process is clearest when examining the electoral ascendance of the Welfare Party in a poor district, Sultanbeyli. Sultanbeyli was the poorest district in greater Istanbul, and absorbed large numbers of rural migrants.[9] The district's population grew from 3,700 in 1980 to 82,000 in 1990 and finally to 175,000 in 2000 (Pinarcioğlu and Işik 2008: 1359). Between 1986 and 1989 alone, 20,000 new informal housing units were built (UN-Habitat 2007: 112). In 1989, the Welfare Party took office. The mayor, Sultan Koçak, used forbearance as a way to demonstrate his defense of the urban poor and expand his appeal beyond religious conservatives. As Tuğal (2009: 115, emphasis added) relates in his ethnography of the district, "Koçak propagated that he was the friend of all the poor, everybody would have their own land and home, and *he would not respect the law until this promise was fulfilled.*" Sultanbeyli residents described Koçak as "one of us" in part because he interpreted construction norms differently than the "urban elite." Forbearance thus communicated the mayor's distributive commitments.

Interviews with bureaucrats confirm that the lack of enforcement was due to political intervention, not weak state capacity. Mayors feared the reputational effects of enforcement and threatened to fire bureaucrats if they tried to enforce against squatters. As one long-serving bureaucrat put it, "Naturally, mayors make political decisions when they govern the district. And since we bureaucrats receive the orders from mayors, we couldn't do anything against squatters as long as the mayor was worried about looking bad in front of the community."[10] Continuing with the example of Sultanbeyli, one bureaucrat explained how Koçak allowed squatter settlements to expand because politicians "were aware of everything, but

[9] Sultanbeyli was part of the Kartal district, governed by ANAP, until it became its own independent district in 1989.

[10] Author interview with director of inspections, District of Beykoz, Istanbul, Turkey, June 9, 2014.

they were firing officials who intervened" (Tuğal 2011: 86). The head inspector in Sultanbeyli told me that politicians discussed each new illegal construction in local council meetings. They "perhaps decided to impose fines," but "never dreamed" of evicting squatters or demolishing constructions in the 1990s.[11] In interviews, almost all of the dozen bureaucrats who had worked in district governments in the 1990s said that mayors lost votes from enforcement in this period, and that political intervention constituted the main constraint on enforcement.

Consistent with the idea that forbearance wins votes among the poor, the Welfare Party drew its strongest support from areas with concentrations of squatters (Başlevent and Silahtar 2013; Özler 2000; Yalçıntan and Erbaş 2003). Of course, these correlations may reflect the fact that, especially in the 1980s, rural migrants tended to be religious Sunnis from inner Anatolia, and thus were more likely to identify with the Welfare Party's religious conservatism. But a number of fringe Islamic parties had failed to capture popular majorities. The Welfare Party's willingness to address the material needs of squatter settlements differentiated it from other small Islamic parties as well as competing centrist parties that had failed to win over squatters' votes (Arslanalp 2015: 100; Bora 1999: 53; Özler 2000: 53; Yalçıntan and Erbaş 2003: 97). A reputation for innovative local management and infrastructure investments in informal settlements helped the Welfare Party broaden its appeal beyond coreligionists (Akinci 1999; White 2002: 255–7, 266).

Positions regarding squatter settlements took center stage in the 1994 election for the mayor of Istanbul. The Welfare Party fielded its own candidate, Erdoğan. The press revealed that Erdoğan, who spent part of his childhood in Sultanbeyli, had tried to build six illegal houses on state forestland. CHP opponents pounced on the case to argue that squatters steal state land to earn profits. They tried to brand Erdoğan as a slum landlord who disrespected "modern" laws. The urban poor saw these charges as an elitist attack, and Erdoğan seized the moment to defend those who lived in informal settlements. Bora (1999: 52) recounts that when Erdoğan declared that "people building illegal housing should not be blamed until the problems leading to migration were solved, the contest was clinched in favor of him." More generally, Erdoğan's references to his humble background helped to reinforce his image as a "man of the people" in contrast to the secular "Republican elites" that had previously

11 Author interview with director of construction and monitoring, District of Sultanbeyli, Istanbul, Turkey, June 10, 2014.

dominated city politics (Aytaç and Öni 2014: 45). The 1994 election was a watershed moment for the Welfare Party, as it took 20 percent of the votes nationally and some of the most important metropolitan posts in the country, including Istanbul and Ankara.[12] It paved the way to the AKP's victory in parliamentary elections in 2002.

In short, the arguments made in this book about how the absence of social policy raises the electoral costs of enforcement resonate remarkably well with Turkey's experience in the 1980s and 1990s. As in Lima and Bogotá, the urban poor looked to informal construction to resolve their housing needs, and then organized around forbearance and post-hoc goods. Local politicians tolerated squatter settlement formation to win votes and signal their concern for poor voters. The fact that politicians intervened to stop bureaucrats from enforcing the law provides disconfirming evidence of capacity-based explanations. The more interesting question is how this system for winning urban elections began to break down in Istanbul.

## 7.3 A DEVELOPMENTAL EXIT FROM THE FORBEARANCE TRAP

Enforcement against both squatters and street vendors changed dramatically in the 2000s. Although few observers doubt that a shift in enforcement occurred, substantial debate exists over why. It would have been logical to expect continued forbearance toward legal violations once the Welfare Party took power at the city level and split into the AKP. As noted above, substitutive social policy is a partial explanation at best. Spending on housing increased, but it was insufficient to meet the needs of the urban poor, and no comparable efforts existed on employment policy. Why, then, did the AKP shift to an enforcement strategy?

Two main factors converged to promote the enforcement turn. First, economic growth allowed the AKP to use a different electoral strategy than the Welfare Party. The fact that the median voter was no longer poor freed the AKP to enforce, even in low-income districts. Second, accelerating Kurdish migration changed the ethnic composition of squatters and street vendors. The AKP blamed legal violations on the Kurdish (as well as

[12] Subnational electoral victories, initially cemented through forbearance, were so critical to softening the Welfare Party's extreme brand that mayors even considered forming a municipal party headed by its local leaders when the Constitutional Court disbanded the Welfare Party in 1997. See "Establishing a Party of the Municipalities," *Hurriyet* February 1, 1997. For a more general discussion of how subnational elections make extreme parties more palatable to the median voter, see Holland (2016c).

Roma and Alevi) minorities, who were less likely to vote for the AKP or elicit public sympathy among Turkey's Sunni majority. Enforcement thus had lower electoral costs due to the higher incomes of voters and social divisions. Politicians also turned to enforcement in part to transform the AKP's reputation from an Islamic to a "modern" party able to represent middle-class and business interests.

### 7.3.1 Economic Development and Enforcement against Squatters

The attempt to enforce against squatters can be seen both in national legislation and local politics. On the legislative side, the AKP reformed the law to criminalize squatting, and blocked the extension of water services to any informal construction built after 2004.[13] The AKP's housing projects were pitched as part of a drive to eliminate squatter settlements. Erdoğan gave a speech at the First Housing Convention in 2006 that foreshadowed enforcement against squatters: "Our biggest ideal is to eradicate the squatter settlements (*gecekondus*) that have surrounded our cities like a tumor" (Kuyucu 2014: 613). The AKP's rise thus heralded the "collapse of the indirect welfare mechanisms" and an important vote-seeking strategy (Eder 2010: 166).

On the enforcement side, local governments took a hard line against new constructions and demolished existing informal settlements to make way for urban renewal projects. Housing bureaucrats in low-income districts reported regular control operations to end illegal land occupations.[14] The elasticity to improvements in enforcement technology has been high: bureaucrats reported using satellite imagery and helicopters to monitor squatter settlement expansion. Mayors contracted with private demolition companies to minimize their direct responsibility for evictions.[15] The national government also targeted for urban renewal centrally located neighborhoods where residents had deeds only to the land, not to the informal housing built on it. According to a United Nations–sponsored inquiry, renewal projects in eight

[13] Law on Zoning, No. 3194, July 26, 2008. Private companies provide electricity and heat, and therefore the government cannot control the provision of these services.

[14] Author interview with director of urban zoning, District of Gaziosmanpaşa, Istanbul, Turkey, June 6, 2014; Author interview with director of construction and monitoring, District of Sultanbeyli, Istanbul, Turkey, June 10, 2014; author interview with director of housing, District of Beyoğlu, Istanbul, Turkey, June 3, 2014.

[15] Author interview with director of urban zoning, District of Sultangazi, Istanbul, Turkey, June 6, 2014.

neighborhoods displaced 80,000 people in the 2000s (AGFE 2009). Because many residents held only land deeds, they received low levels of compensation and many could not afford the mortgage payments in TOKİ housing projects where they were relocated (Kuyucu 2014; Kuyucu and Unsal 2010). Removals ruptured the previous understanding among the urban poor that land deeds were equivalent to full property ownership. In interviews, bureaucrats emphasized that displacements for urban renewal purposes heightened concerns about enforcement even in peripheral areas, and sent a message that illegal land occupations were no longer tolerated.[16]

The growing wealth of voters allowed the AKP to undertake these enforcement actions without losing critical votes. In sharp contrast to the electoral power of the poor in the Latin American cities studied, mayors saw little reason to care about the poor's welfare in Istanbul. A typical comment comes from a bureaucrat who explains, "There is no longer much tolerance for poor people [so] if the district mayor calls us, he wants more enforcement against poor people."[17]

Again, Sultanbeyli illustrates how the expansion of the lower-middle class changed enforcement dynamics. Sultanbeyli seems like an unlikely case for enforcement, given its relatively high poverty rates and its association with Erdoğan. Indeed, Sultanbeyli continued to expand through informal construction when Erdoğan was city mayor in the 1990s; residents received property titles, services, and infrastructure investment. But enforcement against informal settlement increased in the 2000s. The AKP tried to cultivate a reputation for use of "modern" management principles in the district, and an end to negotiations around the law. After the AKP won the 2004 local election, many poor residents asked for forbearance toward their constructions. The mayor and his officials claimed that that they could not interfere in the work of police and bureaucrats to stop enforcement, in contrast to the past (Tuğal 2011: 96–7). Regular patrolling of land began to prevent squatting (Pinarcioğlu and Işik 2008: 1366). Government officials attributed the change in enforcement to the social

[16] In particular, bureaucrats mentioned that demolitions in Zeytinburnu, Sulukule, Tarlabasi, Kucukcekmece, and Fikirtepe (Kadiköy) scared residents in peripheral districts away from informal construction. Author interview with director of construction and monitoring, District of Sultanbeyli, Istanbul, Turkey, June 10, 2014; author interview with director of urban zoning, District of Gaziosmanpaşa, Istanbul, Turkey, June 6, 2014.

[17] Author interview with director of housing, District of Beyoğlu, Istanbul, Turkey, June 3, 2014.

mobility of district residents. Residents came to see squatting as an embarrassment and a threat to their children's prospects to rise into the middle class. Consistent with the changing public sentiment, electoral platforms openly promised enforcement. In 2009, for instance, the AKP mayor won office using the campaign slogan "Don't destroy your children's dreams by constructing illegal houses."[18]

Although housing policies did not provide effective substitutes for the urban poor, the AKP did use them to cushion the political impact of enforcement. Erdoğan appeared at events to inaugurate TOKİ projects, and frequently referenced the social impact of housing projects. For instance, Erdoğan stressed the government's willingness to build housing and relocate squatters in spite of their legal violations. As he put it in a speech to justify the government's enforcement position:

> People were asking us how we were going to demolish these squatter settlements? ... If you are determined ... if you are resolute, you can demolish them. We could do it because we included in our [housing] projects not only those who rightfully own property but also those occupiers who have no rights. Despite the wrongs that they have committed, we still developed our projects in a way that they receive from us the demolition value for their squatter settlements and then are moved into modern buildings. *(qtd. in Kuyucu 2014: 620)*

The AKP's emphasis on enforcement reflected changes in underlying voter demographics and the party's strategic calculations about its core constituency. The AKP began to speak of representing Turkey's "rising middle class," not the poor and marginalized. After breaking with the traditionalist faction of the Welfare Party, Erdoğan wanted to shed the party's association with "backward" practices, including tolerance of squatters, and to straddle social conservatism and modern economic principles (Çinar 2005: 174–7). The AKP also allied with the construction industry and privileged its interests, especially in the pursuit of profitable urban renewal projects.

There were political costs to the AKP's transformation. The AKP arguably lost a pair of district elections in Istanbul due to the popular backlash against urban renewal. Enforcement took many poor residents in districts like Sultanbeyli "by surprise."[19] But urban renewal projects generated substantial rents, and construction contracts could be used to nurture

[18] Author interview with director of construction and monitoring, District of Sultanbeyli, Istanbul, Turkey, June 10, 2014.

[19] Author interview with director of construction and monitoring, District of Sultanbeyli, Istanbul, Turkey, June 10, 2014.

business support, finance political campaigns and private kickbacks, and compensate losers (Arslanalp 2015; Buğra and Savaskan 2014; Erder 2010; Kuyucu and Unsal 2010).

Some may wonder if the strength of the construction industry explains the AKP's enforcement turn. There are two reasons why business interests are an insufficient explanation on their own. First, business opposition preceded enforcement against squatters. A 1994 Chamber of Commerce (*İstanbul Ticaret Odası*, İTO) report estimated that squatters occupied $3.4 billion worth of state land. Blaming politicians for making these transfers to occupants, the chamber called on the Istanbul government to establish a special "urbanization police" to stop illegal construction and eliminate squatter settlements (İTO 1994: 78–9). But Erdoğan made erratic efforts to control squatting as mayor in the 1990s, and peripheral districts expanded substantially during this period. Only once the AKP took national office and incorporated business groups into its electoral coalition did the party change the law and pressure mayors to stop the growth of squatter settlements. Second, the AKP announced its enforcement plans with great fanfare. If the hope was to reward business allies – and then pay off the people affected – it is unclear why the government emphasized its intentions to enforce. Public proclamations support my argument that enforcement against squatters had a growing electoral constituency as well as an economic one. Erdoğan used his support for enforcement to emphasize his strength as a leader and appeal to the growing middle class. Last, as the next section shows, the AKP also enforced against street vendors, despite no comparable business coalition.

### 7.3.2 Economic Development and Enforcement against Street Vendors

The impact of changing voter demographics can also be seen in enforcement against street vending. City and district mayors from the AKP have increased operations and routine sanctions against street vendors. A 2003 household labor force survey – done just after Turkey's economic recession – estimated that there were 451,000 street vendors in Turkey, including 225,000 in Istanbul.[20] Vending has dropped since this peak. My estimate puts the upper-bound number of street vendors in Istanbul at 40,000, and a lower bound of 25,000, which is well below even the

[20] "Istanbul street vendors scarce as Zabıta marks anniversary," *Hurriyet* August 2, 2010.

estimates for Santiago.[21] Although economic recovery partially explains this drop, there also has been substantial enforcement. District police (*zabıta*) under the control of elected mayors are in charge of street vending, and they can fine vendors and decommission their merchandise and equipment. Every district that I surveyed reported regular operations to decommission merchandise from street vendors. Street vendors concur that they are on constant watch to prevent having their merchandise confiscated.[22]

Unsurprisingly, bureaucrats in nonpoor districts report strong electoral pressure to enforce against street vendors, just as in the Latin American cities studied. Bureaucrats said that upper-class constituents associate forbearance with tax evasion, disorder, and corruption. As one long-serving bureaucrat put it, "People used to say, 'Don't touch the poor.' But now it is not like that, neighbors urge us to intervene if there are informal vendors . . . they think, 'I am paying my tax, I am paying my rent, so you should punish the ones who do not pay.'"[23] In line with the idea that mayors want to enforce street-vending regulations, responsiveness to changes in technology has been high. Bureaucrats now use mobile devices so they can match vendors with their identification numbers on the spot. Previously, vendors would report incorrect identification numbers and police would have no way to track down vendors to make them pay their fines. The effectiveness of enforcement thus has increased.[24]

What is more noteworthy is that bureaucrats in the least well-off districts largely reported low electoral costs of enforcement.[25] Bureaucrats

[21] The upper-bound statistic takes the summertime estimate of the number of street vendors from each district that I surveyed and multiplies it by the total number of districts. This approach likely overestimates vendors because my sample includes two of the districts known to have the most vendors in the city: the tourist center of Fatih, and the port center of Kadıköy. The lower-bound estimate comes from taking the yearly average excluding these districts.

[22] "Istanbul's street-food vendors, municipal officers disagree on regulations," *Hurriyet* August 4, 2010. District governments issue licenses (*işgaliyes*) for very select traditional foods; otherwise, a national law bans street vending.

[23] Author interview with sub-director of inspections, District of Beşiktaş, Istanbul, Turkey, June 5, 2014. Beşiktaş even made international news for requiring its licensed vendors to speak more softly. See "No Shouting: Istanbul Tells Its Street Vendors," *PRI* May 17, 2012.

[24] Author interview with director of inspections, District of Beyoğlu, Istanbul, Turkey, June 3, 2014.

[25] One exception was Sultangazi, where the head of inspections thought that the public generally did not like inspectors to take merchandise away. Author interview with sub-director of inspections, District of Sultangazi, Istanbul, Turkey, June 6, 2014.

emphasized that public opinion on street vending shifted in favor of enforcement, and therefore mayors promoted regular enforcement operations. The only exception comes around elections. Take the district of Gaziosmanpaşa, one of the poorest in the city, where about a fifth of residents receive targeted state assistance. The team of inspectors that I interviewed broke into an argument over whether the district was in the "top ten most orderly districts in Istanbul," given that they confiscated vendors' merchandise on a regular basis, but the district's poverty meant that there were still more vendors than in other districts. The inspectors agreed that the mayor won votes through enforcement against street vendors because "even common people don't want to live in ugly cities."[26] Nevertheless, district statistics show a dramatic slowdown in enforcement in election years. More than 500 street vendors had their merchandise decommissioned in non-election years, while around 100 had merchandise taken away in election years. The director explained, "This is, of course, related to politicians" and "represents the mayor's will, priorities, and preferences."[27]

Another way to see the importance of voter demographics is to contrast enforcement in Istanbul with that in other Turkish cities with different economic profiles. While the median voter in Istanbul is lower-middle class, other cities in Turkey are poorer. These cities still rely on forbearance toward street vending as a form of informal welfare provision. For instance, one AKP official explained why it would be impossible to make street vending a criminal (rather than an administrative) offense and enforce regulations across the country:

> Political concerns lead the government not to introduce new legislation because in other cities, many people earn their money through informal street trading, and although it is not a professional business the profits are high. So if you try to pass a law that would cover the nation, it also will cover common people who really are poor and need to work as street vendors for employment.[28]

In sum, the AKP broke with the previous policies of forbearance toward squatters and street vendors in the 2000s. In many settings,

[26] Author interview with director of inspections, District of Gaziosmanpaşa, Istanbul, Turkey, June 6, 2014. Bureaucrats in other districts echoed the political nature of enforcement patterns, saying, "We are laxer before elections, to ensure that no unexpected problems arise." Author interview with sub-director of inspections, District of Maltepe, Istanbul, Turkey, June 10, 2014.

[27] Author interview with director of inspections, District of Gaziosmanpaşa, Istanbul, Turkey, June 6, 2014.

[28] Author interview with director of inspections and AKP party official, District of Fatih, Istanbul, Turkey, June 5, 2014.

politicians and their parties pay high costs when they switch policies (e.g., Roberts 2015). The AKP avoided this electoral price because economic growth expanded the urban lower-middle class that favored enforcement. Of course, economic growth is a gradual process that makes it hard to explain the precise timing of enforcement. The turn to enforcement coincided with changes in the electoral strategy of the AKP, compared to its predecessor the Welfare Party. The AKP reoriented its electoral coalition around an aspiring middle class, and courted the support of the business community. I now turn to the final piece of Istanbul's enforcement turn – the changing portrayal of those in violation of the law.

### 7.3.3 Ethnic Cleavages

Why does embourgeoisement work in some places and not in others? One answer is that Istanbul grew richer and more equal than the Latin American cities studied; this certainly is the explanation emphasized by bureaucrats and politicians. But another part of the story comes from ethnic and religious cleavages. It is easier to enforce against minority groups, especially if they are less likely to vote for a given party or are unpopular. The AKP pitched enforcement as anti-minority rather than anti-poor.

The AKP perceived fewer votes at stake as the composition of migrants shifted. From the 1950s through the 1980s, urban migrants largely were Sunni Muslims, coming from parts of inner Anatolia and the Black Sea region. Violent conflict between the Turkish army and Kurdish separatist forces broke out in the mid-1980s and continued through most of the 1990s. The conflict caused three million Kurdish people to flee from the Southeastern regions of Turkey to cities, including around one million to Istanbul. Ethnic and religious minorities, including the Kurds, tend to vote for parties other than the AKP. According to polls, only 7 percent of Kurds support the AKP, while 84 percent support Kurdish parties (Konda 2006: 60; also see Marschall, Aydogan, and Bulut 2016: 203). The antipathy between the Kurds and the AKP should not be overstated, however. The AKP at times has tried to court Kurdish voters, and in district and city elections, Kurdish voters generally must choose between the major political parties and many have supported the AKP. Regardless, Kurdish voters are not part of the AKP's core constituency.

As mayor of Istanbul in the 1990s, Erdoğan took a split policy toward legal violations, which was consistent with the changing ethnic composition of migrants. On the one hand, he invested in basic services, public transportation, and garbage collection to informal neighborhoods that long had been neglected prior to his ascendance to city hall. These were primarily Sunni, or at least ethnically integrated, neighborhoods. On the other hand, he tried to take a tough line against internal migration and new squatter settlement formation. For instance, he proposed restricting migration into Istanbul through a city permit system to prevent the continued expansion of squatter settlements. The proposal never got off the ground due to national opposition.[29] Bureaucrats emphasized that Erdoğan turned his supporters in favor of enforcement by positioning the government as sympathetic to previous generations of (Sunni) squatters, but opposed to additional law breaking by new (more heavily Kurdish) migrants.[30]

Once the AKP took national power, it played on ethnic prejudice that equated Kurdish migrants with political disloyalty and criminality. For instance, one TOKİ director, Erdoğan Bayraktar, said in a speech that squatter settlements must be controlled because "it is well known that such things as terror, drugs, psychological negativity, health problems and oppositional views all come out of squatter zones and irregular areas" (Lovering and Türkmen 2011: 82). Another TOKİ chairman, Yiğit Gülöksüz, proposed harsh criminal sanctions to prevent illegal construction, claiming that an organized "pillaging minority" stole state land from the "silent majority."[31] Some of the largest urban renewal projects targeted populations marginal to the electoral calculations of the AKP, such as Sulukule, which historically housed Istanbul's Roma population, and Tarlabaşı, which was dominated by Kurdish populations (El-Kazaz 2014: 183). The AKP thus minimized the electoral costs of enforcement by targeting minority neighborhoods and equating enforcement with support for "majority" interests.

Public attitudes turned against squatters and street vendors. Media coverage in the 1980s emphasized structural conditions, such as unemployment and poverty, as justifications for squatting. But by the 1990s, major news outlets shifted their coverage to portray squatters as part of a "social explosion," "political unrest," and an "illegal city." News outlets even changed from using the traditional Turkish nickname for a squatter

[29] Didem Eryar, "No Risk, No Tax; Way of Life," *Hurriyet* May 23, 1996.

[30] Author interview with director of zoning, District of Sarıyer, Istanbul, Turkey, June 12, 2014; author interview with director of urban renewal office, District of Gaziosmanpaşa, Istanbul, Turkey, June 6, 2014.

[31] Eryar, "No risk, no tax."

settlement (*gecekondu*) to a new term suggesting a "threatening other" (*varoslu*) (Akbulut and Başlik 2011: 26–35; Erman 2001: 995–7; Keyder 2005: 131–3). If there are two ways to understand forbearance, one in terms of distributive justice and another in terms of criminality, the growing salience of ethnic divisions may have tilted at least some of the population to see squatting in terms of the latter.

Although there is some evidence that politicians and media outlets pandered to ethnic prejudices, I do not want to exaggerate the role of ethnic cleavages, particularly as compared to economic changes. Far more consensus existed among the bureaucrats and politicians that I interviewed on the role of economic growth in shaping enforcement than on the role of ethnic and religious divisions.[32] Changes in social perceptions can be attributed to the greater wealth of squatters and street vendors, much as I showed in the case of Lima (Chapter 4). For instance, Buğra (1998) argues that the process of squatting, as well as subsequent service provision and formalization, created its own profit-seeking economy in Istanbul. Early generations of squatters built additional stories on their houses and rented out the space; land traffickers brought new migrants to plots and extracted rents. The public therefore may have turned against forbearance as a result of the commercialization of squatter settlements, or as one bureaucrat captures: "Citizens changed their attitudes toward illegal housing once it involved the occupation of public land for profit rather than out of necessity."[33] Ethnic differences and the endogenous economic changes that resulted from decades of forbearance probably both contributed to changing popular attitudes.

### 7.3.4 Alternative Explanations

Could partisan ideology or regime type explain the enforcement turn in Turkey? The AKP is a conservative party, albeit one with a predominantly lower-class constituency. Turkey also has moved toward a competitive authoritarian regime, as the AKP has eroded institutional checks previously provided by the media and courts and harassed critics (Esen and Gumuscu 2016). It is possible that a conservative political ideology led the

[32] Some local officials even emphasized that enforcement was harder in minority communities because tight-knit groups mobilized against government efforts.

[33] Author interview with director of inspections, District of Gaziosmanpaşa, Istanbul, Turkey, June 6, 2014.

AKP to enforce against squatters and street vendors, or that the reduced importance of electoral competition allowed the party to divorce itself from voter demands.

The most basic reason that partisan ideology is a weak explanation of enforcement outcomes comes from the AKP's history. As described above, the AKP emerged from a fissure in the Welfare Party, which had favored squatters. There is nothing inherent in political Islam or conservatism that makes a party favor or oppose forbearance. It is far more indicative to look at changes in the structure of the party's core constituency. As the AKP focused its coalition on middle-class voters and business groups, it moved closer to their enforcement preferences.

The second reason that ideology and regime type are insufficient explanations of enforcement outcomes is that the AKP has retained a lax approach toward other types of regulations, namely, construction violations and small business registration. Illegal construction through the addition of extra floors or rooms to houses remains rampant, and politically negotiated, in Istanbul. Because extralegal construction benefits middle- and lower-middle-class groups, public opinion and district mayors are supportive. For instance, prior to the 2009 local elections, news reports described Sultanbeyli as "more like a construction site than a residential area" because people added floors to their homes on the expectation that the AKP would not enforce building codes or zoning laws.[34] Likewise, while street vending has been controlled, zoning laws that limit commerce to specific areas and affect lower-middle-class business owners go unenforced. Bureaucrats blamed "current structures and conditions" and "electoral sympathies" for the difficulties in enforcing small business regulations, and said they knew to be "gentler before elections, to ensure that no unexpected problems arise."[35] If enforcement were motivated purely by ideological considerations or if competitive authoritarian regimes disregard electoral repercussions, we would expect the AKP to take a hard line against all urban infractions. Its approach has been far more selective. Forbearance has been used in ways that favor its core constituency without threatening its allies in the construction sector.

[34] Enis Tayman, "Ballot Blows Roof off Illegal Homes," *Hurriyet* February 19, 2009.

[35] Author interview with director of inspections, District of Gaziosmanpaşa, Istanbul, Turkey, June 6, 2014; author interview with sub-director of inspections, District of Maltepe, Istanbul, Turkey, June 10, 2014.

## 7.4 CONCLUSION

In much of this book, I emphasized that the informal-sector poor are pivotal voters in urban elections. I showed that enforcement varied with the concentration of poor voters and their incorporation into political coalitions. Here, I used the case of Istanbul to examine how enforcement politics differ when the lower-middle class expands and dominates urban elections. I found that when local politicians depended on the urban poor for votes in the 1980s and 1990s, they avoided enforcement in poor districts. When the lower-middle class then expanded as part of Turkey's economic boom, politicians became less reliant on the votes of the urban poor. They enforced. The case of Istanbul thus strengthens my argument that enforcement outcomes are rooted in local electoral incentives.

Along with the greater level of income equality in Istanbul than in Lima, Santiago, and Bogotá, societal divisions are distinctive. Ethnic heterogeneity often is identified as a damper on public goods and social welfare provision. A look at Istanbul hints at how heterogeneity can have an analogous effect on forbearance. The electoral costs of enforcement can decrease through two possible channels when an ethnic group violates the law. The first is that politicians calculate a lower chance of winning over minority voters. The second effect comes through the political signals conveyed by enforcement. When ethnic cleavages are salient, enforcement no longer is perceived as anti-poor, but rather as anti-minority. Stoking voter prejudices can allow politicians to increase enforcement and still retain the support of most poor voters.

Insight from Istanbul can help us think differently about enforcement dynamics across Latin America. First, the comparison highlights the role that income inequality likely has played in sustaining forbearance in Latin America. Latin America is not the region with the largest number of poor people in the world, but it is the one with the most unequal income distribution. As a result, poverty rates in Latin America are systematically higher than would be expected. A country like Turkey, with similar average income but much lower inequality, has fewer poor residents. This demographic difference altered enforcement incentives for local politicians, and allowed the AKP to maintain large popular majorities as it enforced laws against squatting and street vending.

Second, Latin America is an ethnically diverse region, and the Turkish case forces a reconsideration of the role that racial and ethnic cleavages play in shaping popular attitudes and enforcement politics. The large indigenous population in Lima may have helped to stigmatize vendors as criminal, as shown in Chapter 4. Colombia has a smaller indigenous population (although a substantial Afro-descendent population), which may have contributed to a more compassionate view of vendors among the middle class. Disentangling these effects is tricky, especially without better and longitudinal survey data. The structure of political competition also may explain why I observed less enforcement against minorities in the Latin American cities studied, as compared to Istanbul. As Wilkinson (2006) argues, if politicians need to pool votes from minorities to win elections, then they are more likely to pursue the enforcement policies (in the Indian case, police protection during riots) that minorities favor. Ethnic parties able to capture the votes of indigenous and Afro-descendent groups are very weak or nonexistent in Colombia, Peru, and Chile. Most parties that court poor core constituencies hope to pool votes across ethnic and racial lines, and to appeal to the very heterogeneous urban poor. For instance, Fischer (2008, 2014) documents an initial association between race and Brazil's squatter settlements. But these associations began to fade as the political and economic usefulness of squatter settlements became apparent. Politicians saw electoral advantages in portraying the large number of squatters as mostly hardworking victims of circumstance. Targeting squatters for eviction based on their race or ethnicity would have alienated many poor voters.

A final extension of this logic is that immigration has the potential to reshape enforcement politics in Latin America. My electoral theory holds that much of the political power of squatters and street vendors comes from their status as voters. Intraregional migration, which sometimes brings indigenous groups to more homogeneous societies, could spark an enforcement backlash like that seen in Turkey. Chile and Argentina, for instance, have become hubs for migrants from Peru, Bolivia, and Paraguay. Salvadoran and Honduran migrants increasingly are settling in Mexico, Costa Rica, and Panama, rather than the United States. Many of these migrant populations look to squatting and street vending to establish a foothold in major urban areas, but they do not have the right to vote in local elections. Under my framework, politicians will be more likely to enforce against nonvoters, particularly if they are ethnic minorities who can be defined as an out-group that sparks resentment from an enfranchised in-group. Just as with formal redistribution, extending a theory about informal redistribution requires thinking about how social cleavages change perceptions of poverty and deservingness and how electoral incentives vary based on the size and political incorporation of minority groups.

# 8

# Conclusion

## *Rethinking the Politics of the Poor*

Historically, social expenditures have done little to aid the poor in Latin America. While some countries have made dramatic progress to expand benefits in the 1990s and 2000s, many others have done far less to include those outside the formal sector and redirect spending in their favor. The uneven pace of contemporary reforms raises a wider puzzle about how it is possible that social expenditures barely improve the income distribution in some of the most unequal parts of the world. Why have the informal-sector poor been unable to redirect social expenditures more decisively in their favor?

This question pushed me to investigate what the poor get out of Latin American welfare regimes. I showed that the informal-sector poor often are skeptical that they will benefit from the welfare state for good historical reasons, and therefore do not organize around state programs. Instead, informal welfare provision through forbearance hugely shapes the lives and demands of the poor. Just reflect on a few of the descriptive statistics presented: after decades of informal housing construction more than two-thirds of the urban poor in Lima now are homeowners. A third of the urban poor in Bogotá have depended on income from street vending. By contrast, housing and employment programs have reached comparatively few poor households. A basic message of this book is that the ways that laws are enforced should not be treated as trivial choices, or as apolitical ones.

The tolerance of legal violations has been a deliberate choice in response to popular organizing and democratic elections. To underscore the intentional nature of enforcement decisions, I developed the concept of forbearance and then focused in on its electoral logic. To recap, I argued that two main factors shape how politicians decide to enforce laws that the poor violate. First, the availability of social welfare policies affects the electoral incentives to enforce by changing what the poor want from politicians and what enforcement signals to voters. I distinguished between complementary social policies (minimal, truncated, or cash-based expenditures) and substitutive ones (in-kind and pro-poor expenditures). Complementary social policies leave the poor's distributive needs unmet, displace their demands to local politicians, and lead voters to associate enforcement with anti-poor politicians. This process raises the political costs of enforcement. Substitutive social policies, in contrast, funnel distributive demands to welfare authorities and attenuate the distributive cues sent by enforcement. The stakes decline, so enforcement becomes more frequent and consistent.

Second, where social policies fail to meet basic needs, the poor's political power influences when and where politicians enforce. Politicians gain greater latitude to enforce when they can ignore poor voters and win elections with the support of nonpoor core constituencies, as seen in city-wide elections and nonpoor sub-city districts. Districts that concentrate poor voters lead politicians to attend to their constituency's distributive needs and forgo enforcement. Forbearance serves as a way to boost welfare informally and build a reputation for helping the poor. District poverty, when elections are held at the local level, makes enforcement unlikely.

Together, these propositions suggest that enforcement is malleable and contingent on political incentives, rather than a reflection of underlying levels of state capacity. Decisions about how to organize a welfare state – not just how much to tax and spend, but how much to provide in-kind goods like housing and jobs to the poor – constrain local enforcement decisions under democracy more forcefully than budgets, police, or bureaucrats. And, electoral rules that allocate different degrees of power to the poor explain why enforcement oscillates in some contexts, and why it never happens in others.

Decades of redistribution through forbearance also have feedback effects on how presidents and their parties design welfare programs. Post-hoc policies, which legalize and improve goods secured through legal violations, are attractive ways to reach large numbers of voters quickly. However, they also reinforce the societal legitimacy and the economic payoffs of legal violations. Perversely, formalization policies meant to bring an end to legal violations can perpetuate them.

I looked for a range of empirical implications that distinguish my theory from dominant alternatives moored in state weakness. These included observations that the poor support forbearance and candidates who advocate it (Chapter 2), that politicians block enforcement on welfare and electoral grounds even after bureaucrats perform their jobs (Chapter 3), that enforcement choices vary with politicians' core constituencies irrespective of available resources (Chapter 4), that electoral rules and district demographics predict enforcement patterns even in "strong" states (Chapter 5), and that even presidents and legislators discuss forbearance and post-hoc policies as substitute forms of welfare provision (Chapter 6). The accumulation of anomalies in state capacity-based theories is simply too great to dismiss as an issue of measurement error. Moreover, each of these tests was supported by rich and varied data, including interviews, campaign materials, administrative records, newspaper archives, and secondary sources. These data reinforced that citizens, state officials, and politicians view forbearance as a form of redistribution, albeit inadequate and informal.

Methodologically, this book makes a contribution in showing how we can operationalize forbearance. The challenge of separating situations when governments cannot enforce the law from those when they will not enforce it, as well as the more general difficulty of comparing enforcement effort across space and time, hampered previous work on enforcement politics. A focus on the city and sub-city level allowed me to collect measures of both enforcement and offenses, and to use differences in social policy structure, core constituencies, and electoral rules to generate distinct empirical predictions. The basic methodology employed here could be replicated elsewhere, in this way building an even more comprehensive theory of forbearance across offenses and countries from the subnational level upward. For instance, the same concepts and tools provided leverage to understand enforcement politics in the very different urban setting of Istanbul.

This concluding chapter situates the findings and discusses their implications for debates on political representation, state capacity, weak institutions, and welfare regimes. Woven in this discussion, I consider how the framework may be extended to study laws and regulations with different distributive consequences. I also revisit the normative tension inherent in progressive forbearance: it offers nontrivial forms of material support, especially when compared with inadequate government welfare policies, and has been leveraged by the poor to make distributive claims. Yet forbearance comes at a price – its use can slow the development of a modern welfare state and entrench inequalities in citizenship rights.

## 8.1 POLITICAL REPRESENTATION AND THE POOR

When I began this project, many voiced skepticism that politicians would admit that they did not enforce certain laws and regulations. A study of forbearance, like work on corruption, would be hindered due to its hidden nature. In the course of my fieldwork, however, it became quite clear that politicians did not shy from discussing their enforcement positions. Quite the opposite, I found evidence that enforcement and forbearance were discussed openly in campaign rallies, electoral platforms, and government meetings. Some politicians defended forbearance as an issue of distributive justice and a necessity in the context of weak welfare states. This basic point – that forbearance toward poor voters can be publicly defended and differentiate candidates – raises questions about how forbearance relates to other strategies that politicians use to win the poor's votes. Forbearance does not fit neatly into existing theories of the poor's electoral behavior, which tend to focus on party programs, clientelism, and populism. It is an important complement to these approaches, although I leave it to future work to weigh its relative significance and interaction with other vote-getting strategies.

To briefly review, debates over the voting behavior of the informal-sector poor begin with the idea of a "representation gap." The gold standard is that politicians establish programmatic linkages to voters through political parties. Parties offer packages of policies that they promise to pursue if elected. Voters use party labels to assess which politicians are most likely to represent their interests across a range of issues. But such a model of party-based representation does a poor job explaining the electoral behavior of the poor. In Latin America, as in much of the global South, party identification is low and party systems are volatile. Scholars place some of the blame for party-system destabilization on the growth of the informal sector and deindustrialization (Cameron 1994; Morgan 2011; Roberts 2015; *c.f.* Seawright 2012). Studying Peru's collapsed parties, for example, Cameron (1994: 10) diagnoses that "[t]he flight from the formal economy and the breakdown of the traditional party system were two sides of the same coin." By the 2000s, party representation reemerged in some Latin American countries, where left parties opposed market reforms, patronage budgets shrank, and parties expanded pro-poor social policies (Hagopian Forthcoming; Roberts 2015). But evidence that the informal-sector poor have become durable partisans is weak.

The volatile nature of the poor's vote has led many scholars to focus on the role of clientelism (e.g., Auyero 2000; Stokes 2005; Stokes et al. 2013;

Kitschelt and Wilkinson 2007; Nichter 2008; Szwarcberg 2015; Weitz-Shapiro 2012, 2014). Because of their shorter time horizons and greater marginal utility from small material payouts, poor voters are the targets of clientelistic handouts. As measures of vote buying improve, however, it is increasingly clear that much electoral behavior remains unexplained. Even in countries with high rates of vote buying, such as Argentina, less than 10 percent of poor respondents report being approached with an offer of a gift or good in exchange for their support (Stokes et al. 2013: 40–1).[1] Contingent electoral exchange explains even less of electoral behavior in collapsed party systems, such as Peru, where it is dubious that the necessary party actors exist to monitor voters' behavior. Voters can accept handouts and then choose their favorite candidate. Then, the question becomes, what else leads poor voters to support a given candidate?

Another major explanation of the poor's voting behavior looks to populism. The concept has been stretched and disputed. Resnick (2013), for instance, labels appeals to poor, unorganized groups – including attempts to court street vendors and squatters by promising not to enforce laws in urban Africa – as populism. But such a thin definition provides little analytic leverage to understand the range of politicians and circumstances that make pro-poor appeals, or the difference between programmatic and nonprogrammatic appeals. I follow others in considering the core of populism to involve appeals to mass constituencies by personalistic leaders who challenge established elites and institutions (e.g., Roberts 2006: 127). The programmatic agenda of populists ranges from the political Right, as with neoliberal or security populists, to the Left, and the definition of the masses can be inclusionary or exclusionary (Mudde and Rovira Kaltwasser 2013). The crux is that voters select candidates and mobilize based on anti-establishment appeals. So, under all three of these perspectives, the view of the poor's electoral behavior is rather dim. Informal-sector voters have amorphous interests that lead them to swing erratically among parties, sell their votes, or support politicians based on personality traits and thin ideological appeals.

A major contribution of this book is to identify a coherent material interest of the informal-sector poor, forbearance, and suggest how it can structure preferences, mobilization, and vote choice. To restate my claims, forbearance motivates electoral behavior because it is a targeted and

[1] Reports may be higher in some countries when using list experiments to account for social desirability bias (Gonzalez-Ocantos et al. 2012), but at least in Argentina, estimated rates of vote buying do not change much with these techniques.

credible benefit. The informal-sector poor have shared material interests like their ability to work unchecked or gain security over their land. Given the historic truncation of many welfare programs, the poor often gain little from tax-based forms of "redistribution," especially around housing and unemployment programs. Talk of social welfare provision is cheap. Forbearance provides distributive benefits, but even more importantly, it offers immediate ones in contexts where social policies often fail to come to fruition or exclude the poor. Chapter 2 explicitly compared social policy appeals with those based on forbearance, and showed that only the forbearance platforms led the poor to believe that hypothetical candidates would serve their interests. Evaluating politicians on how many bills they sponsor or even roads they pave, as usually is the case, may miss central issues at stake, especially in increasingly important local elections.

Additionally, the assignment of political responsibility may be easier for forbearance compared to other social policies. A background theme in this book was the visibility of enforcement outcomes in the case of squatting and street vending. Politicians considered how enforcement would affect their local reputation. They feared sanctions at the polls (and sometimes in the streets through protests) if they enforced. As has been shown in the case of other distributive goods, politicians focus on the provision of goods that voters can see (Mani and Mukand 2007). In this sense, I build on work that shows that electoral accountability is improved when voters have better information about policy. Experimental studies show that providing information on policy performance can affect vote choice and government responsiveness under certain conditions (for a review, see Ashworth 2012). But less thought has gone into the types of issues that the poor naturally learn about in their everyday lives. Poor voters may not stumble across reports on budget expenditures or water quality, but they may observe, hear rumors, and learn about visible actions like police sanctions or permitted property law violations. Thus, I suspect that the poor vote and mobilize around forbearance because it is a credible and visible way to improve local welfare.

Forbearance falls short on standard definitions of programmatic policy given that enforcement choices are not codified, and sometimes are clientelistic. However, forbearance can provide a similar structure to political competition when it is extended to all members of a group. Think back on the examples of mayors like Barrantes or Garzón: both articulated a commitment to forbearance as necessary to improve the short-term employment options for the poor until the state could do better. Politicians like Peñalosa,

Andrade, and Villarán countered with a view that enforcement served the poor's long-term interests by boosting growth and investment in the city. None of these proposals required changes to the formal legal structure. But these were substantive philosophies about core social issues. And they had the expected electoral consequences of attracting or repelling poor voters.

I also theorized and showed how forbearance can be distributed in a clientelistic fashion to reward supporters (and combined with enforcement threats to detractors). But perhaps what is most striking about the cases examined is how frequently forbearance and enforcement were *not* linked to any voter behaviors. Three main types of evidence supported this finding. First, enforcement rarely followed against political opponents. For the most part, politicians either enforced in public ways or stopped all sanctions. Second, squatters and street vendors expected candidates to take different enforcement positions in office, just as politicians might invest differently in health care or transportation or border security. But very few squatters or street vendors thought that politicians would impose legal sanctions on them individually or as a group if they failed to support the winning candidate. Third, particularly in the case of squatting, what stood out was the dwindling turnaround time to secure property title. Land invasions chased by legalization make no sense for politicians who want to exploit the continued legal vulnerability of the poor for clientelistic ends. Thus, the empirical evidence suggests numerous ways in which forbearance does not conform to conventional clientelistic exchanges. Rather, I stressed that forbearance was a way for politicians to address local welfare demands and signal a commitment to poor voters. Clientelism thrives in the communities studied, but coercive threats are used sparingly unless other factors, such as direct contact in small districts or ethnic divisions, dilute the reputational consequences.

The use of progressive forbearance to signal affinity with the poor raises questions about its relationship to populism. Indeed, forbearance has been an attractive distributive strategy for populists because it circumvents state institutions and can be rooted in an anti-elite discourse. Politicians can promise to improve the poor's lot regardless of what some out-of-touch legislators and judges might say. Bolivian president Evo Morales, for example, stretched the meaning of social rights claims when he turned a blind eye and registered cars smuggled into Bolivia (*chutos*) with no efforts to end their illegal import. As Morales bent the law, he emphasized his affinity with "poor people" who bought the cars seeking to "improve their status." Enforcement would be unjust in his view because "everyone has a right to a car."[2]

In fact, forbearance helps make sense of the programmatic content that unites a range of populist figures that have appealed to informal-sector voters. Consider the case of Fujimori. The classic interpretation is that Fujimori captured the informal-sector poor's votes through his anti-party, anti-elite appeals, and he did little to serve their interests (after stabilizing the economy). He slashed welfare programs, replacing them gradually with small-scale funds managed in a clientelistic fashion by the President's Office. If we measure the formal welfare benefits that the urban poor received, their enduring loyalty seems inconsistent with voting based on material interests. But Fujimori complemented cuts to the state with a host of informal and post-hoc benefits. His government provided property titles to more than a million Peruvians, which allowed for public service investments in squatter settlements that no previous president had cared to touch. Personal visits to proclaim that property titles made the poor "full legal citizens" and to inaugurate local public works helped resuscitate Fujimori's flagging image. These facts are not meant to defend Fujimori's regime in any way. But they should give us pause when we dismiss the informal-sector poor's loyalty to Fujimori as a vote for charisma or a rejection of elites alone. Informal welfare policies can generate political payoffs just like formal ones.

Although there are some natural complementarities with populism, programmatic political parties also turn to forbearance to win votes. Forbearance was central to the IU and the Polo's party-building projects. Or take the case of Uruguay's institutionalized left party. When Tabaré Vázquez was mayor of Montevideo, Uruguay (1990–1995), his leftist Broad Front (*Frente Amplio*) wanted to invest in housing programs for the poor. The resources to do so existed only at the national level. Vázquez instead tolerated several large land invasions on the city's outskirts and distributed a record number of property titles to squatter settlements that already had formed (Alvarez Rivadulla 2011; Winn and Ferro-Clérico 1997). Forbearance thus appeals to a variety of politicians, including those with programmatic commitments to reduce Latin America's inequalities.

[2] "Escándalo por legalización de carros de contrabando en Bolivia," *Semana* June 24, 2011. Morales changed how laws were written and enforced to favor his supporters in a range of areas like coca growing, informal vending, and gold mining (Crabtree and Chaplin 2013: chapters 3–5; Dargent 2016).

In sum, forbearance should be studied alongside other tools that politicians and parties use to attract the poor's votes, such as programmatic redistributive appeals, vote-buying offers, and charisma, which have received far more attention in the literature. Some of my evidence suggests that forbearance may be more important in urban elections than these other strategies. Future work may try to quantify the electoral payoffs of these different appeals and establish their complementarities.[3] The takeaway is that forbearance can help make sense of the seemingly unpredictable voting behavior by the informal-sector poor.

## 8.2 STATE CAPACITY

Careful attention to how politicians choose to enforce the law is important because it reorients scholars and policymakers away from state weakness as the primary determinant of enforcement outcomes. Much previous work has focused on understaffed, corrupt, or overlapping bureaucracies and police forces that limit the state's ability to detect and sanction legal violations. This view has infused public policy too. International institutions like the World Bank and the Inter-American Development Bank have promoted bureaucratic reform to improve the rule of law. But after two decades of state reforms, property law violations have not disappeared.

Strengthening bureaucracy is a valuable undertaking, but this book's focus on the distributive stakes of enforcement clarifies why it is not a panacea. Efficient small business registration or property titling procedures cannot provide the poor with jobs or houses. If politicians and some citizens prefer legal violations to persist until welfare programs provide basic social goods, as I suggest, then more efficient bureaucracies will produce limited gains. Paradoxically, improvements in administrative capacity – such as faster property titling and infrastructure provision – may even generate more property law violations, if not accompanied by prospective welfare solutions.

State capacity still matters, but not in the ways traditionally discussed in policy circles or studies of enforcement. It is the ability to run substitutive welfare programs that complicates enforcement, and that atrophies

[3] For instance, Diaz-Cayeros, Estévez, and Magaloni (2016: chapter 7) take an important step in this direction by comparing how Mexican voters respond to vote-buying efforts, government social programs, and local public goods investments. A similar exercise could be conducted to understand the electoral yields of forbearance.

after generations of forbearance. Chapter 6 exposed numerous failed attempts to implement housing and employment policies that reach the poor. Some of the problems were inherent to the policy areas studied. Even wealthy countries like the United States have not figured out how to provide decent housing to the poor (Desmond 2016), let alone create jobs for unskilled workers. But decades of reliance on informal welfare substitutes meant that Latin American bureaucracies also learned to specialize in other tasks, such as property titling, slum upgrading, and small business promotion. Perhaps if presidents in Colombia or Peru had the existing state apparatus to run a housing program or expand unemployment insurance, they would have made at least somewhat different investment decisions.

Nevertheless, welfare state construction is an eminently political choice. Saying that governments cannot build housing or run jobs programs misses the rich politics behind these decisions. Some governments do much more than others. Chile, Mexico, Morocco, and South Africa all have invested substantial sums in housing (though with variable effects). Far poorer countries like India have national employment guarantees to provide job alternatives to the poor. Furthermore, Latin America is a middle-income region, and spends substantial sums on these policies for formal-sector workers. The critical point is that welfare politics look very different when informal substitutes are available. The ability to meet the poor's needs through cheaper, quicker, and more certain informal welfare policies has weakened political coalitions to invest in state alternatives.

The cases suggest the need to think through the sequence in which countries develop different components of state strength. My sense is that a police force and bureaucracy with the ability to sanction the poor often develop prior to the architecture of a modern welfare state. To be clear, the laws that the poor violate tend to be relatively simple to enforce. Most states in the developing world still lack the administrative capacity to control complex regulations or white-collar crimes where the rich can use their wealth, power, and lawyers to subvert the law. Violent criminal organizations likewise strain the state's coercive capacity.

A sequence of state development in which politicians can use police repression against the poor prior to the provision of welfare alternatives is apparent across the global South. Even in much poorer contexts, politicians back off the use of coercive power. For instance, Zambia's president Michael Sata (2011–2014) sent an open directive to his government explaining why it should not use its improving local bureaucracy to control the informal economy: "Local government is a very fast growing organization which we need to reorganize [rather] than concentrating on harassing innocent vendors and car washers which will lead to our party being more unpopular." Sata justified forbearance by pointing to social policy deficits: "Those are the people we promised to give employment of which we have not done so."[4] Informal moto-drivers in Uganda similarly became known as "untouchables" when President Yoweri Museveni personally intervened to stop enforcement against them (Goodfellow 2015). Although state weakness poses a stronger constraint in poor democracies like Zambia and Uganda, informal welfare policies are even more necessary to patch over welfare state failings.

The central implication is that improvements in the scale and targeting of social programs can be an alternative route to strengthen law enforcement. As police officers, bureaucrats, and politicians agree, coercion cannot solve social problems. In-kind welfare expenditures matter not just because they resolve basic demands, but also because they change beliefs about the fairness and legitimacy of state enforcement. I showed that citizens with better assessments of the welfare state were more supportive of evictions (Chapter 2). And, citizens were willing to collaborate in the enforcement process when welfare policies were effective, as in Chile, in ways that they refused to do in weak welfare contexts, as in Peru and Colombia (Chapter 3). Hence, reinforcing the welfare state can align politicians' incentives with parchment law and inspire societal collaboration. Welfare state reforms thus are essential complements to existing efforts to streamline and strengthen state bureaucracies.

Some may take forbearance itself as evidence of state weakness. Past scholarship has defined state capacity by the autonomy of state actors to impose their preferences on local actors and pursue long-term developmental goals (Evans 1995; Mann 1984; Skocpol 1985). Migdal (1988, 2001), for instance, emphasizes that many states in the developing world are weak "states in society" because diverse organizations vie to make the de facto rules about how citizens behave. Authorities with informal "tutelary" power, such as religious, military, or traditional leaders, challenge state authority to set the effective rules of the game. Work on subnational authoritarianism shares this impulse that local politicians can weaken

4 "Sata Defends Street Vendors," *Post of Zambia* December 16, 2011, emphasis added. On Sata's campaign to attract vendors and squatters, also see Resnick (2012, 2013: chapter 3).

states by creating enclaves with alternative, often illiberal rules (Gibson 2013; Giraudy 2015).

However, a global wave of political decentralization has created a new set of subnational actors who do not necessarily share the preferences of national legislators and presidents and who can change enforcement to better match their constituents' interests. Consider the example of immigration law in the United States. Dozens of American mayors have joined the "sanctuary city" movement in which they instruct local law enforcement not to share information from routine policing with federal immigration authorities (Ridgley 2013). Whether or not the president forces mayors to provide information on immigrants is hardly an issue of state capacity, in the sense of whether the government can force federal immigration policy on the states or whether local police forces can collect information. It is an issue of federalism. Subnational enforcement preferences may be more or less "liberal" than national ones, and they may be more or less responsive to vulnerable or marginalized citizens. In such cases, the consequences of forbearance for assessments of state strength and democratic quality are not straightforward.

Future research may examine how enforcement politics changes in federal political systems and in the presence of shadow powers. I focused on unitary states where politicians controlled local territory in order to make it easier to identify political responsibility for enforcement. However, the theory can be modified to incorporate multiple tiers of government and challengers to state authority. Recent studies of enforcement politics in federal systems like Brazil find similar electoral dynamics to those uncovered here. For instance, sanctions for violating the conditions of cash transfer programs drop off near elections. These effects are most notable when there is party alignment across the local and state levels, which permits coordination to shift enforcement (Brollo, Kaufmann, and La Ferrara 2014; also see, Ferraz 2007). In addition, many local politicians face challenges to their authority from armed groups, such as drug-trafficking organizations in the *favelas* of Rio de Janeiro or gangs on the streets of San Salvador, El Salvador. In these circumstances, I suspect that the signals conveyed by forbearance change. Enforcement is more likely to be associated with a commitment to the rule of law and tough-on-crime policies. Forbearance says less about a politician's distributive sympathies if motivated by a need for "tacit coexistence" (Staniland 2012) with criminal groups. Even in contexts of organized violence, however, politicians may differ in their inclination – and not just their capacity – to enforce the law.

## 8.3 WEAK INSTITUTIONS AND FORBEARANCE

A core dimension of institutional strength is the degree of enforcement (Levitsky and Murillo 2009, 2013, 2014). But we still know little about the sources of variation in enforcement. This book demonstrates how electoral institutions, and the distributive pressures that they create, drive both spatial and temporal variation in enforcement. Here, I review how an electoral approach adds to existing accounts and can be extended to a range of legal contexts.

The basic idea of intentional non-enforcement is not new. Past scholars have thought about entire categories of laws that their crafters never intended to enforce. International law makes this point clearest. Countries sign international laws to join a community of nations, and laws often carry no enforcement mechanisms. The inclusion of social and economic rights in constitutions similarly is understood as an aspiration, perhaps signaling to domestic and international constituencies a symbolic commitment or a vision of an ideal society. Yet, some symbolic laws can gain "teeth." Courts, politicians, and citizens have made attempts to abide by international laws and enforce social rights. Conversely, some "hard" laws can be reinterpreted as mere (or misguided) symbolic aspirations. Legislators wrote regulations against street vending with the goal of protecting public spaces in Colombia. Some mayors and court justices have reinterpreted these laws as aspirational until the country can offer employment alternatives. Viewing certain laws as purely symbolic brushes aside much of the political debate over when and how enforcement is deemed appropriate.

A different perspective on weak enforcement is that laws remain on the books because there are political costs to remove them. Enforcement can be a de facto mode of institutional change when actors' preferences diverge from written law, but interest groups, bureaucrats, or competing politicians block legal reform. I largely agree with this view. I took the law largely as given due to the barriers to formal institutional change. Local politicians sometimes have limited formal powers to rewrite law. Even when they do, wealthy interest groups like business and construction chambers tend to be most influential at the legislative stage and oppose change. Powerful groups also may prefer arrangements of legal insecurity. Insecure property rights allow politicians to establish power over those who violate the law, and real estate companies, lawyers, and intermediaries to profit off the poor and change the legal order when their interests dictate (e.g., Boone 2009; Fischer 2008; Onoma 2010).

Keeping unenforced laws on the books also can be consistent with popular demands. Chapter 2 showed how a gap between abstract support for the law and sanctions emerges, especially when those affected by sanctions are seen as poor. Such disconnects exist in other legal areas. Ellermann (2009), for example, shows that the American public supports strict immigration laws in the abstract, but rejects deportations (other than for criminals) because they involve concentrated harms on vulnerable populations. Politicians likewise can oppose enforcement to make rules more responsive to the groups that they affect most. The European Union, for instance, allows member countries to violate rules that impose adjustment costs to accommodate governments under strong domestic pressure (Kleine 2013). State officials in Ukraine rejected liberalizing land reforms in areas when the social costs were expected to be high (Allina-Pisano 2012). Forbearance thus can indicate democratic responsiveness to local conditions, not just the power of veto players or flawed laws.

Viewing enforcement as the result of the divergent preferences of elected politicians across levels or units of government provides a tractable framework to understand variation. It can help predict when enforcement deviations occur and stabilize. Forbearance by subnational actors can be a consistent political choice, at which point it can produce informal institutions or give way to formal reforms. But it also can be a volatile, revocable decision. The chapters exposed the role that electoral rules and offense geographies play in producing informal institutions in some contexts as opposed to others. The contrast between the stable forbearance toward squatting and the cyclical patterns in the case of street vending is highly suggestive. The gist of Chapter 3 was that forbearance toward squatting has been unwavering in Peru and Colombia because it occurs precisely in the peripheral districts in which mayors need support from poor voters to win office. Especially under urban decentralization in Peru, it is possible to conclude that there is an informal institution in which the poor take state land for housing purposes, and politicians mainly alter the pace at which they do so. Enforcement varies primarily across urban space. In contrast, Chapter 4 showed that street vending followed a different pattern due to its occurrence across districts. Cyclical enforcement patterns emerged in citywide elections, as in Bogotá, while uneven enforcement patterns dominated in district elections, as in Santiago. In this sense, politically decentralized cities do have areas where some types of law are functionally absent, as O'Donnell (1993) noted. But politically centralized cities have periods in which laws are selectively jettisoned. These periods would be missed if looking for stable institutional outcomes, whether formal or informal, alone.

Many questions about the determinants of attitudes toward enforcement went unexplored due to the need for additional survey research across different cities. How variable are citizen preferences *within* electoral districts? And how do these preferences vary depending on the perceived deservingness, wealth, organization, or ethnic group of those who violate the law? Do experiences of repression strengthen solidarities among the informal-sector poor? Future survey research could deepen our understanding not only of why enforcement varies across time and location, but also tease out the implications of forbearance for the quality of local democracy. Research could probe whether the law itself is mismatched to majority preferences, contested by different groups and areas of a country, or, alternatively as I found, whether citizens approve of the law but not its enforcement. In addition, a fruitful task is to look across different laws, including those with more ambiguous distributive effects, and to expand on why certain legal violations are more prone to clientelistic negotiations than others.

More generally, the framework developed could be extended to understand the enforcement patterns of different types of law. One natural extension is to enforcement against basic service theft, such as electricity and water. Like the laws studied here, service theft involves social claims to water and light that can be imbued with strong social meaning (Simmons 2016). Work on electricity theft in India, the Dominican Republic, and South Africa has found political cycles surrounding violations, and contestation around service payments (Min 2015; Min and Golden 2014; Rufín 2015; von Schnitzler 2016). Future work also may consider how enforcement changes when politicians have varying degrees of control over outcomes. An implication of my electoral theory, for instance, is that the privatization of basic services should result in more uniform enforcement against theft, and greater pressure to subsidize rates for the poor through formal channels. Private companies presumably are less sensitive to (but not exempt from) electoral pressures than politicians. Post's (2014) study of infrastructure privatization in Argentina provides some support for this hypothesis: negotiations around privatization often included formal subsidies for low-income consumers, or in their absence, informal understandings that the private companies still would let the poor's bills go unpaid.

Street vending also is but one component of the broader informal economy, and future extensions may look at other informal economic activities. In the case of informal businesses, meaning small shops that violate zoning, registration, tax, or labor regulations, I suspect that my electoral framework applies relatively seamlessly. Local politicians in Pernambuco, Brazil, for instance, provide "blanket" legal exemptions to win the political support of more than 30,000 informal business owners. Like the forbearance trap that I describe, Tendler (2002: 3) concludes that leniency toward Pernambuco's business owners "causes informality to become *more* attractive, and formalization *less* attractive" and "stalls the necessary reforms and initiatives meant to restructure the economy." Outside of Latin America, legal favors similarly are used to win the support of informal business owners. For instance, small business taxes (as well as land regulations) are enforced much less in election years in Greece (Skouras and Christodoulakis 2014).

Applying my electoral theory to informal labor *within* large firms is a more complicated undertaking due to the disputed distributive consequences and competing interest groups. There are many laws where people disagree about who benefits from enforcement, including most firm regulations like minimum wage, worker safety, and environmental standards. In the case of firm regulations, fines are imposed on business owners so the direct incidence of forbearance is regressive. Organized business has little reason to push for regulatory reforms as long as it can rely on forbearance to create a cheap, informal workforce (Schneider 2013: 109). Nevertheless, seeing forbearance simply as a favor to business is too simplistic. Regulatory trade-offs involve, inter alia, worker safety, employment levels, development, and environmental degradation. Schrank (2009), for example, shows how labor inspectors in the Dominican Republic use their discretion to balance the need for worker protection with economic growth and efficiency.

Politicians can have competing visions of the public interest in mind when they adjust enforcement levels against firms. Gordon and Hafer (2014) show in the case of coal mining regulation in the United States that the Republican and Democratic parties dispute the relative importance of miner employment and safety. Although regulatory capture can occur in which industry lobbies pay off politicians or bureaucrats to reduce enforcement, ideological beliefs that strict control endangers the coal industry and jobs also can lead politicians to support forbearance. Some low-income voters share these concerns. A pattern of forbearance emerges in which different – but plausible and "electorally sanctioned" – interpretations of the public interest lead to changes in worker safety enforcement by partisan administration. In such cases where the incidence of enforcement is disputed, my suspicion is that electoral institutions matter less than the dynamics of party competition and interest group representation.

Finally, my electoral theory applies to laws with regressive consequences with some modifications. Privileged elites tend to be more influential at the legislative stage. They can use their lobbying and expertise to craft the law in their favor, especially in low-salience areas of "quiet politics" (Culpepper 2010). However, if the public pays attention (and politicians care about public opinion), the rich may be unable to change the rules of the game. In these circumstances, forbearance often emerges. Tax laws are perhaps the most obvious example. The rich often trade their electoral support (usually in the form of campaign contributions) for favorable exemptions and loopholes in the tax code. But for more politicized taxes, such as the income tax, the rich have an incentive to evade payment and then negotiate for forbearance.

The electoral dynamics of legal violations by the rich are quite different than those of the poor because they often have no public justification. Continuing with the tax example, one of the most frequent topics that I encountered in local election campaigns and that motivated citizens to go to mayors' offices in Lima was tax amnesty. Politicians did not promise to change the tax rate; they offered to forgive past nonpayment. Forbearance toward taxes that "ordinary" citizens pay often is part of open, distributive political competition. In contrast, Chapter 2 found that tax violations by the rich generated almost uniform condemnation. Even the wealthy seemed to concur that offenses like industrial electricity theft and tax evasion were unambiguously "bad." Social desirability bias may lead to underestimates of private levels of support, but it confirms my central point: politicians rarely campaign for office on a policy that is broadly censured.[5] Indeed, one study in Italy shows hefty electoral *rewards* for politicians who rigorously enforce against tax evasion (Casaburi and Troiano 2016). Progressive forms of forbearance thus hold out a relatively unique potential to structure electoral competition in public ways. Regressive forbearance is more likely to involve backroom dealings for campaign contributions and private gain.

This contrast suggests different policy recommendations to promote enforcement of laws that the poor and rich violate. Transparency often is proposed to reduce legal violations. Indeed, many types of white-

[5] President Donald Trump is an exception in admitting his pride in tax avoidance. However, Williamson (2017) demonstrates that most Americans view paying taxes as a civic duty and condemn tax avoidance by the rich.

collar crime persist because they are unobservable to voters until *after* elections have passed, if at all. If the public condemns these acts, then real-time information on legal violations allows voters to hold politicians accountable and increase enforcement. This is not the case for legal violations by the poor. Information about enforcement often polarizes the electorate, leading to less support among poor voters and more among nonpoor ones. The implication of this book is that investments in social policy alternatives – and information about their availability – may do more to increase enforcement, if that is the social goal.

## 8.4 INFORMAL WELFARE REGIMES

Although the substantive focus of this book was enforcement politics, it was motivated by broad questions about Latin American welfare states. I put in dialogue literatures on enforcement politics and social policy that rarely speak to each other. To date, research on the comparative political economy of welfare states has generally overlooked the extensive linkages between legal violations and social policy, and thus missed a central means through which governments shape the incomes and risks faced by citizens. Similarly, as noted above, work on property rights has focused on issues of state weakness while minimizing the distributive consequences of enforcement. Highlighting these linkages can anchor future work on both social policy and enforcement within a broader framework. It also suggests modifications to how we assess welfare regimes in the global South.

Comparative welfare state scholars tend to study a handful of formal policies to assess how governments aid the poor and use these policy areas to draw conclusions about who benefits from redistributive politics writ large. Incorporating forbearance is necessary to understand what the informal-sector poor get out of the system and how welfare policies are set. In emphasizing informal welfare provision, this book joins an emerging literature that has expanded the landscape of welfare policies, ranging from mandatory private welfare provision (Hacker 2002) and tax entitlements (Howard 1999) to non-state service provision (Cammett and MacLean 2011, 2014), consumer credit (Rajan 2010), and industrial policy (Estévez-Abe 2008). Such efforts risk opening a Pandora's box in which all actions that shape citizens' income and risks are game for inclusion. For both theoretical and pragmatic reasons, I concur with Hacker's (2002: 32) warning that welfare regimes should be limited to those forms of provision with "an essential *political* relationship." The broadest thesis of this book is that enforcement is a political choice, and a central lever of social policy in developing countries when deployed to assist the poor. In this way, my view differs from past work that has identified an informal component to welfare regimes in the global South but largely seen informality as a "safety valve" that relieved pressure on state systems (e.g., Barrientos 2004, 2009; Buğra 1998; Ferrera 1996; Gilbert and Ward 1985; Gough and Wood 2006, 2008; Martinez Franzoni 2008). Informal welfare policies do not just involve an "opting out" of the state to rely on family-based aid or self-employment. Choices to refrain from enforcement are choices nonetheless, and they affect access to essential welfare goods and structure electoral politics.

Informal welfare policies may change our view of the size and incidence of welfare regimes in developing countries because the effects can be so substantial. To bring in an example on the revenue side, consider that value-added taxes are regressive on paper in Peru. Since the mid-1990s, indirect taxes constitute the bulk of revenue compared to nominally progressive income taxes in most Latin American countries. The decreased tax progressivity has offset many of the improvements in social policy (Mahon Jr. 2013). However, most rural and urban poor escape consumption taxes through purchases in the informal sector. The rich have a harder time skirting consumption taxes because they tend to shop in registered stores, use credit cards, and buy goods only available on the formal market (Jaramillo 2014: 406). The choice to move away from a formally progressive income tax in which the wealthy evaded taxes to a formally regressive consumption tax in which the poor are allowed to purchase outside the system thus ironically might represent a move toward a more pro-poor tax incidence.[6] Latin American governments may do more for the poor, albeit in somewhat unconventional ways, then commonly recognized when we look at formal policies alone.

This broader conceptualization of welfare regimes also has implications for our theories that relate changes in economic conditions or inequality to redistribution. Classic political economy models predict that economic downturns lead to more demands for redistribution from those hardest hit to help smooth consumption and spread risk. Governments respond to increased demands by boosting social expenditures, leading to countercyclical spending patterns under democracy. Yet, social expenditures in developing countries tend to be procyclical. International borrowing

[6] Gordon and Li (2009) similarly explain the greater reliance on distortionary excise taxes, rather than income taxes, in developing countries through the different enforcement challenges.

constraints and pressures to spend during good times partially can explain the phenomenon. But Latin American governments maintain social security and benefits to the organized middle class when economies sour; they cut benefits to the poor who are unable to pressure for their continuance (Wibbels 2006: 440).

Although I do not doubt the poor's limited power to press their interests, adding informal redistribution to the mix of policy tools available to governments gives us a different perspective on redistributive politics in times of austerity. Informal welfare policies stabilize public programs in the developing world during recessions. Street vending and squatting are strongly countercyclical (Chapter 4; Hidalgo, Naidu, and Richardson 2010). A key demand of the poor in economic downturns may be the ability to work in streets unimpeded, invade land, or stop paying electricity bills, rather than positive state provision. Again, my point is not that informal welfare is the best system for the poor. Levels of indigence escalated dramatically during Latin America's debt crises. Many workers got stuck in informal jobs that pay little and provide no social protection. But the reality is that governments offered no better solution, and may even have acted to cut social expenditures on the expectation that they could use informal mechanisms to compensate the losers. The largely countercyclical nature of informal redistribution thus provides a possible alternative explanation for why procyclical and regressive expenditure patterns endure under democracy.

A focus on informal welfare also provides a new perspective on welfare state persistence and change. In a twist to conventional models where policy insiders block social policy extensions, I showed that outsiders often act in ways that sustain their exclusion. Moves to substitutive social policies become harder, even when they would result in long-term gains, following past forbearance because the poor do not expect to benefit from state policies. As Helmke and Levitsky (2006: 18) propose, informal rules can "crowd out" formal institutions by dampening demands for formal services and encouraging actors to invest in the informal rules of the game. Similarly, informal welfare policies have delayed needed social policy reforms and reinforced a focus on short-term upgrades with immediate political returns.

What role will informal welfare play in Latin America in the future? In looking at squatter settlements and street markets, this book focused on legal violations that have dominated debates about popular movements and law for more than a century in Latin America (for a terrific intellectual history of informality, see Fischer 2014). It is possible that the period of tolerance toward squatting and street vending finally will pass. The Turkish case provides reason to suspect that forbearance toward squatters and street vendors may fade from the political agenda in Latin American capital cities, if governments continue to progress in the reduction of poverty and extension of social welfare programs. But these "old" legal violations also have been shaped by new developments, such as the rise of social rights, political decentralization, and a commodities boom, which I suspect will continue to shape forbearance in Latin America in three ways.

First, social rights may continue to transform enforcement politics. The Colombian Constitutional Court has passed several important judgments recognizing that the government has an obligation to avoid enforcement actions that harm the poor. In this reasoning, the Court follows an international trend that often is traced to the South African Constitutional Court's famous *Grootboom* case in 2000. There, the Court suspended the eviction of squatters until the government attended to the housing needs of the poorest. Such interventions make it harder for politicians to enforce against legal violations. They also can change the politics of enforcement, as politicians make more programmatic enforcement choices and claim to interpret competing laws. The optimistic interpretation of this trend is that constitutional courts will prod governments to invest more in welfare substitutes. The less rosy picture comes from South Africa, where Ms. Grootboom passed away still waiting for a house.

Second, the issue that motivated much of the empirical strategy and demarcated the period of study was political decentralization. As the empirical chapters demonstrated, decentralization gives subnational authorities the latitude to take divergent enforcement positions. It also requires thinking of forbearance beyond capital cities. Issues of informal welfare policy may become even more relevant in the fast-growing secondary cities of Latin America, where poverty rates are higher and there is more open land. Arequipa, not Lima, has been the center of land invasions in Peru. Smaller cities like Bucaramanga, Barranquilla, and Santa Marta have the most heated political negotiations surrounding street vending in Colombia. The commodities boom also made salient enforcement issues around illegal deforestation, mining, and land invasions in rural areas. Forbearance increasingly may fade from electoral agendas in the capital and surge outside of it.

Third, an economic slowdown may expose the resilience of the informal welfare regime. Latin America expanded targeted social policies during a commodities boom; they have yet to demonstrate their ability to maintain countercyclical social policies. Even in more developed countries, forbearance can be important when public welfare comes under strain during recessions. The economic crisis in Spain, for instance, rekindled squatting as a response to foreclosures and inaccessible housing prices (Solanas Domínguez 2013: 173). As economic growth slows, many Latin American governments will learn whether the social policies designed to cushion the poor in boom times have sufficient stakeholders and financing to survive austerity measures.

As a last word, it is worth returning to the tricky question of what the persistence of informal welfare means for the poor. I largely have avoided the normative questions raised by forbearance. In part, this silence reflects the fact that this is a work of positive social science. My aim was to demonstrate that forbearance – good or bad – is part of the political landscape and thinking about poverty in Latin America. But my silence also reflects a deep ambivalence. On the one hand, forbearance is an undesirable, second-best way to provide basic goods. It leaves the poor vulnerable to exploitative intermediaries, physical risks, and relationships of political dependency. As T.H. Marshall (2000[1949]) famously argues, social citizenship constitutes the essential idea of a modern welfare state. Allowing the poor to violate the law to secure basic goods is the opposite of a commitment to social rights. While perhaps better than nothing, forbearance occurs precisely because the state fails in its positive duties of welfare provision. Worse yet, I revealed the ways that forbearance has stalled the implementation of rights-based social policies. To the extent that forbearance falls short of the poor's distributive demands and has retarded the construction of modern welfare states, its usage has done real damage to Latin America's most vulnerable.

On the other hand, forbearance fills a gap in welfare states that still lag far beyond the ideal for unequal societies. In the absence of forbearance, it is not clear that the political system would rise to the occasion. Few governments in the developing world are able to provide expensive and complicated goods like housing and jobs to their citizens. It is only against this backdrop that we can understand why so many actors, from ordinary citizens to politicians to constitutional court justices, hold the paradoxical view that forbearance improves the poor's lot and even advances social rights. It also forces us to question the caricature of forbearance as a relationship of political dependency and stunted citizenship rights. Forbearance gives rise to demands on local politicians that show real political power and engagement on the part of urban poor. It is part of a process of "insurgent citizenship," to use Holston's (2008) term, in which the poor have learned to claim resources, elect leaders who provide tangible goods, and tip the legal system in their favor.

Seen in this light, democratic elections have aligned politicians' behavior with the poor's desires for concrete benefits that reach them. The central issue is not how to socialize the urban poor to understand their class interests or to train bureaucrats to enforce the law. Rather, it is how to strengthen welfare provision and provide vital social goods so that the poor get more and expect more from expansions in the welfare state.

# APPENDIX A

## Public Opinion Data on Enforcement and Social Policy

I designed and implemented a face-to-face public opinion survey of 900 voters in Bogotá, Colombia. The Bogotá-based polling firm Cifras y Conceptos administered the survey between August 5 and 29, 2013. On average, the survey interview lasted twenty-five minutes.

A clustered random sample was generated for the city. Thirty-six polling stations were selected as the primary sampling units (PSUs), with twenty-five interviews conducted in each PSU. To ensure sufficient power for the survey experiment, twelve polling stations were selected from lower-class groups (Strata 1 and 2), twelve polling stations from lower-middle-class groups (Strata 3), and twelve polling stations from middle- and upper-class groups (Strata 4, 5, and 6). Survey weights must be used to adjust for the oversampling of upper-class groups to make population-representative statements. Interviewers began from a randomly selected corner in the PSU and proceeded in a clockwise direction. The survey included two survey experiments, resulting in twelve unique paper questionnaires. Interviewers used the twelve different questionnaires in sequential order and rotated between asking for a male and female respondent in the household.

Enumerators were part of the survey firm's trained professionals. Training was conducted for enumerators on the logistics of the survey instrument and issues of respondent protection such as anonymity and privacy. On a separate sheet from the questionnaire, interviewers recorded the first name and phone number of each respondent for the purposes of later data quality checks. Post-sampling verification was conducted on a randomly selected 30 percent of the sample by telephone, after which point

TABLE A.1 *Summary Statistics, Public Opinion on Informality and Social Policy in Bogotá*

| Variable | Mean | Std. Dev. | Min. | Max. | N |
|---|---|---|---|---|---|
| Dependent Variables, Forbearance | | | | | |
| Forbearance Index | 0 | 1 | −2.462 | 2.194 | 878 |
| Street Vending | 0.513 | 0.382 | 0 | 1 | 896 |
| Squatting | 0.251 | 0.332 | 0 | 1 | 895 |
| Decommission | 0.836 | 0.37 | 0 | 1 | 898 |
| Eviction (Abstract) | 0.463 | 0.499 | 0 | 1 | 896 |
| Eviction (Concrete) | 0.606 | 0.489 | 0 | 1 | 889 |
| Dependent Variables, Redistribution | | | | | |
| Redistribution Index | 0 | 1 | −1.896 | 1.599 | 884 |
| Cash Transfers | 0.497 | 0.398 | 0 | 1 | 899 |
| Tax | 0.701 | 0.361 | 0 | 1 | 896 |
| Inequality | 0.822 | 0.291 | 0 | 1 | 895 |
| Pension | 0.597 | 0.387 | 0 | 1 | 896 |
| Housing | 0.467 | 0.404 | 0 | 1 | 896 |
| Employment | 0.44 | 0.405 | 0 | 1 | 899 |
| Independent Variables | | | | | |
| Class | 0.433 | 0.307 | 0 | 1 | 900 |
| Education | 0.637 | 0.304 | 0 | 1 | 900 |
| Female | 0.492 | 0.5 | 0 | 1 | 891 |
| Age | 0.538 | 0.314 | 0 | 1 | 900 |
| Right | 0.54 | 0.301 | 0 | 1 | 763 |
| Vendor Past | 0.228 | 0.42 | 0 | 1 | 896 |
| Squatter Past | 0.112 | 0.315 | 0 | 1 | 895 |
| Informal | 0.524 | 0.341 | 0 | 1 | 902 |
| Variables for Mechanism Analysis | | | | | |
| Tax Loopholes | 0.075 | 0.181 | 0 | 1 | 896 |
| Electricity | 0.106 | 0.218 | 0 | 1 | 896 |
| Benefits | 0.39 | 0.327 | 0 | 1 | 888 |
| Housing Availability | 0.746 | 0.316 | 0 | 1 | 887 |

contact information was destroyed. The response rate for the survey was 15.6 percent; the cooperation rate was 23.7 percent, the refusal rate was 23.3 percent, and the contact rate was 36.4 percent.

The full questionnaires in English and Spanish are available as part of the supplemental online materials. Table A.1 presents the summary statistics for the variables used. Table A.2 provides the question wording for the main items analyzed. I multiply impute left–right ideology using socioeconomic characteristics and past vote choice,

TABLE A.2 *Question Wording*

| Variable | Question Wording |
|---|---|
| Legal Violations (Compliance) | |
| *How strongly do you approve or disapprove ...* | *(from strongly disapprove "1" to strongly approve "4")* |
| Street Vending | Of people informally selling merchandise on the street? |
| Squatting | Of people occupying land informally to access housing? |
| Tax Loopholes | Of companies that use loopholes to lower their taxes? |
| Electricity | Of companies that pay for less than their electricity use? |
| Sanctions (Enforcement) | |
| *How strongly do you agree or disagree ...* | *(from strongly disagree "1" to strongly agree "4")* |
| Eviction (Abstract) | The government should evict people who occupy land informally. |
| Eviction (Concrete) | A family with few resources occupies a piece of land and builds a home despite not having title to the land. The government orders them evicted. How much do you approve of the eviction? |
| Street Vending (Concrete) | A man loses his job and begins to sell goods in the streets. The government decommissions his merchandise. How much do you agree with the decommission? |
| Redistribution | |
| *How strongly do you agree or disagree ...* | *(from strongly disagree "1" to strongly agree "4")* |
| Inequality | The government should implement strong policies to reduce income inequality between the rich and the poor. |
| Cash Transfers | The government should increase taxes to spend more on programs that provide monthly assistance to poor families. |
| Tax | The government should collect more taxes from the rich to redistribute to the poor. |
| Pension | The government should increase taxes to spend more on pensions for the elderly. |
| Housing | The government should increase taxes to spend more on housing programs. |
| Employment | The government should increase taxes to spend more on programs to promote employment and job training. |
| Benefits | State social policies help people like you. |
| Housing Availability | The poor need to occupy land informally or buy from pirate landlords to access housing. |

and present the results of regressions, including the perceived availability of welfare alternatives in the online supplement.

Turning to the experimental results, Table A.3 presents balance tests on pretreatment covariates. An omnibus F-test also found no imbalance (the first candidate pair $p < 0.9492$, the second candidate pair, $p < 0.5498$).

Although Chapter 2 presented the results for each candidate, difference-of-means tests produce similar results by breaking down the candidate pairs into the: (1) enforcement-forbearance and (2) redistribution-business candidates. My key hypothesis is that there should be a significant difference between the first pair of candidates, but not the second. In other words, enforcement positions are more polarizing than standard social policy ones. Gender and political ideology do come close to statistical significance, so I also corroborate my results using regression analyses in which the experimental treatment is included as an independent variable with and without covariates, namely, gender, age, education, political ideology, and vending past in Table A.4. The results are substantively unchanged.

Turning to the region-wide data, I rely on the Latin American Public Opinion Project's Americas Barometer (publicly available at http://datasets.americasbarometer.org/). I use the 2008, 2010, and 2012 waves because they included the relevant block of questions about protest behaviors and redistribution. Table A.5 presents summary statistics.

To construct the index of property seizure attitudes, I used questions *e14*, *e15*, *e3*, *prot* (*prot1*, *prot2*, or *prot3* depending on the wave), *e5*, and *d2*, respectively.[1] Applying the method of principal components, all variables load positively on the first component, and the first component explains a third of the variation in the data. I refer to this index as *Protest approval.* The second component loads negatively for illegal behaviors – seizing property and plotting to overthrow the government – and positively for less disruptive protest behaviors – including peaceful protests and protest participation.

[1] To create a comparable measure of protest across waves, I create an indicator variable *prot:* for 2010 and 2012, it codes individuals who have participated in a protest in the past twelve months as "1" (participants) and those who have not as "0" (nonparticipants), while for 2008 it includes respondents as having participated in a protest if they say they did "a few times" in the past year.

TABLE A.3 *Balance Tests on Pretreatment Covariates*

| | Candidate 1 | | Candidate 2 | | Balance Tests | | | |
|---|---|---|---|---|---|---|---|---|
| | Redistribution (A) | Business (B) | Forbearance (C) | Enforcement (D) | Difference of Means (A-B) | Difference of Means (C-D) | $p$-value (A-B) | $p$-value (C-D) |
| *Class* | 0.433 | 0.433 | 0.434 | 0.433 | 0.000 | 0.000 | 1.00 | 0.965 |
| *Education* | 0.635 | 0.639 | 0.632 | 0.642 | −0.003 | −0.010 | 0.869 | 0.622 |
| *Female* | 0.484 | 0.499 | 0.524 | 0.458 | −0.015 | 0.065 | 0.662 | 0.052 |
| *Age* | 48.32 | 47.00 | 47.35 | 47.98 | 1.32 | −0.630 | 0.891 | 0.278 |
| *Right* | 0.545 | 0.535 | 0.560 | 0.520 | 0.090 | 0.040 | 0.671 | 0.068 |
| *Vendor Past* | 0.225 | 0.231 | 0.225 | 0.231 | −0.006 | −0.006 | 0.831 | 0.820 |

*Note:* The $p$-values in the final column give the probability of observing a $t$-statistic as large in absolute value as the observed value, if the groups are drawn from the same distribution. $N$ = 899 respondents total.

TABLE A.4 *Treatment Effects with Covariates*

| | (1) | (2) | (3) | (4) | (5) | (6) | (7) | (8) |
|---|---|---|---|---|---|---|---|---|
| | Benefits the Poor | | Benefits Me | | Vote Intention | | Ideological Placement | |
| *Redistribution Treatment* | −0.007 | | 0.001 | | −0.045 | | 0.081* | |
| | (0.02) | | (0.02) | | (0.03) | | (0.03) | |
| *Forbearance Treatment* | | −0.342* | | −0.206* | | −0.237* | | 0.136* |
| | | (0.02) | | (0.02) | | (0.03) | | (0.03) |
| *Class* | 0.018 | 0.124* | −0.114* | 0.016 | 0.017 | 0.083 | −0.048 | −0.010 |
| | (0.05) | (0.05) | (0.05) | (0.05) | (0.05) | (0.05) | (0.05) | (0.06) |
| *Female* | 0.049* | 0.001 | 0.035 | −0.002 | 0.039 | −0.005 | −0.008 | −0.017 |
| | (0.02) | (0.02) | (0.02) | (0.02) | (0.03) | (0.03) | (0.03) | (0.03) |
| *Education* | −0.024 | −0.087 | 0.060 | −0.016 | 0.031 | −0.036 | 0.087 | 0.073 |
| | (0.05) | (0.05) | (0.05) | (0.05) | (0.05) | (0.05) | (0.06) | (0.06) |
| *Age* | 0.000 | 0.001 | −0.000 | −0.000 | 0.000 | 0.001 | −0.001 | 0.000 |
| | (0.00) | (0.00) | (0.00) | (0.00) | (0.00) | (0.00) | (0.00) | (0.00) |
| *Ideology* | −0.006 | −0.060 | −0.031 | −0.085* | −0.015 | −0.055 | 0.110* | 0.040 |
| | (0.04) | (0.04) | (0.04) | (0.04) | (0.05) | (0.05) | (0.05) | (0.05) |
| *Vendor Past* | 0.017 | −0.023 | 0.033 | 0.001 | 0.029 | 0.018 | −0.023 | −0.014 |
| | (0.03) | (0.03) | (0.03) | (0.03) | (0.03) | (0.03) | (0.03) | (0.04) |
| $R^2$ | 0.007 | 0.229 | 0.014 | 0.100 | 0.009 | 0.114 | 0.029 | 0.039 |

*Notes:* The redistribution treatment reflects the difference between the pro-redistribution and pro-business candidate information; the forbearance treatment shows the difference between the forbearance and enforcement candidate information. All dependent variables are rescaled from 0 to 1 and run from "very unlikely" to "highly likely," or in the case of ideological placement, from the right to left.

TABLE A.5 *Summary Statistics, AmericasBarometer, Pooled 2008, 2010, and 2012 Waves*

| Variable | Mean | Std. Dev. | Min. | Max. | N |
|---|---|---|---|---|---|
| Forbearance | 0 | 1 | −4.059 | 5.342 | 81,707 |
| Redistribution | 0 | 1 | −3.071 | 0.787 | 87,815 |
| Income | 8.196 | 2.915 | 0 | 16.345 | 78,003 |
| Wealth | 0.475 | 0.317 | 0 | 1 | 90,571 |
| Education | 0.510 | 0.252 | 0 | 1 | 90,329 |
| Rural | 0.302 | 0.459 | 0 | 1 | 90,837 |
| Female | 0.513 | 0.500 | 0 | 1 | 90,836 |
| Right | 0.513 | 0.279 | 0 | 1 | 72,644 |
| Age | 0.280 | 0.193 | 0 | 1 | 90,531 |
| Self-Employed | 0.187 | 0.390 | 0 | 1 | 90,837 |

Blocking roads falls in the middle with a loading near zero. The second component (*Legality*) appears to capture a common attitude toward law breaking and violence. Cumulatively, the first and second components explain over half of the variance. Including the second component in the first-stage regression does not change the results.

# APPENDIX B

## Coding Rules for Campaign Platform, Newspaper, and Administrative Sources

I constructed a database of campaign platforms (*Plan de Gobierno*) from the 2010 district elections in Lima, Peru. These platforms are available for each district and political party through the National Electoral Authority's Governance Observatory (*Jurado Nacional de Elecciones, Observatorio para la Gobernabilidad*). Given that I was interested in the contrast between poor and nonpoor districts, I left out thirteen mixed-income districts. This restriction generates 201 platforms in poor districts, and 105 in nonpoor districts. Given the small size of the database, platforms were hand-coded by a research assistant (rather than using automated text analysis) based on the types of enforcement and housing commitments they mentioned toward squatting.

Some of the harder decisions concerned how to code platforms that promised to improve the land cadaster. In many cases, an updated land cadaster is an important step to improve monitoring and enforcement of district lands. However, the cadaster can also be used to improve property titling and tax collection. It therefore seemed too ambiguous to treat a cadaster as a commitment to enforce against squatters, unless accompanied by an explicit reference to enforcement operations. I also do not include platforms that promise to respect or create zoning plans unless they include more specific provisions for the control of squatting.

For the newspaper article database in Chapter 4, I relied on *El Tiempo*'s online archive to locate articles on street vendors; in contrast, I used physical archives to locate articles on street vending from *El Comercio*, given that the online archive only begins in 2002 and has partial coverage. I also reviewed the physical archives of *El Tiempo* through the categorized newspaper archive maintained by the Center for Research and Popular

Education (*Centro de Investigación y Educación Popular*, CINEP). This difference in methodology may have resulted in some discrepancy in the set of stories located. In particular, stories with briefer mentions of street vending, such as those that only involved a paragraph in a broader story or a sentence in a letter to an editor, were more difficult to locate using the physical archive. I attempted to standardize by only including articles from the online archive that included a substantial discussion of street vending. In practice, this meant that stories that interviewed street vendors on unrelated content or mentioned that a street had been occupied by vendors without commentary were excluded.

Articles were pulled on street vending from 1990 through 2010 (and through 2014, in the case of Lima). The articles were classified as one of four types: (1) news item, (2) letter to the editor, (3) short note, and (4) platforms, speeches, or interviews with politicians. Articles were then given a primary coding based on their dominant theme (sympathetic narrative, sympathetic polemic, unsympathetic narrative, and unsympathetic polemic), as well as secondary markers for the specific types of issues mentioned. For the sympathetic categories, these included: (1) *unemployment* if there is mention of high unemployment rates, lack of jobs, etc., (2) *displacement* if there is mention of the civil war, migration, or internal displacement, or (3) *criminalization of poverty* if there is mention of "persecution" of innocent poor. Within the unsympathetic categories, there were several sub-categorizations: (1) *public space* if the article denounces street vendors for monopolizing public areas like sidewalks or parks; (2) *traffic* if there is mention of blocking traffic; (3) *business competition* if there is mention of business being harmed, less private sector investment, tax evasion, or effects on local businesses; (4) *public safety risk* if there is mention of bad sanitation, unsafe electricity connections, blocking emergency exits, etc.; and (5) *crime* if there is discussion of how street vendors make streets unsafe, shelter criminals, serve as facades for drug organizations, etc. More details and examples can be found in the online supplementary material.

In addition to the platforms and newspaper sources, I relied on several government sources to calculate the number of squatters, street vendors, and government expenditures. In Lima, I approximated the number of squatters using the annual household surveys, *Encuesta Nacional de Hogares* (ENAHO) module on housing (*Características de la Vivienda y del Hogar*). All calculations are done for the Lima metropolitan area. I rely on a question that asks households if their house is (1) a rental, (2) their own, completely paid for, (3) their own, by invasion, (4) their own, purchasing in installments, (5) given to them by a job, or (6) given to them by another person or institution. I count households that answer that their house is "their own, by invasion" as squatters.

To estimate the worth of land transfers, I rely on a question that asks households how much they would be willing to accept in rent for their house. On average, households that accessed their property through invasions said someone would pay $60 (191 soles) in monthly rent; as expected, invasion households without property title rent for less than those with title ($47 versus $66). I estimate that households spend about $3,000 on the construction of the house itself (the average reported on the household survey), and that these costs are amortized over about fifteen years for a given house. This amounts to about $15 each month in construction costs. The government also may generate additional value to the household when it formally transfers the property: two-thirds of households formed through a land invasion have a property title. This transfer could be counted as a onetime surplus payment beyond the rental stream to the household, but I exclude it given that I cannot attribute differences in home prices to the property title itself.

To calculate the wealth of squatters, I rely on an index of questions about consumer durables – landline phone, cell phone, TV with cable, water, sewerage, and internet – and then compare these households to the rest of the Lima population. On the wealth index, 82 percent of squatter households are in the bottom third of the distribution, whereas just 4 percent are in the top third.

To analyze the number and wealth of street vendors in Lima, I rely on the same household survey, but use the module on independent workers (*Ingresos del Trabajador Independiente*). Individuals who respond that they are independent workers on an initial work module (32 percent of the population in 2011) answer a special set of questions about where they work, including the category "as a street vendor (*ambulante*)." In 2011, ENAHO leads to an estimate of 341,237 street vendors, which is far higher than the number reported by district governments. The discrepancy in the estimates likely reflects the weights used to inflate the survey data, and the ambiguity in the question wording (the term *ambulante* refers to any commercial vendor in public space, whether licensed or unlicensed). Given that the sample probably includes many formal vendors, the household survey also probably overestimates the income of unlicensed street vendors.

Turning to the government expenditures data, more so than in other social policy areas, national accounts data on housing expenditures are rarely comparable. The IMF, for instance, reports a vague category of public expenditures on "housing and other." The inaccuracy of this categorization arises from two issues – many housing ministries lump together a variety of housing, infrastructure, and environmental functions, such as water provision and road construction, and second, some housing expenditures occur through non-housing entities, such as pension funds. Accordingly, I turned to line-item budget reports and studies that attempt to standardize reports to estimate expenses on government supply- and demand-side interventions. I calculate only expenditures on social interest housing programs here, which necessarily means leaving aside some complementary expenses meant to improve the quality of these projects. The supplementary online material discusses the sources and coding challenges in each country.

# APPENDIX C

## Local Government Enforcement Survey

The survey of local governments involved an in-person interview with the director or sub-director of the office in charge of street vending and housing in each district. The precise office depends on the district's administrative structure. Rather than seek an office with a specific title, the selection criterion is the office that manages operations against street vending and squatting. In most cases, a local commerce or inspections office is in charge of street vending. The exceptions are districts that have a special office for street commerce, or that group vending in an economic "rents" office. Housing or building offices tend to be in charge of squatting issues. The structured survey lasted thirty minutes, although unstructured conversations with officials often continued for up to two hours and are archived through the Qualitative Data Repository (QDR).

The sample does not include districts that are classified as more than 75 percent rural or have populations under 5,000. This means that the sample excludes Sumapaz in Bogotá, and Ancón, Pucusana, Punta Hermosa, Punta Negra, San Bartolo, and Santa Rosa in Lima. In Santiago, I include the thirty-four districts that comprise Greater Santiago (thirty-two *comunas* in Santiago, plus San Bernardo and Puente Alto in the provinces of Maipo and Cordillera, respectively).

In Istanbul, I conducted the survey only in a subset of the city's thirty-nine districts. I first stratified the sample into lower-, mixed-, and upper-income districts based on the fraction of the population that is eligible to receive free health assistance from the government ("green card" holders). Green card holders provided the best proxy for district income or poverty, which were unavailable. I considered 12 percent of households as green card holders to be the cut point for a low-income district;

I consider a nonpoor district to have less than 4 percent of households with green cards. I selected four districts from each category (although I was unable to complete one interview in the low-income district of Çatalca). The districts surveyed included Gaziosmanpaşa, Sultanbeyli, and Beyoğlu (lower); Arnavutköy, Beykoz, Fatih, and Kadıköy (mixed); and Beşiktaş Maltepe, Sarıyer, and Sultangazi (upper). Seven of the districts selected were governed by the AKP, which roughly reflects their control over two-thirds of Istanbul district governments in 2009. All interviews were conducted in Turkish with the assistance of a translator. Additional details on the construction of all the variables and robustness checks are available in the supplementary material of Holland (2015).

The questionnaire for bureaucrats included three main sections. The first asked about the bureaucrat's experience in the district, the resources at his disposal, and the types of political intervention that occurred in the district. The second section asked about the types and frequency of control activities that the district undertook. The third section asked about bureaucrats' perceptions of politics and law enforcement in the district before concluding with demographic information. The third section began with the following set of instructions:

> People have different ideas about street vending/squatting. I am going to read you some opinions and ask you where you would situate your own opinions on this scale where "1" means that you agree completely with the first statement, and "10" means that you agree completely with the second statement. The statements are opposites. If your opinions are somewhere in the middle, you can choose any intermediate number.

Here, I reproduce the questions analyzed in Chapters 3 and 5. The full questionnaires in English and Spanish, as well as a full list of the interviews conducted (for those participants who allowed me to release identifying information), are available with the online supplementary material.

1. *Loses Votes*

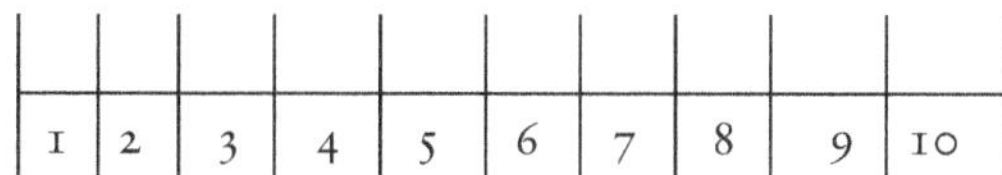


| The mayor loses electoral support when he evicts street vendors/squatters. | The mayor gains electoral support when he evicts street vendors/squatters. |
|---|---|

2. *Political Constraint*

| 1 | 2 | 3 | 4 | 5 | 6 | 7 | 8 | 9 | 10 |
|---|---|---|---|---|---|---|---|---|---|

The lack of resources is the biggest obstacle to the control of street vending/squatting.

Political intervention is the biggest obstacle to the control of street vending/squatting.

3. *Tolerant Left*

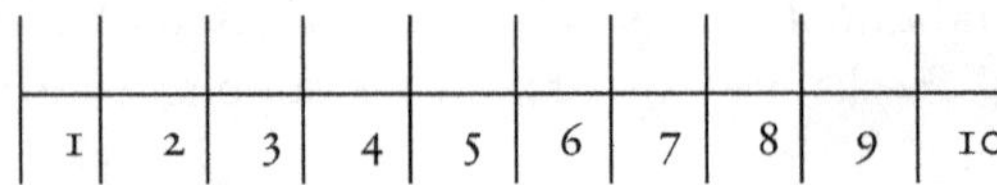


Politicians on the Right are more willing to tolerate street vendors/squatters due to their aversion to using the state to create jobs.

Politicians on the Left are more willing to tolerate street vendors/squatters due to their social sympathies.

4. *Corruption*

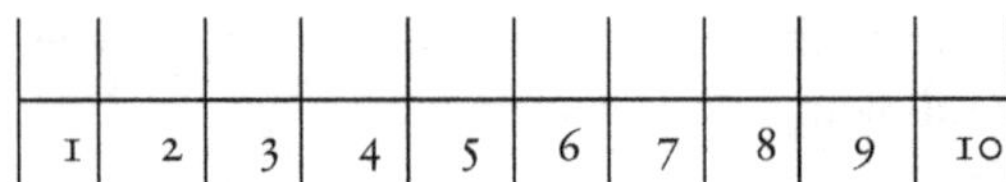


It is common that street vendors/squatters pay bureaucrats or the police to remain in the streets/on their property.

It is uncommon that street vendors/squatters pay bureaucrats or the police to remain in the streets/on their property.

APPENDIX D

# Information Available in Online Supplement

1. Interview list
2. Additional tables and figures
3. Additional survey instruments
   a. Public Opinion Questionnaire (English)
   b. Public Opinion Questionnaire (Spanish)
   c. Housing Survey Questionnaire (English)
   d. Housing Survey Questionnaire (Spanish)
   e. Street Vending Survey Questionnaire (English)
   f. Street Vending Survey Questionnaire (Spanish)
4. Newspaper coding examples
5. Housing budget statistics

# References


Acemoglu, Daron, and James A. Robinson. 2006. *Economic Origins of Dictatorship and Democracy*. New York: Cambridge University Press.

Adelman, Jeremy, and Miguel Á. Centeno. 2002. "Between Liberalism and Neoliberalism: Law's Dilemma in Latin America." In *Global Prescriptions*, ed. Yves Dezalay and Bryant G. Garth. Ann Arbor: University of Michigan Press, 139–61.

Adrianzén, Alberto. 2012. *Apogeo y crisis de la izquierda Peruana: Hablan sus protagonistas*. Lima: IDEA Internacional and Universidad Antonio Ruiz de Montoya.

AGFE (Advisory Group on Forced Evictions). 2009. "Mission to Istanbul, Republic of Turkey, June 8–11, 2009." *Report to the Executive Director of the UN Habitat Program*.

Akbulut, Mehmet R., and Seher Başlik. 2011. "Transformation of Perception of the Gecekondu Phenomenon." *METU Journal of the Faculty of Architecture* 28(2): 1–44.

Akinci, Ugur. 1999. "The Welfare Party's Municipal Track Record: Evaluating Islamist Municipal Activism in Turkey." *Middle East Journal* 53(1): 75–94.

Albertus, Michael. 2015. *Autocracy and Redistribution*. New York: Cambridge University Press.

Aldrich, John H. 1995. *Why Parties? The Origin and Transformation of Political Parties in America*. Chicago: University of Chicago Press.

Alesina, Alberto, and Edward L. Glaeser. 2004. *Fighting Poverty in the US and Europe: A World of Difference*. New York: Oxford University Press.

Alfonso, Óscar. 2012. "¿Ciudad prioritaria, Ciudad social? Análisis de la política nacional de vivienda para familias de bajos ingresos en Bogotá (1991–2009)." In *Dimensiones del hábitat popular latinoamericano*, ed. Teolinda Bolívar and Jaime Erazo Espinosa. Quito, Ecuador: FLACSO Ecuador, 19–44.

Aliaga Linares, Lissette. 2010. "Informal Economy Budget Analysis in Peru and Metropolitan Lima." *WIEGO Inclusive Cities Project* 5: 1–39.

2012. "Shaping Informality in the Free Market City: A Comparative Spatial Analysis of Street Vending Policies in Lima and Bogotá." PhD diss. University of Texas-Austin.

Allina-Pisano, Jessica. 2012. "Sub Rosa Resistance and the Politics of Economic Reform: Land Redistribution in Post-Soviet Ukraine." *World Politics* 56(4): 554–81.

Alvarez Rivadulla, María José. 2012. "Clientelism or Something Else? Squatter Politics in Montevideo." *Latin American Politics and Society* 54(1): 37–63.

Amengual, Matthew. 2015. *Politicized Enforcement: Labor and Environmental Regulation in Argentina*. New York: Cambridge University Press.

Ansell, Ben W., and David J. Samuels. 2015. *Inequality and Democratization: An Elite-Competition Approach*. New York: Cambridge University Press.

Ansolabehere, Stephen, Jonathan Rodden, and James M. Snyder. 2008. "The Strength of Issues: Using Multiple Measures to Gauge Preference Stability, Ideological Constraint, and Issue Voting." *American Political Science Review* 102(2): 215–32.

Apoyo. 1999. "Intención de voto, Campaña electoral del 2000." Lima: Encuestas Ipsos Perú-Apoyo, March.

2002. "Porqué razones no votaría por Alberto Andrade?" Lima: Encuestas Ipsos Perú-Apoyo, November.

Arriagada Luco, Camilo, and Juan Moreno Crossley. 2006. *Atlas de la evolución del déficit habitacional en Chile 1992–2002*. Santiago, Chile: Pehuen.

Arslanalp, Mert. 2015. "Claiming Rights, Negotiating Exceptions: Politics of Urban Citizenship in Istanbul and Buenos Aires." PhD diss. Northwestern University.

Ashworth, Scott. 2012. "Electoral Accountability: Recent Theoretical and Empirical Work." *Annual Review of Political Science* 15(1): 183–201.

Auerbach, Adam. 2016. "Clients and Communities: The Political Economy of Party Network Organization and Development in India's Urban Slums." *World Politics* 68(1): 111–48.

Auyero, Javier. 2000. *Poor People's Politics: Peronist Survival Networks and the Legacy of Evita*. Durham, NC: Duke University Press Books.

Auyero, Javier, and Debora A. Swistun. 2009. *Flammable: Environmental Suffering in an Argentine Shantytown*. New York: Oxford University Press.

Aytaç, Selim E., and Ziya Öni. 2014. "Varieties of Populism in a Changing Global Context: The Divergent Paths of Erdoğan and Kirchnerismo." *Comparative Politics* 47(1): 41–59.

Azevedo, Joao Pedro, and Aziz Atamanov. 2014. "Pathways to the Middle Class in Turkey: How Have Reducing Poverty and Boosting Shared Prosperity Helped?" World Bank Policy Research Working Paper No. 6834.

Baker, Andy. 2010. *The Market and the Masses in Latin America: Policy Reform and Consumption in Liberalizing Economies*. New York: Cambridge University Press.

Barnhardt, Sharon, Erica Field, and Rohini Pande. 2015. "Moving to Opportunity or Isolation? Network Effects of a Slum Relocation Program in India." NBER Working Paper No. 21419.

Barrientos, Armando. 2004. "Latin America: Toward a Liberal-Informal Welfare Regime." In *Insecurity and Welfare Regimes in Asia, Africa and Latin America: Social Policy in Development Contexts*, ed. Ian Gough and Geof Wood. New York: Cambridge University Press, 68–121.

2009. "Labour Markets and the (Hyphenated) Welfare Regime in Latin America." *Economy and Society* 38(1): 87–108.

Başlevent, Cem, and Eyüp Silahtar. 2013. "Socio-Demographic Determinants of the Support for Turkey's Justice and Development Party." *Economics Bulletin* 33(2): 1215–28.

Başlevent, Cem, and Meltem Dayıoğlu. 2005. "The Effect of Squatter Housing on Income Distribution in Urban Turkey." *Urban Studies* 42(1): 31–45.

Bayat, Asef. 1998. *Street Politics*. New York: Columbia University Press.

Beccassino, Angel. 2000. *Peñalosa y una ciudad 2600 metros más cerca de las estrellas*. Bogotá, Colombia: Grijalbo.

Becker, Gary. 1968. "Crime and Punishment: An Economic Approach." *Journal of Political Economy* 76(2): 169–217.

Becker, Gary, and George Stigler. 1974. "Law Enforcement, Malfeasance, and the Compensation of Enforcers." *Journal of Legal Studies* 3(1): 1–19.

Bénabou, Roland. 1997. "Inequality and Growth." *NBER Macroeconomics Annual* 11: 11–74.

Bergman, Marcelo. 2009. *Tax Evasion and the Rule of Law in Latin America: The Political Culture of Cheating and Compliance in Argentina and Chile*. University Park: Pennsylvania State University Press.

Berney, Rachel. 2010. "Learning from Bogotá: How Municipal Experts Transformed Public Space." *Journal of Urban Design* 15(4): 539–58.

Blofield, Merike, and Juan Pablo Luna. 2011. "Public Opinion on Income Inequalities in Latin America." In *The Great Gap: Inequality and the Politics of Income Redistribution in Latin America*, ed. Merike Blofield. University Park: Pennsylvania State University Press, 147–85.

Bogotá Cómo Vamos. 2003. *Encuesta de Percepción 2003*. Bogotá: Bogotá Cómo Vamos.

2005. *Encuesta de Percepción 2005*. Bogotá: Bogotá Cómo Vamos.

Boix, Carles. 2003. *Democracy and Redistribution*. New York: Cambridge University Press.

Bonner, Christine, and Dave Spooner. 2012. *The Only School We Have: Learning from Organizing Experiences Across the Informal Economy*. Cambridge, MA: Women in Informal Employment: Globalizing and Organizing (WIEGO).

Boone, Catherine. 2009. "Electoral Populism Where Property Rights Are Weak: Land Politics in Contemporary Sub-Saharan Africa." *Comparative Politics* 41(2): 183–201.

Bora, Tanil. 1999. "Istanbul of the Conqueror: The Alternative Global City Dreams of Political Islam." In *Istanbul: Between the Global and the Local*, ed. Çağlar Keyder. Lanham, MD: Rowman & Littlefield, 47–59.

Borg, Marian J., and Karen F. Parker. 2001. "Mobilizing Law in Urban Areas: The Social Structure of Homicide Clearance Rates." *Law & Society Review* 35(2): 435–66.

Bouillon, César Patricio. 2012. *Room for Development: Housing Markets in Latin America and the Caribbean*. Washington, DC: Inter-American Development Bank, Palgrave Macmillan.

Brinks, Daniel M., and William Forbath. 2014. "The Role of Courts and Constitutions in the New Politics of Welfare in Latin America." In *Law and Development of Middle-Income Countries: Avoiding the Middle-Income Trap*, ed. Randall Peerenboom and Tom Ginsburg. New York: Cambridge University Press, 221–45.

Brollo, Fernanda, Katja Kaufmann, and Eliana La Ferrara. 2014. "The Political Economy of Enforcing Conditional Welfare Programs: Evidence from Brazil." Working Paper.

Bromley, Ray. 1978. "The Urban Informal Sector: Why Is It Worth Discussing?" *World Development* 6(9–10): 1033–9.

2000. "Street Vending and Public Policy: A Global Review." *International Journal of Sociology and Social Policy* 20(1/2): 1–28.

Buğra, Ayşe. 1998. "The Immoral Economy of Housing in Turkey." *International Journal of Urban and Regional Research* 22(2): 303–317.

2007. "Poverty and Citizenship: An Overview of the Social-Policy Environment in Republican Turkey." *International Journal of Middle East Studies* 39(1): 33–52.

Buğra, Ayşe, and Çağlar Keyder. 2006. "The Turkish Welfare Regime in Transformation." *Journal of European Social Policy* 16(3): 211–28.

Buğra, Ayşe, and Osman Savaskan. 2014. *New Capitalism in Turkey: The Relationship Between Politics, Religion and Business*. Cheltenham: Edward Elgar Publisher.

Caldeira, Teresa. 2000. *City of Walls: Crime, Segregation, and Citizenship in São Paulo*. Berkeley: University of California Press.

Calderón Cockburn, Julio. 2006. *Mercado de tierras urbanas, propiedad y pobreza*. Cambridge, MA: Lincoln Institute of Land Policy.

2009. "El efecto MiVivienda: Política de vivienda para la clase media." *Ecuador Debate* 76(3): 107–22.

2013a. "Affordable Housing Policies and Urban Land Markets in Peru." Lincoln Institute of Land Policy Working Paper: 1–36.

2013b. "La ciudad ilegal en el Perú." In *Perú hoy, el Perú subterráneo*, ed. Werner Jungbluth. Lima, Peru: DESCO, 39–56.

Camacol (Cámara Colombiana de la Construcción). 2009. *Costos de la vivienda de interés prioritario*. Bogotá: Camacol.

Camargo, Angélica, and Adriana Hurtado. 2011. *La urbanización informal en Bogotá: Panorama a partir del Observatorio del mercado informal de suelo y vivienda*. Bogotá: Universidad Piloto de Colombia.

2013. "Urbanización informal en Bogotá: Agentes y lógicas de producción del espacio urbano." *Invi* 28(78): 77–107.

Cameron, Maxwell A. 1991. "Political Parties and the Worker-Employer Cleavage: The Impact of the Informal Sector on Voting in Lima, Peru." *Bulletin of Latin American Research* 10(3): 293–313.

1994. *Democracy and Authoritarianism in Peru: Political Coalitions and Social Change*. New York: St. Martin's Press.

2011. "Peru: The Left Turn That Wasn't." In *The Resurgence of the Latin American Left*, ed. Steven Levitsky and Kenneth Roberts. Baltimore, MD: Johns Hopkins University Press, 375–98.

Cammett, Melani. 2015. *Compassionate Communalism: Welfare and Sectarianism in Lebanon*. New York: Cambridge University Press.

Cammett, Melani, and Lauren M. MacLean. 2011. "Introduction: The Political Consequences of Non-State Social Welfare in the Global South." *Studies in Comparative International Development* 46(1): 1–21.

2014. *The Politics of Non-state Social Welfare*. Ithaca, NY: Cornell University Press.

Campbell, Andrea L. 2005. *How Policies Make Citizens: Senior Political Activism and the American Welfare State*. Princeton, NJ: Princeton University Press.

Candan, Ayfer B., and Biray Kolluoglu. 2008. "Emerging Spaces of Neoliberalism: A Gated Town and a Public Housing Project in Istanbul." *New Perspectives on Turkey* 39(39): 5–46.

Çanga, A. 2002. *Housing Policies and Housing Demand Analysis for the 2000–2010 Period*. Istanbul, Turkey: General Assembly on Housing, Chamber of City Planners.

Carnes, Matthew E. 2014. *Continuity Despite Change: The Politics of Labor Regulation in Latin America*. Stanford: Stanford University Press.

Carnes, Matthew E., and Isabela Mares. 2015. "Explaining the 'Return of the State' in Middle-Income Countries: Employment Vulnerability, Income, and Preferences for Social Protection in Latin America." *Politics & Society* 43(4): 525–50.

Carpenter, Daniel. 2014. "Detecting and Measuring Capture." In *Preventing Regulatory Capture: Special Interest Influence and How to Limit It*, ed. Daniel Carpenter and David A. Moss. New York: Cambridge University Press, 57–68.

Carrión, Julio. 2006. "Public Opinion, Market Reforms, and Democracy in Fujimori's Peru." In *The Fujimori Legacy: The Rise of Electoral Authoritarianism in Peru*, ed. Julio Carrión. University Park: Pennsylvania State Press, 126–49.

Carvallo, Marcelo. 2000. "Desafios actuales del Programa Chile Barrio." *Jornadas de Vivienda Social* 3 (May): 54–62.

Casaburi, Lorenzo, and Ugo Troiano. 2016. "Ghost-House Busters: The Electoral Response to a Large Anti Tax Evasion Program." *Quarterly Journal of Economics* 131(1): 273–314.

Casasfranco, María Virginia, and Oscar Arcos. 2007. *10 años de Metrovivienda: Modelos de gestión del suelo, vivienda y hábitat*. Bogotá: Alcaldía Mayor de Bogota, Metrovivienda.

Castañeda, Alberto, and Jon García Bañales. 2007. *Hábitat y espacio público: El caso de los vendedores informales en el espacio público físico de Bogotá*. Bogotá: Alcaldía Mayor de Bogotá, Secretaría de Gobierno.

Castells, Manuel. 1971. *Campamentos de Santiago: Movilización urbana*. Milwaukee: University of Wisconsin.

CChC (Cámara Chilena de Construcción). 2008, 2011. *Balance de la vivienda en Chile*. Santiago, Chile: CChC, Comisión Permanente de la Vivienda.

Centeno, Miguel A., and Alejandro Portes. 2006. "The Informal Economy in the Shadow of the State." In *Out of the Shadows: Political Action and the Informal Economy in Latin America*, ed. Patricia Fernández-Kelly and Jon Shefner. University Park: Pennsylvania State Press, 23–48.

CEP (Centro de Estudios Públicos). 1991. "*Estudio Social y de Opinión Pública, Marzo 1991*." Santiago, Chile: CEP.

Chatterjee, Partha. 2004. *The Politics of the Governed: Reflections on Popular Politics in Most of the World*. New York: Columbia University Press.

2011. *Lineages of Political Society: Studies in Postcolonial Democracy*. New York: Columbia University Press.

Chirinos, Luis. 1980. *Municipios, un debate mas allá de lo electoral*. Lima: Centro de Investigación, Documentación y Asesoria Poblacional (CIDAP).

Chubb, Judith. 1982. *Patronage, Power and Poverty in Southern Italy: A Tale of Two Cities*. New York: Cambridge University Press.

Çinar, Alev. 2005. *Modernity, Islam, and Secularism In Turkey: Bodies, Places, and Time*. Minneapolis: University of Minnesota Press.

COFOPRI (Organismo de Formalización de la Propiedad Informal). 2004. *La formalización de propiedad en el Perú: Develando el misterio*. Lima: COFOPRI.

Collier, David. 1976. *Squatters and Oligarchs: Authoritarian Rule and Policy Change in Peru*. Baltimore, MD: Johns Hopkins Press.

Collier, Ruth Berins, and David Collier. 1991. *Shaping the Political Arena: Critical Junctures, the Labor Movement, and Regime Dynamics in Latin America*. Princeton, NJ: Princeton University Press.

Collier, Ruth Berins, and Samuel Handlin. 2009. "Popular Representation in the Interest Area." In *Reorganizing Popular Politics: Participation and the New Interest Regime in Latin America*. University Park: Pennsylvania State University Press, 3–32.

Contreras, Victoria. 1988. *Sobrevivir en la calle: el comercio ambulante en Santiago*. Geneva: PREALC, OIT.

Cook, Philip J. 1979. "The Clearance Rate as a Measure of Criminal Justice System Effectiveness." *Journal of Public Economics* 11: 135–42.

Cornelius, Wayne A. 1975. *Politics and the Migrant Poor in Mexico City*. Stanford, CA: Stanford University Press.

CPI. 2013. *Encuesta Revocatoria*. Lima: Compañía peruana de estudios de mercados y opinión pública, February 23, 2013.

Crabtree, John. 1992. *Peru Under García: An Opportunity Lost*. Pittsburgh, PA: University of Pittsburgh Press.

Crabtree, John, and Ann Chaplin. 2013. *Bolivia: Processes of Change*. New York: Zed Books.

Cross, John. 1998. *Informal Politics: Street Vendors and the State in Mexico City*. Stanford: Stanford University Press.

Cuervo, Nicolás, and Samuel Jaramillo. 2009. "Dos décadas de política de vivienda en Bogotá apostando por el mercado." Documentos CEDE Working Paper 006651: 1–36.

Culpepper, Pepper D. 2010. *Quiet Politics and Business Power: Corporate Control in Europe and Japan*. New York: Cambridge University Press.

DADEP. 2010. "Informe Final Auditoría Gubermental, DADEP," Dirección Sector Control Urbano, Departamento Administrativo de la Defensoría del Espacio Público, Bogotá, Colombia, December 12, 2010.

Dahl, Robert A. 1961. *Who Governs? Democracy and Power in an American City*. New Haven: Yale University Press.

Dargent, Eduardo. 2015. *Technocracy and Democracy in Latin America: Experts Running the Government*. New York: Cambridge University Press.

2016. "The Politics of Enforcement: Social Actors as Sources of Institutional Strength and Weakness in Bolivia and Peru." Working Paper.

DaMatta, Roberto. 1991. *Carnivals, Rogues, and Heroes: An Interpretation of the Brazilian Dilemma*. Notre Dame, IN: Notre Dame Press.

DANE (Departamento Administrativo Nacional de Estadística). 2005. *Boletín Déficit de Vivienda*. Bogotá: DANE.

2012. *Estadísticas por tema: empleo y desempleo*. Bogotá: DANE.

Davis, Diane. 1994. *Urban Leviathan: Mexico City in the Twentieth Century*. Philadelphia, PA: Temple University Press.

2013. "Zero-Tolerance Policing, Stealth Real Estate Development, and the Transformation of Public Space: Evidence from Mexico City." *Latin American Perspectives* 40(2): 53–76.

De La O Torres, Ana. 2015. *Crafting Policies to End Poverty in Latin America: The Quiet Transformation*. New York: Cambridge University Press.

De Soto, Hernando. 1989. *The Other Path: The Invisible Revolution in the Third World*. New York: Harper and Row.

2000. *The Mystery of Capital: Why Capitalism Triumphs in the West and Fails Everywhere Else*. New York: Basic Books.

De Soto, Hernando, Enrique Ghersi, and Mario Ghibellini. 1986. *El otro sendero: la revolución informal*. Lima: El Barranco.

Deininger, Klaus, and Gershon Feder. 2009. "Land Registration, Governance, and Development: Evidence and Implications for Policy." *World Bank Research Observer* 24(2): 233–66.

Delgado Silva, Angel. 1994. "Autocracia y régimen local." *Socialismo y Participación* 65(2): 1–10.

Desmond, Matthew. 2016. *Evicted: Poverty and Profit in the American City*. New York: Deckle Edge.

Diaz-Cayeros, Alberto, and Beatriz Magaloni. 2009. "Aiding Latin America's Poor." *Journal of Democracy* 20(4): 36–48.

Diaz-Cayeros, Alberto, Federico Estévez, and Beatriz Magaloni. 2016. *The Political Logic of Poverty Relief: Electoral Strategies and Social Policy in Mexico*. New York: Cambridge University Press.

Dietz, Henry. 1985. "Political Participation in the Barriadas: An Extension and Reexamination." *Comparative Political Studies* 18(3): 323–55.

1989. "Political Participation in the Barriadas: A Research Update." *Comparative Political Studies* 22(1): 122–30.

1998. *Urban Poverty, Political Participation, and the State: Lima, 1970–1990*. Pittsburgh, PA: University of Pittsburgh Press.

Dietz, Henry, and David Myers. 2002. *Capital City Politics in Latin America: Democratization and Empowerment*. Boulder, CO: Lynne Reiner.

Dimitrov, Martin K. 2009. *Piracy and the State: The Politics of Intellectual Property Rights in China*. New York: Cambridge University Press.

Dion, Michelle L., and Vicki Birchfield. 2010. "Economic Development, Income Inequality, and Preferences for Redistribution." *International Studies Quarterly* 54(2): 315–34.

DiTella, Rafael, Sebastian Galiani, and Ernesto Schargrodsky. 2007. "The Formation of Beliefs: Evidence from the Allocation of Land Titles to Squatters." *Quarterly Journal of Economics* 122(1): 209–41.

DNP (Departamento Nacional de Planeación). 2007. *Estado comunitario: Desarrollo para todos*. Bogotá: Gaceta del Congreso, DNP.

Doebele, William A. 1977. "The Private Market and Low Income Urbanization: The 'Pirate' Subdivisions of Bogota." *The American Journal of Comparative Law* 25(3): 531.

Donovan, Michael. 2002. "Space Wars in Bogotá: The Recovery of Public Space and Its Impact on Street Vendors." Master's Thesis. MIT.

2008. "Informal Cities and the Contestation of Public Space: The Case of Bogota's Street Vendors, 1988–2003." *Urban Studies* 45(1): 29–51.

Dorlach, Tim. 2015. "The Prospects of Egalitarian Capitalism in the Global South: Turkish Social Neoliberalism in Comparative Perspective." *Economy and Society* 44(4): 519–44.

Dorman, W. Judson. 2007. "The Politics of Neglect: The Egyptian State in Cairo, 1974–98." PhD diss. University of London.

Dosh, Paul. 2010. *Demanding the Land: Urban Popular Movements in Peru and Ecuador, 1990–2005*. University Park: Pennsylvania State Press.

Driant, Jean-Claude. 1991. *Las barriadas de Lima: Historia e interpretación*. Lima: IFEA and DESCO.

Dunning, Thad. 2009. "Direct Action and Associational Participation: Problem-Solving Repetoires of Individuals." In *Reorganizing Popular Politics: Participation and the New Interest Regime in Latin America*, ed. Ruth B. Collier and Samuel Handlin. University Park: Pennsylvania State University Press, 95–131.

Eaton, Kent. 2004. *Politics Beyond the Capital: The Design of Subnational Institutions in South America*. Stanford: Stanford University Press.

ECLAC (Economic Commission for Latin America and the Caribbean). 2009. *Urban Growth Rates*. Santiago, Chile: CEPAL Population Division (DEPUALC).

2011. *CEPALSTAT: Database of Social, Economic, and Environmental Indicators for Latin America and the Caribbean*. Santiago, Chile: CEPAL.

Egusquiza, Abel T. 2000. "Reubicación de la venta ambulante: Experiencias con éxito para la recuperación del espacio público en Lima." UN-Habitat Best Practices Database.

El-Kazaz, Sarah. 2014. "Building Politics: Urban Transformation and Governance in Cairo and Istanbul." PhD diss. Princeton University.

Ellermann, Antje. 2009. *States Against Migrants: Deportation in Germany and the United States*. New York: Cambridge University Press.

Erder, Sema. 1996. *İstanbul'a bir kent kondu Ümraniye*. İstanbul: İletişim Yayınları.

Erman, Tahire. 2001. "The Politics of Squatter (Gecekondu) Studies in Turkey: The Changing Representations of Rural Migrants in the Academic Discourse." *Urban Studies* 38(7): 983–1002.

Esen, Berk, and Sebnem Gumuscu. 2016. "Rising Competitive Authoritarianism in Turkey." *Third World Quarterly* 37(9): 1581–606.

Estévez-Abe, Margarita. 2008. *Welfare and Capitalism in Postwar Japan: Party, Bureaucracy, and Business*. New York: Cambridge University Press.

Evans, Peter. 1995. *Embedded Autonomy: States & Industrial Transformation*. Princeton, NJ: Princeton University Press.

Falleti, Tulia G. 2010. *Decentralization and Subnational Politics in Latin America*. New York: Cambridge University Press.

Feierherd, German G. 2014. "Bypassing the Gates to the Enemy's Backyard: Land-Titling in Authoritarian Peru." Yale University Working Paper.

Ferranti, David De, Guillermo Perry, and Francisco Ferreira. 2004. *Inequality in Latin America: Breaking with History?* Washington, DC: World Bank.

Ferraz, Claudio. 2007. "Electoral Politics and Bureaucratic Discretion: Evidence from Environmental Licenses and Local Elections in Brazil." Instituto de Pesquisa Economica Aplicada Working Paper: 1–43.

Ferrera, Maurizio. 1996. "The 'Southern Model' of Welfare in Social Europe." *Journal of European Social Policy* 6: 17–37.

Field, Erica. 2007. "Entitled to Work: Urban Property Rights and Labor Supply in Peru." *Quarterly Journal of Economics* 122(4): 1451–1602.

Figueroa, Yanny. 2003. "Campamento Esperanza Andina." In *Ampliando la ciudadanía, promoviendo la participación*, ed. Antonieta Surawski and Julia C. Romo. Santiago: Instituto de Asuntos Públicos, 559–93.

Fischer, Brodwyn. 2008. *A Poverty of Rights: Citizenship and Inequality in Twentieth-Century Rio de Janeiro*. Stanford: Stanford University Press.

2014. "A Century in the Present Tense." In *Cities from Scratch: Poverty and Informality in Urban Latin America*, ed. Javier Auyero, Brodwyn Fischer, and Bryan McCann. Durham, NC: Duke University Press, 9–67.

Florian, Alejandro. 1991. "Fedevivienda: The National Federation of Self-Help Community Housing Organizations in Colombia." *Environment and Urbanization* 3(2): 87–91.

France, Anatole. 1905. *The Red Lily*. Paris: Maison Mazarin.

FVP (Fondo de Ventas Populares). 2004. *Encuesta socio-económica línea de base*. Bogotá: Alcaldía Mayor de Bogotá, FVP.

Galiani, Sebastian, and Ernesto Schargrodsky. 2010. "Property Rights for the Poor: Effects of Land Titling." *Journal of Public Economics* 94(9–10): 700–29.

Gans-Morse, Jordan. 2012. "Threats to Property Rights in Russia: From Private Coercion to State Aggression." *Post-Soviet Affairs* 28(3): 263–95.

Garay, Candelaria. 2007. "Social Policy and Collective Action: Unemployed Workers, Community Associations, and Protest in Argentina." *Politics & Society* 35(2): 301–28.

2017. *Including Outsiders: Social Policy Expansion in Latin America*. New York: Cambridge University Press.

García Villegas, Mauricio. 2009. *Normas de papel: la cultura del incumplimiento de reglas*. Bogotá: Siglo de Hombres Editores.

Gauri, Varun, and Daniel M. Brinks. 2010. *Courting Social Justice: Judicial Enforcement of Social and Economic Rights in the Developing World.* New York: Cambridge University Press.

Gaviria, Alejandro, and Jorge Tovar. 2011. "El potencial de la política de vivienda en Colombia." Presented at the III Foro de Vivienda, Bogotá, Colombia.

Gay, Robert. 1994. *Popular Organization and Democracy in Rio De Janeiro: A Tale of Two Favelas.* Philadelphia: Temple University Press.

Geddes, Barbara. 1994. *Politician's Dilemma: Building State Capacity in Latin America.* Berkeley: University of California Press.

Gerring, John. 2007. "Is There a (Viable) Crucial-Case Method?" *Comparative Political Studies* 40(3): 231–53.

Gibson, Edward L. 2013. *Boundary Control: Subnational Authoritarianism in Federal Democracies.* New York: Cambridge University Press.

Gibson, James L. 2008. "Group Identities and Theories of Justice: An Experimental Investigation into the Justice and Injustice of Land Squatting in South Africa." *Journal of Politics* 70(3): 700–16.

Gilbert, Alan. 1981. "Pirates and Invaders: Land Acquisition in Urban Colombia and Venezuela." *World Development* 9(7): 657–78.

1997. "Colombian Housing Policy during the 1990s." In *Colombia: The Politics of Reforming the State*, ed. Eduardo Posada-Carbo. New York: Saint Martin's Press, 155–83.

2002. "On the Mystery of Capital and the Myths of Hernando de Soto: What Difference Does Legal Title Make?" *International Development Planning Review* 24(1): 1–19.

2004. "Helping the Poor through Housing Subsidies: Lessons from Chile, Colombia and South Africa." *Habitat International* 28(1): 13–40.

2008. "Un alcalde de Izquierda: Los logros y fracasos de Lucho Garzón." In *Bogotá: Progreso, gobernabilidad y pobreza*, ed. Alan Gilbert and María Teresa Garcés. Bogotá: Universidad del Rosario Press, 244–89.

2012. "The Struggle for Good Governance: The Difficulty in Reconciling Democracy, Honesty, and Effective Administration." University College of London Working Paper: 1–14.

Gilbert, Alan, and Peter Ward. 1985. *Housing, the State and the Poor: Policy and Practice in Three Latin American Cities.* New York: Cambridge University Press.

Gilens, Martin. 2000. *Why Americans Hate Welfare: Race, Media, and the Politics of Antipoverty Policy.* Chicago: University of Chicago Press.

Giraudy, Agustina. 2015. *Democrats and Autocrats: Pathways of Subnational Undemocratic Regime Continuity Within Democratic Countries.* New York: Oxford University Press.

Glewwe, Paul, and Hall Gillette. 1992. *Poverty and Inequality during Unorthodox Adjustment: The Case of Peru, 1985–1990.* Washington, DC: World Bank.

Gobel, Christian. 2011. "Uneven Policy Implementation in Rural China." *China Journal* 65(1): 53–76.

Göçmen, Ipek. 2014. "Religion, Politics and Social Assistance in Turkey: The Rise of Religiously Motivated Associations." *Journal of European Social Policy* 24(1): 92–103.

Golden, Miriam, and Brian K. Min. 2013. "Distributive Politics Around the World." *Annual Review of Political Science* 16(1): 1–72.

Gonzalez-Ocantos, Ezequiel, Chad K. de Jonge, Carlos Meléndez, Javier Osorio, and David W. Nickerson. 2012. "Vote Buying and Social Desirability Bias: Experimental Evidence from Nicaragua." *American Journal of Political Science* 56(1): 202–17.

Goodfellow, Tom. 2012. "State Effectiveness and the Politics of Urban Development in East Africa: A Puzzle of Two Cities, 2000–2010." PhD diss. London School of Economics.

2015. "Taming the 'Rogue' Sector: Studying State Effectiveness in Africa through Informal Transport Politics." *Comparative Politics* 47(2): 127–47.

Gordon, Roger, and Wei Li. 2009. "Tax Structures in Developing Countries: Many Puzzles and a Possible Explanation." *Journal of Public Economics* 93(7–8): 855–66.

Gordon, Sanford C., and Catherine Hafer. 2014. "Conditional Forbearance as an Alternative to Capture." In *Preventing Regulatory Capture: Special Interest Influence and How to Limit It*, ed. Daniel Carpenter and David A. Moss. New York: Cambridge University Press, 208–39.

Gough, Ian, and Geof Wood. 2006. "A Comparative Welfare Regime Approach to Global Social Policy." *World Development* 34(10): 1696–712.

2008. *Insecurity and Welfare Regimes in Asia, Africa and Latin America: Social Policy in Development Contexts*. New York: Cambridge University Press.

Graham, Carol. 1991. "The APRA Government and the Urban Poor: The PAIT Programme in Lima's Pueblos Jóvenes." *Journal of Latin American Studies* 23(01): 91–130.

1994. *Safety Nets, Politics, and the Poor: Transition to Market Economies*. Washington, DC: Brookings Institution.

Graham, Carol, and Cheikh Kane. 1998. "Opportunistic Spending or Sustaining Reform? Electoral Trends and Public-Expenditure Patterns in Peru, 1990–1995." *Latin American Research Review* 33(1): 67–104.

Güneş-Ayata, Ayşe. 1987. "Migrants and Natives: Urban Bases of Social Conflict." In *Migrants, Workers, and the Social Order*, ed. Jeremy Eades. New York: Tavistock, 234–48.

Guzmán, Romina, Henry Renna, Alejandra Sandoval, and Camila Silva. 2009. *Movimiento de pobladores en lucha: A tomarse Peñalolén para conquistar la ciudad*. Santiago, Chile: Ediciones Sur.

Hacker, Jacob S. 2002. *The Divided Welfare State: The Battles Over Private and Public Social Benefits in the United States*. New York: Cambridge University Press.

Haggard, Stephan, and Robert R. Kaufman. 2008. *Development, Democracy, and Welfare States: Latin America, East Asia, and Eastern Europe*. Princeton, NJ: Princeton University Press.

Haggard, Stephan, Robert R. Kaufman, and James D. Long. 2013. "Income, Occupation, and Preferences for Redistribution in the Developing World." *Studies in Comparative International Development* 48: 113–40.

Hagopian, Frances. Forthcoming. *Reorganizing Representation in Latin America: Parties, Program, and Patronage in Argentina, Brazil, Chile, and Mexico.* New York: Cambridge University Press.

Hall, Peter, and David Soskice. 2001. *Varieties of Capitalism: The Institutional Foundations of Comparative Advantage.* New York: Oxford University Press.

Handlin, Samuel. 2013. "Survey Research and Social Class in Venezuela: Evaluating Alternative Measures and Their Impact on Assessments of Class Voting." *Latin American Politics and Society* 55(1): 141–67.

Harberger, Arnold C. 1978. "On the Use of Distributional Weights in Social Cost-Benefit Analysis." *Journal of Political Economy* 86(2): 87–120.

1984. "Basic Needs versus Distributional Weights in Social Cost-Benefit Analysis." *Economic Development and Cultural Change* 32(3): 455–74.

Hays-Mitchell, M. 1993. "The Ties That Bind: Informal and Formal Sector Linkages in Streetvending." *Environment and Planning A* 25(8): 1085–102.

Helmke, Gretchen, and Steven Levitsky. 2006. *Informal Institutions and Democracy: Lessons from Latin America.* Baltimore, MD: The Johns Hopkins University Press.

Herbst, Jeffrey. 1989. "How the Weak Succeed: Tactics, Political Goods, and Institutions in the Struggle over Land in Zimbabwe." In *Everyday Forms of Peasant Resistance*, ed. Forrest D. Colburn. Armonk, NY: M.E. Sharpe, 198–221.

Hicken, Allen. 2007. "How Do Rules and Institutions Encourage Vote Buying?" In *Elections for Sale: The Causes and Consequences of Vote Buying*, ed. Frederic C. Schaffer. Boulder, CO: Lynne Rienner Publishers, 47–61.

Hidalgo, Daniel, Suresh Naidu, Simeon Nichter, and Neal Richardson. 2010. "Economic Determinants of Land Invasions." *Review of Economics and Statistics* 92(3): 505–23.

Hilgers, Tina. 2008. "Causes and Consequences of Political Clientelism: Mexico's PRD in Comparative Perspective." *Latin American Politics and Society* 50(4): 123–53.

Hipsher, Patricia L. 1996. "Democratization and the Decline of Urban Social Movements in Chile and Spain." *Comparative Politics* 28(3): 273–97.

Hochstetler, Kathryn, and Margaret E. Keck. 2007. *Greening Brazil: Environmental Activism in State and Society.* Durham: Duke University Press.

Holland, Alisha C. 2015. "The Distributive Politics of Enforcement." *American Journal of Political Science* 59(2): 357–71.

2016a. "Forbearance." *American Review of Political Science* 110(2): 232-246.

2016b. "Redistributive Preferences in Truncated Welfare States." Working Paper.

2016c. "Insurgent Successor Parties: Scaling Down to Build a Party After War." In *Challenges of Party-Building in Latin America*, ed. Brandon Van Dyck, James Loxton, Steven Levitsky, and Jorge Domínguez. New York: Cambridge University Press, 273–304.

Holland, Alisha C., and Brian Palmer-Rubin. 2015. "Beyond the Machine: Clientelist Brokers and Interest Organizations in Latin America." *Comparative Political Studies* 48(9): 1186–223.

Holland, Alisha C., and Ben Ross Schneider. 2017. "Easy and Hard Redistribution: The Political Economy of Welfare States in Latin America." Working Paper.

Holston, James. 2008. *Insurgent Citizenship: Disjunctions of Democracy and Modernity in Brazil.* Princeton, NJ: Princeton University Press.

Howard, Christopher. 1999. *The Hidden Welfare State: Tax Expenditures and Social Policy in the United States.* Princeton, NJ: Princeton University Press.

Htun, Mala. 2003. *Sex and the State: Abortion, Divorce, and the Family under Latin American Dictatorships and Democracies.* New York: Cambridge University Press.

Huber, Evelyne, and John D. Stephens. 2012. *Democracy and the Left: Social Policy and Inequality in Latin America.* Chicago: University of Chicago Press.

Hummel, Calla. 2017. "Disobedient Markets: Street Vendors, Enforcement, and State Intervention in Collective Action," *Comparative Political Studies*, Online.

İnan, Feride. 2013. "Turkey." In *Civil 20 Proposals for Strong, Sustainable, Balanced and Inclusive Growth.* Moscow: Logos Press, G20 Research Group, 192–201.

INEI (Instituto Nacional de Estadísticañ e Informática). 2004–2014. *Encuesta Nacional de Hogares (ENAHO).* Lima: INEI.

IOP (Instituto de Opinión Pública). 2008–2012. *Estado de la opinion pública sobre Lima.* Lima: IOP.

İTO (İstanbul Ticaret Odası). 1994. *İstanbul Ticaret Odası'nın Önerisi.* Istanbul: İTO.

IU (Izquierda Unida). 1986. *Plan de Gobierno Municipal de Izquierda Unida 1987–89.* Lima: Petit Thouars.

Jaramillo, Miguel. 2014. "The Incidence of Social Spending and Taxes in Peru." *Public Finance Review* 42(3): 391–412.

Jaramillo, Pilar D., Andrés C. Villamil, and Jon G. Bañales. 2008. *Espacio público y derecho a la ciudad: La política de espacio público físico y la venta informal en Bogotá.* Bogotá: Javegraf.

Jaramillo, Samuel, Oscar Alfonso, and Noriko Hataya. 1996. *Urban Development and People's Organization in Bogota.* Tokyo: Institute of Developing Economics.

Jha, Saumitra, Vijayendra Rao, and Michael Woolcock. 2007. "Governance in the Gullies: Democratic Responsiveness and Leadership in Delhi's Slums." *World Development* 35(2): 230–46.

Karaman, Ozan. 2014. "Resisting Urban Renewal in Istanbul." *Urban Geography* 35(2): 290–310.

Karl, Terry L. 2003. "The Vicious Cycle of Inequality in Latin America." In *What Justice? Whose Justice?*, ed. Susan E. Eckstein and Timothy P. Wickham-Crowley. Berkeley: University of California Press, 133–57.

Karpantschof, René. 2011. "Bargaining and Barricades: The Political Struggle over the Freetown Christiania, 1971–2011." In *Space for Urban Alternatives?*

*Christiania 1971–2011*, ed. Håkan Thörn, Cathrin Wasshede, and Tomas Nilson. Hedemora: Gidlunds Förlag, 38–67.

Karpat, Kemal H. 1976. *The Gecekondu: Rural Migration and Urbanization*. New York: Cambridge University Press.

Karst, Kenneth. 1971. "Rights in Land and Housing in an Informal Legal System: The Barrios of Caracas." *American Journal of Comparative Law* 19(3): 550–74.

Kaufman, Robert R. 2009. "The Political Effects of Inequality in Latin America: Some Inconvenient Facts." *Comparative Politics* 41(3): 21.

Keleş, Rusen. 2010. *Kentlesme Politikası [Urbanization Policies]*. 11th ed. Ankara: Imge Publications.

Kelling, George L., and James Q. Wilson. 1982. "Broken Windows." *Atlantic* 249(March): 29–38.

Keyder, Çağlar. 1999. "The Housing Market from Informal to Global." In *Istanbul: Between the Global and the Local*. Lanham, MD: Rowman & Littlefield, 143–60.

2005. "Globalization and Social Exclusion in Istanbul." *International Journal of Urban and Regional Research* 29(1): 124–35.

Khemani, Stuti. 2007. "Can Information Campaigns Overcome Political Obstacles to Serving the Poor?" In *The Politics of Service Delivery in Democracies: Better Access for the Poor*, ed. Shantayanan Devarajan and Ingrid Widlund. Stockholm: EGDI Secretariat Edita, 56–69.

Kitschelt, Herbert. 2000. "Linkages between Citizens and Politicians in Democratic Polities." *Comparative Political Studies* 33(6–7): 845–79.

Kitschelt, Herbert, Kirk Hawkins, Guillermo Rosas, and Elizabeth J. Zechmeister. 2010. "Patterns of Programmatic Party Competition in Latin America." In *Latin American Party Systems*, ed. Herbert Kitschelt, Kirk A. Hawkins, Juan Pablo Luna, Guillermo Rosas, and Elizabeth J. Zechmeister. New York: Cambridge University Press, 14–69.

Kitschelt, Herbert, and Steven Wilkinson. 2007. "Citizen-Politician Linkages: An Introduction." In *Patrons, Clients and Policies: Patterns of Democratic Accountability and Political Competition*, ed. Herbert Kitschelt and Steven Wilkinson. New York: Cambridge University Press, 1–49.

Klaarhamer, Raul. 1989. "The Chilean Squatter Movement and the State." In *Urban Social Movements in the Third World*, ed. Frans Schuurman and Ton Van Naerssen. New York: Routledge Press, 177–97.

Kleine, Mareike. 2013. *Informal Governance in the European Union*. Ithaca: Cornell University Press.

Konda. 2006. *Social Structure Survey*. Istanbul: Konda Research and Consultancy.

Kurtz, Marcus J. 2004. "The Dilemmas of Democracy in the Open Economy: Lessons from Latin America." *World Politics* 56(2): 262–302.

Kusnetzoff, Fernando. 1987. "Urban and Housing Policies under Chile's Military Dictatorship 1973–1985." *Latin American Perspectives* 14(2): 157–86.

Kuyucu, Tuna. 2014. "Law, Property and Ambiguity: The Uses and Abuses of Legal Ambiguity in Remaking Istanbul's Informal Settlements." *International Journal of Urban and Regional Research* 38(2): 609–27.

Kuyucu, Tuna, and Özlem Unsal. 2010. "'Urban Transformation' as State-Led Property Transfer: An Analysis of Two Cases of Urban Renewal in Istanbul." *Urban Studies* 47(7): 1479–99.

Lagos, Ricardo. 2012. *The Southern Tiger: Chile's Fight for a Democratic and Prosperous Future*. New York: Palgrave Macmillan.

Landau, David. 2012. "The Reality of Social Rights Enforcement." *Harvard International Law Journal* 53(1): 402–58.

Latinobarometer. 1995–2000. *Latinobarómetro Banco de Datos*. Santiago, Chile: Corporación Latinobarómetro.

Leeds, Elizabeth. 1974. "Forms of 'Squatment' Political Organization: The Politics of Control in Brazil." Master's Thesis. University of Texas at Austin.

Levi, Margaret. 1988. *Of Rule and Revenue*. Berkeley, CA: University of California Press.

Levitsky, Steven, and Kenneth Roberts. 2011. "Latin America's 'Left Turn.'" In *The Resurgence of the Latin American Left*. Baltimore, MD: Johns Hopkins University Press, 1–28.

Levitsky, Steven, and María Victoria Murillo. 2009. "Variation in Institutional Strength." *Annual Review of Political Science* 12(1): 115–33.

2013. "Building Institutions on Weak Foundations." *Journal of Democracy* 24(2): 93–107.

2014. "Building Institutions on Weak Foundations: Lessons from Latin America." In *Reflections on Uneven Democracies: The Legacy of Guillermo O'Donnell*, ed. Daniel Brinks, Marcelo Leiras, and Scott Mainwaring. Baltimore, MD: John Hopkins University Press, 189–213.

Levitsky, Steven, and Maxwell A. Cameron. 2003. "Democracy without Parties? Political Parties and Regime Change in Fujimori's Peru." *Latin American Politics and Society* 45(3): 1–33.

Levy, Santiago. 2008. *Good Intentions, Bad Outcomes: Social Policy, Informality, and Economic Growth*. Washington, DC: Brookings Institution Press.

Lieberman, Evan S. 2003. *Race and Regionalism in the Politics of Taxation in Brazil and South Africa*. New York: Cambridge University Press.

Lindert, Kathy, Emmanuel Skoufias, and Joseph Shapiro. 2010. "Globalization and the Role of Public Transfers in Redistributing Income in Latin America and the Caribbean." *World Development* 38(6): 895–907.

Lindert, Peter. 2004. *Growing Public*. New York: Cambridge University Press.

Lima Cómo Vamos. 2011. *Informe de Percepción sobre Calidad de Vida*. Lima: Lima Cómo Vamos.

Lipsky, Michael. 1980. *Street Level Bureaucracy: Dilemmas of the Individual in Public Services*. New York: Russell Sage Foundation.

Lovering, John, and Hade Türkmen. 2011. "Bulldozer Neo-Liberalism in Istanbul: The State-Led Construction of Property Markets, and the Displacement of the Urban Poor." *International Planning Studies* 16(1): 73–96.

Lowi, Theodore J. 1964. "American Business, Public Policy, Case-Studies, and Political Theory." *World Politics* 16(4): 677–715.

Luna, Juan Pablo. 2010. "Segmented Party – Voter Linkages in Latin America: The Case of the UDI." *Journal of Latin American Studies* 42(02): 325–56.

2015. *Segmented Representation: Political Party Strategies in Unequal Democracies.* New York: Oxford University Press.

Luna, Juan Pablo, and Cristóbal Kaltwasser Rovira. 2014. "The Right in Contemporary Latin America: A Framework for Analysis." In *The Resilience of the Latin American Right.* Baltimore, MD: John Hopkins University Press, 1–25.

Luna, Juan Pablo, and Rodrigo Mardones. 2010. "Chile: Are the Parties Over?" *Journal of Democracy* 21(3): 107–21.

Lustig, Nora, Carola Pessino, and John Scott. 2014. "The Impact of Taxes and Social Spending on Inequality and Poverty in Argentina, Bolivia, Brazil, Mexico, Peru, and Uruguay." *Public Finance Review* 42(3): 287–303.

Luttmer, Erzo. 2001. "Group Loyalty and the Taste for Redistribution." *Journal of Political Economy* 109(3): 500–28.

Mahon Jr., James E. 2013. "Tax Reforms and Income Distribution in Latin America." In *The Great Gap: Inequality and the Politics of Income Redistribution in Latin America*, ed. Merike Blofield. University Park: Pennsylvania State University Press, 313–47.

Mahoney, James, and Kathleen Thelen. 2010. "A Theory of Gradual Institutional Change." In *Explaining Institutional Change: Ambiguity, Agency, and Power*, ed. James Mahoney and Kathleen Thelen. New York: Cambridge University Press, 1–37.

Maldonado Copello, Mercedes. 2009. "¿Es posible anticiparse a la urbanización informal?" *Lincoln Institute of Land Policy* 10: 325–43.

Malthus, Thomas. 2008[1803]. *An Essay on the Principle of Population.* New York: Oxford University Press.

Mangin, William. 1967. "Latin American Squatter Settlements: A Problem and a Solution." *Latin American Research Review* 2(3): 65–98.

Mani, Anandi, and Sharun Mukand. 2007. "Democracy, Visibility and Public Good Provision." *Journal of Development Economics* 83(2): 506–29.

Mann, Michael. 1984. "The Autonomous Power of the State: Its Origins, Mechanisms, and Results." *European Journal of Sociology* 25(2): 185–213.

Marcano, Luis, and Inder J. Ruprah. 2008. "An Impact Evaluation of Chile's Progressive Housing Program." Inter-American Development Bank Working Paper 0207: 1–19.

Mares, Isabela. 2003. *The Politics of Social Risk: Business and Welfare State Development.* New York: Cambridge University Press.

2005. "Social Protection Around the World: External Insecurity, State Capacity, and Domestic Political Cleavages." *Comparative Political Studies* 38(6): 623–51.

Mares, Isabela, and Lauren Young. 2016. "Buying, Expropriating, and Stealing Votes." *Annual Review of Political Science* 19: 267–288.

Mares, Isabela, and Matthew E. Carnes. 2009. "Social Policy in Developing Countries." *Annual Review of Political Science* 12(1): 93–113.

Markus, Stanislav. 2015. *Property, Predation, and Protection: Piranha Capitalism in Russia and Ukraine.* New York: Cambridge University Press.

Marschall, Melissa, Abdullah Aydogan, and Alper Bulut. 2016. "Does Housing Create Votes? Explaining the Electoral Success of the AKP in Turkey." *Electoral Studies* 42: 201–12.

Marshall, Thomas H. 2000[1949]. "Citizenship and Social Class." In *The Welfare State Reader*, ed. Christopher Pierson. Malden, MA: Polity, 30–50.

Martinez Franzoni, Juliana. 2008. "Welfare Regimes in Latin America: Capturing Constellations of Markets, Families, and Policies." *Latin American Politics and Society* 50(2): 67–100.

Mayo, Stephen, and Shlomo Angel. 1993. *Housing: Enabling Markets to Work.* Washington, DC: World Bank.

McCubbins, Mathew D., Roger G. Noll, and Barry R. Weingast. 1987. "Administrative Procedures as Instruments of Political Control." *Journal of Law, Economics, & Organization* 3(2): 243–77.

McKeown, Timothy J. 1999. "Case Studies and the Statistical Worldview." *International Organization* 53(1): 161–90.

Medina, Luis Fernando, and Susan C. Stokes. 2007. "Monopoly and Monitoring: An Approach to Political Clientelism." In *Patrons, Clients and Policies: Patterns of Democratic Accountability and Political Competition*, ed. Herbert Kitschelt and Steven Wilkinson. New York: Cambridge University Press, 68–83.

MEF (Ministerio de Economía y Finanzas). 2003. *El Impacto del programa "A Trabajar Urbano": Ganancias de ingreso y utilidad de las obras.* Lima: MEF.

Mello, Joao De, Daniel Mejía, and Lucía Suárez. 2013. "The Pharmacological Channel Revisited: Alcohol Sales Restrictions and Crime Revisited." *Inter-American Development Bank Working Paper* 394: 1–36.

Meltzer, Allan H., and Scott F. Richard. 1981. "A Rational Theory of the Size of Government." *Journal of Political Economy* 89(5): 914–27.

Méndez, Juan E., Guillermo A. O'Donnell, and Paulo S. Pinheiro. 1999. *The (Un) Rule of Law and the Underprivileged in Latin America.* Notre Dame: University of Notre Dame Press.

Mettler, Suzanne. 2011. *The Submerged State: How Invisible Government Policies Undermine American Democracy.* Chicago: University of Chicago Press.

Migdal, Joel S. 1988. *Strong Societies and Weak States: State-Society Relations and State Capabilities in the Third World.* Princeton, NJ: Princeton University Press.

2001. *State in Society: Studying How States and Societies Transform and Constitute One Another.* New York: Cambridge University Press.

Min, Brian. 2015. *Power and the Vote: Elections and Electricity in the Developing World.* New York: Cambridge University Press.

Min, Brian, and Miriam Golden. 2014. "Electoral Cycles in Electricity Losses in India." *Energy Policy* 65: 619–25.

MINVU (Ministerio de Vivienda y Urbanismo). 2013. *Mapa social de campamentos.* Santiago, Chile: MINVU.

Mockus, Antanas. 2002. "Co-Existence as Harmonization of Law, Morality, and Culture." *Prospects* 32(1): 19–37.

2005. "Balance pedagógico en la recuperación del espacio público." In *Espacio público y ciudad*, ed. Andrés Gaviria Garcia. Bogotá: Cámara de Comercio de Bogotá, Alcaldía Distrital de Bogotá, 18–25.

2012. "Make Unfamiliar the Familiar." Presentation at the MIT DUSP Conference on Reframing International Development, Cambridge, MA, April 2.

Mockus, Antanas, Henry Murrain, and Maria Villa. 2012. *Antipodas de la violencia: Desafios de cultura ciudadana para la crisis de (in)seguridad en America Latina*. Washington, DC: Inter-American Development Bank.

Moene, Karl O., and Michael Wallerstein. 2003. "Earnings Inequality and Welfare Spending: A Disaggregated Analysis." *World Politics* 55(4): 485–516.

Moncada, Eduardo. 2016. *Cities, Business, and the Politics of Urban Violence in Latin America*. Stanford: Stanford University Press.

Morgan, Jana. 2011. *Bankrupt Representation and Party System Collapse*. University Park: Penn State University Press.

Mudde, Cas Mudde and Cristóbal Rovira Kaltwasser. 2013. "Exclusionary vs. Inclusionary Populism: Comparing Contemporary Europe and Latin America." *Governance and Opposition* 48(2): 147–74.

Muñoz, Paula. 2014. "An Informational Theory of Campaign Clientelism." *Comparative Politics* 47(1): 79–98.

Murillo, Maria Victoria. 2001. *Labor Unions, Partisan Coalitions, and Market Reforms in Latin America*. New York: Cambridge University Press.

Murillo, María Victoria, and Andrew Schrank. 2005. "With a Little Help from My Friends: Partisan Politics, Transnational Alliances, and Labor Rights in Latin America." *Comparative Political Studies* 38(8): 971–99.

Murphy, Edward. 2015. *For a Proper Home: Housing Rights in the Margins of Urban Chile, 1960–2010*. Pittsburgh, PA: University of Pittsburgh Press.

MVCS (Ministerio de Vivienda, Construcción y Saneamiento). 2005. *Situación de los barrios urbano- marginales en el Perú*. Lima: MVCS.

2006. *Políticas y estrategias 2007–2011*. Lima: MVCS.

2011. *Indicadores de vivienda*. Lima: MVCS.

MVCT (Ministerio de Vivienda, Ciudad y Territorio). 2014. *Colombia: Cien años de políticas habitacionales*. Bogotá: MVCT.

Nelson, Joan. 1970. "The Urban Poor: Disruption or Political Integration in Third World Cities?" *World Politics* 22(3): 393–414.

Nelson, Nancy L. 1992. "Public Order and Private Entrepreneurs: The Pocket Economy of Street Vending in Bogota, Colombia." PhD diss. University of New Mexico.

Nichter, Simeon. 2008. "Vote Buying or Turnout Buying? Machine Politics and the Secret Ballot." *American Political Science Review* 102(01): 19–31.

North, Douglass C. 1990. *Institutions, Institutional Change and Economic Performance*. New York: Cambridge University Press.

Oates, Wallace E. 1972. *Fiscal Federalism*. Cheltenham, UK: Edward Elgar.

O'Brien, Kevin, and Lianjiang Li. 1999. "Selective Policy Implementation in Rural China." *Comparative Politics* 31(2): 167–86.

O'Donnell, Guillermo. 1993. "On the State, Democratization, and Some Conceptual Problems." *World Development* 21(8): 1355–69.

OECD. 2011. "Unemployment Insurance." Social Expenditure Database (SOCX).

O'Neill, Kathleen. 2005. *Decentralizing the State: Elections, Parties, and Local Power in the Andes*. New York: Cambridge University Press.

Onoma, Ato Kwamena. 2009. "The Contradictory Potential of Institutions: The Rise and Decline of Land Documentation in Kenya." In *Explaining Institutional Change: Ambiguity, Agency, and Power*, ed. James Mahoney and Kathleen Thelen. New York: Cambridge University Press, 63–94.

2010. *The Politics of Property Rights Institutions in Africa*. New York: Cambridge University Press.

Ostiguy, Pierre. 2009. "The High and Low in Politics: A Two-Dimensional Political Space for Comparative Analysis and Electoral Studies." Helen Kellogg Institute for International Studies Working Paper 360: 1–64.

Oxhorn, Philip. 1995. *Organizing Civil Society: The Popular Sectors and the Struggle for Democracy in Chile*. University Park: Pennsylvania State Press.

1998. "The Social Foundations of Latin America's Recurrent Populism: Problems of Popular Sector Class Formation and Collective Action." *Journal of Historical Sociology* 11(June): 212–46.

Özdemir, Dilek. 2011. "The Role of the Public Sector in the Provision of Housing Supply in Turkey, 1950–2009." *International Journal of Urban and Regional Research* 35(6): 1099–117.

Özler, S. Ilgu. 2000. "Politics of the Gecekondu in Turkey: The Political Choices of Urban Squatters in National Elections." *Turkish Studies* 1(2): 39–58.

Pagés, Carmen, Gaëlle Le B. Pierre, and Stefano Scarpetta. 2009. *Job Creation in Latin America and the Caribbean: Recent Trends and Policy Challenges*. Washington, DC: World Bank Publications.

Panfichi, Aldo. 1997. "The Authoritarian Alternative: 'Anti-Politics' in the Popular Sectors of Lima," In *The New Politics of Inequality in Latin America*, ed. Douglas A. Chalmers. New York: Oxford University Press, 217–36.

Pasotti, Eleonora. 2009. *Political Branding in Cities: The Decline of Machine Politics in Bogotá, Naples, and Chicago*. New York: Cambridge University Press.

Pease Garcia, Henry. 1989. *Democracia local: Reflexiones y experiencias*. Lima: DESCO.

Peñalosa Londoño, Enrique. 2000. "La Bogotá de los peatones: Una ciudad para la gente." La ciudad peatonal, Report by the Alcaldía Mayor de Bogotá.

Peñalver, Eduardo Moisés, and Sonia Katyal. 2010. *Property Outlaws: How Squatters, Pirates and Protesters Improve the Law of Ownership*. New Haven: Yale University Press.

Perlman, Janice. 1974. *The Myth of Marginality: Urban Poverty and Politics in Rio de Janeiro*. Berkeley, CA: University of California Press.

Perotti, Roberto. 1996. "Growth, Income Distribution, and Democracy: What the Data Say." *Journal of Economic Growth* 1(2): 149–87.

Perry, Guillermo. 2007. *Informality: Exit and Exclusion*. Washington, DC: World Bank.

Pierson, Paul. 1993. "When Effect Becomes Cause: Policy Feedback and Political Change." *World Politics* 45(4): 595–628.

1994. *Dismantling the Welfare State? Reagan, Thatcher and the Politics of Retrenchment.* New York: Cambridge University Press.

2000. "Increasing Returns, Path Dependence, and the Study of Politics." *American Political Science Review* 94(2): 251–67.

Pinarcioğlu, Melih, and Oğuz Işik. 2008. "Not Only Helpless but Also Hopeless: Changing Dynamics of Urban Poverty in Turkey, the Case of Sultanbeyli, Istanbul." *European Planning Studies* 16(1): 1353–70.

Piven, Frances F. and Richard A. Cloward. 1971. *Regulating the Poor: The Functions of Public Welfare.* New York: Pantheon.

Pontusson, Jonas. 2005. *Inequality and Prosperity: Social Europe vs. Liberal America.* Ithaca, NY: Cornell University Press.

Portes, Alejandro. 1989. "Latin American Urbanization during the Years of the Crisis." *Latin American Research Review* 24(3): 7–44.

Portes, Alejandro, and John Walton. 1976. *Urban Latin America: The Political Position from Above and Below.* Austin: University of Texas Press.

Portes, Alejandro, and Kelly Hoffman. 2003. "Latin American Class Structures: Their Composition and Change during the Neoliberal Era." *Latin American Research Review* 38(1): 41–82.

Portes, Alejandro, and Manuel Castells. 1989. "World Underneath: The Origins, Dyanamics, and Effects of the Informal Economy." In *The Informal Economy: Studies in Advanced and Less Developed Countries*, ed. Alejandro Portes, Manuel Castells, and Laura Benton. Baltimore, MD: Johns Hopkins University Press, 11–41.

Post, Alison E. 2014. *Foreign and Domestic Investment in Argentina: The Politics of Privatized Infrastructure.* New York: Cambridge University Press.

Pribble, Jennifer. 2010. "Worlds Apart: Social Policy Regimes in Latin America." *Studies in Comparative International Development* 46(2): 191–216.

2013. *Welfare and Party Politics in Latin America.* New York: Cambridge University Press.

2015. "The Politics of Building Municipal Institutional Effectiveness in Chile." *Latin American Politics & Society* 57(3): 100–21.

Rajan, Raghuram G. 2010. *Fault Lines: How Hidden Fractures Still Threaten the World Economy.* Princeton, NJ: Princeton University Press.

Ramírez Corzo, Daniel, and Gustavo Riofrío. 2006. *Formalización de la propiedad y mejoramiento de barrios: Bien legal, bien informal.* Lima: DESCO.

Ray, Talton F. 1969. *The Politics of the Barrios of Venezuela.* Berkeley: University of California Press.

Razmilic, Slaven. 2010. "Property Values, Housing Subsidies and Incentives: Evidence from Chile's Current Housing Policies." MA Thesis. Massachusetts Institute of Technology.

Remmer, Karen L. 1985. "Redemocratization and the Impact of Authoritarian Rule in Latin America." *Comparative Politics* 17(3): 253–75.

Resnick, Danielle. 2012. "Opposition Parties and the Urban Poor in African Democracies." *Comparative Political Studies* 45(11): 1351–78.

2013. *Urban Poverty and Party Populism in African Democracies*. New York: Cambridge University Press.

Ridgley, Jennifer. 2013. "Cities of Refuge: Immigration Enforcement, Police, and the Insurgent Genealogies of Citizenship in US Sanctuary Cities." *Urban Geography* 29(1): 53–77.

Riofrío, Gustavo. 1991. *Producir la ciudad popular de los '90: Entre el mercado y el estado*. Lima: DESCO.

2003. "The Case of Lima, Peru." In *Understanding Slums: Case Studies for the UN-Habitat Global Report on Human Settlements*, ed. Patrick Wakely. London: University College London, 195–228.

Roberts, Kenneth. 1995. "Neoliberalism and the Transformation of Populism in Latin America: The Peruvian Case." *World Politics* 48: 82–116.

1998. *Deepening Democracy?: The Modern Left and Social Movements in Chile and Peru*. Stanford, CA: Stanford University Press.

2002. "Social Inequalities without Class Cleavages in Latin America's Neoliberal Era." *Studies in Comparative International Development* 36(4): 3–33.

2006. "Populism, Political Conflict, and Grass-Roots Organization in Latin America." *Comparative Politics* 38(2): 127.

2015. *Changing Course in Latin America: Party Systems in the Neoliberal Era*. New York: Cambridge University Press.

Roberts, Kenneth, and Moisés Arce. 1998. "Neoliberalism and Lower-Class Voting Behavior in Peru." *Comparative Political Studies* 31(2): 217–46.

Robinson, James A. 2010. "The Political Economy of Redistribution." In *Declining Inequality in Latin America: A Decade of Progress?*, ed. Luis López-Calva and Nora Lustig. New York and Washington, DC: United Nations Development Programme and Brookings Institution Press, 39–71.

Robinson, James A., and Thierry Verdier. 2013. "The Political Economy of Clientelism." *Scandinavian Journal of Economics* 115(2): 260–91.

Rocha, Ricardo, Fabio Sánchez, and Leonardo García. 2009. "Ventas callejeras y espacio público: Efectos sobre el comercio de Bogotá." *Desarrollo y Sociedad* 63(1): 245–68.

Rodríguez, Alfredo, and Ana Sugranyes. 2005. *Los Con Techo: Un desafío para la política de vivienda social*. Santiago, Chile: Ediciones Sur.

Rodríguez, Jorge, Juan A. Roeschmann, Antonio Garrido, and Carla Vanelli. 2006. *Gasto público en vivienda*. Santiago, Chile: Estudio de Finanzas Públicas, Ministerio de Hacienda.

Rodríguez-Franco, Diana. 2016. "Internal Wars, Taxation, and State Building." *American Sociological Review* 81(1): 190–213.

Rodríguez-Garavito, César, and Diana Rodríguez-Franco. 2015. *Radical Deprivation on Trial: The Impact of Judicial Activism on Socioeconomic Rights in the Global South*. New York: Cambridge University Press.

Rodrik, Dani. 2012. "The Turkish Economy after the Global Financial Crisis." *Ekonomi-tek* 1(1): 41–62.

Roever, Sally. 2005. "Negotiating Formality: Informal Sector, Market, and State in Peru." PhD diss. University of California, Berkeley.

2006. "Street Trade in Latin America: Demographic Trends, Legal Issues, and Vending Organizations in Six Cities." Wiego Urban Policies Programme.

Romer, Thomas. 1975. "Individual Welfare, Majority Voting, and the Properties of a Linear Income Tax." *Journal of Public Economics* 4(2): 163–85.

Ronconi, Lucas. 2010. "Enforcement and Compliance with Labor Regulations in Argentina." *Industrial and Labor Relations Review* 63(4): 719–36.

Ronda, Stéphanie. 2000. "Estrategias de legitimaciones y discursos: La utilización de las políticas de rehabilitación de los centros históricos." In *Desarrollo cultural y gestión en centros históricos*, ed. Fernando Carrión. Quito, Ecuador: FLACSO, 86–103.

Rueda, David and Daniel Stegmueller. 2016. "The Externalities of Inequality: Fear of Crime and Preferences for Redistribution in Western Europe," *American Journal of Political Science* 60(2): 472–89.

Rufín, Carlos. 2015. "Politics of Utility Service Provision in Brazil's Favelas." Working Paper.

Sabatini, Francisco, Guillermo Wormald, Carlos Sierralta, and Paul A. Peters. 2009. "Residential Segregation in Santiago: Scale-Related Effects and Trends, 1992–2002." In *Urban Segregation and Governance in the Americas*, ed. Bryan R. Roberts and Robert H. Wilson. New York: Palgrave Macmillan, 121–45.

Santos, Rafael. 2007. "Bogotá: El Colapso de una maquinaria política." *Documentos de Trabajo en Análisis Económico* 6(13): 1–28.

Sarica, Salih O. 2012. "Turkish Housing Policies: A Case Study on Mass Housing Provision in the Last Decade." MA Thesis. University of Louisville.

Schady, Norbert R. 2000. "The Political Economy of Expenditures by the Peruvian Social Fund (FONCODES), 1991–95." *American Political Science Review* 94(2): 289–304.

Schamis, Hector E. 1991. "Reconceptualizing Latin American Authoritarianism in the 1970s: From Bureaucratic-Authoritarianism to Neoconservatism." *Comparative Politics* 23(2): 201–20.

Schneider, Ben Ross. 2013. *Hierarchical Capitalism in Latin America: Business, Labor, and the Challenges of Equitable Development*. New York: Cambridge University Press.

Schneider, Cathy. 1995. *Shantytown Protest in Pinochet's Chile*. Philadelphia, PA: Temple University Press.

Schönwälder, Gerd. 2002. *Linking Civil Society and the State: Urban Popular Movements, the Left, and Local Government in Peru, 1980–1992*. University Park: Pennsylvania State University Press.

Schrank, Andrew. 2009. "Professionalization and Probity in a Patrimonial State: Labor Inspectors in the Dominican Republic." *Latin American Politics & Society* 51(2): 91–115.

Scott, James C. 1969. "Corruption, Machine Politics, and Political Change." *American Political Science Review* 63(4): 1142–58.

Seawright, Jason. 2012. *Party-System Collapse: The Roots of Crisis in Peru and Venezuela*. Stanford: Stanford University Press.

Segura-Ubiergo, Alex. 2007. *The Political Economy of the Welfare State in Latin America: Globalization, Democracy, and Development*. New York: Cambridge University Press.

Şenyapılı, Tansı. 2004. "Charting the 'Voyage' of Squatter Housing in Urban Spatial 'Quadruped'." *European Journal of Turkish Studies* 1: 1–43.

SDP (Secretaría Distrital de Planeación). 2011. *Base de Legalización de Barrios*. Bogotá: SDP, and Observatorio del Mercado Informal de Suelo y Vivienda.

Shayo, Moses. 2009. "A Model of Social Identity with an Application to Political Economy: Nation, Class, and Redistribution." *American Political Science Review* 103(2): 147–174.

Simmons, Erica. 2016. *Meaningful Resistance: Market Reforms and the Roots of Social Protest in Latin America*. New York: Cambridge University Press.

Skocpol, Theda. 1985. "Bringing the State Back In: Strategies of Analysis in Current Research." In *Bringing the State Back In*, ed. Peter B. Evans, Dietrich Rueschemeyer, and Theda Skocpol. New York: Cambridge University Press, 3–39.

1995. *Protecting Soldiers and Mothers: The Political Origins of Social Policy in United States*. Cambridge, MA: Belknap Press.

Skouras, Spyros, and Nicos Christodoulakis. 2014. "Electoral Misgovernance Cycles: Evidence from Wildfires and Tax Evasion in Greece." *Public Choice* 159(3): 533–59.

Slater, Dan, and Daniel Ziblatt. 2013. "The Enduring Indispensability of the Controlled Comparison." *Comparative Political Studies* 46(10): 1301–27.

Slater, Dan, and Diana Kim. 2015. "Standoffish States: Nonliterate Leviathans in Southeast Asia." *TRaNS: Trans-Regional and -National Studies of Southeast Asia* 3(1): 25–44.

Soifer, Hillel D. 2013. "State Power and the Economic Origins of Democracy." *Studies in Comparative International Development* 48(1): 1–22.

2015. *State Building in Latin America*. New York: Cambridge University Press.

Solanas Domínguez, Marta. 2013. "Andalucía hace camino: Ocupaciones populares y respuesta institucional." In *La tierra es nuestra*, ed. Charlotte Mathivet. Paris: Passerelle, 170–5.

Solt, Frederick. 2016. "The Standardized World Income Inequality Database." *Social Science Quarterly* 97, SWIID Version 5.0, October 2014.

Staniland, Paul. 2012. "States, Insurgents, and Wartime Political Orders." *Perspectives on Politics* 10(2): 243–64.

Stepan, Alfred C. 1978. *The State and Society: Peru in Comparative Perspective*. Princeton, NJ: Princeton University Press.

Stigler, George. 1970. "The Optimum Enforcement of Laws." *Journal of Political Economy* 78(3): 526–36.

Stokes, Susan. 1991. "Politics and Latin America's Urban Poor: Reflections from a Lima Shantytown." *Latin American Research Review* 26(2): 75–101.

1995. *Cultures in Conflict: Social Movements and the State in Peru*. Berkeley: University of California Press.

2005. "Perverse Accountability: A Formal Model of Machine Politics with Evidence from Argentina." *American Political Science Review* 99(3): 315–25.

Stokes, Susan, Thad Dunning, Marcelo Nazareno, and Valeria Brusco. 2013. *Brokers, Voters, and Clientelism: The Puzzle of Distributive Politics*. New York: Cambridge University Press.

Sulmont, David, and Alvaro Gordillo. 2011. "Elecciones municipales 2010: Factores explicativos de la orientación de voto de los Limeños." In *El nuevo poder en las regiones*, ed. Omar Coronel and María Ana Rodríguez. Lima: Pontificia Universidad Católica del Perú, 58–72.

Sun, Xin. 2015. "Selective Enforcement of Land Regulations: Why Large-Scale Violators Succeed." *The China Journal* 74(1): 66–90.

Szalachman, Raquel, and María Paz Collinao. 2010. "Estimaciones de gasto social en vivienda y desarrollo urbano para algunos países de América Latina y el Caribe." CEPAL Working Paper 142.

Szwarcberg, Mariela. 2015. *Mobilizing Poor Voters: Machine Politics, Clientelism, and Social Networks in Argentina*. New York: Cambridge University Press.

Tanaka, Martín. 2002. *La dinámica de los actores regionales y el proceso de descentralización*. Lima: Instituto de Estudios Peruanos (IEP).

Taylor, Lewis. 1990. "One Step Forward, Two Steps Back: The Peruvian Izquierda Unida." *Journal of Communist Studies* 6(3): 108–19.

Tendler, Judith. 2002. "Small Firms, the Informal Sector, and the Devil's Deal." *Institute of Development Studies Bulletin* 33(3): 1–14.

Thachil, Tariq. 2015a. *Elite Parties, Poor Voters: How Social Services Win Votes in India*. New York: Cambridge University Press.

2015b. "Does Police Repression Increase Cooperation Between Migrants? A Study of Informal Urban Marketplaces in India." Working Paper.

Titmuss, Richard M. 1965. "The Role of Redistribution in Social Policy." *Social Security Bulletin* 28(1): 14–20.

Torcal, Mariano, and Scott Mainwaring. 2003. "The Political Recrafting of Social Bases of Party Competition: Chile, 1973–95." *British Journal of Political Science* 33(1): 55–84.

Torres Tovar, Carlos A. 2009. *Ciudad Informal Colombiana: Barrios construidos por la gente*. Bogotá: Universidad Nacional de Colombia.

Tripp, Aili M. 1997. *Changing the Rules: The Politics of Liberalization and the Urban Informal Economy in Tanzania*. Berkeley: University of California Press.

Tsai, Lily L. 2015. "Constructive Noncompliance." *Comparative Politics* 47(3): 253–79.

Tuesta Soldevilla, Fernando. 2014. *Una Onda Expansiva: Las revocatorias en el Perú y América Latina*. Lima: PUCP-Fondo Editorial.

Tuğal, Cihan. 2009. *Passive Revolution: Absorbing the Islamic Challenge to Capitalism*. Stanford: Stanford University Press.

2011. "The Islamic Making of a Capitalist Habitus." In *Comparing European Workers: Experiences and inequalities*, ed. David Brady. Bingley, UK: Emerald Group Publishing, 85–115.

UN-Habitat. 2007. *Enhancing Urban Safety and Security: Global Report on Human Settlements*. London: Earthscan.

2011. *State of the World's Cities 2010/11: Bridging the Urban Divide*. London: Earthscan.

2015. "Forced Evictions: Fact Sheet." No. 25. Washington, DC: UN-Habitat.

Urrutia, Miguel. 1991. "On the Absence of Economic Populism in Colombia." In *The Macroeconomics of Populism in Latin America*, ed. Rudiger Dornbusch and Sebastian Edwards. Chicago: University of Chicago Press, 369–91.

Vargas Llosa, Mario. 2011. *A Fish in the Water: A Memoir*. New York: Farrar, Straus and Giroux.

Von Schnitzler, Antina. 2016. *Democracy's Infrastructure: Techno-Politics and Protest after Apartheid*. Princeton, NJ: Princeton University Press.

Ward, Peter. 1976. "The Squatter Settlement as Slum or Housing Solution: Evidence from Mexico City." *Land Economics* 52(3): 330–47.

Webb, Richard, Diether Beuermann, and Revilla Carla. 2006. *La Construcción del derecho de propiedad: El caso de los asentamientos humanos en el Perú*. Lima: Colegio de Notarios de Lima.

Webb, Richard, and Graciela Fernández Baca. 1999. *Anuario estadístico: Perú en numeros*. Lima: Cuanto.

Weitz-Shapiro, Rebecca. 2012. "What Wins Votes: Why Some Politicians Opt Out of Clientelism." *American Journal of Political Science* 56(3): 568–83.

2014. *Curbing Clientelism in Argentina: Politics, Poverty, and Social Policy*. New York: Cambridge University Press.

Weyl, E. Glen. Forthcoming. "Price Theory." *Journal of Economic Literature*.

Weyland, Kurt. 1996a. *Democracy without Equity: Failures of Reform in Brazil*. Pittsburgh, PA: University of Pittsburgh Press.

1996b. "Neopopulism and Neoliberalism in Latin America: Unexpected Affinities." *Studies in Comparative International Development* 31(3): 3–31.

2002. "Limitations of Rational-Choice Institutionalism for the Study of Latin American Politics." *Studies in Comparative International Development* 37(1): 57–85.

White, Jenny. 2002. *Islamist Mobilization in Turkey: A Study in Vernacular Politics*. Seattle: University of Washington Press.

Wibbels, Erik. 2006. "Dependency Revisited: International Markets, Business Cycles, and Social Spending in the Developing World." *International Organization* 60(2): 433–68.

Forthcoming. *Trade, Development and Social Insurance in the other 85 Percent of the World*. New York: Cambridge University Press.

Wibbels, Erik, and John S. Ahlquist. 2011. "Development, Trade, and Social Insurance." *International Studies Quarterly* 55(1): 125–49.

Wilkinson, Steven I. 2006. *Votes and Violence: Electoral Competition and Ethnic Riots in India*. New York: Cambridge University Press.

Williamson, John. 2003. "The Washington Consensus as Policy Prescription for Development." Institute for International Economics: 1–33.

Williamson, Vanessa. 2017. *Read My Lips: Why Americans are Proud to Pay Taxes*. Princeton, NJ: Princeton University Press.

Winn, Peter, and Lillia Ferro-Clérico. 1997. "Can a Leftist Government Make a Difference? The Frente Amplio Administration of Montevideo, 1990–1994." In *The New Politics of Inequality in Latin America*, ed. Douglas A. Chalmers,

Carlos M. Vilas, Katherine Hite, Scott B. Martin, Kerianne Piester, and Monique Segarra. New York: Oxford University Press, 447–68.

Wood, Geof, and Ian Gough. 2006. "A Comparative Welfare Regime Approach to Global Social Policy." *World Development* 34(10): 1696–712.

Woodruff, Christopher. 2001. "Review of De Soto's 'The Mystery of Capital.'" *Journal of Economic Literature* 39(4): 1215–23.

Working, Elmer J. 1927. "What Do Statistical 'Demand Curves' Show?" *Quarterly Journal of Economics* 41(2): 212–35.

World Bank. 2012. *Mexico's System for Social Protection in Health and the Formal Sector*. Washington, DC: World Bank.

Yalçıntan, Murat C., and Adem E. Erbaş. 2003. "Impacts of 'Gecekondu' on the Electoral Geography of Istanbul." *International Labor and Working-Class History* 64(October): 91–111.

Zeiderman, Austin. 2016. *Endangered City: The Politics of Security and Risk in Bogotá*. Durham: Duke University Press.

# Index

Other Books in the Series (*continued from page ii*)

Laia Balcells, *Rivalry and Revenge: The Politics of Violence during Civil War*
Lisa Baldez, *Why Women Protest? Women's Movements in Chile*
Kate Baldwin, *The Paradox of Traditional Chiefs in Democratic Africa*
Stefano Bartolini, *The Political Mobilization of the European Left, 1860–1980: The Class Cleavage*
Robert Bates, *When Things Fell Apart: State Failure in Late-Century Africa*
Mark Beissinger, *Nationalist Mobilization and the Collapse of the Soviet State*
Pablo Beramendi, *The Political Geography of Inequality: Regions and Redistribution*
Nancy Bermeo, ed., *Unemployment in the New Europe*
Nancy Bermeo and Deborah J. Yashar, eds., *Parties, Movements, and Democracy in the Developing World*
Carles Boix, *Democracy and Redistribution*
Carles Boix, *Political Order and Inequality: Their Foundations and their Consequences for Human Welfare*
Carles Boix, *Political Parties, Growth, and Equality: Conservative and Social Democratic Economic Strategies in the World Economy*
Catherine Boone, *Merchant Capital and the Roots of State Power in Senegal, 1930–1F985*
Catherine Boone, *Political Topographies of the African State: Territorial Authority and Institutional Change*
Catherine Boone, *Property and Political Order in Africa: Land Rights and the Structure of Politics*
Michael Bratton and Nicolas van de Walle, *Democratic Experiments in Africa: Regime Transitions in Comparative Perspective*
Michael Bratton, Robert Mattes, and E. Gyimah-Boadi, *Public Opinion, Democracy, and Market Reform in Africa*
Valerie Bunce, *Leaving Socialism and Leaving the State: The End of Yugoslavia, the Soviet Union, and Czechoslovakia*
Daniele Caramani, *The Nationalization of Politics: The Formation of National Electorates and Party Systems in Europe*
John M. Carey, *Legislative Voting and Accountability*
Kanchan Chandra, *Why Ethnic Parties Succeed: Patronage and Ethnic Headcounts in India*
Eric C. C. Chang, Mark Andreas Kayser, Drew A. Linzer, and Ronald Rogowski, *Electoral Systems and the Balance of Consumer-Producer Power*
José Antonio Cheibub, *Presidentialism, Parliamentarism, and Democracy*
Ruth Berins Collier, *Paths toward Democracy: The Working Class and Elites in Western Europe and South America*
Daniel Corstange, *The Price of a Vote in the Middle East: Clientelism and Communal Politics in Lebanon and Yemen*
Pepper D. Culpepper, *Quiet Politics and Business Power: Corporate Control in Europe and Japan*
Sarah Zukerman Daly, *Organized Violence after Civil War: The Geography of Recruitment in Latin America*
Christian Davenport, *State Repression and the Domestic Democratic Peace*

Donatella della Porta, *Social Movements, Political Violence, and the State*
Alberto Diaz-Cayeros, *Federalism, Fiscal Authority, and Centralization in Latin America*
Alberto Diaz-Cayeros, Federico Estévez, Beatriz Magaloni, *The Political Logic of Poverty Relief*
Jesse Driscoll, *Warlords and Coalition Politics in Post-Soviet States*
Thad Dunning, *Crude Democracy: Natural Resource Wealth and Political Regimes*
Gerald Easter, *Reconstructing the State: Personal Networks and Elite Identity*
Margarita Estevez-Abe, *Welfare and Capitalism in Postwar Japan: Party, Bureaucracy, and Business*
Henry Farrell, *The Political Economy of Trust: Institutions, Interests, and Inter-Firm Cooperation in Italy and Germany*
Karen E. Ferree, *Framing the Race in South Africa: The Political Origins of Racial Census Elections*
M. Steven Fish, *Democracy Derailed in Russia: The Failure of Open Politics*
Robert F. Franzese, *Macroeconomic Policies of Developed Democracies*
Roberto Franzosi, *The Puzzle of Strikes: Class and State Strategies in Postwar Italy*
Timothy Frye, *Building States and Markets After Communism: The Perils of Polarized Democracy*
Geoffrey Garrett, *Partisan Politics in the Global Economy*
Scott Gehlbach, *Representation through Taxation: Revenue, Politics, and Development in Postcommunist States*
Edward L. Gibson, *Boundary Control: Subnational Authoritarianism in Federal Democracies*
Jane R. Gingrich, *Making Markets in the Welfare State: The Politics of Varying Market Reforms*
Miriam Golden, *Heroic Defeats: The Politics of Job Loss*
Jeff Goodwin, *No Other Way Out: States and Revolutionary Movements*
Merilee Serrill Grindle, *Changing the State*
Anna Grzymala-Busse, *Rebuilding Leviathan: Party Competition and State Exploitation in Post-Communist Democracies*
Anna Grzymala-Busse, *Redeeming the Communist Past: The Regeneration of Communist Parties in East Central Europe*
Frances Hagopian, *Traditional Politics and Regime Change in Brazil*
Mark Hallerberg, Rolf Ranier Strauch, Jürgen von Hagen, *Fiscal Governance in Europe*
Henry E. Hale, *The Foundations of Ethnic Politics: Separatism of States and Nations in Eurasia and the World*
Stephen E. Hanson, *Post-Imperial Democracies: Ideology and Party Formation in Third Republic France, Weimar Germany, and Post-Soviet Russia*
Michael Hechter, *Alien Rule*
Timothy Hellwig, *Globalization and Mass Politics: Retaining the Room to Maneuver*
Gretchen Helmke, *Institutions on the Edge: The Origins and Consequences of Inter Branch Crises in Latin America*
Gretchen Helmke, *Courts Under Constraints: Judges, Generals, and Presidents in Argentina*

Yoshiko Herrera, *Imagined Economies: The Sources of Russian Regionalism*
Alisha C. Holland, *Forbearance as Redistribution: The Politics of Informal Welfare in Latin America*
J. Rogers Hollingsworth and Robert Boyer, eds., *Contemporary Capitalism: The Embeddedness of Institutions*
John D. Huber, *Exclusion by Elections: Inequality, Ethnic Identity, and Democracy*
John D. Huber and Charles R. Shipan, *Deliberate Discretion? The Institutional Foundations of Bureaucratic Autonomy*
Ellen Immergut, *Health Politics: Interests and Institutions in Western Europe*
Torben Iversen, *Capitalism, Democracy, and Welfare*
Torben Iversen, *Contested Economic Institutions*
Torben Iversen, Jonas Pontussen, and David Soskice, eds., *Unions, Employers, and Central Banks: Macroeconomic Coordination and Institutional Change in Social Market Economics*
Thomas Janoski and Alexander M. Hicks, eds., *The Comparative Political Economy of the Welfare State*
Joseph Jupille, *Procedural Politics: Issues, Influence, and Institutional Choice in the European Union*
Stathis Kalyvas, *The Logic of Violence in Civil War*
Stephen B. Kaplan, *Globalization and Austerity Politics in Latin America*
David C. Kang, *Crony Capitalism: Corruption and Capitalism in South Korea and the Philippines*
Junko Kato, *Regressive Taxation and the Welfare State*
Orit Kedar, *Voting for Policy, Not Parties: How Voters Compensate for Power Sharing*
Robert O. Keohane and Helen B. Milner, eds., *Internationalization and Domestic Politics*
Herbert Kitschelt, *The Transformation of European Social Democracy*
Herbert Kitschelt, Kirk A. Hawkins, Juan Pablo Luna, Guillermo Rosas, and Elizabeth J. Zechmeister, *Latin American Party Systems*
Herbert Kitschelt, Peter Lange, Gary Marks, and John D. Stephens, eds., *Continuity and Change in Contemporary Capitalism*
Herbert Kitschelt, Zdenka Mansfeldova, Radek Markowski, and Gabor Toka, *Post-Communist Party Systems*
David Knoke, Franz Urban Pappi, Jeffrey Broadbent, and Yutaka Tsujinaka, eds., *Comparing Policy Networks*
Ken Kollman, *Perils of Centralization: Lessons from Church, State, and Corporation*
Allan Kornberg and Harold D. Clarke, *Citizens and Community: Political Support in a Representative Democracy*
Amie Kreppel, *The European Parliament and the Supranational Party System*
David D. Laitin, *Language Repertoires and State Construction in Africa*
Fabrice E. Lehoucq and Ivan Molina, *Stuffing the Ballot Box: Fraud, Electoral Reform, and Democratization in Costa Rica*
Mark Irving Lichbach and Alan S. Zuckerman, eds., *Comparative Politics: Rationality, Culture, and Structure, 2nd edition*
Evan Lieberman, *Race and Regionalism in the Politics of Taxation in Brazil and South Africa*

Richard M. Locke, *The Promise and Limits of Private Power: Promoting Labor Standards in a Global Economy*

Julia Lynch, *Age in the Welfare State: The Origins of Social Spending on Pensioner's Workers and Children*

Pauline Jones Luong, *Institutional Change and Political Continuity in Post-Soviet Central Asia*

Pauline Jones Luong and Erika Weinthal, *Oil is Not a Curse: Ownership Structure and Institutions in Soviet Successor States*

Doug McAdam, John McCarthy, and Mayer Zald, eds., *Comparative Perspectives on Social Movements*

Lauren M. MacLean, *Informal Institutions and Citizenship in Rural Africa: Risk and Reciprocity in Ghana and Côte d'Ivoire*

Beatriz Magaloni, *Voting for Autocracy: Hegemonic Party Survival and its Demise in Mexico*

James Mahoney, *Colonialism and Postcolonial Development: Spanish America in Comparative Perspective*

James Mahoney and Dietrich Rueschemeyer, eds., *Historical Analysis and the Social Sciences*

Scott Mainwaring and Matthew Soberg Shugart, eds., *Presidentialism and Democracy in Latin America*

Melanie Manion, *Information for Autocrats: Representation in Chinese Local Congresses*

Isabela Mares, *From Open Secrets to Secret Voting: Democratic Electoral Reforms and Voter Autonomy*

Isabela Mares, *The Politics of Social Risk: Business and Welfare State Development*

Isabela Mares, *Taxation, Wage Bargaining, and Unemployment*

Cathie Jo Martin and Duane Swank, *The Political Construction of Business Interests: Coordination, Growth, and Equality*

Anthony W. Marx, *Making Race, Making Nations: A Comparison of South Africa, the United States, and Brazil*

Bonnie M. Meguid, *Party Competition between Unequals: Strategies and Electoral Fortunes in Western Europe*

Joel S. Migdal, *State in Society: Studying How States and Societies Constitute One Another*

Joel S. Migdal, Atul Kohli, and Vivienne Shue, eds., *State Power and Social Forces: Domination and Transformation in the Third World*

Scott Morgenstern and Benito Nacif, eds., *Legislative Politics in Latin America*

Kevin M. Morrison, *Nontaxation and Representation: The Fiscal Foundations of Political Stability*

Layna Mosley, *Global Capital and National Governments*

Layna Mosley, *Labor Rights and Multinational Production*

Wolfgang C. Müller and Kaare Strøm, *Policy, Office, or Votes?*

Maria Victoria Murillo, *Political Competition, Partisanship, and Policy Making in Latin American Public Utilities*

Maria Victoria Murillo, *Labor Unions, Partisan Coalitions, and Market Reforms in Latin America*

Monika Nalepa, *Skeletons in the Closet: Transitional Justice in Post-Communist Europe*
Ton Notermans, *Money, Markets, and the State: Social Democratic Economic Policies since 1918*
Aníbal Pérez-Liñán, *Presidential Impeachment and the New Political Instability in Latin America*
Roger D. Petersen, *Understanding Ethnic Violence: Fear, Hatred, and Resentment in 20th Century Eastern Europe*
Roger D. Petersen, *Western Intervention in the Balkans: The Strategic Use of Emotion in Conflict*
Simona Piattoni, ed., *Clientelism, Interests, and Democratic Representation*
Paul Pierson, *Dismantling the Welfare State?: Reagan, Thatcher, and the Politics of Retrenchment*
Marino Regini, *Uncertain Boundaries: The Social and Political Construction of European Economies*
Kenneth M. Roberts, *Changing Course in Latin America: Party Systems in the Neoliberal Era*
Marc Howard Ross, *Cultural Contestation in Ethnic Conflict*
Roger Schoenman, *Networks and Institutions in Europe's Emerging Markets*
Ben Ross Schneider, *Hierarchical Capitalism in Latin America: Business, Labor, and the Challenges of Equitable Development*
Lyle Scruggs, *Sustaining Abundance: Environmental Performance in Industrial Democracies*
Jefferey M. Sellers, *Governing from Below: Urban Regions and the Global Economy*
Yossi Shain and Juan Linz, eds., *Interim Governments and Democratic Transitions*
Beverly Silver, *Forces of Labor: Workers' Movements and Globalization since 1870*
Theda Skocpol, *Social Revolutions in the Modern World*
Prerna Singh, *How Solidarity Works for Welfare: Subnationalism and Social Development in India*
Austin Smith et al, *Selected Works of Michael Wallerstein*
Regina Smyth, *Candidate Strategies and Electoral Competition in the Russian Federation: Democracy Without Foundation*
Richard Snyder, *Politics after Neoliberalism: Reregulation in Mexico*
David Stark and László Bruszt, *Postsocialist Pathways: Transforming Politics and Property in East Central Europe*
Sven Steinmo, *The Evolution of Modern States: Sweden, Japan, and the United States*
Sven Steinmo, Kathleen Thelen, and Frank Longstreth, eds., *Structuring Politics: Historical Institutionalism in Comparative Analysis*
Susan C. Stokes, *Mandates and Democracy: Neoliberalism by Surprise in Latin America*
Susan C. Stokes, ed., *Public Support for Market Reforms in New Democracies*
Susan C. Stokes, Thad Dunning, Marcelo Nazareno, and Valeria Brusco, *Brokers, Voters, and Clientelism: The Puzzle of Distributive Politics*
Milan W. Svolik, *The Politics of Authoritarian Rule*
Duane Swank, *Global Capital, Political Institutions, and Policy Change in Developed Welfare States*

Sidney Tarrow, *Power in Movement: Social Movements and Contentious Politics*

Sidney Tarrow, *Power in Movement: Social Movements and Contentious Politics, Revised and Updated Third Edition*

Tariq Thachil, *Elite Parties, Poor Voters: How Social Services Win Votes in India*

Kathleen Thelen, *How Institutions Evolve: The Political Economy of Skills in Germany, Britain, the United States, and Japan*

Kathleen Thelen, *Varieties of Liberalization and the New Politics of Social Solidarity*

Charles Tilly, *Trust and Rule*

Daniel Treisman, *The Architecture of Government: Rethinking Political Decentralization*

Guillermo Trejo, *Popular Movements in Autocracies: Religion, Repression, and Indigenous Collective Action in Mexico*

Rory Truex, *Making Autocracy Work: Representation and Responsiveness in Modern China*

Lily Lee Tsai, *Accountability without Democracy: How Solidary Groups Provide Public Goods in Rural China*

Joshua Tucker, *Regional Economic Voting: Russia, Poland, Hungary, Slovakia and the Czech Republic, 1990–1999*

Ashutosh Varshney, *Democracy, Development, and the Countryside*

Yuhua Wang, *Tying the Autocrat's Hand: The Rise of The Rule of Law in China*

Jeremy M. Weinstein, *Inside Rebellion: The Politics of Insurgent Violence*

Stephen I. Wilkinson, *Votes and Violence: Electoral Competition and Ethnic Riots in India*

Andreas Wimmer, *Waves of War: Nationalism, State Formation, and Ethnic Exclusion in the Modern World*

Jason Wittenberg, *Crucibles of Political Loyalty: Church Institutions and Electoral Continuity in Hungary*

Elisabeth J. Wood, *Forging Democracy from Below: Insurgent Transitions in South Africa and El Salvador*

Elisabeth J. Wood, *Insurgent Collective Action and Civil War in El Salvador*

Daniel Ziblatt, *Conservative Parties and the Birth of Democracy*

CPSIA information can be obtained
at www.ICGtesting.com
Printed in the USA
LVHW111346250320
651170LV00001B/68

9 781316 626351